*A World Bank Group
Flagship Report*

JANUARY 2023

Global Economic Prospects

ISBN (paper): 978-1-4648-1906-3
ISBN (electronic): 978-1-4648-1950-6
DOI:10.1586/978-1-4648-1906-3

Cover design: Bill Pragluski (Critical Stages)

Library of Congress Control Number: 2022923405.

The cutoff date for the data used in the report was December 19, 2022.

Summary of Contents

Contents

Acknowledgments

This World Bank Group Flagship Report is a product of the Prospects Group in the Equitable Growth, Finance and Institutions (EFI) Vice Presidency. The project was managed by M. Ayhan Kose and Franziska Ohnsorge, under the general guidance of Indermit Gill and Pablo Saavedra.

Global and regional surveillance work was led by Carlos Arteta. The report was prepared by a team that included John Baffes, Jongrim Ha, Samuel Hill, Osamu Inami, Sergiy Kasyanenko, Philip Kenworthy, Jeetendra Khadan, Patrick Kirby, Peter Nagle, Nikita Perevalov, Franz Ulrich Ruch, Kersten Stamm, Ekaterine Vashakmadze, Dana Vorisek, Collette Mari Wheeler, and Takefumi Yamazaki.

Research assistance was provided by Jiayue Fan, Arika Kayastha, Maria Hazel Macadangdang, Mohamad Nassar, Muneeb Ahmad Naseem, Vasiliki Papagianni, Lorëz Qehaja, Juan Felipe Serrano, Shijie Shi, Kaltrina Temaj, Yujia Yao, and Juncheng Zhou. Modeling and data work were provided by Rajesh Kumar Danda and Shijie Shi.

Online products were produced by Graeme Littler. Joe Rebello managed communications and media outreach with a team that included Nandita Roy and Paul Blake and extensive support from the World Bank's media and digital communications teams. Graeme Littler provided editorial support, with contributions from Adriana Maximiliano and Janice Tuten.

The print publication was produced by Adriana Maximiliano, in collaboration with Andrew Berghauser, Cindy Fisher, Maria Hazel Macadangdang, and Jewel McFadden.

Regional projections and write-ups were produced in coordination with country teams, country directors, and the offices of the regional chief economists.

Many reviewers provided extensive advice and comments. The analysis also benefited from comments and suggestions by staff members from World Bank Group country teams and other World Bank Group Vice Presidencies as well as Executive Directors in their discussion of the report on December 19, 2022. However, both forecasts and analysis are those of the World Bank Group staff and should not be attributed to Executive Directors or their national authorities.

Foreword

The crisis facing development is intensifying.

Our latest forecasts indicate a sharp, long-lasting slowdown, with global growth declining to 1.7 percent in 2023 from 3.0 percent expected just six months ago. The deterioration is broad-based: in virtually *all* regions of the world, per-capita income growth will be slower than it was during the decade before COVID-19. The setback to global prosperity will likely persist: By the end of 2024, GDP levels in emerging-market and developing economies (EMDEs) will be about 6 percent below the level expected on the eve of the pandemic. Median income levels, moreover, are being eroded significantly—by inflation, currency depreciation and under-investment in people and the private sector.

The latest *Global Economic Prospects* report highlights why the outlook is particularly devastating for many of the poorest economies, where poverty reduction has already ground to a halt. Total debt among EMDEs is at a 50-year high, and Russia's invasion of Ukraine has added major new costs. This leaves no room for fiscal support at a time when people are still suffering from COVID-related setbacks in health, education and nutrition.

Over the next two years, per-capita income growth in EMDEs is expected to average only 2.8 percent—a full percentage point less than the 2010-2019 average. Between 2020 and 2024, per-capita income growth in EMDEs other than China is projected to be roughly the same as per-capita income growth in advanced economies, meaning income convergence is now effectively stalled. In fragile and conflict-affected areas, average per-capita incomes are expected to decline by 2024. In small states, an important focus of this edition of *Global Economic Prospects*, the output decline during the pandemic was about seven times the average decline in other EMDEs partly because of prolonged disruptions to tourism. Recoveries are expected to be weak, with large and persistent reductions in the level of output.

Restoring progress will be especially difficult where poverty rates are highest. In Sub-Saharan Africa, which is home for 60 percent of the world's poor, per-capita income growth is expected to average just 1.2 percent over the next two years—a rate that could cause poverty rates to rise, not fall.

This report also takes a detailed look at the shortfall in the new investment needed to overcome the reversals hitting development. Gross investment in EMDEs is projected to grow by just 3.5 percent on average from 2022 through 2024. That's less than half the average rate in the previous two decades and less than the rate needed to maintain capital stocks. Amid sharply rising global interest rates, the large fiscal demand on global capital by the governments of advanced economies points to a channeling of critical resources *away* from EMDEs. Today, roughly one in five EMDEs is effectively locked out of global debt markets, up from one in 15 in 2019.

The ongoing shortfall in investment in EMDEs casts a cloud over *all* development and climate objectives. Sluggish investment weakens the rate of growth of potential output, reducing the capacity of economies to increase median incomes, promote shared prosperity and repay debts. Slow capital accumulation obstructs advances in technology and productivity, impeding overall economic growth. It also hinders the ability of countries to tackle climate change and achieve the full array of development needs such as access to electricity, clean water and sufficient hours in school to achieve foundational learning skills.

With the global economy under pressure, five critical steps must be taken. Boosting median incomes and shared prosperity in EMDEs will require:

More investment to create jobs and increase output, allowing growth in consumption. This report underscores the urgent need for EMDEs to design policies that attract and incentivize new investment. This will require a comprehensive strategy featuring fiscal, structural and regulatory measures to boost public and private investment, in ways that meet the needs of individual countries. Fiscal and monetary policies that support stable, market-based currencies and productive investment are particularly critical to promote growth, higher median income, and poverty reduction.

Improvements in the business-enabling environment. In about 60 EMDEs for which data is available, investment growth was about 7 percentage points higher on average in years when investment-climate reforms were implemented. In low-income countries that rely on public-private partnerships for infrastructure investment, it is critical to establish a robust regulatory framework. Corruption and restrictions on foreign direct investment are key factors limiting the quantity and quality of cross-border investment. Reducing business start-up costs and strengthening property rights can also help enable business growth.

Greater debt transparency and sustainability, especially for the rising share of poor countries at high risk of debt distress. A faster, more decisive debt reconciliation and restructuring process will be vital to avoid the damage associated with delays and incremental steps.

Integrating climate and development in ways that increase energy access and speed up the transition to lower-carbon energy. These objectives need to be complemented by increased investment in climate adaptation. Meeting the challenge of increasing global public goods will require better mobilization of public-private partnerships, sustained international cooperation, and large new concessional funding and grants by the global community.

Stronger cooperation to increase cross-border trade. Greater efforts are needed to diversify products and markets, gain access to trade finance and strengthen trade facilitation through arrangements such as customs agreements. Governments should reduce arbitrary barriers to both imports and exports alike. Protectionist measures including the latest wave of export bans on food and fertilizers should be shunned.

Thus, even in a time of scarce resources, there is much that policy makers can do to encourage the right investments to materialize. One global starting point is to veer away from the wasteful subsidies that prevail and redirect the savings to more productive uses including private sector investment, targeted time-bound subsidies, and impactful climate investments.

Even though the world is now in a very tight spot, there should be no room for defeatism. The latest *Global Economic Prospects* report makes it clear that there are significant reforms that could be undertaken now to strengthen the rule of law, improve the outlook and build stronger economies with more robust private sectors and better opportunities for people around the world.

David Malpass
President
World Bank Group

Executive Summary

Global growth is projected to decelerate sharply this year, to its third weakest pace in nearly three decades, overshadowed only by the 2009 and 2020 global recessions. This reflects synchronous policy tightening aimed at containing very high inflation, worsening financial conditions, and continued disruptions from the Russian Federation's invasion of Ukraine. Investment growth in emerging market and developing economies (EMDEs) is expected to remain below its average rate of the past two decades. Further adverse shocks could push the global economy into yet another recession. Small states are especially vulnerable to such shocks because of their reliance on external trade and financing, limited economic diversification, elevated debt, and susceptibility to natural disasters. Urgent global action is needed to mitigate the risks of global recession and debt distress in EMDEs. Given limited policy space, it is critical that national policy makers ensure that any fiscal support is focused on vulnerable groups, that inflation expectations remain well anchored, and that financial systems continue to be resilient. Policies are also needed to support a major increase in EMDE investment, including new financing from the international community and from the repurposing of existing spending, such as inefficient agricultural and fuel subsidies.

Global outlook. Global growth is expected to decelerate sharply to 1.7 percent in 2023—the third weakest pace of growth in nearly three decades, overshadowed only by the global recessions caused by the pandemic and the global financial crisis. This is 1.3 percentage points below previous forecasts, reflecting synchronous policy tightening aimed at containing very high inflation, worsening financial conditions, and continued disruptions from Russia's invasion of Ukraine. The United States, the euro area, and China are all undergoing a period of pronounced weakness, and the resulting spillovers are exacerbating other headwinds faced by emerging market and developing economies (EMDEs). The combination of slow growth, tightening financial conditions, and heavy indebtedness is likely to weaken investment and trigger corporate defaults. Further negative shocks—such as higher inflation, even tighter policy, financial stress, deeper weakness in major economies, or rising geopolitical tensions—could push the global economy into recession. In the near term, urgent global efforts are needed to mitigate the risks of global recession and debt distress in EMDEs. Given limited policy space, it is critical that national policy makers ensure that any fiscal support is focused on vulnerable groups, that inflation expectations remain well anchored, and that financial systems continue to be resilient. Policies are also needed to support a major

increase in EMDE investment, which can help reverse the slowdown in long-term growth exacerbated by the overlapping shocks of the pandemic, the invasion of Ukraine, and the rapid tightening of global monetary policy. This will require new financing from the international community and from the repurposing of existing spending, such as inefficient agricultural and fuel subsidies.

Regional prospects. The forecast for growth in 2023 and 2024 combined has been downgraded for every EMDE region. Monetary policy tightening, and restrictive global financial conditions are slowing growth, especially in LAC, SAR and SSA. Persistently elevated energy prices are expected to dampen outlooks for energy-importers in all regions, while falling metals prices will weigh on terms of trade in LAC and SSA. The projected slowdown in advanced economy import demand is expected to especially impact EAP and ECA. Added to the pandemic-recession and incomplete recovery, the outlook implies feeble per capita income growth in LAC, MNA and SSA in the half decade to 2024. Risks to the baseline forecasts are skewed to the downside in all regions. They include the possibility of financial stress and greater spillovers from major advanced economy weakness (especially in EAP, ECA, LAC and SSA), commodity price shocks (especially in ECA, EAP and SAR), conflict (particularly in ECA, MNA, and SSA), and natural disasters (with elevated risk in sub-regions in EAP, LAC and SAR).

This edition of *Global Economic Prospects* also includes analytical pieces on prospects for investment after the pandemic and the multiple challenges faced by small states.

Investment growth after the pandemic. Investment growth in EMDEs is expected to remain below its average rate of the past two decades through the medium term. This subdued outlook follows a geographically widespread investment growth slowdown in the decade before the COVID-19 pandemic. During the past two decades, investment growth was associated with strong real output growth, robust real credit growth, terms of trade improvements, growth in capital inflows, and investment environment reform spurts. All of these factors have seen a declining trend since the 2007-09 global financial crisis. Weak investment growth is a concern because it dampens potential growth, is associated with weak trade, and makes achieving development and climate-related goals more difficult. Policies to boost investment growth need to be tailored to country circumstances but include comprehensive fiscal and structural reforms, including repurposing of expenditure on inefficient subsidies. Given EMDEs' limited fiscal space, the international community will need to signifi-cantly scale up international cooperation and official financing and grants as well as help leverage private sector financing for sufficient investment to materialize.

Small States: Overlapping crises, multiple challenges. Small states' economies were hit particularly hard by COVID-19, largely due to prolonged disruptions to global tourism. Now facing spillovers from Russia's invasion of Ukraine and the global monetary tightening cycle, small states are expected to have weak recoveries with large and possibly permanent losses to the level of output. Small states are diverse in their economic features, but they share attributes that make them especially vulnerable to shocks, including dependence on imports of essential goods, highly concentrated economies, elevated levels of debt, reliance on external financing, and susceptibility to natural disasters and climate change. Policy makers in small states can improve long-term growth prospects by building fiscal space, fostering effective economic diversification, and improving resilience to climate change. There is a need for intensified international cooperation to support small states in addressing their challenges. The global community can assist small states in these efforts by maintaining the flow of official assistance, helping restore and preserve debt sustainability, facilitating trade, and supporting climate change adaptation.

Abbreviations

ACLED	Armed Conflict Location & Event Data Project
AE	advanced economy
CA	Central Asia
CE	Central Europe and Baltic Countries
CPI	consumer price index
EAP	East Asia and Pacific
ECA	Europe and Central Asia
ECB	European Central Bank
EE	Eastern Europe
EMBI	emerging markets bond index
EMDE	emerging market and developing economy
EU	European Union
FAO	Food and Agriculture Organization
FCS	fragile and conflict-affected situations
FDI	foreign direct investment
FSIN	Food Security Information Network
FY	fiscal year
G7	Group of Seven: Canada, France, Germany, Italy, Japan, the United Kingdom, and the United States
G20	Group of Twenty: Argentina, Australia, Brazil, Canada, China, France, Germany, India, Indonesia, Italy, Japan, Republic of Korea, Mexico, Russia, Saudi Arabia, South Africa, Türkiye, the United Kingdom, the United States, and the European Union
GCC	Gulf Cooperation Council
GDP	gross domestic product
GEP	Global Economic Prospects
GFC	Global Financial Crisis
GMM	generalized method of moments
GNAFC	Global Network Against Food Crises
GNFS	goods and nonfactor services
ICRG	International Country Risk Guide
IEA	International Energy Agency
ILO	International Labour Organization
IMF	International Monetary Fund
IPC	Integrated Food Security Phase Classification
IPCC	Intergovernmental Panel on Climate Change
LAC	Latin America and the Caribbean
LIC	low-income country
MNA/MENA	Middle East and North Africa
OAD	official development assistance
OECD	Organization for Economic Co-operation and Development
OLS	ordinary least squares
OPEC	Organization of the Petroleum Exporting Countries
OPEC+	OPEC and Azerbaijan, Bahrain, Brunei Darussalam, Kazakhstan, Malaysia, Mexico, Oman, the Russian Federation, South Sudan, and Sudan
PMI	Purchasing Managers' Index

Abbreviations *(continued)*

PPP	purchasing power parity
PPPs	public-private partnerships
RHS	right-hand scale
SAR	South Asia
SCC	South Caucasus
SDG	Sustainable Development Goal
SOE	state-owned enterprise
SSA	Sub-Saharan Africa
TFP	total factor productivity
UN	United Nations
UNCTAD	United Nations Conference on Trade and Development
VAR	vector autoregression
WAEMU	West African Economic and Monetary Union
WDI	World Development Indicators
WFP	World Food Programme
WTO	World Trade Organization

CHAPTER 1

GLOBAL OUTLOOK

Global growth is expected to decelerate sharply to 1.7 percent in 2023—the third weakest pace of growth in nearly three decades, overshadowed only by the global recessions caused by the pandemic and the global financial crisis. This is 1.3 percentage points below previous forecasts, reflecting synchronous policy tightening aimed at containing very high inflation, worsening financial conditions, and continued disruptions from the Russian Federation's invasion of Ukraine. The United States, the euro area, and China are all undergoing a period of pronounced weakness, and the resulting spillovers are exacerbating other headwinds faced by emerging market and developing economies (EMDEs). The combination of slow growth, tightening financial conditions, and heavy indebtedness is likely to weaken investment and trigger corporate defaults. Further negative shocks—such as higher inflation, even tighter policy, financial stress, deeper weakness in major economies, or rising geopolitical tensions—could push the global economy into recession. In the near term, urgent global efforts are needed to mitigate the risks of global recession and debt distress in EMDEs. Given limited policy space, it is critical that national policy makers ensure that any fiscal support is focused on vulnerable groups, that inflation expectations remain well anchored, and that financial systems continue to be resilient. Policies are also needed to support a major increase in EMDE investment, which can help reverse the slowdown in long-term growth exacerbated by the overlapping shocks of the pandemic, the invasion of Ukraine, and the rapid tightening of global monetary policy. This will require new financing from the international community and from the repurposing of existing spending, such as inefficient agricultural and fuel subsidies.

Summary

Global growth has slowed to the extent that the global economy is perilously close to falling into recession—defined as a contraction in annual global per capita income—only three years after emerging from the pandemic-induced recession of 2020. Very high inflation has triggered unexpectedly rapid and synchronous monetary policy tightening around the world to contain it, including across major advanced economies (figure 1.1.A). Although this tightening has been necessary for price stability, it has contributed to a significant worsening of global financial conditions, which is exerting a substantial drag on activity. This drag is set to deepen given the lags between changes in monetary policy and its economic impacts, and the fact that real rates are expected to continue to increase.

Asset prices have been in broad, synchronous decline, investment growth has weakened substantially, and housing markets in many countries are worsening rapidly. Shockwaves continue to emanate from the Russian Federation's invasion of Ukraine, especially in energy and other

commodity markets. Against this backdrop, confidence has fallen precipitously. The world's three major engines of growth—the United States, the euro area, and China—are undergoing a period of pronounced weakness, with adverse spillovers for emerging market and developing economies (EMDEs), many of which are already struggling with weakening domestic conditions.

Global inflation has been pushed higher by demand pressures, including those from the lagged effects of earlier policy support, and supply shocks, including disruptions to both global supply chains and the availability of key commodities. In some countries, inflation has also been spurred by large currency depreciations relative to the U.S. dollar, as well as tight labor market conditions.

Inflation remains high worldwide and well above central bank targets in almost all inflation-targeting economies. Although inflation is likely to gradually moderate over the course of the year, there are signs that underlying inflation pressures could be becoming more persistent. In response, central banks around the world have been tightening policy faster than previously expected. Monetary policy tightening in advanced economies, a strong U.S. dollar, geopolitical tensions, and high inflation have dampened risk appetite and led to widespread capital outflows and slowing bond issuance across EMDEs. Financial conditions have particularly worsened

Note: This chapter was prepared by Carlos Arteta, Samuel Hill, Jeetendra Khadan, Patrick Kirby, Nikita Perevalov, and Collette Wheeler, with contributions from Jongrim Ha, Osamu Inami, Sergiy Kasyanenko, Phil Kenworthy, Peter Nagle, and Ekaterine Vashakmadze.

TABLE 1.1 Real GDP[1]

(Percent change from previous year unless indicated otherwise)

Percentage point differences from June 2022 projections

	2020	2021	2022e	2023f	2024f	2022e	2023f	2024f
World	-3.2	5.9	2.9	1.7	2.7	0.0	-1.3	-0.3
Advanced economies	-4.3	5.3	2.5	0.5	1.6	-0.1	-1.7	-0.3
United States	-2.8	5.9	1.9	0.5	1.6	-0.6	-1.9	-0.4
Euro area	-6.1	5.3	3.3	0.0	1.6	0.8	-1.9	-0.3
Japan	-4.3	2.2	1.2	1.0	0.7	-0.5	-0.3	0.1
Emerging market and developing economies	-1.5	6.7	3.4	3.4	4.1	0.0	-0.8	-0.3
East Asia and Pacific	1.2	7.2	3.2	4.3	4.9	-1.2	-0.9	-0.2
China	2.2	8.1	2.7	4.3	5.0	-1.6	-0.9	-0.1
Indonesia	-2.1	3.7	5.2	4.8	4.9	0.1	-0.5	-0.4
Thailand	-6.2	1.5	3.4	3.6	3.7	0.5	-0.7	-0.2
Europe and Central Asia	-1.7	6.7	0.2	0.1	2.8	3.2	-1.4	-0.5
Russian Federation	-2.7	4.8	-3.5	-3.3	1.6	5.4	-1.3	-0.6
Türkiye	1.9	11.4	4.7	2.7	4.0	2.4	-0.5	0.0
Poland	-2.0	6.8	4.4	0.7	2.2	0.5	-2.9	-1.5
Latin America and the Caribbean	-6.2	6.8	3.6	1.3	2.4	1.1	-0.6	0.0
Brazil	-3.3	5.0	3.0	0.8	2.0	1.5	0.0	0.0
Mexico	-8.0	4.7	2.6	0.9	2.3	0.9	-1.0	0.3
Argentina	-9.9	10.4	5.2	2.0	2.0	0.7	-0.5	-0.5
Middle East and North Africa	-3.6	3.7	5.7	3.5	2.7	0.4	-0.1	-0.5
Saudi Arabia	-4.1	3.2	8.3	3.7	2.3	1.3	-0.1	-0.7
Iran, Islamic Rep.[2]	1.9	4.7	2.9	2.2	1.9	-0.8	-0.5	-0.4
Egypt, Arab Rep.[3]	3.6	3.3	6.6	4.5	4.8	0.5	-0.3	-0.2
South Asia	-4.5	7.9	6.1	5.5	5.8	-0.7	-0.3	-0.7
India[2]	-6.6	8.7	6.9	6.6	6.1	-0.6	-0.5	-0.4
Pakistan[3]	-0.9	5.7	6.0	2.0	3.2	1.7	-2.0	-1.0
Bangladesh[3]	3.4	6.9	7.2	5.2	6.2	0.8	-1.5	-0.7
Sub-Saharan Africa	-2.0	4.3	3.4	3.6	3.9	-0.3	-0.2	-0.1
Nigeria	-1.8	3.6	3.1	2.9	2.9	-0.3	-0.3	-0.3
South Africa	-6.3	4.9	1.9	1.4	1.8	-0.2	-0.1	0.0
Angola	-5.8	0.8	3.1	2.8	2.9	0.0	-0.5	-0.3
Memorandum items:								
Real GDP[1]								
High-income countries	-4.3	5.3	2.7	0.6	1.6	0.0	-1.6	-0.4
Middle-income countries	-1.2	6.9	3.2	3.4	4.3	-0.1	-0.8	-0.2
Low-income countries	1.6	3.9	4.0	5.1	5.6	0.0	-0.1	0.0
EMDEs excl. China	-3.9	5.7	3.8	2.7	3.6	1.1	-0.7	-0.4
Commodity-exporting EMDEs	-3.7	4.9	2.8	1.9	2.8	1.6	-0.7	-0.4
Commodity-importing EMDEs	-0.4	7.6	3.6	4.1	4.8	-0.8	-0.8	-0.2
Commodity-importing EMDEs excl. China	-4.2	6.8	5.0	3.8	4.5	0.4	-0.7	-0.4
EM7	-0.4	7.4	3.0	3.5	4.5	-0.3	-0.8	-0.2
World (PPP weights)[4]	-2.8	6.1	3.1	2.2	3.2	0.0	-1.2	-0.3
World trade volume[5]	**-8.2**	**10.6**	**4.0**	**1.6**	**3.4**	**0.0**	**-2.7**	**-0.4**

Commodity prices[6]

Level differences from June 2022 projections

	2020	2021	2022e	2023f	2024f	2022e	2023f	2024f
Energy price index	52.7	95.4	151.7	130.5	118.3	7.1	4.4	7.2
Oil price (US$ per barrel)	42.3	70.4	100.0	88.0	80.0	0.0	-4.0	0.0
Non-energy commodity price index	84.4	112.0	123.7	113.7	113.0	-8.4	-7.6	-4.6

Source: World Bank.

Note: e = estimate; f = forecast. World Bank forecasts are frequently updated based on new information. Consequently, projections presented here may differ from those contained in other World Bank documents, even if basic assessments of countries' prospects do not differ at any given date. For the definition of EMDEs, developing countries, commodity exporters, and commodity importers, please refer to table 1.2. EM7 includes Brazil, China, India, Indonesia, Mexico, the Russian Federation, and Türkiye. The World Bank is currently not publishing economic output, income, or growth data for Turkmenistan and República Bolivariana de Venezuela owing to lack of reliable data of adequate quality. Turkmenistan and República Bolivariana de Venezuela are excluded from cross-country macroeconomic aggregates.

1. Headline aggregate growth rates are calculated using GDP weights at average 2010-19 prices and market exchange rates. The aggregate growth rates may differ from the previously published numbers that were calculated using GDP weights at average 2010 prices and market exchange rates.

2. GDP growth rates are on a fiscal year basis. Aggregates that include these countries are calculated using data compiled on a calendar year basis. The column labeled 2022 refers to FY2022/23.

3. GDP growth rates are on a fiscal year basis. Aggregates that include these countries are calculated using data compiled on a calendar year basis. Pakistan's growth rates are based on GDP at factor cost. The column labeled 2022 refers to FY2021/22.

4. World growth rates are calculated using average 2010-19 purchasing power parity (PPP) weights, which attribute a greater share of global GDP to emerging market and developing economies (EMDEs) than market exchange rates.

5. World trade volume of goods and nonfactor services.

6. Energy price index is in nominal U.S. dollars (2010=100) and it includes coal (Australia), crude oil (Brent), and natural gas (Europe, Japan, and the United States). Oil price refers to the Brent crude oil benchmark. The non-energy index is in nominal U.S. dollars (2010=100) and it is the weighted average of 39 commodity prices (7 metals, 5 fertilizers, and 27 agricultural commodities). For additional details, please see https://www.worldbank.org/commodities.

for less creditworthy EMDEs, especially if they are also energy importers (figure 1.1.B).

Fiscal space has narrowed considerably, and concerns over debt sustainability in many countries have risen as global financial conditions have made it more difficult to service debt loads that have accumulated rapidly in recent years, particularly during the pandemic. Nonetheless, many governments have announced new support measures to shield households and firms from the effects of sharply rising prices, slowing the pace of fiscal consolidation as pandemic-related stimulus is withdrawn.

Most commodity prices have eased, to varying degrees, largely due to the slowdown in global growth and concerns about the possibility of a global recession. By historical standards, however, they remain elevated, prolonging challenges associated with energy and food insecurity. Crude oil prices have steadily declined from their mid-2022 peak; meanwhile, natural gas prices in Europe soared to an all-time high in August but have since fallen back toward pre-invasion levels. Non-energy prices, particularly metal prices, have declined alongside weak demand. While food prices have eased from earlier peaks, food price inflation remains very high in some EMDEs.

Against this backdrop, global growth is forecast to slow to 1.7 percent in 2023 (figure 1.1.C). This pace of growth would be the third weakest in nearly three decades, overshadowed only by the global recessions caused by the pandemic in 2020 and the global financial crisis in 2009. This forecast is 1.3 percentage points lower than in June, largely reflecting more aggressive monetary policy tightening, deteriorating financial conditions, and declining confidence. Growth projections have been downgraded for almost all advanced economies and about two-thirds of EMDEs in 2023, and for about half of all countries in 2024 (figure 1.1.D). Global trade is also expected to slow sharply alongside global growth, despite support from a continued recovery in services trade. Downgrades to growth project-ions mean that global activity is now expected to fall even further below its pre-pandemic trend over the forecast horizon, with EMDEs accounting for

FIGURE 1.1 Global prospects

High global inflation has prompted rapid, synchronous monetary tightening. This has contributed to worsening financial conditions, particularly for less creditworthy emerging market and developing economies (EMDEs). Global growth in 2023 is expected to be the third weakest in nearly three decades, overshadowed only by global recessions. Most country forecasts have been downgraded. The recovery from the pandemic recession is far from complete, especially in EMDEs, and the per-capita income outlook is particularly subdued for poverty-stricken countries.

A. G7 policy rates

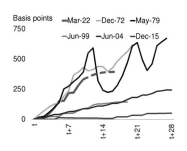

B. EMDE sovereign spread changes in 2022, by credit rating and energy exporter status

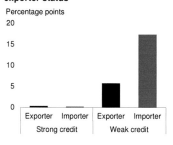

C. Global growth

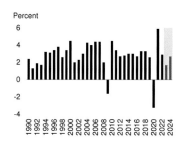

D. Share of countries with downgrades in growth forecasts

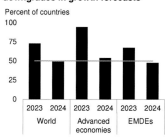

E. Deviation of output from pre-pandemic trends

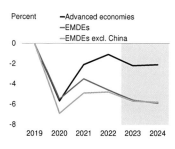

F. EMDE per capita GDP growth, by bottom and top quartile poverty headcount ratio

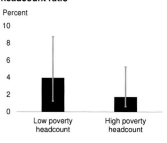

Sources: BIS (database); Bloomberg; Haver Analytics; Moody's; JP Morgan; World Bank.
Note: EMBI = Emerging Markets Bond Index; EMDEs = emerging market and developing economies. Unless otherwise indicated, aggregate growth rates are calculated using real U.S. dollar GDP weights at average 2010-19 prices and market exchange rates. Shaded areas indicate forecasts.
A. Short-term policy rate weighted by nominal GDP in current U.S. dollars. "t" is the month before the U.S. policy rate increases. Cycle ends when the G7-weighted policy rate peaks. Judgement used to define "double-peak" cycles. March 2022 cycle extended using market-implied interest rate expectations from January 2023 onward, observed on December 16, 2022.
B. Change in EMBI spreads since January 2022, using Moody's sovereign foreign currency ratings. Sample includes 11 EMDE energy exporters and 35 EMDE energy importers. Strong credit defined as ratings from Aaa to Baa3. Weak credit defined as ratings from Caa to Ca. Sample excludes Belarus, the Russian Federation, and Ukraine. Last observation is December 13, 2022.
C. Sample includes up to 37 advanced economies and 144 EMDEs.
D. Figure shows share of countries with forecast downgrades since the June 2022 *Global Economic Prospects*.
E. Figure shows deviation between current forecasts and January 2020 *Global Economic Prospects*. January 2020 baseline extended into 2023 and 2024 using projected growth for 2022.
F. "Low poverty headcount" are EMDEs with poverty headcount in the 25th percentile, and "high poverty headcount" are those in the 75th percentile. Bars show average per capita GDP growth over 2023-24 for 39 EMDEs. Whiskers show minimum-maximum range. Sample excludes Belarus and the Russian Federation. Poverty data are the poverty headcount ratio at $2.15 a day (2017 PPP).

most of the shortfall from trend (figure 1.1.E). This suggests that the negative shocks of the past three years—namely the pandemic, the invasion of Ukraine, and the rapid increase in inflation and associated tightening of monetary policy worldwide—are having a lasting impact on economic prospects.

In advanced economies, conditions have deteriorated sharply, owing to declining confidence alongside high inflation and rapid monetary policy tightening. In the United States, one of the most aggressive monetary policy tightening cycles in recent history is expected to slow growth sharply. The euro area is also contending with severe energy supply disruptions and price hikes associated with the Russian Federation's invasion of Ukraine. In all, growth in advanced economies is forecast to slow from 2.5 percent in 2022 to 0.5 percent in 2023.

In EMDEs, growth prospects have worsened materially, with the forecast for 2023 downgraded 0.8 percentage point to a subdued 3.4 percent. The downward revision results in large part from weaker external demand and tighter financing conditions. EMDE growth is anticipated to remain essentially unchanged in 2023 relative to last year, as a pickup in China offsets a decline in other EMDEs. Excluding China, EMDE growth is forecast to decelerate from 3.8 percent in 2022 to 2.7 percent in 2023 as significantly weaker external demand is compounded by high inflation, tighter financial conditions, and other domestic headwinds. The deviation between EMDE investment and its pre-pandemic trend is expected to remain substantial. EMDE investment growth is envisaged to remain below its 2000-21 average pace, dampened significantly by weakening activity, heightened uncertainty, and rising borrowing costs. Low-income countries (LICs) are expected to grow 5.1 percent in 2023, with forecasts downgraded in about 65 percent of countries. Cost-of-living increases and a deterioration in the external environment are weighing heavily on activity in many LICs and compounding weakness in LICs with fragile and conflict affected situations (FCS).

As a result of the sharp slowdown in global growth, per capita income is not expected to surpass 2019 levels until at least 2024 in about one-third of EMDEs. Per capita income growth is expected to be slowest where poverty is highest (figure 1.1.F). In Sub-Saharan Africa—which accounts for about 60 percent of the world's poor—growth in per capita income over 2023-24 is forecast to average only 1.2 percent, far less than the pace that would be needed over the remainder of the decade to reach a 3 percent poverty rate by 2030.

Soaring inflation reflects a combination of supply and demand factors, including large price increases for food and energy products priced in U.S. dollars. Inflation has risen particularly rapidly in poorer countries, partially due to the greater share of food in consumer spending. Relative to previous projections, global inflation is assumed to remain higher for longer. After peaking at 7.6 percent in 2022, global headline CPI inflation is expected to remain elevated at 5.2 percent in 2023 before easing to 3.2 percent in 2024, above its 2015-19 average of 2.3 percent.

Risks to the growth outlook are tilted to the downside. In light of high inflation and repeated negative supply shocks, there is substantial uncertainty about the impact of central bank policy in terms of both magnitude and timing. As a result, the risk of policy missteps is elevated. Global inflation may be pushed higher by renewed supply disruptions, including to key commodities, and elevated core inflation may persist. To bring inflation under control, central banks may need to hike policy rates more than is currently expected. Financial stress among sovereigns, banks, and nonbank financial institutions may result from the combination of additional monetary tightening, softer growth, and falling confidence in an environment of elevated debt. Given already-weak global growth, a combination of sharper monetary policy tightening and financial stress could result in a more pronounced slowdown or even a global recession this year (figures 1.2.A and 1.2.B). Weaker-than-expected activity in China amid pandemic-related disruptions and stress in the real estate sector, rising geopolitical tensions and trade fragmentation, and climate change could also result in markedly slower growth.

The weak global outlook and the heightened downside risks highlight the challenges facing policy makers around the world. Urgent action is needed to attenuate the risk of global recession stemming, in part, from the fastest and most synchronized monetary tightening in decades. As they focus on reducing record-high inflation, central banks in advanced economies and EMDEs need to take into account the possibility that cross-border spillovers from other monetary authorities' actions may tighten financial conditions more than expected. Discussions among central banks can help mitigate risks associated with financial stability and avoid an excessive global economic slowdown in the pursuit of inflation objectives.

The international community needs to intensify its support to large numbers of displaced people and others affected by conflict or food insecurity, particularly in LICs (figure 1.2.C). In responding to food and energy shocks, governments need to avoid imposing export restrictions and instead attenuate the impact on the poor through support measures targeted at low-income groups. The international community also needs to reduce the risk of debt crises in EMDEs, including by supporting timely debt restructuring. Given the rising human and economic costs of more frequent climate-related disasters, particularly in small states, speedy action to foster the energy transition is critical for mitigating climate change.

Global efforts need to be complemented by decisive policy action at the national level. While monetary policy cycles are peaking in some EMDEs, further tightening may be needed in others to rein in inflation. Financial stability risks stoked by global and domestic policy tightening can be mitigated by strengthening macroprudential regulation and promptly addressing financial vulnerabilities such as rising nonperforming loans. Preemptively alleviating currency mismatches in EMDE corporate and financial sectors with proper financial policy can also reduce crisis risks. EMDE policy makers can take steps to bolster foreign exchange buffers as appropriate, which can be utilized in episodes of excessive volatility. Deployed appropriately, foreign exchange interventions can help stem temporary exchange rate pressures.

FIGURE 1.2 Global risks and policy challenges

Risks are tilted to the downside. Central banks may need to tighten more than expected to bring inflation under control. Given already-weak global growth, this could result in a sharper slowdown or even a global recession this year. A rising number of people are affected by food insecurity, especially in low-income countries. Fiscal challenges in emerging market and developing economies (EMDEs) have become more acute, as exemplified by a precipitous drop in bond issuance. The long-term effects of the adverse shocks of the past three years have led to substantial losses, particularly for EMDE investment and output, which could grow larger if downside scenarios materialize.

A. Global interest rates and inflation under different scenarios

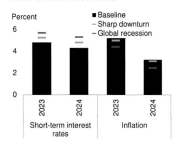

B. Global growth under different scenarios

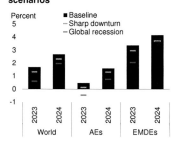

C. Food insecurity in LICs

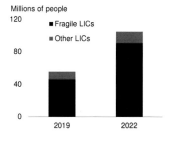

D. Change in bond issuance in EMDEs

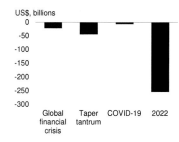

E. Deviation of investment from pre-pandemic trends in 2024

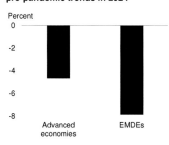

F. Cumulative output losses, 2020-24

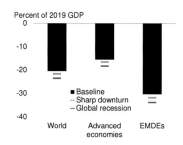

Sources: Bloomberg; Consensus Economics; Dealogic; FSIN and GNAFC (2022); GNAFC (2022); Guenette, Kose, and Sugawara (2022); Haver Analytics; Oxford Economics; World Bank.
Note: AEs = advanced economies; EMDEs = emerging market and developing economies; LICs = low-income countries; Fragile LICs = LICs with fragile and conflict affected situations. Unless indicated, aggregate growth rates calculated using real U.S. dollar GDP weights at average 2010-19 prices and market exchange rates. Data are estimates for 2022 and forecasts for 2023-24.
A.B. Scenarios use Oxford Economics *Global Economic Model*.
B. Growth aggregates computed by Oxford Economics using 2015 market exchange rates and prices.
C. Bars show the number of people in food crisis as classified by the Integrated Food Security Phase Classification (IPC/CH) Phase 3, that is, in acute food insecurity crisis or worse. Data for 2022 are estimates adapted from GNAFC (2022).
D. Bars indicate the change in public and private bond issuance during the ten months after the start of the event compared to the same period one year prior. The starting dates are August 2008 for Global financial crisis, June 2013 for Taper tantrum, March 2020 for COVID-19, and February 2022 for 2022.
E. Deviation between current forecasts and those of the January 2020 *Global Economic Prospects* report. For 2024, the January 2020 baseline is extended using projected growth for 2022.
F. Figure shows expected losses over 2020-24 relative to pre-pandemic trend as a percentage of 2019 GDP. Pre-pandemic trend based on January 2020 baseline extended using 2022 projections.

Tighter financing conditions, weaker growth, and elevated debt levels create significant fiscal challenges for EMDEs, exemplified by the recent precipitous fall in bond issuance (figure 1.2.D). Timely and carefully calibrated fiscal consolidation needs to be guided by credible medium-term frameworks, with a focus on reducing wasteful spending, such as inefficient agricultural and fuel subsidies, and ensuring that support for the poor and most vulnerable is well-targeted. Although increasing tax rates may be a challenge in the near term given weak growth prospects, revenues can nonetheless be bolstered by broadening the tax base through removing exemptions, progressively expanding coverage of under-taxed activities, and strengthening collection and administration mechanisms.

The long-term scarring effects of the overlapping adverse shocks of the past three years have led to large cumulative losses, especially with respect to EMDE output and investment (figure 1.2.E). These losses would be even larger in a sharper global downturn or recession (figure 1.2.F). To offset these losses and bolster green, resilient, and inclusive growth, EMDEs will need to make substantial investments in all forms of capital—human, physical, social, and natural. Given limited fiscal space, these investments will require private-sector involvement and new concessional financing from the international community. This can be complemented by structural reforms that improve the investment climate and reallocate public expenditures toward growth-enhancing investment. Such efforts will need to be accompanied by measures to strengthen social protection systems, foster gender equality, promote investments in human capital, and facilitate more resilient food systems.

Global context

Weakening global demand is weighing on global trade. Most commodity prices have eased, to varying degrees, although they are expected to remain well above their average of the past five years. High inflation is expected to persist for longer than previously expected. Monetary tightening and risk aversion have led to widespread currency depreciations and steep capital outflows from EMDEs.

Global trade

Global trade growth decelerated in the second half of 2022, in tandem with deteriorating activity in major economies. Weakening trade mirrored the slowdown in global industrial production, as demand shifted toward its pre-pandemic composition and away from goods. Despite this moderation, goods trade surpassed pre-pandemic levels last year; meanwhile, services trade continued to recover, supported by the gradual shift in demand toward services. Tourism flows rebounded as many countries eased travel restrictions but remained well below pre-pandemic levels and uneven across regions (WTO 2022).

Although global supply chain pressures are still above pre-pandemic levels, they have eased since mid-2022, as reflected in lower transportation costs and normalization of inventories (figures 1.3.A and 1.3.B). Weakening demand for goods is expected to reduce these pressures further in 2023.

After softening to 4 percent in 2022, global trade growth is expected to decelerate further to 1.6 percent in 2023, largely reflecting weakening global demand (figure 1.3.C). Trade is envisaged to be particularly subdued in EMDEs with strong trade linkages to major economies where demand is expected to slow sharply. In all, the current post-recession rebound in global trade is on course to be among the weakest on record (figure 1.3.D). Travel and tourism are expected to pick up further but will be constrained by slower global activity and high input costs. Goods trade is expected to moderate owing to subdued demand and a gradual shift in consumption toward services.

Weaker-than-expected global demand and renewed supply chain bottlenecks pose downside risks to the global trade outlook. In addition, an intensification in trade protectionism, fragmentation of trade networks, and security concerns about supply chains could increase trade costs and slow trade growth (Góes and Bekkers 2022; Rubínová and Sebti 2021).

Commodity markets

Most commodity prices have eased since June, to varying degrees, due to slowing global growth (figure 1.4.A; World Bank 2022a). Oil prices declined from their mid-2022 peak amid demand concerns; for the year as a whole, the price of Brent crude oil averaged $100/bbl. European natural gas prices surged to an all-time high in August but have since fallen back toward pre-invasion levels as inventories filled and mild weather reduced demand for natural gas for heating. Coal prices reached a record high in the third quarter before starting to soften in the fourth.

Meanwhile, metal prices fell in the second half of 2022 owing to slowing demand, particularly from China (figure 1.4.B; Baumeister, Verduzco-Bustos, and Ohnsorge 2022). Agricultural prices remain high but have also declined, particularly for wheat and vegetable oils, reflecting higher-than-expected crop yields, as well as a resumption of some exports from Ukraine. Concerns about food availability due to the invasion of Ukraine prompted many countries to impose export bans and other trade restrictions (figure 1.4.C). The extent of these restrictions, in both absolute numbers and as a share of caloric intake, have been comparable with those during the 2008 food price spike. However, because recent restrictions have been applied to a broad set of commodities, they have not affected global markets as much as those imposed in 2008 (which were applied mostly to rice and wheat and were also accompanied by large purchases from major importers).

Currency depreciations in many countries have resulted in higher commodity prices in local currency terms compared to the price in U.S. dollars. For instance, from February to November 2022, the price of Brent crude oil in U.S. dollars fell nearly 5 percent, but rose by 7 percent in domestic currency terms, on average, in advanced economies (excluding the United States) and by 5 percent in oil-importing EMDEs. As a result, commodity-driven inflationary pressures in many countries may be more persistent than indicated by recent declines in global commodity prices.

Going forward, energy prices are expected to ease in 2023 but remain higher than previously forecast, primarily reflecting an upward revision to coal prices. Crude oil prices are projected to

FIGURE 1.3 Global trade

Supply chain pressures continue to ease and are returning to historical averages amid rising inventories and falling shipping costs, while supplier delivery times are increasing at a slower pace. Global trade growth has been revised down substantially, in part reflecting deteriorating global demand. The recovery of global trade following the 2020 global recession is on course to be substantially weaker than the rebounds seen after previous global recessions.

A. Global supply chain pressures

B. Manufacturing PMIs

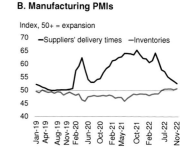

C. Global trade growth

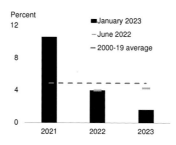

D. Global trade growth after global recessions

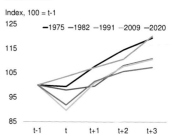

Sources: Federal Reserve Bank of New York; Haver Analytics; Kose, Sugawara, and Terrones (2020); World Bank.
A. Figure shows the Global Supply Chain Pressure Index, as produced by the Federal Reserve Bank of New York. The index is normalized such that zero indicates the average value for the period January 1998-November 2022, while positive (negative) values represent how many standard deviations the index is above (below) the average value. Last observation is November 2022.
B. Figure shows manufacturing Purchasing Managers' Index (PMI) subcomponents. PMI data for delivery times are inverted by subtracting data from 100; therefore, increasing (decreasing) PMI data indicate faster (slower) delivery times. Last observation is November 2022.
C. Trade is measured as the average of export and import volumes. June 2022 refers to forecasts presented in the June 2022 edition of the *Global Economic Prospects* report.
D. Figure shows global trade recoveries after global recessions (1975, 1982, 1991, 2009, and 2020). Global recession is defined as a contraction in global per capita GDP, as described in Kose, Sugawara, and Terrones (2020).

moderate to an average of $88/bbl in 2023, $4/bbl below previous projections. The downward revision is primarily due to slower global growth and the subsequent weakness in oil demand in 2023, particularly in Europe. Russian oil exports are expected to fall in 2023 due to additional EU sanctions that started in December 2022 for crude oil and will begin in February 2023 for oil products. The overall reduction in Russia's exports is likely to be smaller than initially expected, however, as the G7 oil price cap will enable countries that import oil from Russia to continue

FIGURE 1.4 Commodity markets

Most commodity prices have eased due to slowing global growth. Metals demand growth has seen a particularly marked slowdown. Concerns about food availability due to the invasion of Ukraine resulted in a number of countries implementing food export restrictions in 2022. OPEC+ announced a 2 mb/d reduction in their production target; however, the group is already producing below their official target.

A. Commodity prices

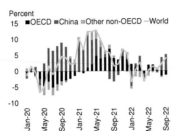

B. Metals demand growth

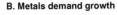

C. Number of countries implementing food export restrictions

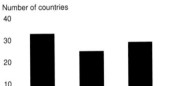

D. OPEC+ production shortfall

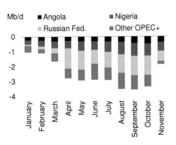

Sources: Bloomberg; IEA (2022a); Laborde and Mamun (2022); World Bank; World Bureau of Metal Statistics.
Note: OPEC = Organization of the Petroleum Exporting Countries.
A. Last observation is November 2022.
B. Figure shows percent change in metal demand relative to same period in previous year. Last observation is September 2022.
C. Bars show the peak of number of countries during each period implementing food export restrictions.
D. Figure shows the difference in crude oil production compared to the target set by OPEC+ countries for 2022 based on IEA (2022a).

to access EU and UK insurance services, provided they adhere to the price cap (IEA 2022a). Beyond Russia, oil supply will increase modestly, mainly from the United States, while OPEC+ output will remain subject to their production agreement.

For natural gas, annual average prices are forecast to moderate in 2023. Demand for natural gas is expected to decline in 2023 as households and industrial users reduce consumption, while rapid growth in renewable energy generation will help moderate demand for natural gas for electricity generation. Nonetheless, further price spikes are possible. Exports from Russia are envisaged to remain significantly lower than before the onset of

the war in Ukraine. In addition, competition for liquefied natural gas (LNG) will remain intense at the global level, as European countries continue to import large volumes of LNG to replace lower imports from Russia. Coal prices will ease from extremely elevated levels as production rises, especially in China and India.

The main downside risk to the energy price forecast is weaker-than-expected global growth. Oil consumption could also be lower as a result of more persistent pandemic-related restrictions in China. Upside risks chiefly relate to supply factors. U.S. shale oil production could disappoint as producers focus on returning cash to shareholders rather than increasing production. Disruption to Russia's exports could be larger than expected, while a cessation of the war in Ukraine could ease supply issues. Spare capacity among OPEC members is minimal, and OPEC+ members continue to produce well below target, in part because of low levels of investment in new production in recent years (figure 1.4.D). In addition, strategic inventories have been drawn down, leaving limited buffers in the event of unexpected new shocks. For natural gas and, to a lesser extent, coal, a cold winter in Europe could cause natural gas inventories to fall to very low levels, requiring additional refilling in 2023, and Europe could struggle to refill inventories ahead of the 2023 winter season.

Agricultural prices are projected to decline 5 percent in 2023 after rising 13 percent in 2022, largely reflecting better global production prospects and easing input costs, particularly for fertilizers. However, prices are expected to remain above pre-pandemic levels. Upward risks to food prices include the possibility that fertilizer prices will rise in response to higher natural gas prices and the closure of several fertilizer manufacturers in Europe, as well as the effects of a third consecutive year of La Niña in 2022.

Food insecurity remains a critical challenge in some EMDEs, reflecting the high number of food trade restrictions imposed last year, weather-related events, and the impact of the invasion of Ukraine and conflict elsewhere. As a result, about 220 million people are projected to face severe food insecurity in 2022, a number which could rise further if upward risks to food prices materialize.

Metal prices are expected to decline 15 percent in 2023 reflecting slowing global growth. Weakness in China's property market will weigh on demand, though this may be tempered by infrastructure spending. Demand for metals from the renewable energy sector—made more competitive by high fossil fuel prices—is likely to remain strong in 2023. Metal prices may be higher than expected if elevated energy costs cause smelters to close and reduce production of refined metals. Conversely, weaker-than-expected growth, particularly in China, is a downside risk to prices.

Global inflation

Inflation rose throughout 2022 in almost all economies. Median global headline inflation exceeded 9 percent in the second half of the year, its highest level since 1995. Inflation reached almost 10 percent in EMDEs, its highest level since 2008, and in advanced economies just over 9 percent, the highest since 1982. Inflation was above target in virtually all countries that have adopted inflation targeting.

Soaring inflation in 2022 reflected a combination of demand and supply factors (Ha, Kose, and Ohnsorge 2022; Shapiro 2022). On the demand side, the acceleration of growth during the initial rebound from the 2020 global recession, as well as the lagged effects of earlier macroeconomic support, contributed to persistent price pressures. Price increases were particularly large in sectors such as shipping and air travel, where compositional shifts in demand encountered ongoing capacity constraints and supply chain disruptions (Kalemli-Özcan et al. 2022). On the supply side, shortages of key commodities, exacerbated by Russia's invasion of Ukraine, contributed substantially to higher energy and food prices. In some countries, tight conditions and mismatches in labor markets further added to rising wages and higher input and production costs. Finally, many countries experienced large currency depreciations that passed through into higher import, producer, and consumer prices. The higher share of food in consumer spending has caused inflation to

accelerate more in low-income countries compared to other EMDEs.

Inflation has risen across a broad range of goods and services (Ball, Leigh, and Mishra 2022). Global core inflation has risen markedly, reaching over 6 percent late last year, its highest level since 1992. As a result, short-term (one-year-ahead) inflation expectations have risen in most econ-omies (figure 1.5.A). In contrast, long-term (five-year-ahead) inflation expectations have been relatively more stable, edging up by only about 0.15 percentage point in both advanced econ-omies and EMDEs since the onset of the pandemic. This stability may reflect the credibility of the commitment of most central banks to confront inflation, reinforced by recent policy tightening.

Inflationary pressures started to abate toward the end of 2022, reflecting weakening demand and easing commodity prices. The share of countries where inflation is accelerating is trending down (figure 1.5.B). In the face of substantial monetary tightening, slowing activity, easing supply chain disruptions, and moderating prices for many non-energy commodities, both core and headline inflation are expected to decline over the forecast horizon. In many countries, however, high core inflation has been unexpectedly persistent, suggesting that global inflation will remain elevated for longer than previously envisaged.

Financial developments

Global financial conditions have tightened sharply, with risk appetite dampened by slowing global growth, persistently elevated inflation, and faster-than-expected monetary tightening (figure 1.5.C). Long-term government bond yields in the United States and Germany increased at their fastest pace in nearly three decades in 2022, reaching their highest levels since 2007 and 2011, respectively, in October. In the United Kingdom, a sharp deterioration in liquidity related to collateral calls on pension fund derivative posi-tions prompted central bank intervention in gilt markets for financial stability purposes. Equity markets worldwide saw substantial declines—by December, the MSCI World equity index had

FIGURE 1.5 Global inflation and financial developments

Global inflation surged in 2022. Short-term inflation expectations have risen in most countries; however, long-term expectations have been more stable. Global inflation has started to abate as fewer countries experience accelerating price increases. Amid faster-than-expected advanced-economy monetary policy tightening, the currencies of emerging market and developing economies (EMDEs) with large fiscal deficits have depreciated sharply. Bond issuance in EMDEs has also declined markedly, while sovereign borrowing spreads have risen particularly sharply in energy importers with weak credit ratings.

A. Inflation expectations

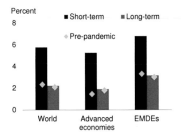

B. Share of economies with rising inflation

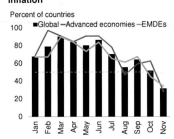

C. U.S. and euro area interest rate expectations

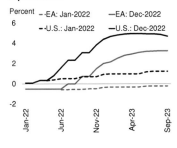

D. EMDE currency depreciation against the U.S. dollar in 2022

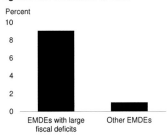

E. EMDE bond issuance, by region

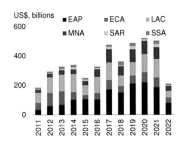

F. EMDE sovereign spread changes in 2022, by credit rating and energy exporter status

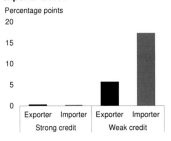

Sources: BIS (database); Bloomberg; Consensus Economics; Dealogic; Haver Analytics; JP Morgan; Moody's; WEO (database); World Bank.
Note: EAP = East Asia and Pacific, ECA = Europe and Central Asia, LAC = Latin America and the Caribbean, MNA = Middle East and North Africa, SAR = South Asia, SSA = Sub-Saharan Africa; EA = Euro area; EMBI = Emerging Markets Bond Index; EMDEs = emerging market and developing economies.
A. Median one-year-ahead (short-term) and five-year-ahead (long-term) CPI inflation expectations for up to 33 advanced economies and 50 EMDEs, based on December 2022 surveys. Yellow diamonds indicate pre-pandemic levels based on January 2020 surveys.
B. Last observation is November 2022. Median inflation for 32 advanced economies and 48 EMDEs.
C. Policy rate expectations, starting on January 2023, derived from futures curves observed on December 16, 2022.
D. Simple average of change in U.S. dollar exchange rates for 114 EMDEs with estimated fiscal deficits greater (less) than 3 percent of GDP in 2022. Last observation is December 16, 2022.
E. Sovereign and corporate bond issuance, January to November. Unbalanced sample of up to 76 EMDEs (9 EAP, 16 ECA, 17 LAC, 10 MNA, 4 SAR, and 20 SSA).
F. Change in EMBI spreads since January 2022, using Moody's sovereign foreign currency ratings. Sample includes 11 EMDE energy exporters and 35 EMDE energy importers. Strong credit defined as ratings from Aaa to Baa3. Weak credit defined as ratings from Caa to Ca. Sample excludes Belarus, the Russian Federation, and Ukraine. Last observation is December 13, 2022.

declined nearly 20 percent since the start of the year, with equity market indexes down more than 15 percent (in U.S. dollar terms) in about half of countries.

As in past tightening episodes, tighter monetary policy in advanced economies weighed on EMDE capital flows. China experienced sizable debt market outflows in 2022, while other EMDEs remained in a protracted period of generally weak debt and equity flows that started in 2021. The U.S. dollar also appreciated markedly in 2022, by about 14 percent on a GDP-weighted basis by October, before moderating somewhat later in the year. Most EMDE currencies depreciated against the U.S. dollar, but economies with fiscal deficits greater than 3 percent of GDP saw eight times more depreciation, on average, than other EMDEs (figure 1.5.D).

Dollar strength has squeezed a wide range of borrowers with net dollar exposures and has contributed to inflation in countries with depreciating currencies. To forestall more acute capital outflows and currency depreciation pressures, many EMDE monetary authorities extended domestic tightening cycles or used foreign exchange reserves to lean against currency pressures. Increasingly difficult market conditions led EMDE bond issuance in 2022 to fall to its lowest level in 10 years (figure 1.5.E). Investors increasingly shied away from the debt of the most vulnerable EMDEs, where financial crisis risks are mounting. Energy importers with weak credit ratings saw especially sharp increases in sovereign spreads, adding to the difficulty of financing large current account deficits (figure 1.5.F). Spreads on dollar-denominated debt exceed 10 percentage points in about one-in-five EMDEs, effectively locking them out of global debt markets. This is up from less than one-in-fifteen in 2019.

Major economies: Recent developments and outlook

Conditions in advanced economies have deteriorated sharply since mid-2022 amid high inflation, rapid monetary tightening, reduced fiscal support, and major energy disruptions in Europe. The monetary tightening cycle and continued energy supply pressures are projected to slow growth further in 2023, especially in the euro area. In China, activity weakened last year and remains vulnerable to a prolonged drag from the real estate sector and continued pandemic-related disruptions.

Advanced economies

Advanced economy growth slowed from 5.3 percent in 2021 to an estimated 2.5 percent in 2022—the fourth fastest deceleration of the past five decades. Economic conditions deteriorated substantially in the second half of 2022 as high inflation eroded household purchasing power and dented confidence, while rapid monetary policy tightening weighed on demand. Housing prices and property-related activity have cooled. Gas supply to the euro area was disrupted by Russia's invasion of Ukraine, pushing up energy prices and inflation, hampering industrial production, and stoking uncertainty.

Growth in advanced economies is projected to slow sharply in 2023, to 0.5 percent, as central banks continue to tighten monetary policy to contain inflationary pressures, labor markets soften, and energy market disruptions in Europe persist. Growth is expected to pick up modestly in 2024, as policy headwinds abate and energy markets stabilize. Persistent high inflation requiring an even more aggressive monetary policy response represents a major downside risk, as do prolonged energy supply disruptions in Europe.

In the **United States**, rising food and energy prices, together with a tight labor market, pushed inflation to multi-decade highs in 2022, before price pressures began easing toward the end of the year (figure 1.6.A). This has prompted the most rapid monetary policy tightening in more than 40 years (figure 1.6.B). Activity contracted in the first half of 2022, and domestic demand remained weak in the second half, with particular softness in residential investment. In all, growth for 2022 is estimated to have slowed to 1.9 percent as substantial fiscal consolidation—worth about 5 percent of GDP—added to monetary policy headwinds.

Continued macroeconomic policy tightening to contain inflationary pressures this year is envisaged

FIGURE 1.6 Major economies: Recent developments and outlook

In the United States, inflation rose to multidecade highs, prompting the most rapid tightening of monetary policy in more than 40 years. In the euro area, energy prices soared as natural gas supplies were severely disrupted. Activity in China slowed due to pandemic-related restrictions and ongoing stress in the property sector.

A. CPI inflation in the United States

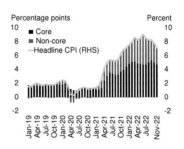

B. Rate hikes and U.S. dollar appreciation during U.S. monetary tightening episodes

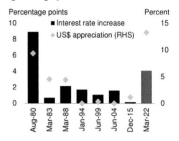

C. Euro area electricity prices

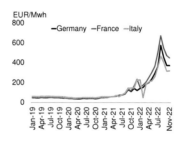

D. Industrial production, retail sales, export, and import growth in China

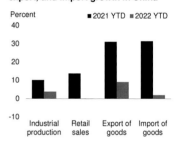

Sources: BIS (database); Bloomberg; Federal Reserve Economic Data; Haver Analytics; U.S. Bureau of Labor Statistics; World Bank.
A. CPI refers to consumer price index. Bars show contributions to year-on-year headline CPI inflation. Line shows year-on-year headline CPI inflation. Last observation is November 2022.
B. Bars represent the extent of the U.S. interest rate increase in the first 9 months of tightening cycle. Yellow diamonds represent the peak appreciation in the U.S. dollar nominal effective exchange rate in the first 9 months of tightening cycle. U.S. dollar depreciations during tightening cycles starting in 1994 and 2004 not shown. Horizontal axis represents the start of each tightening cycle since 1980. Last observation for nominal effective exchange rate is October 2022.
C. Figure shows one-year-forward baseload electricity prices. Last observation is November 2022.
D. Bars denote the year-to-date real growth of industrial production from January to November and year-to-date nominal growth of retail sales and goods exports and imports from January to November. Last observation is November 2022.

to compound the lagged effects of substantial interest rate increases in 2022 and further weigh on U.S. activity. Growth is projected to slow to 0.5 percent in 2023—1.9 percentage points below previous forecasts—the weakest performance outside official recessions since 1970. Inflation is expected to moderate in 2023 as labor markets soften and wage pressures abate.

In the **euro area**, activity in the first half of 2022 exceeded expectations, resulting in annual growth being revised up to 3.3 percent. In the second half of the year, however, activity weakened substantially as a result of soaring energy prices and supply uncertainty, compounded by rising borrowing costs. Inflation rose to record highs as Russia's invasion of Ukraine led to natural gas supply cuts and surging energy prices—which, despite some recent moderation, remain well above pre-invasion levels (figure 1.6.C). Broad-ranging fiscal measures introduced by European governments, estimated at 1.2 percent of GDP in 2022 and up to almost 2 percent of GDP in 2023, aimed to cushion the impact of energy price increases on households and businesses (European Commission 2022).

In 2023, euro area growth is forecast at zero percent—a downward revision of 1.9 percentage points, owing to ongoing energy supply disruptions and more monetary policy tightening than expected. Activity is expected to contract in the first half of 2023 before stabilizing later in the year. Inflation is envisaged to moderate as labor markets cool and energy prices decline.

In **Japan**, growth slowed in 2022 as high energy prices and supply bottlenecks eroded household purchasing power and dampened consumption. Deteriorating terms of trade and weakening global demand added to these headwinds. Growth is expected to slow further to 1 percent in 2023, alongside a slowdown in other advanced economies.

China

Economic activity in China deteriorated markedly in 2022 (figure 1.6.D). COVID-19 related restrictions, unprecedented droughts, and ongoing property sector stress restrained consumption, production, and residential investment (World Bank 2022b). Property sales, housing starts, and new-home prices have continued to decline, and several property developers have defaulted on their debt obligations. Infrastructure-focused fiscal support, policy rate and reserve requirement ratio cuts, and regulatory easing measures—including cash subsidies and lower down payment requirements—have only partially offset these headwinds. In all, growth is estimated to have slowed to 2.7 percent in 2022, 1.6 percentage points below previous forecasts—and, with the

exception of 2020, the weakest pace of growth since the mid-1970s.

Growth is projected to pick up to 4.3 percent in 2023 as the lifting of pandemic restrictions releases pent-up consumer spending. This is 0.9 percentage point below previous forecasts, primarily due to longer-than-expected pandemic-related disruptions, weaker external demand, and protracted weakness in the real estate sector. Continued disruptions from COVID-19, extreme weather events, and prolonged real estate sector stress are key downside risks.

Emerging market and developing economies

The outlook for EMDEs has deteriorated markedly due to tighter financial conditions and weaker external demand. High inflation, monetary policy tightening, and adverse effects from the Russian Federation's invasion of Ukraine are expected to weigh on EMDE activity. LICs are being particularly affected by high prices and shortages of food.

Recent developments

Activity in EMDEs decelerated sharply in 2022 as global financial conditions tightened, high inflation weighed on consumer spending, weakness in the world's largest economies dampened external demand, and spillovers from the Russian Federation's invasion of Ukraine persisted. Growth nearly halved from 6.7 percent in 2021 to an estimated 3.4 percent in 2022—the sharpest deceleration in EMDE growth outside of the 2009 and 2020 global recessions (figure 1.7.A). A steep fall in activity in the second half of the year contributed to downgrades in growth estimates for 2022 in many EMDEs and is set to be a drag on growth in 2023 (figure 1.7.B).

Inflation in many EMDEs has outpaced nominal wage growth. Price increases have dented real incomes, particularly for vulnerable households, and weighed on consumption (figure 1.7.C; Argente and Lee 2021; Ha, Kose, and Ohnsorge 2019a). Private investment has been feeble, reflecting higher borrowing costs, weakened confidence, and elevated uncertainty. Decelerating global demand has weighed on EMDE export growth, especially in economies with strong trade linkages with the United States, the euro area, and China. However, a rebound in tourism led to stronger-than-expected growth in tourism-reliant economies, including many small states (figure 1.7.D).

Growth estimates for 2022 in energy-exporting EMDEs were revised up, as the positive effects of high energy prices offset domestic demand weakness (figure 1.7.E). The improvement, however, was held back by supply constraints in some oil exporters, owing to a prolonged period of subdued investment (chapter 3). Activity among metal exporters was weaker than expected in 2022, reflecting softening external demand, especially from China, and the high cost of production, which tends to be energy intensive (World Bank 2022a). Estimated growth last year in many agricultural exporters was revised down as a result of supply disruptions, high input costs, and unfavorable weather. In commodity importers, growth is estimated to have fallen from 7.6 percent in 2021 to 3.6 percent in 2022, partly reflecting the impact from high food and energy prices.

Activity in LICs deteriorated over the course of the year as food insecurity and poverty worsened, with inflation in the median LIC doubling since early 2022. Cost-of-living increases and surging import bills have weighed on growth, particularly in LICs without the policy space to shield vulnerable populations from rising food and fuel prices. Activity in LICs is also suffering from slowing external demand, debt distress, and ongoing conflict and fragility (figure 1.7.F).

Outlook

EMDE outlook

Following last year's sharp deceleration, growth in EMDEs is forecast to remain essentially unchanged at 3.4 percent in 2023. However, excluding China—where growth is expected to partially recover after a weak 2022—EMDE activity is forecast to again slow markedly this year, to 2.7 percent (figure 1.8.A). Spillovers from weaker growth in the euro area and the United States are expected to dampen activity in EMDEs,

FIGURE 1.7 Recent developments in emerging market and developing economies

Growth in emerging market and developing economies (EMDEs) slowed significantly in 2022, particularly in the second half of the year, owing to tighter global financial conditions and ongoing effects of the Russian Federation's invasion of Ukraine. The acceleration in inflation dampened private consumption, while weak external demand weighed on EMDE exports. Growth estimates for 2022 have been revised up for many energy exporters and tourism-reliant economies; in contrast, downgrades have been particularly prevalent in non-energy commodity exporters. In low-income countries, conflict and fragility have weighed on activity.

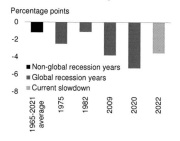

A. Slowdown in EMDE growth

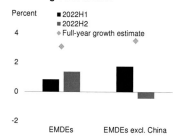

B. EMDE growth in 2022

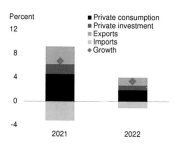

C. Contributions to EMDE growth

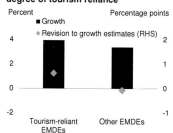

D. Growth estimates in 2022, by degree of tourism reliance

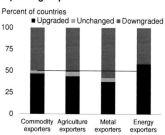

E. Revisions to EMDE growth estimates in 2022, by commodity exporter group

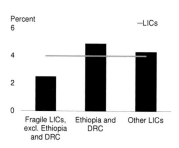

F. LICs growth estimates in 2022

Sources: Haver Analytics; Kose, Sugawara, and Terrones (2020); United Nations World Tourism Organization; World Bank.

Note: DRC = Democratic Republic of Congo; EMDEs = emerging market and developing economies; LICs = low-income countries; Fragile LICs = LICs with fragile and conflict affected situations. Unless otherwise indicated, aggregate growth rates are calculated using real U.S. dollar GDP weights at average 2010-19 prices and market exchange rates. Forecast revisions are the change in 2022 growth forecasts between the June 2022 and January 2023 editions of *Global Economic Prospects*. Growth rates may differ than what is presented in table 1.1 due to sample size.

A. Blue bar denotes the average EMDE growth slowdown in non-global recession years since 1962. Red bars denote EMDE growth slowdowns that coincided with global recession years (1975, 1982, 2009, and 2020). Global recession is a contraction in global per capita GDP, as described in Kose, Sugawara, and Terrones (2020). Sample includes 101 EMDEs.

B. Growth for period averages is calculated from quarterly growth rates, which are seasonally adjusted annual rates. Balanced sample includes 31 EMDEs.

D. "Tourism-reliant" EMDEs are those in the top quartile of inbound tourism expenditures as a share of GDP (2015-19 average). Sample size includes 35 tourism-reliant economies and 109 other EMDEs.

E. Sample includes 90 EMDE commodity exporters.

F. Sample includes 23 LICs, including 13 fragile LICs.

BOX 1.1 Regional perspectives: Outlook and risks

The forecast for growth in 2023 and 2024 combined has been downgraded for every emerging market and developing economy (EMDE) region. Monetary policy tightening, and restrictive global financial conditions are slowing growth, especially in LAC, SAR, and SSA. Persistently elevated energy prices are expected to dampen outlooks for energy importers in all regions, while falling metals prices will weigh on terms of trade in LAC and SSA. The projected slowdown in advanced economy import demand is expected to especially impact EAP and ECA. Added to the pandemic-induced recession and incomplete recovery, the outlook implies feeble per capita income growth in LAC, MNA, and SSA in the half decade to 2024. Risks to the baseline forecasts are skewed to the downside in all regions. They include the possibility of financial stress and greater spillovers from major advanced economy weakness (especially in EAP, ECA, LAC, and SSA), commodity price shocks (especially in ECA, EAP, and SAR), conflict (particularly in ECA, MNA, and SSA), and natural disasters (with elevated risk in subregions in EAP, LAC, and SAR).

Introduction

Emerging market and developing economy (EMDE) regions are contending with varied headwinds. These include spillovers from subdued conditions in major economies; the repercussions of the Russian Federation's invasion of Ukraine, including high food and energy prices; tightening financial conditions; and continued fiscal consolidation. These factors are expected to hinder EMDE growth in 2023 and 2024, to varying degrees across the regions. Growth is expected to be weakest in ECA, where the effects of the war and a sharp slowdown in the euro area are greatest, and in LAC, where commodity tailwinds are unwinding amid sharp policy tightening to contain inflation. MNA is projected to experience rapid slowing from a decade-high growth rate in 2022, driven by surging oil prices. The outlook remains comparatively resilient in SAR, due to limited spillovers to India from a projected global slowdown, but growth is nonetheless expected to decelerate notably in 2023. Growth is set to gradually firm in EAP and SSA in 2023 and 2024, but from low starting points due to weakness in large regional economies. The baseline projection of broadly lackluster growth leaves EMDE regions vulnerable to further negative shocks. These could take the form of balance of payments difficulties, debt crises, weaker external demand, food and energy price shocks, and climate-related natural disasters.

Against this backdrop, this box considers two questions:

- What are the cross-regional differences in the outlook for growth?

- What are the key risks to the outlook for each region?

_____

Note: This box was prepared by Phil Kenworthy

Outlook

EMDE regions face numerous spillovers from the darkening global economic outlook, along with weakening domestic conditions. The forecast for growth in 2023 and 2024 combined has been downgraded for every EMDE region since June (figure B1.1.1.A). Growth is projected to be weakest in ECA, with output virtually flat in 2023 for a second consecutive year, reflecting a deep contraction in Russia and weak growth elsewhere. The outlook in LAC is also for anemic growth in 2023, as a recovery boosted by commodity tailwinds unwinds, with only a limited rebound in 2024. After growth at a decade-high rate in 2022, driven by surging energy prices, MNA's economy is expected to decelerate rapidly toward its average 2010s growth rate. Weakness in China weighed on activity in EAP in 2022, though expansion was firmer in the rest of the region. Some improvement in activity is forecast in 2023 and 2024, underpinned by a partial recovery in China, but growth overall is projected to remain slower than in the pre-pandemic decade.

In SSA, a firming but still mediocre growth outlook suggests only limited progress with poverty reduction. Though set to decelerate, SAR is expected to remain the fastest growing EMDE region accross the forecast horizon, driven by India. Nonetheless, Pakistan faces mounting economic difficulties and Sri Lanka remains in crisis. In all regions, improvements in living standards over the half-decade to 2024 are expected to be slower than from 2010-19 (figure B1.1.1.B). In LAC and SSA, per capita incomes are expected to further diverge from those in advanced economies, rather than catching up.

Restrictive global financial conditions and domestic monetary tightening are weighing on most regional outlooks by discouraging investment and raising debt

BOX 1.1 Regional perspectives: Outlook and risks (*continued*)

FIGURE B1.1.1 Regional outlooks

Growth forecasts have been downgraded in all EMDE regions since June, reflecting external headwinds as well as weakening domestic conditions. In almost all regions, per capita income growth in 2020-24 is expected to be far below 2010-19 averages. Monetary policies have been tightened in many EMDEs to combat inflation and stave off external financing pressures. Amid high inflation, real effective exchange rates have appreciated in most EMDE regions.

A. Output growth

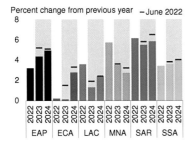

B. Average annual per capita GDP growth

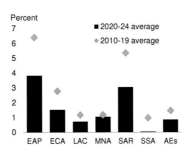

C. Changes in real policy interest rates and real effective exchange rates in 2022

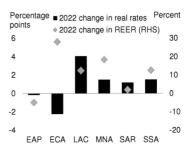

Sources: BIS (database); Bloomberg; Consensus Economics; Haver Analytics; International Monetary Fund; United Nations Population Division; World Bank.
Note: AEs = advanced economies; EAP = East Asia and Pacific, ECA = Europe and Central Asia, LAC = Latin America and the Caribbean, MNA = Middle East and North Africa, SAR = South Asia, SSA = Sub-Saharan Africa; REER = real effective exchange rate.
A.B. Aggregate growth rates are calculated using GDP weights at average 2010-19 prices and market exchange rates.
A. June 2022 refers to forecasts presented in the June 2022 edition of the *Global Economic Prospects* report. Shaded areas indicate forecasts.
C. Real interest rates are policy rates minus one-year-ahead inflation expectations. One-year-ahead expectations are calculated as a weighted average of Consensus Economics or Bloomberg private forecasters median expectations for annual inflation in 2022 and 2023. Regional values are GDP-weighted averages of the three largest economies in each region, excluding economies where inflation is above 50 percent year-on-year (Argentina and Türkiye). The change in real interest rates is from the end of 2021 to November, 2022. Change in real effective exchange rate is a GDP-weighted average of the change from December 31, 2021, to December 16, 2022. REERs are based on consumer price inflation. Sample contains 54 EMDEs (9 in EAP, 12 in ECA, 14 in LAC, 7 in MNA, 2 in SAR, and 10 in SSA).

service costs, with the most pronounced effects in LAC, SAR, and SSA. Many EMDEs are also pursuing necessary fiscal adjustments, which nonetheless dampen near-term growth prospects. The sharpest tightening of monetary policy has taken place in LAC, where inflation-targeting central banks reacted to accelerating prices with steep rate hikes earlier than in other regions. Higher interest rates, in real as well as nominal terms, may help to limit currency depreciations and ensure macroeconomic stability in the medium-term, but are expected to dampen domestic demand in 2023 and 2024 (figure B1.1.1.C).

In SAR and SSA, fiscal and monetary policies have become less accommodative more recently, as authorities seek lower fiscal deficits and higher real interest rates to stem external financing pressures and bear down on rising inflation. In MNA, monetary policy has tightened in both net oil importers and exporters—in the former, to curb soaring inflation and current account deficits; in the latter, in line with pegged exchange rates and in recognition of substantial

price pressures on households. In ECA, nominal policy rates have risen to multidecade highs in many countries but have been outstripped by soaring prices; real rates have fallen sharply as a result. Many ECA authorities have also implemented emergency fiscal measures to support populations facing plummeting real incomes due to war-related energy supply disruptions. Monetary and fiscal policy has eased somewhat in China, where activity has been weak and inflation below target. Elsewhere in EAP, policy has started to tighten due to mounting inflation and price pressures, albeit with inflation still lower than in other regions.

As growth in advanced economies slows sharply, EMDE export growth will weaken. The projected contraction in the euro area is set to weigh on ECA and net oil importers in MNA. A subdued global growth outlook also implies limited demand growth for primary commodity exports, including from LAC and SSA, though gradually firming import demand in China should provide some offset. Producers of manufactured goods in EAP and LAC are heavily exposed to the sharp

BOX 1.1 Regional perspectives: Outlook and risks (*continued*)

deceleration projected for the United States. In SAR, in contrast, limited trade openness reduces direct vulnerability to trade spillovers. High inflation and substantial weakening of several advanced economy currencies have also contributed to appreciating real effective exchange rates in most EMDE regions, eroding competitiveness. In ECA, real appreciation reflects falls in the euro and sterling, the appreciation of the Russian ruble, and broad-based double-digit domestic inflation. In LAC, high inflation has been paired with resilient domestic currencies, reflecting strong commodity exports and rising real interest rates. Energy producers in MNA and SSA have also seen large real appreciations due to export windfalls (combined with fixed exchange rates, in many cases). EAP and SAR are the only regions where real effective exchange rates did not strengthen significantly in 2022, due to the weakening Chinese renminbi and sharp nominal currency depreciations in Pakistan and Sri Lanka, respectively.

Diverging commodity prices are another key factor driving regional prospects. Despite slowing global growth, energy prices are expected to remain elevated. In contrast, most metal prices fell appreciably in 2022 and are expected to decline by a further 15 percent (in U.S. dollar terms) in 2023 (World Bank 2022a). The only EMDE region where growth is bolstered by the commodity price outlook is MNA, due to the preponderance of energy exporters. In LAC and SSA, while fossil fuel exporters are benefitting from high energy prices, exporters of industrial metals are suffering from worsening terms of trade that are expected to weaken investment and output growth. The effects of commodity price movements are also mixed in ECA. Energy exporters are likely to continue seeing elevated export earnings, but sharply higher energy and food prices will suppress regionwide consumption. Most large economies in EAP and SAR depend on imported energy, with heavy use of coal and gas for which prices are expected to remain especially elevated. In some countries this implies a continued squeeze in consumer spending; in others, price controls and subsidies may initially shield households, but fiscal burdens and distortions associated with such policies will grow (World Bank 2022b).

Risks

The baseline projection is subject to a range of downside risks, stemming from additional global policy tight-

ening, adverse geopolitical developments, and varied domestic challenges. Additional tightening of global financial conditions poses substantial risks in ECA, LAC, and SSA, given the size and composition of regional debt stocks. Further increases in energy and food prices, potentially linked to an intensifying war in Ukraine, would weigh heavily on SAR and SSA, and on energy importers in ECA and MNA. Trade spillovers from weaker-than-anticipated economic activity in advanced economies could undermine manufacturing output in EAP and LAC. On the domestic front, EMDE regions also face risks from worsening conflicts (in ECA, MNA, and SSA), and extreme climate-related weather events (especially in small states in EAP and LAC).

A disorderly tightening of financial conditions is a key risk facing EMDEs. It could be triggered by further increases in advanced-economy interest rates in response to persistent elevated inflation, combined with deteriorating global risk sentiment (Obstfeld 2022a). The EMDEs at greatest risk of financial stress are those with large stocks of externally held debt, especially at short maturities or denominated in foreign currency. These liabilities could become increasingly costly to service and roll over, generating stress in sovereign, corporate, or financial sectors. Risks appear greatest in ECA, LAC, and SSA, owing to different combinations of high corporate indebtedness (ECA and LAC), large sovereign debts (ECA and SSA), and sizable currency depreciations against the U.S. dollar (SSA; figure B1.1.2.A). Difficulties accessing external credit are especially likely in countries with large fiscal and current account deficits. In LAC, SAR, and SSA, there are large regional economies where these risks are substantial, though all regions contain some countries where they are elevated (figure B1.1.2.B).

If energy prices are higher than projected, several EMDE regions could see further commodity-driven deterioration in their terms of trade (figure B1.1.2.C). A broad range of factors could prompt an energy price spike, including a spell of unusually cold weather in Europe, continued sluggish supply responses from U.S. shale producers, and further geopolitical turmoil involving energy exporters. The resulting impacts on regionwide import prices and current account balances could be large in EAP and SAR, where energy importers make up the vast majority of regional GDP (figure B1.1.2.D). In ECA, though there could be windfall

BOX 1.1 Regional perspectives: Outlook and risks (*continued*)

FIGURE B1.1.2 Regional risks

Against a backdrop of tightening financial conditions and a strong U.S. dollar, regions with large external debts or wide fiscal and external deficits are at particular risk of financial stress. Further increases in energy prices could weigh on EMDEs that rely on energy imports, while weakening global demand could have outsized effects on metal exporters. Weaker-than-expected growth in advanced economies would dampen EMDE export demand. Weather-related natural disasters are an ever-present risk, especially for parts of SAR and small states in EAP and LAC, and climate change is increasing their frequency.

A. External debt

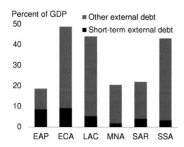

B. Current account and fiscal balances in 2023

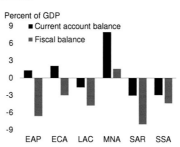

C. Change in commodity terms of trade in 2022

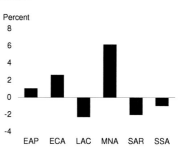

D. Proportion of GDP from energy and metals exporters

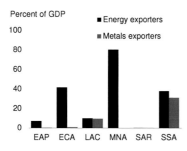

E. Exports to the United States and European Union

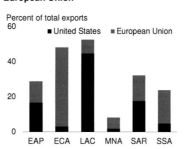

F. Extreme weather events in EMDEs

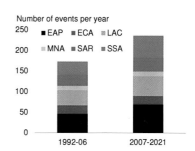

Sources: Comtrade (database); EM-DAT (database); International Monetary Fund; Kose et al. (2022); World Bank.

Note: AEs = advanced economies; EAP = East Asia and Pacific, ECA = Europe and Central Asia, EMDE = emerging market and developing economy, LAC = Latin America and the Caribbean, MNA = Middle East and North Africa, SAR = South Asia, SSA = Sub-Saharan Africa.

A. GDP-weighted average of gross debt held by nonresidents as a share of GDP. Short-term external debt is external debt maturing is less than one year. Data for 2021, except for SSA (2020 data). Debt holdings across different countries within a region are counted as external.

B. GDP-weighted averages of forecast current account and general government balances in 2023.

C. GDP-weighted average of regional change in commodity terms of trade between December 2021 and October 2022. Commodity terms of trade is based on commodity net export price index, constructed from commodities weighted by ratio of net exports to total commodity trade, with rolling weights. Sample includes 146 EMDEs (20 in EAP, 22 in ECA, 32 in LAC, 18 in MNA, 8 in SAR, and 46 in SSA).

D. An economy is defined as an exporter of energy or metals when, on average in 2017-19, exports of that commodity category accounted for 20 percent or more of total exports. Economies for which the thresholds were met as a result of re-exports are excluded. When data are not available, judgment is used. This taxonomy results in the exclusion of some well-diversified economies with a broad range of exports, even if they are exporters of certain commodities. Data for 2023, based on forecasts.

E. Sources of export demand for 2019 and 2020 combined. Percent of gross regional exports (that is, total regional exports include intraregional exports).

F. Simple average of events per year throughout the specified time periods. Storms, droughts, floods, and extreme heat episodes are classified as extreme weather events.

gains for energy exporters, the already intense pressure on terms of trade in Central and Eastern Europe would worsen, and negative trade spillovers from the euro area could intensify. The adverse implications for global growth could also prompt sharper than assumed falls in metals prices, which would widen external imbalances

and exacerbate downside risks for metal exporters in LAC and SSA (Baumeister, Verduzco-Bustos, and Ohnsorge 2022; Di Pace, Juvenal, and Petrella 2020).

The headwinds facing EMDEs would intensify if the materialization of global downside risks resulted in

BOX 1.1 Regional perspectives: Outlook and risks (*continued*)

additional economic weakness in advanced economies and China. This would weigh heavily on export-oriented EMDEs, particularly those in ECA and LAC which have the greatest direct exposure (figure B1.1.2.E; Bems, Johnson, and Yi 2010). Even in regions where direct export exposures are less pronounced, the effects of reduced consumer spending would propagate through supply chains, reducing demand for intermediate goods and primary commodities.

EMDEs are increasingly vulnerable to shocks from natural disasters, including extreme weather events such as floods, storms, and droughts (Mallucci 2020). With climate change, such events are becoming more common (figure B1.1.2.F). Extreme weather presents a severe economic threat in small states in EAP and LAC: as a group, EMDE small states experience annual average disaster-related losses amounting to close to 5 percent of GDP. Some areas of SAR also face

particularly elevated risks, as illustrated by the damage wrought by recent flooding in Pakistan.

A broad range of social and political challenges could also worsen in the context of rising food insecurity in EMDEs, proliferation of armed conflict in some regions, and slow progress on poverty reduction (World Bank 2022a). In parts of SSA, violence and armed conflict has recently increased, with dire implications for safety, food security, and childhood development. Food insecurity is also rising in MNA among net oil importers and several economies that have long grappled with fragility and conflict. In LAC, stagnating living standards could heighten risks of disruptive social unrest and make it harder for authorities to combat elevated crime and corruption in some countries. Meanwhile, the ECA region faces the profound uncertainty and extreme downside risks of a protracted war.

especially those with tighter economic linkages to these major economies (ECA, LAC, SSA; box 1.1).

The forecast for 2023 EMDE growth has been downgraded 0.8 percentage point, reflecting weaker external demand and tighter financing conditions than previously assumed (figure 1.8.B). The overlapping adverse shocks of recent years are expected to keep output in EMDEs 5.6 percent below pre-pandemic trends in 2023—considerably worse than in advanced economies, where output is expected to be only 2.2 percent below pre-pandemic trends this year (figure 1.8.C).

Despite weakening demand and negative output gaps, inflation is expected to remain above central bank targets in most EMDEs, including large economies (figure 1.8.D). High prices for food, energy, and other inputs—especially in local currency terms, given the strength of the U.S. dollar—will remain a burden for households and businesses. Investment will be restrained by higher borrowing costs, weak sentiment, expectations of slow growth, and elevated policy and geopolitical uncertainty (chapter 3). Higher borrowing costs are envisaged to be particularly disruptive among

EMDEs with debt that is largely denominated in foreign currency, issued with short maturities, and already facing high servicing costs.

Exports are not expected to provide much support to activity, especially in economies closely linked to the United States, the euro area, or China. High inflation has outpaced currency depreciation in some EMDE regions, which may weigh on export competitiveness. The recovery in international tourism, however, should buoy tourism-reliant economies (WTTC 2022).

EMDE energy exporters will generally benefit from elevated energy prices over the near-term. In contrast, subdued demand from China, which imports more than half of global metal exports, is likely to dampen activity in metal exporters this year. Agricultural exporters will need to contend with high fertilizer costs during planting season. In commodity importers, growth is forecast to remain subdued in 2023 as a result of high prices for many commodities, inflation, tightening monetary policy, and limited fiscal space. EMDE growth is projected to firm to 4.1 percent in 2024 asexternal demand gradually improves, price pressures abate, and the drag from policy tightening eases.

EMDE potential growth is expected to continue to decelerate as recent output losses exacerbate the slowdown in the underlying drivers of long-term growth, including investment growth and human capital accumulation. Even prior to the pandemic, earlier gains from increases in human and physical capital had faded while reform momentum slowed. Learning and job losses from the pandemic have interrupted the accumulation of skills and human capital and are likely to weigh on incomes and potential growth for years to come (Schady et al. forthcoming). High food prices have increased food insecurity, including for children, which could lower long-term productivity as malnutrition early in life can permanently impair learning abilities. The adverse effects of the pandemic and the invasion of Ukraine on confidence and uncertainty are expected to linger and weigh on investment (figure 1.8.E; Dieppe 2021). Projected investment growth is below the individual country trend of the past 20 years in about three-fifths of EMDEs, which will reduce long-term growth and the ability to reach key development goals (chapter 3).

LICs outlook

LICs are forecast to grow 5.1 percent this year. However, projections have been revised down in nearly two-thirds of LICs due to worsening external conditions and rising domestic vulnerabilities (box 1.2). The deterioration of growth prospects in key trading partners is projected to weaken external demand, while high inflation, tighter global financing conditions, and debt distress are anticipated to restrain domestic consumption and investment (figure 1.8.F). Subdued activity in many economies—particularly in LICs with fragile conflict affected situations (FCS)—will further delay the reduction of poverty and food insecurity to pre-pandemic levels.

A substantial share of the LIC population is on the brink of famine and starvation due to various factors, including the effects of climate change, an intensification of conflict and violence, reduced food affordability, and a decline in foreign aid

FIGURE 1.8 Outlook in emerging market and developing economies

Growth in emerging market and developing economies (EMDEs) excluding China is expected to slow further in 2023. Widespread downgrades reflect weaker external demand and much tighter financial conditions. As a result of overlapping shocks over the past three years, aggregate output and investment in EMDEs are anticipated to remain well below pre-pandemic trends. Despite negative output gaps and weak demand, inflation is likely to remain elevated, including in large EMDEs. The outlook remains challenging for low-income countries, particularly those nearing or facing debt distress.

A. Contributions to EMDE growth

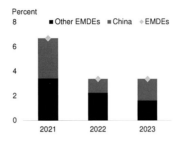

B. Forecast revisions to 2023 growth

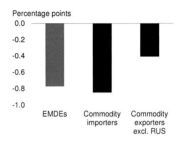

C. Deviation of output from pre-pandemic trends

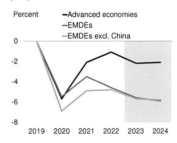

D. Output gaps and inflation in EM7

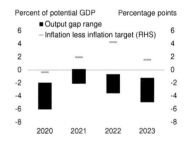

E. Deviation of investment from pre-pandemic trends in 2024

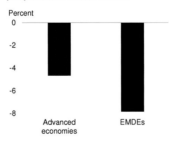

F. Growth in LICs

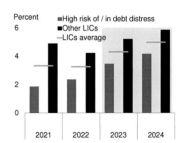

Sources: Haver Analytics; IMF (2022a); World Bank.
Note: EMDEs = emerging market and developing economies; LICs = low-income countries; RUS = Russian Federation; UKR = Ukraine. Unless otherwise indicated, aggregate growth rates are calculated using real U.S. dollar GDP weights at average 2010-19 prices and market exchange rates. Shaded areas indicate forecasts.
A. Figure shows the contributions to EMDE growth estimates and forecasts.
B. Forecast revisions are the change in 2023 growth forecasts between the June 2022 and January 2023 editions of *Global Economic Prospects*.
C.E. Figure shows the percent deviation between the current estimates and forecasts released in the January 2020 edition of *Global Economic Prospects*. For 2023 and 2024, the January 2020 baseline is extended using projected growth for 2022.
D. EM7 includes Brazil, China, India, Indonesia, Mexico, the Russian Federation, and Türkiye. "Output gap range" reflects one standard deviation range.
F. Sample size includes 23 LICs, of which 12 are in high risk of debt distress, and 11 in debt distress, as of November 2022 (IMF 2022a). Aggregates calculated using simple averages.

BOX 1.2 Recent developments and outlook for low-income countries

Growth in low-income countries (LICs) is forecast to be 5.1 percent in 2023. Despite this year's aggregate pickup, projections have been revised down for about two-thirds of LICs. Moreover, per capita income growth is expected to be a more subdued 2.2 percent in 2023. LICs are facing severe cost-of-living pressures, worsened by disruptions to global commodity markets—particularly for energy and staple cereals—following Russia's invasion of Ukraine. Many more people have fallen into extreme poverty and food insecurity due to soaring food and fuel prices. The outlook for many LICs has deteriorated amid surging inflation, tightening financial conditions, fiscal and debt pressures, slowing activity in key trading partners, and heightened fragility. Risks to the baseline projections are mainly to the downside, including high inflation, resurgence of violence, debt distress in several countries, new COVID-19 outbreaks, and adverse weather events owing to climate change.

Introduction

Although, the recovery in low-income countries (LICs) from the COVID-19 pandemic is expected to continue this year, many countries are facing substantial headwinds as prices of fuel and staple foods have increased further following Russia's invasion of Ukraine. Food affordability, especially for poorer households, has deteriorated sharply and many more people have fallen into extreme poverty (World Bank 2022c). Weakening global demand has dampened activity in many LICs, while tightening global financial conditions have worsened existing fiscal vulnerabilities. In several LICs, rising violence and adverse weather events have led to more disruptions, especially in farming, deepening food insecurity and heightening famine risks.

The baseline projections are subject to many downside risks. Deteriorating living standards for many, and increased poverty, may stoke social unrest in some countries, while already tight fiscal space to support the poor may shrink further with many governments facing unfavorable debt dynamics. A deeper and more protracted global economic slowdown than currently envisaged could further weigh on growth in many LICs through lower export demand and global commodity prices.

Against this backdrop this box addresses the following questions.

- What have been the main recent economic developments in LICs?

- What is the outlook for LICs?

- What are the risks to the outlook?

Note: This box was prepared by Sergiy Kasyanenko.

Recent developments

Output in LICs grew by an estimated 4.0 percent in 2022—only marginally faster than in 2021 even as the pandemic continued to abate and vaccination rates increased. Although revised 2022 growth estimates are on par with the June projections, they are sharply below the 5.4 percent average growth rate that LICs registered in 2000-19. Despite some large exporters benefitting from elevated global commodity prices, costlier imports and declining metal prices have led to a deterioration in LICs' terms of trade (figure B1.2.1.A). Activity in non-resource sectors strengthened in several large LICs (Democratic Republic of Congo, Uganda) spurred by the removal of COVID-19 restrictions. But the boost from economic reopening failed to deliver strong growth in many other countries: surging inflation, slowing global activity, increasing borrowing costs, limited fiscal space, and rising debt prompted growth downgrades for about 60 percent of LICs.

There is a large degree of heterogeneity among the growth revisions for individual countries. Small upgrades to previous projections for 2022 growth in larger resource-rich LICs (Democratic Republic of Congo, Mozambique), countries with less dependence on imported food (Uganda), and oil exporters (Chad) have been offset by large downgrades for many smaller LICs (Central African Republic, Eritrea, The Gambia, Mali), where cost-of-living and terms-of-trade shocks were amplified by high levels of fragility, soaring inflation and import bills, debt distress, and limited fiscal space. In addition, adverse weather events, such as severe floods in South Sudan and Sudan, have dampened activity in agriculture and mining.

With food accounting for over 40 percent of consumer spending, accelerating inflation is eroding domestic demand across many LICs; consumer prices in LICs

BOX 1.2 Recent developments and outlook for low-income countries (*continued*)

FIGURE B1.2.1 LICs: Recent developments

The sharp slowdown in global growth and the surge in global inflation have dampened economic recoveries across low-income countries (LICs). Terms of trade across LICs worsened further last year amid a sharp weakening of demand for industrial metals in key trading partners. The cost-of-living crisis has pushed many more people into poverty and food insecurity, especially in LICs where fragility was already elevated before Russia's invasion of Ukraine.

A. Terms of trade changes in LICs

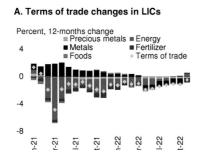

B. Consumer price inflation in LICs

C. Food insecurity in LICs

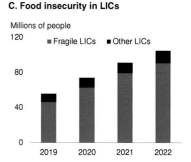

Sources: Haver Analytics; FSIN and GNAFC (2022); World Bank.
Note: EMDEs = emerging market and developing economies; Fragile LICs = LICs with fragile and conflict-affected situations; LICs = low-income countries.
A. Similar to Gruss and Kebhaj (2019), commodity terms-of-trade are calculated as changes in real commodity prices weighted by each commodity's net export share in GDP. Figure calculated using median net export shares for the sample of 15 non-oil exporting LICs. A negative change indicates deterioration in the terms of trade. Last observation is November 2022.
B. Sample includes 9 LICs. Dashed lines indicate interquartile range. Last observation is October 2022.
C. Bars show the number of people in food crisis as classified by the Integrated Food Security Phase Classification (IPC/CH) Phase 3, that is, in acute food insecurity crisis or worse. Data for 2022 are estimates as of September 2022.

increased more than five times faster in 2022 than before the COVID-19 pandemic (figure B1.2.1.B). Food affordability deteriorated considerably last year and millions more people fell into acute food insecurity, especially in LICs where poverty rates were already elevated because of the pandemic and fragility (figure B1.2.1.C; FSIN and GNAFC 2022). Several countries (Afghanistan, Somalia, South Sudan, Yemen) are facing catastrophic conditions with the shares of populations facing famine or starvation rising substantially as the negative impact of food price inflation is amplified by disruptions to humanitarian aid, droughts and flooding, and insecurity (WFP and FAO 2022). Violence and conflict escalated in a number of LICs last year, further disrupting farming, exacerbating food insecurity, and contributing to sharp growth slowdowns in several countries (Ethiopia, Mali, South Sudan). A recent ceasefire agreement in Ethiopia should facilitate the resumption of humanitarian aid to the Tigray region where millions of people were displaced by the two-year conflict.

Fiscal and debt sustainability pressures worsened in many LICs—budget deficits widened last year in almost half of all countries amid rising borrowing costs and muted growth. Additional measures to protect the poor—including subsidies, cuts to consumption taxes and custom duties, and transfers to vulnerable populations—have further strained fiscal budgets in some countries (The Gambia, Madagascar, Rwanda). Government debt in the median LIC, excluding energy-exporting Chad and South Sudan, hit almost 60 percent of GDP in 2022, its highest level since 2007. As a result, nearly 60 percent of all LICs were in, or at high risk of, debt distress at the end of 2022.

Outlook

Growth in LICs is projected to firm gradually to 5.1 percent in 2023 and 5.6 percent in 2024 as cost-of-living increases moderate, post-pandemic recoveries regain strength, and several countries complete the expansion of large extractive projects (figure B1.2.2.A). A small downward revision to this year's aggregate growth forecast masks a wide range of downward forecast revisions. The negative impact from high inflation is anticipated to persist in many smaller countries, being further amplified by the expected sharp

BOX 1.2 Recent developments and outlook for low-income countries (*continued*)

global economic slowdown and tight global financing conditions. Although, growth in the three largest LICs—Democratic Republic of Congo, Ethiopia, and Uganda, which account for over a half the group output—was revised upward slightly; projections for 2023 and 2024 had been revised down for about 65 and 50 percent of LICs, respectively. As a result, aggregate growth projections for LICs, excluding three largest economies, were revised down by 0.5 percentage point for 2023 and by 0.3 percentage point for 2024.

Among energy and metal exporters, growth prospects are mixed. The boost from elevated energy prices is envisaged to fade in some countries (Chad, South Sudan) where high levels of insecurity and policy uncertainty, adverse weather events, and aging oil fields are likely to deter oil output expansion. Increased demand for Africa's liquified natural gas is expected to lift growth in Mozambique, albeit with a delay because elevated insecurity in the northern part of the country has interrupted the development of a large offshore natural gas project; similarly, growth is anticipated to firm in Niger as oil production and exports take off. In contrast, a sharp slowdown in key trading partners, particularly China, which accounts for over a third of all exports in some LICs, is anticipated to weigh on recoveries in many countries, especially in metal exporters, as most commodity prices continue to ease (World Bank 2022a). In some countries (the Democratic Republic of Congo, Zambia) the negative impact of the global slowdown is expected to be partly offset by the continuing expansion of production in mining.

Growth in fragile and conflict-affected LICs is projected to average 5.4 percent in 2023-24, broadly in line with previous forecasts. However, if Ethiopia (the largest fragile LIC) and several fragile states that are expected to complete large mining projects (Democratic Republic of Congo, Mozambique) are excluded from the growth forecast, the outlook for fragile LICs has substantially worsened, with downgrades of 0.4 percentage point both in 2023 and 2024. Insecurity, elevated levels of debt—nearly 70 percent of fragile LICs are in, or at high risk of, debt distress—policy uncertainty, and a sharp deterioration in food affordability are expected to dampen activity in many fragile LICs (Eritrea, Mali, South Sudan). Growth in Ethiopia is anticipated to remain under 6 percent on average in 2023-24—well below its pre-pandemic average—amid debt distress, continued fragility in the Tigray region, currency depreciation, and soaring inflation.

Conflict, adverse weather events, and rising production costs are anticipated to keep LIC food supplies tight. Reduced use of fertilizer and other farming inputs whose costs have risen sharply is envisaged to result in below-average agricultural production this year. Severe drought conditions are expected to persist in some countries, while high levels of violence are projected to disrupt farming activities, access to food markets and humanitarian aid (Eritrea, Ethiopia, Somalia). Some countries, however, may benefit from improved rainfall—production of coffee in Uganda, SSA's biggest coffee exporter, could increase to record levels in the 2022-23 crop year.

Fragility, conflict, and climate change are set to continue to drive poverty and food insecurity and restrain growth in many countries by amplifying the weakness in domestic demand. Progress with poverty alleviation, which has already stalled prior to the start of the COVID-19 pandemic, is anticipated to remain slow as subdued per-capita income growth persists in many LICs (World Bank 2022c). Although per capita income growth in LICs is forecast to increase at 2.5 percent on average in 2023-24, it is expected to remain slow in LICs with more prevalent poverty further delaying the reversal of pandemic-induced poverty increases. In LICs where over half of the population live in extreme poverty, average per capita income growth has been falling behind other LICs, a trend that began before the pandemic. For this group of countries, per capita incomes will only barely return to 2019 levels in 2024. In LICs with less prevalent poverty, per capita incomes never fell below 2019 levels, but they are still projected to remain 7 percent below the 2000-19 trend through 2023 (figure B1.2.2.B).

Risks

Risks to the outlook are mainly to the downside. Although growth is expected to firm this year and next as price pressures ease somewhat, a sharper-than-expected global economic deceleration could lead to further declines in commodity prices and export revenues, adversely affecting activity in many LICs, particularly energy and metal exporters.

BOX 1.2 Recent developments and outlook for low-income countries (*continued*)

FIGURE B1.2.2 LICs: Outlook and risks

Activity in low-income countries (LICs) is expected to firm somewhat in the forecast horizon, albeit with substantial heterogeneity among individual countries. Weaker per capita income growth, together with elevated levels of violence, would make it particularly challenging to rapidly reverse recent increases in food insecurity and poverty.

A. GDP growth

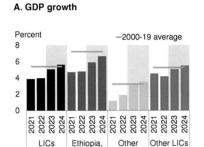

B. Per capita income in LICs

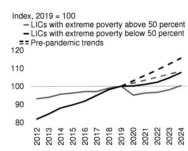

C. Reported violent events in LICs during the first 11 months of each year

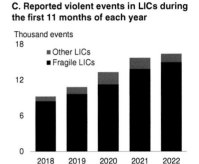

Source: Armed Conflict Location & Event Data Project (ACLED), https://www.acleddata.com; World Bank.
Note: Shaded area indicates forecast. Fragile LICs = LICs with fragile and conflict-affected situations; LICs = low-income countries.
A. DRC = Democratic Republic of Congo, MOZ = Mozambique, and NER = Niger; Democratic Republic of Congo, Ethiopia, Mozambique, and Niger age fragile LICs. Average GDP growth rates calculated using constant GDP weights at average 2010-19 prices and market exchange rates. Sample comprises 22 LICs, which include 13 fragile LICs.
B. Extreme poverty rate is measured as the share of people living on less than $2.15 per day. Per capita income is calculated as each group's GDP divided by each group's population. Dashed lines indicate per capita income assuming its growth rate equals to 2000-19 average after 2019. Sample excludes Democratic Republic of Congo and Niger—both with over half of population experiencing extreme poverty.
C. Violent events include battles, explosions, violence against civilians, riots, and protests reported since the start of the year. Last observation is December 2, 2022.

Debt sustainability risks have escalated for many LICs last year, as current account deficits widened and debt service costs surged. If global economic activity is weaker than projected, or if global interest rates rise further than assumed because of persistent inflation and faster-than-expected policy tightening, fiscal, currency, and debt sustainability pressures for many LICs could intensify sharply, with more countries pushed to the brink of debt distress.

LICs remain vulnerable to further deteriorations in food security, including from additional disruptions to already tight food supplies, especially of staple grains. Weak income growth also weighs on food security. Uncertainty surrounding the Black Sea Grain Initiative could lead to more volatility in global food prices, with possible price spikes further reducing food affordability (World Bank 2022d). Greater intensity, frequency, and duration of adverse weather events because of climate change could continue to disrupt farming and livelihoods in many LICs (OSCDS and UNHCR 2022; UNDRR 2022). Soaring import bills, shortages of

foreign exchange reserves, and debt distress could further constrain imports of staple food, fuel, and fertilizer. Agricultural productivity, already stressed by soaring production costs and climate change, could suffer lasting damage because of reduced use of fertilizer. Increased violence and fragility could exacerbate the impact of these developments on poverty and food security (figure B1.2.2.C; Maino and Emrullahu 2022).

Healthcare systems in LICs, severely stressed by the two years of the COVID-19 pandemic, could be further strained by new outbreaks of infectious diseases (for example, a recent Ebola outbreak in Uganda). Furthermore, even as the COVID-19 pandemic abates across LICs, very low vaccination rates, emerging variants, and waning immunity could lead to new virus outbreaks and disruptions in activity. Only 25 percent of the LIC population had been fully vaccinated against COVID-19 as of end-December and an even lower proportion in fragile LICs.

BOX 1.2 Recent developments and outlook for low-income countries (*continued*)

TABLE B1.2.1 Low-income country forecasts[a]

(Real GDP growth at market prices in percent, unless indicated otherwise) Percentage point differences from June 2022 projections

	2020	2021	2022e	2023f	2024f	2022e	2023f	2024f
Low-Income Country, GDP [b]	**1.6**	**3.9**	**4.0**	**5.1**	**5.6**	**0.0**	**-0.1**	**0.0**
Afghanistan [c]	-2.4	-20.7	..	..	..	..	..	..
Burkina Faso	1.9	6.9	4.3	5.0	5.3	-0.5	-0.4	0.0
Burundi	0.3	1.8	2.1	3.0	4.0	-0.4	-0.3	-0.1
Central African Republic	1.0	1.0	1.5	3.0	3.8	-1.7	-0.4	-0.2
Chad	-1.6	-1.2	3.1	3.3	3.3	0.3	-0.2	-0.6
Congo, Dem. Rep.	1.7	6.2	6.1	6.4	6.6	0.1	0.0	0.5
Eritrea	-0.5	2.9	2.5	2.7	2.9	-2.2	-0.9	-0.8
Ethiopia [d]	6.1	6.3	3.5	5.3	6.1	0.2	0.1	0.2
Gambia, The	0.6	4.3	3.5	4.0	5.5	-2.1	-2.2	-1.0
Guinea	4.9	3.9	4.6	5.3	5.6	0.3	-0.6	-0.2
Guinea-Bissau	1.5	5.0	3.5	4.5	4.5	0.0	0.0	0.0
Liberia	-3.0	5.0	3.7	4.7	5.7	-0.7	-0.1	0.5
Madagascar	-7.1	4.4	2.6	4.2	4.6	0.0	0.0	0.0
Malawi	0.8	2.8	1.5	3.0	3.4	-0.6	-1.3	-0.8
Mali	-1.2	3.1	1.8	4.0	4.0	-1.5	-1.3	-1.0
Mozambique	-1.2	2.3	3.7	5.0	8.0	0.1	-1.0	2.2
Niger	3.6	1.4	5.0	7.1	10.1	-0.2	0.0	-0.3
Rwanda	-3.4	10.9	6.0	6.7	7.0	-0.8	-0.5	-0.4
Sierra Leone	-2.0	4.1	3.7	3.7	4.4	-0.2	-0.7	-0.4
South Sudan [d]	9.5	-5.1	-2.8	-0.8	2.1	-2.0	-3.3	-1.9
Sudan	-3.6	-1.9	0.3	2.0	2.5	-0.4	0.0	0.0
Syrian Arab Republic	-3.9	-2.9	-3.5	-3.2	..	-0.9	..	..
Togo	1.8	5.3	4.8	5.6	6.4	-0.2	-0.2	0.0
Uganda [d]	3.0	3.5	4.7	5.5	6.1	1.0	0.4	-0.4
Yemen, Rep.	-8.5	-1.0	1.0	1.0	..	0.2	-1.5	..
Zambia	-3.0	3.6	3.0	3.9	4.1	-0.3	0.3	0.1
Memorandum items:								
GDP per capita (U.S. dollars)								
LICs	-1.3	1.0	1.1	2.2	2.8	-0.1	-0.2	0.1
LICs, poverty rate below 50 percent [g]	0.1	0.9	1.2	2.4	2.8	0.0	-0.1	-0.1
LICs, poverty rate above 50 percent [g]	-5.3	1.0	0.2	1.4	2.2	-0.4	-0.4	0.2

Source: World Bank.
Note: e = estimate; f = forecast. World Bank forecasts are frequently updated based on new information and changing (global) circumstances. Consequently, projections presented here may differ from those contained in other Bank documents, even if basic assessments of countries' prospects do not significantly differ at any given moment in time.
a. The Democratic People's Republic of Korea and Somalia are not forecast on account of data limitations.
b. Aggregate growth rates are calculated using GDP weights at average 2010-19 prices and market exchange rates.
c. Forecasts for Afghanistan (beyond 2021), the Syrian Arab Republic (beyond 2023), and the Republic of Yemen (beyond 2023) are excluded because of a high degree of uncertainty.
d. GDP growth rates are on a fiscal year basis. For example, the column labeled 2022 refers to FY2021/22.
g. Extreme poverty rate is measured as the share of people living on less than $2.15 per day. Per capita income is calculated as each group's GDP divided by each group's population. Sample excludes Democratic Republic of Congo and Niger—both with over half of population experiencing extreme poverty.

(Afghanistan, South Sudan, Somalia). LICs' food supplies are likely to remain stressed due to limited grain imports, reduced fertilizer use, and persistent and severe drought conditions in several countries (Ethiopia, Madagascar, Malawi). In LICs with fragile and conflict-affected situations, increasing levels of violence will continue to disrupt farming activities and limit access to markets and humanitarian aid (Central African Republic, Ethiopia, Mali). Local food prices will be kept high by elevated global prices for fuel and fertilizer, which have become more costly due to weaker currencies, reducing food affordability, real incomes, and growth, and possibly worsening some countries' security situation.

Per capita income growth

EMDE per capita income growth is anticipated to average 2.8 percent over 2023-24—1 percentage point weaker than its 2010-19 average—with wide variation across countries. In most energy exporters, per capita income growth over 2023-24 is expected to exceed its 2010-19 average, largely reflecting windfall gains from high energy prices. In commodity importers and non-energy exporters, high food and fuel prices have dented real incomes, with per capita income growth expected to fall short of long-term trends. In both metal and agricultural exporters, per capita income growth is forecast to be well below 1 percent over 2023-24, reflecting tepid global demand for metals and elevated input costs for agriculture. In almost 40 percent of LICs, per capita income growth in 2024 is projected to remain below its 2010-19 average.

EMDE catch-up with per capita incomes of advanced economies will remain slow—EMDE per capita income growth is anticipated to exceed that of advanced economies by only 1.9 percentage points on average over 2023-24 compared to 2.8 percentage points in 2000-19. Furthermore, income per capita is expected to remain below its 2019 level in over 40 percent of EMDEs this year and in more than 30 percent in 2024.

The subdued near-term outlook, combined with weakness in the long-term drivers of growth, suggests that EMDEs will make limited progress at reducing poverty. Per capita income growth is

expected to be especially subdued in countries with high levels of extreme poverty, leaving poverty rates above pre-pandemic trends (figures 1.9.A and 1.9.B; World Bank 2022c). In Sub-Saharan Africa (SSA)—home to almost 60 percent of the world's extreme poor—output growth will only slightly outpace population growth; as a result, per capita income growth over 2023-24 is forecast to be among the weakest of the EMDE regions, at 1.2 percent, and lag the EMDE average by about 1.5 percentage points. As such, the goal of eradicating extreme poverty by 2030 appears well out of reach (World Bank 2022c).

Global outlook and risks

Global growth is slowing sharply in the face of high inflation, synchronous policy tightening to contain it, worsening financial conditions, disruptions resulting from Russia's invasion of Ukraine, and feeble confidence. The world's major engines of growth are undergoing a period of pronounced weakness, and the ensuing spillovers are exacerbating other headwinds faced by EMDEs. Elevated debt burdens and already-weak growth indicate that a further negative shock—in the form of higher inflation, additional policy tightening, or financial stress—could push the global economy into recession.

Global outlook

Global growth prospects have darkened substantially since June amid the continued effects of negative shocks. To rein in high inflation and address concerns about diminished inflation-fighting credibility, major central banks have pivoted toward tighter policy at the fastest pace in more than 40 years (figure 1.10.A). This has contributed to a significant tightening of global financial conditions. At the same time, fiscal support policies introduced earlier in the pandemic have been scaled back in a context of rising borrowing costs and fears of stoking inflation. Despite wide variation across countries, fiscal policy is expected to be a slight drag on global growth (figure 1.10.B). The adverse effects of Russia's invasion of Ukraine persist, particularly those related to commodity supply disruptions. The weakening outlook has been accompanied by consumer sentiment falling to lows not seen since the global financial crisis (figure 1.10.C).

FIGURE 1.9 **Per capita income growth**

Per capita income growth is expected to be anemic in economies with high poverty rates, placing poverty reduction goals further from reach.

A. EMDE per capita GDP growth, by bottom and top quartile poverty headcount ratio

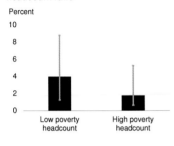

B. Global population in poverty

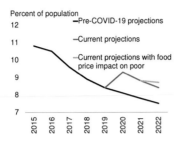

Sources: Mahler, Yonzan, and Lakner (2022); WDI (database); World Bank (2022c); World Bank.
Note: EMDE = emerging market and developing economies. Unless otherwise indicated, aggregate growth rates are calculated using real U.S. dollar GDP weights at average 2010-19 prices and market exchange rates.
A. "Low poverty headcount" are EMDEs with poverty headcount in the 25th percentile, and "high poverty headcount" are those in the 75th percentile. Bars show average per capita GDP growth over 2023-24 for 39 EMDEs. Whiskers indicate the minimum-maximum range. Sample excludes Belarus and the Russian Federation. Poverty data are the poverty headcount ratios at $2.15 a day (2017 PPP).
B. Data show the global poverty headcount rates at the $2.15 per day poverty line. Pre-COVID-19 projections are based on per capita GDP growth forecasts published in the January 2020 edition of the *Global Economic Prospects* report; current projections reflect the estimated impact of COVID-19 on poverty in 2020 and the distribution-neutral per capita GDP-based poverty projections for 2021 and 2022; the orange line indicates the scenario that accounts for the differential short-run impact of food price inflation on poorer households relative to richer ones (Mahler, Yonzan, and Lakner 2022; World Bank 2022c).

The magnitude and synchronous nature of policy tightening is exerting a significant drag on the recovery from the 2020 global recession. Global growth is forecast to slow from 2.9 percent in 2022 to 1.7 percent in 2023, substantially weaker than expected in June, before rebounding to 2.7 percent in 2024. Projected growth in 2023 is the third weakest in nearly three decades, over-shadowed only by the global recessions caused by the pandemic and the global financial crisis. The world's major engines of growth—the United States, the euro area, and China—are all expected to grow substantially below potential, and their contributions to global growth will be far below recent norms (figure 1.10.D). The associated spillover effects will compound the challenges facing EMDEs already struggling with weakening domestic conditions. The slowdown has been especially pronounced for interest-rate sensitive activities. In particular, residential investment is in outright contraction in many countries amid a sharp rise in mortgage rates, while business investment has slowed substantially.

Growth projections have been downgraded for almost all advanced economies and about two-thirds of EMDEs in 2023, and about half of all countries in 2024 (figure 1.10.E). These mark-downs are substantial, averaging 1.3 percentage points in 2023 and 0.8 percentage point in 2024, and tend to be larger among countries with lower credit ratings, which are more vulnerable to tightening financial conditions.

Globally, inflation has proven more persistent than previously assumed, and the rise in core inflation, wages, and short-term inflation expectations suggests that inflation may remain above pre-pandemic averages and central bank targets in many countries for an extended period. Both model- and survey- based inflation forecasts suggest that core and non-core components of global CPI inflation peaked in late 2022 and will gradually slow as activity softens and the price of many commodities moderates. Inflation is expected to fall from 7.6 percent in 2022 to 5.2 percent in 2023 and 3.2 percent in 2024, still above the 2015-19 average of 2.3 percent (figure 1.10.F). The deceleration in headline inflation this year is envisaged to be primarily driven by moderating prices for many commodities; furthermore, core inflation is expected to slow substantially next year but remain above pre-pandemic levels.

Risks to the outlook

The combination of slowing growth, persistently high inflation, and tightening financial conditions amid high levels of debt increases the risks of stagflation, financial strains, continued fiscal pressures, and weak investment in many countries. The baseline forecasts assume that central banks tighten monetary policy broadly in line with market expectations and are able to bring inflation down without triggering significant financial stress. These assumptions may prove optimistic in two ways. First, more persistent inflation could prompt significantly more monetary tightening. Second, sharper monetary tightening and rising global borrowing costs, in a context of weak growth prospects, could prompt investors to reassess the sustainability of large and rising debt burdens in many countries. This could trigger a broad-based flight to safety and substantial capital outflows, leading to financial stress affecting a large swath of EMDEs. If these risks were to materialize, model simulations suggest that the global economy could fall into recession in 2023, defined as a contraction in per capita income—which, currently, is equal to annual global GDP growth of less than about 0.9 percent.

In addition to the risks around monetary tightening and global financial conditions, a number of other developments could worsen the trajectory of the global economy. First, activity in China could be weaker than expected as a result of worsening disruptions from COVID-19 or stress in the real estate sector. Second, geopolitical tensions, which rose markedly after Russia's invasion of Ukraine, could increase further and encompass a larger set of countries. In addition to their humanitarian implications, escalating tensions could hasten the trend toward un-productive re-shoring of supply chains, put the financial system under strain, and disrupt the supply of commodities (Caldara and Iacoviello 2022). Finally, the risks associated with climate change are growing, as changing weather patterns contribute to increasingly disruptive events, such as heat waves and floods. In the near term, climate-related disasters can substantially weigh on activity; in the longer term, climate change can render some populated area uninhabitable, lower productivity, and worsen global poverty.

High inflation and additional monetary tightening

Repeated negative shocks to both global supply chains and the supply of key commodities have played an important role in driving up global inflation. Some of these shocks have started to wane, especially those related to supply chain bottlenecks; however, they may reemerge in various forms. Worsening geopolitical tensions—most notably those related to Russia's invasion of Ukraine—or additional export cutoffs may lead to shortages and higher prices for food, fertilizers, and energy. These shocks could again exacerbate inflation pressures and prompt additional mone-tary tightening.

In the context of these shocks and the elevat ed level of inflation, there is unusually high

FIGURE 1.10 Global outlook

Ongoing monetary tightening among major advanced economies is the fastest in recent history. Fiscal policy is expected to be a slight drag on global activity, with wide variations across countries. Confidence has fallen to lows not seen since the global financial crisis. Global growth is forecast to slow sharply in 2023, with weakness in all major engines of activity and downgrades in most economies. Elevated inflation is expected to persist for longer than previously anticipated, even as it slows due to weak activity and moderating commodity prices.

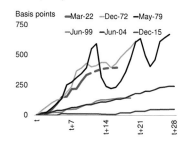

A. G7 policy rates

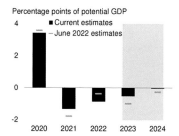

B. Global fiscal impulse

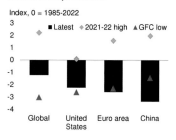

C. Consumer confidence and economic expectations

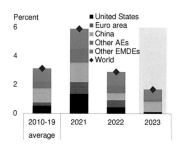

D. Contributions to global growth

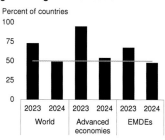

E. Share of countries with down-grades in growth forecasts

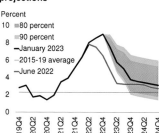

F. Model-based global CPI inflation projections

Sources: BIS (database); Bloomberg; Consensus Economics; European Commission (2022); Federal Reserve Economic Data; Haver Analytics; IMF (2022b; 2022c); Oxford Economics; World Bank.

Note: AEs = advanced economies; EMDEs = emerging market and developing economies; G7 = Canada, France, Germany, Italy, Japan, the United Kingdom, and the United States. CPI = consumer price index. GFC = global financial crisis. Shaded areas indicate forecasts. Unless otherwise indicated, aggregates are calculated using real U.S. dollar GDP weights at average 2010-19 prices and market exchange rates.

A. Increases in short-term policy interest rate weighted by nominal GDP in current U.S. dollars. "t" is the month before the U.S. federal funds rate starts to increase. A cycle ends when the weighted policy rate peaks. Judgement used to define "double-peak" cycles (1972 and 1979). The March 2022 cycle is extended using market-implied interest rate expectations from January 2023 onward, observed on December 16, 2022. Prior to 1999, German and Italian rates are discount rates; French rates are interest rates on French treasury bills.

B. Fiscal impulse is the negative annual change in the structural balance for 80 countries, using data from the IMF (2022b, 2022c) and the European Commission (2022).

C. Figure shows z-scores. Last observation is December 2022 for global, November 2022 for euro area, and October 2022 for China and United States.

E. Figure shows share of countries with forecast downgrades since the June 2022 *Global Economic Prospects*.

F. Model-based projections of year-on-year global CPI inflation using Oxford Economics' Global Economic Model, using global oil price forecasts presented in table 1.1. Uncertainty bands constructed from distribution of forecast errors for total CPI from Consensus Economics for an unbalanced panel of 18 countries.

FIGURE 1.11 **Risks to the outlook**

Large exchange rate depreciations have the potential to cause unexpectedly rapid increases in inflation. Rising U.S. interest rates arising from a perceived pivot by the Federal Reserve toward a more hawkish stance materially increase the probability of financial crises in emerging market and developing economies (EMDEs). Already, the volume of bond issuance in EMDEs has fallen precipitously. A high share of riskier types of debt makes some countries particularly vulnerable to financial stress.

A. Unconditional pass-through during significant currency depreciations, 1998-2017

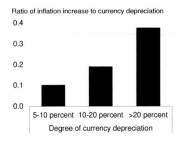

B. Likelihood of EMDE crises due to changes in the Federal Reserve's reaction function

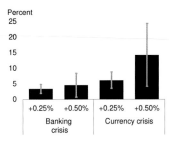

C. Change in bond issuance in EMDEs

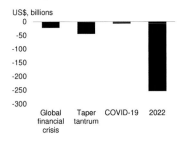

D. EMDE debt characteristics

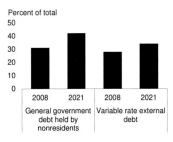

Sources: Arteta, Kamin, and Ruch (2022); Bloomberg; Caselli and Roitman (2016); Dealogic; Ha, Kose, and Ohnsorge (2019a); International Debt Statistics (database); Kose et al. (2022); Laeven and Valencia (2020); World Bank.

Note: EMDEs = emerging market and developing economies.

A. Currency depreciations are defined as negative quarterly changes in the nominal effective exchange rate. The sample includes 138 EMDEs from 1998 to 2017. Pass-through to inflation is defined as the change in consumer prices after one quarter divided by the depreciation of the nominal effective exchange rate, as described in Ha, Kose, and Ohnsorge (2019a). Sample includes 34 advanced economies and 138 EMDEs.

B. Figure shows impact on crisis probability of an increase in 2-year U.S. yields due to a "reaction-function" shock—a change in perceptions of how the Federal Reserve reacts to incoming information. It is based on a sign-restricted Bayesian VAR and a panel logit model as described in Arteta, Kamin, and Ruch (2022). "+0.25%" and "+0.50%" indicate the crisis probabilities in the case of 25 and 50 basis point increase in the 2-year U.S. yield driven by a reaction-function shock. Whiskers reflect 95 percent confidence intervals. Crisis events based on Laeven and Valencia (2020).

C. Bars indicate the change in public and private bond issuance during the ten months after the start of the event compared to the same period one year prior. The starting dates are August 2008 for Global financial crisis, June 2013 for Taper tantrum, March 2020 for COVID-19, and February 2022 for 2022.

D. Bars indicate the EMDE median. Unbalanced sample includes 42 EMDEs for the general government debt held by nonresidents and 114 EMDEs for the variable rate external debt. For details, refer to Kose et al. (2022) and the World Bank's *International Debt Statistics*.

uncertainty about the impact of central bank policy in terms of both magnitude and timing (Doh and Foerster 2022). As a result, the risk of policy missteps is elevated, and market expectations about the necessary degree of tightening are likely to continue being revised (Reis 2022).

Historically, at the start of policy tightening episodes, market-based interest rate expectations in the United States have underestimated the subsequent cumulative rate increases by an average of 85 basis points (Wessel 2022). The shift in expectations during the current policy tightening cycle has been considerably larger—between the beginning and the end of 2022, the average policy rate expectation for 2023 was revised up by more than 325 basis points, and further upward revisions remain possible.

These uncertainties are magnified by the possibility of non-linear relationships between key macroeconomic parameters. As inflation declines, the marginal degree of monetary tightening to bring it down further may increase, which may manifest as inflation remaining stubbornly above target and requiring unanticipated additional tightening (Forbes, Gagnon, and Collins 2022). In the context of large currency movements this year, the possible non-linearities in the relationship between currency depreciations and inflation are important, with larger depreciations causing proportionally larger increases in prices (Ha, Kose, and Ohnsorge 2019b). If the pass-through from a substantial currency depreciation is many times larger than expected, this could drive inflation far above target in some countries (figure 1.11.A). In either of these circumstances, the persistence of high inflation increases the risk that it becomes embedded in expectations.

If inflation remains persistently above target, central banks would likely raise interest rates more quickly and to higher levels than currently expected, and keep them elevated for longer to re-anchor expectations and return inflation to target (Ha, Kose, and Ohnsorge 2022; World Bank 2022e). Particularly tight monetary policy in the United States could result in a stronger U.S. dollar, which has substantial spillovers given its role as the primary currency for trade and finance. As the invoicing currency for many commodities and traded goods, a strong dollar can drive up prices in local currencies and cause inflation to persist. The dollar is also the funding currency for global banking and capital markets, and a higher value is associated with greater constraints on many institutions' balance sheets, resulting in deleveraging in the banking sector and tighter global credit conditions (Hofmann, Mehrotra, and Sandri 2022).

Financial stress across EMDEs

Several EMDEs have experienced financial stress featuring rapid capital outflows, currency depreciation, and difficulty servicing debt. Unlike during the global financial crisis, the countries affected thus far have been frontier markets with limited cross-border spillovers, and markets have been discerning about individual country risks. In a global economy characterized by slowing growth and rising borrowing costs, however, the growing pressures on EMDEs could result in currency crises or widespread private and public defaults, with potential cross-border spillovers. Historically, the probability that EMDEs experience a banking crisis or, especially, a currency crisis in a given year has increased when the market perceives that the Federal Reserve's reaction function is shifting toward a more hawkish policy stance, as has occurred recently (figure 1.11.B; Arteta, Kamin, and Ruch 2022; Kose et al. 2021a).

Rising interest rates and falling EMDE currencies add to the cost of refinancing debt for both private and sovereign borrowers (Obstfeld and Zhou 2022). Already, the value of bond issuance in EMDEs has dropped by an unprecedented amount (figure 1.11.C). More countries may lose access to international capital markets if creditors become increasingly concerned that large, growing debt burdens are unsustainable. Current record-high debt levels and sizable fiscal and current account deficits make EMDEs vulnerable to financial stress and balance of payments difficulties in the event of further capital outflows and sharp currency depreciation (Hoek, Kamin, and Yoldas 2022). In the private sector, tightening credit conditions and slowing growth could lead to loan losses, impaired balance sheets, and liquidity problems among both banks and nonbank financial institutions (IMF 2022d).

Risks of financial stress are particularly acute among those EMDEs with large current account deficits and heavy reliance on foreign capital inflows, as well as EMDEs with high levels of short-term or foreign-currency denominated government or private debt. The shares of

government debt held by nonresidents and of external debt with variable rates have both risen in many EMDEs since the global financial crisis (figure 1.11.D). These characteristics increase the risk that some countries may lose the confidence of global capital markets and struggle to refinance debt as it rolls over (Rogoff 2022). EMDEs are also rendered more vulnerable where they have shallow and illiquid local currency debt markets and excessive reliance on domestic bank financing of sovereign entities. In contrast, EMDEs with more developed local currency financial markets, and which implemented reforms following the global financial crisis to enhance financial stability, are likely to be more resilient.

Weaker growth in China

Growth in China slowed sharply last year as a result of recurrent pandemic-related restrictions and strains in the real estate market (World Bank 2022f). The recent shift toward reopening has been faster than expected, and there is significant uncertainty about the trajectory of the pandemic and how households, businesses, and policy makers in China will respond. The economic recovery may be delayed if reopening results in major outbreaks that overburden the health sector and sap confidence.

The real estate sector is particularly important in China, as it accounts for about 25 percent of both gross value added and fixed asset investment, a far higher share than in other countries. A number of major property developers have defaulted or are at risk of doing so amid a significant decline in housing prices and the pace of new construction. Financial vulnerabilities in the country are a long-standing concern. Since 2008, corporate credit has increased by nearly 60 percentage points of GDP to 160 percent of GDP in 2022, well above the increase of about 18 percentage points in the average EMDE. This pace of credit growth is well above the rate typically associated with credit booms and well above thresholds identified as early warning indicators for financial stress. State-owned enterprises are estimated to account for about two-thirds of corporate debt. Although policy buffers are likely sufficient to prevent systematic market stress, continued defaults by heavily leveraged real estate developers and a broadening downturn in the real estate sector may trigger domestic financial strains and weigh on household balance sheets, consumer confidence, local government finances, and growth. Financial strains may also be channeled through linkages with non-traditional financial intermediaries that play an important role in the financial system. Even if financial stress is avoided, longer-term growth may be affected if a substantial share of the credit expansion were allocated to unproductive uses.

A slowdown in China would add further headwinds to global activity, with adverse spillovers to global trade, commodity markets, and financial markets (Ahmed et al. 2019). Direct trade spillovers would be most significant for the EAP region, including for countries integrated into China's supply chains, and some trade-reliant advanced economies. Falling demand in China, which accounts for half of global metals demand and one-third of global energy demand, could also have particularly adverse impacts on commodity exporters in South America, where China is the single largest export market. Outbound lending, investment, and remittances from China could come under pressure, compromising an important financing source for many EMDEs (Horn, Reinhart, and Trebesch 2021).

Geopolitical turmoil and trade fragmentation

Geopolitical tensions are at a high level. An intensification of the war in Ukraine, or rising conflict elsewhere, could have significant economic repercussions through commodity and financial markets, trade and migration linkages, uncertainty, confidence, and increased likelihood of financial stress in affected countries.

Following the trade and financial dislocations due to the pandemic, the current level of geopolitical tensions has led some policy makers to take further steps to delink from global financial and trade networks, which has heightened global trade policy uncertainty. Many countries are seeking to re-orient supply chains such that key inputs are produced either domestically or with a narrow set of partners. Similarly, some countries are seeking ways to reduce the vulnerability of their financial systems and foreign assets to policy actions by other nations. Energy markets, in particular those in Europe, are going through major disruptions as a result of sanctions due to Russia's invasion of Ukraine and related spillovers.

In the near term, geopolitical turmoil and the possible segmentation of finance, trade, and commodity markets into regional blocks could lead to a new wave of production disruptions and higher prices for globally traded goods and commodities—as occurred during the pandemic and the invasion of Ukraine—with global spillovers through supply chains. Even if the war does not worsen, persistent uncertainty and a push toward trade reshoring through domestic subsidies and import barriers have the potential to slow investment, trade, productivity, and progress against poverty (Brenton, Ferrantino, and Maliszewska 2022; Caldera et al. 2020).

Worsening effects of climate change

The world is experiencing an increasing number of costly, record-breaking weather events linked to climate change. For instance, recent severe heat waves, including in Europe and China, have imposed a significant human cost and strained power systems. Major rivers have run dry in Europe, North America, and China, impeding transport and water supplies. Floods in Pakistan have inundated one-third of the country, while droughts in South America threaten agricultural production and larger ecosystems. Such extreme events are become increasingly likely as global warming heightens the expected losses and damages related to climate change (IPCC 2022).

The global climate may be approaching "tipping points" at which changes become self-perpetuating and accelerate in damaging ways (McKay et al. 2022). These include rising sea levels from melting ice sheets, the rapid collapse of major biomes such as the Amazon rainforest or coral reefs, or runaway carbon release from thawing permafrost.

In the near term, these or other climate-related disasters can inflict substantial human costs, damage infrastructure, and disrupt activity.

Disasters can also add to the number of displaced people, with disproportionate impacts on the poor. They can also worsen government fiscal positions through lower tax receipts and lower productivity alongside increased spending on reconstruction and public services. They may prove especially disruptive at the current juncture by interrupting the supply of already-scarce commodities, disrupting supply chains, or increasing the need for heating or cooling in an environment of already-high energy prices. Changes in climate may further increase food insecurity in regions with large numbers of subsistence farmers that lack the resources to easily adjust production. In the longer term, climate change may render some populated areas uninhabitable, lower productivity, and worsen global poverty.

Alternative downside scenarios

In the baseline forecast, global activity is expected to grow by only 1.7 percent in 2023 before rebounding to a still subdued 2.7 percent in 2024. The baseline forecast for global inflation is 5.2 percent in 2023 and 3.2 percent in 2024. A global macroeconomic model is used to quantify the downside risks to growth of higher anticipated inflation, additional monetary tightening in response, and the potential resultant financial stress. Two downside scenarios are considered—a *sharp downturn* scenario and a *global recession* scenario (figure 1.12.A).[1] These alternative scenarios would imply even more persistent losses relative to the pre-pandemic trend of global activity—and, in the case of global recession, an outright contraction in per capita GDP (figures 1.12.B and 1.12.C).

In the first scenario, central banks tighten monetary policy more quickly and to a rate above the market expectations embedded in the baseline forecast in response to rising inflation

_____

[1] Each scenario is prepared using the Oxford Economics Global Economic Model, a global semi-structural macro projection model which includes 81 individual country blocks, most of which are available at a quarterly frequency, with behavioral equations governing domestic economic activity, monetary and fiscal policy, global trade, and commodity prices (Oxford Economics 2019).

FIGURE 1.12 Alternative downside scenarios

The materialization of downside risks would lead to substantially weaker growth and further widen the gap between global GDP and its pre-pandemic trend, potentially leading to a global recession. In a sharp downturn scenario, central banks hike policy rates more than is currently expected to bring inflation under control; in a global recession scenario, this triggers widespread financial crises and a sharper fall in inflation.

A. Global growth under different scenarios

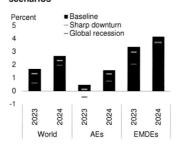

B. Evolution of global GDP

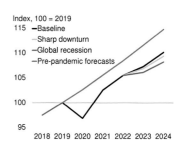

C. Global per capita GDP under different scenarios

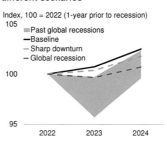

D. U.S. policy interest rates

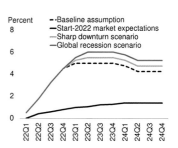

E. Global short-term interest rates

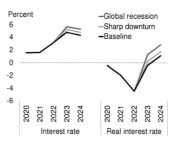

F. Global inflation

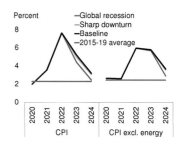

Sources: Bloomberg; Consensus Economics; Federal Reserve Bank of St. Louis; Haver Analytics; Guenette, Kose, and Sugawara (2022); Oxford Economics; World Bank.
Note: AEs = advanced economies; EMDEs = emerging market and developing economies. CPI = consumer price index. Scenarios produced using the Oxford Economics *Global Economic Model*. Unless otherwise indicated, aggregate growth rates are calculated using real U.S. dollar GDP weights at average 2010-19 prices and market exchange rates. Data are estimates for 2022 and forecasts for 2023-24.
A. Global growth aggregate is computed by Oxford Economics using 2015 market exchange rates and prices.
B. The pre-pandemic forecasts are based on the January 2020 long-term Consensus forecasts over 2020-24.
C. For past global recessions, the range shows the minimum-maximum range of past five global recessions, and the values one year prior to each global recession (for example, 1974 for the 1975 global recession, and 2019 for the 2020 global recession) are equal to 100.
D. Start-2022 market expectations are derived from future overnight index swaps (OIS) curves, observed on December 31, 2021. Baseline interest rate assumptions consistent with market expectations through 2023Q3. Beyond 2023 baseline assumptions are broadly in line with Federal Reserve's summary of economic projections as of December 14th, 2022.
E. Global nominal short-term interest rate is measured as GDP-weighted averages of national rates. The baseline assumptions are broadly in line with Consensus expectations 3 months and 12 months ahead.
F. Model-based projection of annual global year-on-year CPI inflation using Oxford Economics *Global Economic Model*. Projection embeds global oil price forecast presented in table 1.1.

expectations. This comes at a substantial cost to output, even absent significant and broad financial stress in EMDEs. In this scenario, 5-year inflation expectations rise by an average of 0.7 percentage points in 2023Q1-Q2 (equivalent to half of the standard deviation of realized inflation in major economies from 2010 to 2019). This further increases the persistence of the global inflation shock. In response, central banks in the United States, other advanced economies, and major EMDEs are assumed to raise their benchmark policy rates by 50 basis points above market assumptions over 2023Q1-Q2 and sustain this differential through 2024 (figure 1.12.D). This additional policy tightening, alongside slowing inflation, causes the global real short-term interest rate to rise from -4.5 percent in 2022 to an average of 1.0 percent over 2023-24, slightly over 60 basis points higher than in the baseline scenario and the fastest pace since the global oil shock of the late 1970s (figure 1.12.E).[2] The higher global policy rates are sufficient to offset the initial shock to inflation and keep both total global inflation and inflation excluding energy from deviating significantly from the baseline (figure 1.12.F).

While the global economy avoids a recession, global GDP growth falls to 1.3 percent in 2023—comparable to the global downturn of 1991. Activity in this scenario rebounds in 2024, but the projected GDP growth rate of 2.3 percent remains 0.4 percentage point below baseline, largely reflecting the lagged impacts of additional monetary tightening. The downturn is more severe for EMDEs, particularly those that are heavily exposed to the United States via trade and financial channels, as well as commodity-exporting EMDEs affected by substantially lower commodity prices.

In the second scenario, not only are major central banks' policy rates even more restrictive, but tighter financial conditions are assumed to lead to widespread and significant financing difficulties across EMDEs, leaving the world in a *global recession*. In this scenario, policy makers in major

economies observe signs of an even larger increase in inflation expectations than assumed in the first risk scenario and respond by raising policy rates by 100 basis points above the baseline over 2023Q1-2023Q2, keeping them there until the end of 2024. This raises concerns that debt in a growing number of EMDEs is becoming unsustainable, leading to heightened investor risk aversion in the form of widening borrowing spreads, capital outflows, and currency depreciations. EMDE governments, particularly those with limited fiscal space, are forced to further tighten fiscal policy by reducing expenditures, while the ability of central banks to provide relief to stressed financial markets is limited by the need to focus on containing inflation. Uncertainty about the extent of exposure to widespread market losses prompts a surge in financial volatility and a sharp fall in consumer and business confidence. Most economies face markedly negative spillovers from abroad via financial, trade, and commodity price channels.

In this scenario, global GDP grows by only 0.6 percent in 2023, comparable to the global recession of 1982. This translates into a contraction of 0.3 percent in per capita terms. Weak growth is widespread in this scenario, with EMDE growth slowing to 2.0 percent in 2023, the lowest rate of expansion since the early 1990s, excluding the pandemic. Meanwhile, advanced economies contract by 0.5 percent in 2023. A gradual recovery begins in 2024, hampered by limited countercyclical policy support in major economies.

The global recession modeled in this scenario would also lead to severe disruptions in labor markets. The scenario-consistent model-based path for the global unemployment rate would rise about 0.5 percentage point above the baseline in 2024, slightly less than the change during the global financial crisis. Worsening unemployment would push even more people into poverty. In addition, the reduction in per capita incomes in the global recession scenario is likely to be more severely felt by those at the lower end of the global income distribution, resulting in further increases in global income inequality (Mahler, Yonzan, and Lakner 2022).

---

[2] Global real short-term interest rate is measured as a GDP-weighted average of national rates, minus the global headline CPI inflation rate.

Global inflation falls to 2.5 percent in 2024, close to the 2015-19 average of 2.3 percent, as unexpected weakness in demand pulls inflation down globally. Part of the deceleration in headline inflation is explained by inflation excluding energy, which slows to 2.9 percent in 2024 in this scenario, compared to 3.7 percent in the baseline. The sharp tightening of global financial conditions in this scenario is especially damaging for EMDEs with large current account deficits that rely heavily on foreign capital inflows, as well as those with high levels of short-term or foreign-currency-denominated debt.

Policy challenges

Urgent global policy efforts are needed to mitigate the risk of global recession and debt distress in EMDEs, address climate change, and support people affected by crises and hunger. EMDEs will need to pursue a carefully calibrated macroeconomic policy mix that reins in inflation without triggering financial stress, ensures any additional fiscal support is targeted to vulnerable groups, restores fiscal sustainability, and preserves financial stability. To offset the long-term damage from the adverse shocks of the past three years, EMDEs need to substantially increase investment. Given limited fiscal space, this will require new financing from the international community and from the repurposing of existing spending, such as inefficient agricultural and fuel subsidies.

Key global challenges

The key challenge for policy makers around the world is to lower the likelihood of a global recession, especially one that could result from rapid and synchronous monetary policy tightening that causes widespread financial stress. The unexpected rise in inflation last year highlights the uncertainties about the relationship between changes in central bank policy rates, growth, and inflation. The unusual pace and synchronous nature of the current tightening cycle has heightened these uncertainties. To mitigate them, central banks need to fully factor in the cross-border effects of their decisions to ensure policy is not tightened more than is needed to return inflation to target. Discussions among national monetary policy makers are needed to mitigate

financial stability risks associated with synchronous tightening of policies and avoid undue economic costs.

EMDEs are particularly vulnerable to spillovers from sharply higher policy rates in the United States and other advanced economies. Unlike increases in U.S. interest rates that result from changes in real economic activity, increases due to perceived shifts in the Federal Reserve's reaction function, such as a move toward a more hawkish position, can have particularly damaging effects on the financial conditions of EMDEs (figure 1.13.A; Arteta et al. 2015; Arteta, Kamin, and Ruch 2022). These can lead to higher bond yields and sovereign risk spreads in EMDEs, alongside capital outflows and currency depreciation, which can render dollar-denominated external debt unsustainable. In addition, higher import prices can worsen already high inflation. In this context, the risks to EMDEs of unprecedented global monetary tightening can be mitigated by a range of tools, including enhanced communication among central banks aimed at mitigating financial stability risks, monitoring cross-border spillovers, and increased support from international financial institutions (Avdjiev et al. 2020; Obstfeld 2022b).

Minimizing the probability of crisis will also require a sound macroeconomic policy mix where fiscal policy does not add to inflationary pressures and prompt additional monetary policy tightening. This risk can be mitigated by ensuring that fiscal support is carefully targeted toward the poor. Above all, macroeconomic authorities need to avoid heightening policy uncertainty, which could add further pressure to global financial markets already threatened by rising borrowing costs and generate additional adverse spillovers to growth (figure 1.13.B; Kose et al. 2017a).

In a context of rising global borrowing costs, slower growth, and already-limited fiscal space, the international community needs to bolster efforts to reduce debt distress and attenuate the risk of debt crises in EMDEs. Access to timely, fair, and adequate debt restructuring is essential, particularly among the growing share of LICs at high risk of debt distress. The G20 Common Framework can help countries overcome debt restructuring challenges resulting from unaffordable

FIGURE 1.13 Global policy challenges

To reduce the risk of global recession, global policy efforts are needed to address the potential spillovers from pivots toward more aggressive monetary policy tightening or heightened uncertainty. Global action is needed to respond to the adverse consequences of increasingly frequent and severe natural disasters on vulnerable countries, such as small states, as well as the substantial rise in food insecurity amid high inflation.

A. Impact of 25 basis point U.S. interest rate shock on EMDEs, by type of shock

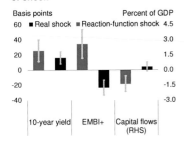

B. Impact of 10-percent rise in U.S. economic policy uncertainty on growth

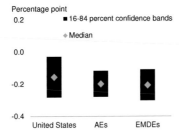

C. Natural disasters in small states

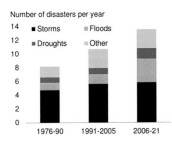

D. Food inflation, by region

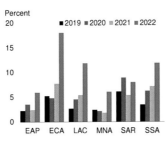

Sources: Arteta, Kamin, and Ruch (2022); EM-DAT (database); Haver Analytics; International Monetary Fund; JP Morgan; Kose et al. (2017a); World Bank.
Note: AEs = advanced economies; EMBI + = Emerging Markets Bond Index Plus; EMDE = emerging market and developing economies; EAP = East Asia and Pacific, ECA = Europe and Central Asia, LAC = Latin America and the Caribbean, MNA = Middle East and North Africa, SAR = South Asia, SSA = Sub-Saharan Africa. Small states are EMDEs with populations less than 1.5 million.
A. Figure shows impulse responses after one quarter from panel local projection models with fixed effects and robust standard errors, to reaction-function shocks (for example, a pivot toward a more hawkish monetary policy stance) and real shocks (for example, positive news about U.S. activity). Shocks are estimated from a sign-restricted Bayesian VAR. Positive "capital flow" values reflect an increase in net liabilities of portfolio and other investments for EMDEs. Whiskers reflect 90 percent confidence intervals.
B. Figure shows the cumulative impulse responses after one year on output growth in the United States, 23 other AEs, and 18 EMDEs to a 10-percent increase in the U.S. Economic Policy Uncertainty Index.
C. Disasters are counted as the total number in all small states per year. Other disasters include earthquakes, landslides, and volcanic activity. Sample includes 26 EMDE small states.
D. Figure shows annual averages of food consumer price inflation. Sample includes 46 EMDEs. Regional inflation rates are based on median across countries.

debt owed to a diverse set of creditors. Decisive debt restructuring at an early stage can help avoid the long and costly adjustment process that sometimes accompanies more incremental efforts and can result in more favorable outcomes for both borrowers and lenders (Kose et al. 2021b; World Bank 2022g).

Climate change is a key global challenge, as it is increasing the frequency and severity of natural disasters and can exacerbate extreme poverty by reducing agricultural productivity, increasing food prices, and worsening food and water insecurity in EMDEs. Climate-related disasters are becoming more common, and they weigh particularly heavily on vulnerable countries such as small states (chapter 4; figure 1.13.C). Strong global cooperation is essential to meet the goals of the Paris Agreement on Climate Change. After falling in 2020, global carbon dioxide emissions rebounded in 2021, with early estimates pointing to further increases in 2022 (IEA 2022b; WMO et al. 2022). Disruptions to natural gas flows related to the war in Ukraine have temporarily set back efforts to transition away from coal in both advanced economies and EMDEs.

EMDEs will need to make substantial investments in all forms of capital—human, physical, social and natural—to bolster green, resilient, and inclusive growth. Substantial resources can be redeployed from expensive and, in many cases, inefficient subsidies, which work against global development objectives—for example, agriculture and fuel subsidies alone amount to $1.2 trillion globally (World Bank 2022h). However, given the lack of fiscal space and the scale of the investment needs in many countries, strong global cooperation is needed to increase access to official financing for EMDEs, in addition to supporting reforms that encourages private finance (World Bank 2021a, 2022i).

Sustained international cooperation is also needed to accelerate the clean energy transition, help countries improve both energy security and affordability, and incentivize renewable energy and energy efficiency. For example, carbon pricing instruments can incentivize new investment and dampen fossil fuel demand while generating government revenue; however, they remain underutilized (World Bank 2022j). Border carbon adjustment mechanisms can also help reduce global emissions, but they must not be used as a form of trade protectionism.

Food price inflation has increased substantially across all EMDE regions (figure 1.13.D). Soaring food prices have worsened food insecurity and increased the number of people affected by hunger. In particular, Russia's invasion of Ukraine led to disruptions in exports of key food commodities, which exacerbated food price inflation in many poor and vulnerable countries. Although the Black Sea Grain Initiative has helped to facilitate exports of food and agricultural products from Ukraine since August, uncertainty remains about its continuation. Global cooperation is needed on several fronts to overcome global food insecurity.

The international community needs to safeguard the global commodity trading system by avoiding restrictive measures, such as export bans on food and fertilizer. Such protectionist policies often amplify volatility in prices and worsen food insecurity and nutrition globally (Laborde, Lakatos, and Martin 2019). Enhancing the resilience of the trading system to shocks, including from intensifying geopolitical tensions, requires stronger international cooperation to support diversification of products and markets and improve access to trade finance, especially for the most vulnerable countries. Sustained collective action is also required to enhance resilience to food systems, including adopting measures to limit shortages of key agricultural inputs such as fertilizer, supporting fertilizer innovations and methods to improve fertilizer use efficiency, and by coordinating research to develop and implement agricultural innovations that are climate-resilient (Voegele 2022).

Greater international efforts are needed to mitigate humanitarian crises stemming from war and conflict. International coordination of relief efforts can help to limit humanitarian costs in affected areas, especially through the delivery of food, water, medicine, shelter, and financial aid. Coordinated efforts by multilateral institutions can support countries hosting refugees and those affected by the direct and indirect economic impacts of war and conflict. In addition, COVID-19 remains a global health challenge, highlighting the need for improved vaccination coverage and strengthened pandemic preparedness, especially in LICs (Glennerster, Snyder, and Tan 2022). International financial and technical assistance is needed to buttress the ability of health care systems in the poorest countries to confront current and future health crises.

Challenges in emerging market and developing economies

EMDE monetary and financial policy challenges

Monetary policy is expected to continue tightening as slowing inflation causes global real policy rates to gradually rise from their current deeply negative levels (figure 1.14.A). Elevated inflation tends to inflict the greatest harm on low- and middle-income households. Inflation often outstrips growth in wages, which these households disproportionately rely on. Poorer households also suffer more when high inflation is driven by rising prices for food and fuel, which take up a greater share of their income—in EMDEs, the lowest-income households spend roughly 50 percent of their income on food (Gill and Nagle 2022).

EMDE monetary and financial authorities will need to continue to calibrate domestic monetary conditions taking into account the effects of both domestic tightening and cross-border spillovers from higher policy rates in advanced economies (Guénette, Kose, and Sugawara 2022; Obstfeld 2022a). A shifting policy mix in advanced economies, where more supportive fiscal policy could add to inflation pressures, represents a potential added challenge. Tightening financial conditions and depreciation pressures are likely to lead to a further rise in EMDE financial volatility and an increased probability of balance of payments strains, financial crises, and economic downturns. Some EMDE monetary authorities may have limited the rise in inflation and averted disruptive exchange rate dynamics through relatively early and swift increases in policy rates. In countries where inflation remains elevated, however, authorities may have to continue tightening monetary policy to support macroeconomic stability and to prevent inflation expectations from becoming de-anchored (figure 1.14.B).

Critically, communicating monetary policy decisions clearly, leveraging credible monetary frameworks, and safeguarding central bank independence will help EMDEs anchor inflation expectations and avoid disruptive capital outflows. This would help limit the adverse economic im-

FIGURE 1.14 Monetary policy challenges in emerging market and developing economies

Monetary policy is expected to continue tightening as slowing inflation causes global real policy rates to gradually rise from their current deeply negative levels. Among emerging market and developing economies, monetary policy has been tightening more markedly in response to larger inflation increases, which were generally accompanied by large currency depreciations. Foreign exchange reserve buffers, which have been used to cushion depreciation amid high inflation, need to be rebuilt.

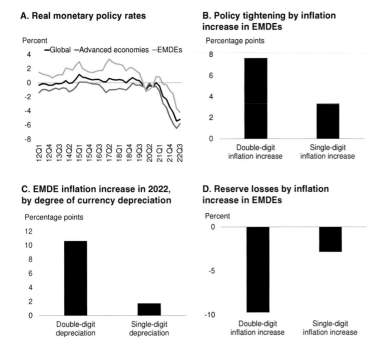

A. Real monetary policy rates

B. Policy tightening by inflation increase in EMDEs

C. EMDE inflation increase in 2022, by degree of currency depreciation

D. Reserve losses by inflation increase in EMDEs

Sources: Haver Analytics; International Financial Statistics (database); Oxford Economics; World Bank.
Note: EMDEs = emerging market and developing economies.
A. Figure shows nominal 3-month government rates deflated by realized consumer price inflation for a sample of 27 EMDEs and 26 advanced economies, sourced from Oxford Economics' *Global Economic Model*.
B.D. Data are average cumulative changes in policy interest rates and increases in inflation rates since 2021. Foreign reserve losses are since end-2021. "Single-digit inflation increase" includes some countries where inflation declined. Sample include 71 EMDEs, of which 22 EMDEs faced double-digit and 49 EMDEs faced single-digit inflation increases.
C. Average rise in headline consumer price index inflation in 2022. "Double-digit depreciation" and "Single-digit depreciation" are relative to the U.S. dollar in 2022. Balanced sample includes 84 EMDEs.

pacts of tightening cycles. Falling currencies have contributed to domestic inflation in many EMDEs, and this would likely accelerate if monetary policy credibility were eroded (figure 1.14.C).

EMDEs can also reduce their vulnerability to volatile capital flows and exchange rate fluctuations by strengthening macroprudential regulation. In 2022, about one-fifth of EMDEs liquidated more than 15 percent of gross official reserves to cushion the fall in domestic currencies, with larger losses among countries contending with higher inflation (figure 1.14.D). To smooth disruptive short-term volatility in currency markets and bolster investor sentiment, EMDEs can consider foreign exchange interventions where reserves are judged to be adequate. While these actions may alleviate immediate pressures, policy makers will eventually need to rebuild foreign exchange reserve buffers and realign prudential policy to prepare for the possibility of financial stress. Prudential policy efforts will need to prioritize, among other things, adequate bank capital and liquidity, better currency alignment of assets and liabilities, and appropriate levels of leverage in the household and corporate sectors.

Banking system exposures to exchange rate risk and rollover risk need to be monitored carefully and contained through macro- and micro-prudential policies. Credit quality, nonperforming loans, and currency mismatches need to be reported transparently such that prompt corrective action can be taken. There is an elevated risk of episodes of market dislocation in response to adverse events, given the sharp increase in interest rates after a prolonged period of low borrowing costs. The buffers of both banks and non-bank financial institutions therefore need to be sufficient to absorb sizable shocks, and should be stress-tested where institutions pose potentially systemic risks. In addition, risks from highly indebted corporate sectors can be allayed through insolvency reform and rapid, transparent treatment of nonperforming loans.

EMDE fiscal policy challenges

Governments face the difficult task of supporting vulnerable households and meeting other public spending needs while shoring up fiscal sustainability. EMDE debt levels rose sharply during the pandemic, with the median rising from 49 percent of GDP in 2019 to 55 percent of GDP in 2022, compounding earlier increases. With fiscal deficits that are still above pre-pandemic averages, debt levels are set to remain elevated, and many economies are vulnerable to rising borrowing costs, especially those with already high debt servicing costs and sizable external or foreign-currency denominated debt (figure 1.15.A; Rogoff 2022). LICs have also become more vulnerable, as their debt has increasingly shifted from concessional to market financing. More broadly, commodity importers—particularly those heavily reliant on food and fuel imports for domestic consumption and production—have experienced a sharp drawdown of their fiscal buffers. In contrast, many energy exporters have taken advantage of high energy prices to replenish revenues and stabilization funds.

After a sharp fiscal adjustment in 2021, when nearly 80 percent of EMDE pandemic-related fiscal support was unwound, fiscal consolidation paused in many EMDEs in 2022. The aggregate EMDE fiscal stance turned expansionary in 2022, with fiscal policy becoming more supportive in about half of EMDEs, especially in large economies (figures 1.15.B and 1.15.C). The EMDE fiscal stance is expected to be slightly contractionary in 2023. In all, about 70 percent of EMDEs are expected to consolidate fiscal balances in both 2023 and 2024.

Last year's pause in fiscal consolidation efforts reflected the fact that many EMDEs responded to higher food and fuel prices by implementing tax cuts, subsidies, loans, and trade measures to mitigate the impact on households and firms (figures 1.15.D and 1.15.E; Amaglobeli et al. 2022). In many cases, support to households has been largely untargeted and may add to inflationary pressures and work against monetary policy tightening. In addition to being costly, untargeted tax cuts and subsidies on fossil fuels support demand for environmentally-damaging and carbon-intensive energy sources, eroding incentives for energy conservation and creating tension with longer-term climate goals.

Reprioritizing fiscal support away from broad and costly subsidies can free up resources that can be redirected to low-income households and viable firms (Bridle et al. 2018). In particular, governments can provide vulnerable households with means-tested cash transfers, which tend to be less costly than food and fuel subsidies, especially when implemented with automatic sunset clauses (World Bank 2022k). Protecting spending in categories such as health, climate, and education is critical given setbacks from the pandemic, increased costs due to inflation, and large investment gaps.

FIGURE 1.15 Fiscal policy challenges in emerging market and developing economies

Many emerging market and developing economies (EMDEs) are vulnerable to rising borrowing costs, especially those with already high debt servicing costs and sizable external or foreign-currency denominated debt. In some EMDEs, fiscal consolidation efforts in 2022 slowed or were further delayed due to government support in response to high food and energy prices. Tax revenues in many EMDEs fall short of the amount needed to make progress toward development goals, highlighting the need for greater domestic revenue mobilization.

A. EMDE debt service costs, by credit rating

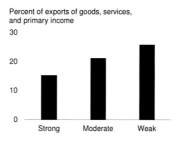

B. Share of EMDEs with tightening fiscal policy

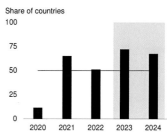

C. Fiscal impulse

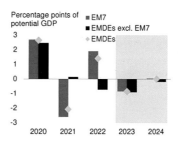

D. Government support packages in response to high food and energy prices, 2022 survey

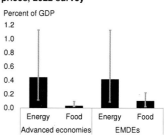

E. Government measures in response to high energy and food prices, 2022 survey

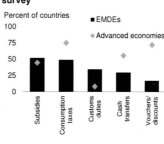

F. Government revenues, 2022

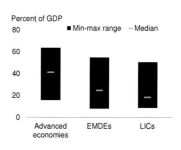

Sources: IMF (2022b); Kose et al. (2022); Moody's Corporation; WEO (database); World Bank.
Note: EMDEs = emerging market and developing economies; EM7 = Brazil, China, India, Indonesia, Mexico, the Russian Federation, and Türkiye; LICs = low-income countries. Shaded areas indicate forecasts. Unless otherwise indicated, aggregates are calculated using real U.S. dollar GDP weights at average 2010-19 prices and market exchange rates.
A. Bars show median debt service for each category and whiskers indicate the minimum-maximum range. Strong credit is defined as countries with investment grade ratings (ratings from AAA to BBB). Moderate credit is defined as countries with ratings between BB and B. Weak credit is defined as countries with ratings between CCC and C. Sample size includes 72 EMDEs.
B.C. Fiscal impulse is calculated as the negative change in the structural balance from previous year. Sample includes 43 EMDEs.
B. Tightening fiscal policy shows the share of countries with a negative fiscal impulse.
D.E. Survey of 174 countries on the measures taken during the period from January to June 2022 in response to rising food and energy prices, as described in IMF (2022b).
D. Bars show the median and whiskers show the 20th and 80th percentile, based on IMF (2022b).
F. Sample size includes 137 EMDEs, 37 advanced economies, and 23 LICs.

EMDEs can also renew their adherence to fiscal rules, as appropriate, which may set debt on a more sustainable path and help buttress market confidence. Improvements to the expenditure review process—such as strengthening mechanisms that prioritize and evaluate the efficacy of public projects—can enhance the quality and efficiency of public spending. Policies that aim at strengthening public procurement practices, administrative capacity, and transparency can also bolster public investment efficiency, foster a more favorable business climate for private investment, and help reinvigorate productivity. Several EMDEs (Malaysia, Namibia, Russia) activated escape clauses, modified fiscal rule limits, and suspended fiscal rules in response to the pandemic (Davoodi et al. 2022). It is critical to re-establish rules and strengthen medium-term expenditure frameworks to create a predictable policy environment.

EMDE government revenue as a share of GDP is expected to remain below pre-pandemic levels until at least 2024 in over half of EMDEs—particularly commodity importers. Even prior to the pandemic, EMDE government revenues trailed advanced-economy levels by about 15 percentage points of GDP; since then, the gap has widened, particularly in LICs (figure 1.15.F). Much of the challenge reflects weak domestic revenue mobilization. Tax revenues in nearly half of EMDEs fell short of the amount needed to provide basic services, increasing the challenge of financing the Sustainable Development Goals (SDGs; OECD 2018).

Increasing tax rates may be difficult to pursue in the near term given weak growth prospects, but EMDEs have a variety of other options to bring government revenues closer to advanced-economy levels. They can broaden tax bases and curb revenue leakages by reducing exemptions and closing loopholes, adopting tax expenditure analysis, and aligning policy with international rules such as the OECD/G20 Inclusive Framework on Base Erosion and Profit Shifting. To this end, international tax agreements that improve automatic information sharing can also help combat revenue losses. Governments can also focus on ensuring under-taxed activities are appropriately taxed and explore options to better utilize taxes that can be both progressive and efficient, including property taxes. Tax administration and collection mechanisms can be strengthened to reduce avoidance and ensure revenue is collected efficiently. This can be complemented by efforts to bolster taxpayers' intrinsic willingness to pay taxes by improving the fairness and efficiency of taxes and public spending (Hoy 2022). Revenue reforms, where appropriate, should be carefully sequenced to avoid macro-economic instability. For example, restructuring tax rates, particularly on capital, in tandem with a pronounced tightening in global financing conditions, could exacerbate portfolio outflows and deter investment.

EMDE structural policy challenges

The longer-term challenges facing EMDEs have been aggravated by the pandemic, Russia's invasion of Ukraine, and the sharp deceleration in global growth. These developments have weighed on investment growth in EMDEs, worsened food insecurity in the world's poorest countries, and stalled progress in promoting gender equality. Reversing the impact of these negative shocks and better preparing vulnerable groups for future crises will require structural reforms that bolster long-term growth prospects. This will involve policies that boost investment and human capital development, as well as those that buttress resilience and crisis preparedness, especially in agriculture and food systems.

Bolstering investment

The lasting damage inflicted by the pandemic, the invasion of Ukraine, and other negative shocks over the past three years has led to substantial and growing cumulative output losses in EMDEs (figure 1.16.A). In particular, the recovery in investment—a key driver of long-term growth—after these negative shocks is expected to be substantially weaker than the one that followed the 2009 global recession (figure 1.16.B; Kose et al. 2017b). Weak investment growth can worsen potential growth, weaken trade growth, and hamper the ability of countries to achieve the SDGs (chapter 3). Absent reforms, investment growth in EMDEs will likely continue falling during the next decade, reflecting trends in fundamental drivers along with scarring from the negative shocks of recent years.

Well-targeted investments can create jobs, lower income inequality, and boost productivity.[3] Substantial investment is also needed to help EMDEs meet the SDGs in education, health, and infrastructure (Vorisek and Yu 2020). For example, low- and middle-income countries need to invest $1.5-2.7 trillion per year (about 5-8 percent of their combined annual GDP) during 2015-30 to close SDG-related infrastructure gaps (figure 1.16.C; Rozenberg and Fay 2019). These gaps are reflected in low school enrollment and completion rates, poor health indicators, low female labor force participation, product and labor market distortions, and high rates of informality. Disruptions to schooling during the pandemic have worsened learning outcomes, especially among poorer households and countries, and have likely damaged future productivity, earnings, and innovation (Moscoviz and Evans 2022). Similarly, while better health outcomes are associated with higher growth rates, EMDEs require significant investment to reverse stubbornly poor health outcomes and achieve the health-related SDGs targets. Given the scale of these investments, EMDE efforts will need to be supported by the global community through greater access to official financing and measures to leverage private finance.

Sound investments aligned with climate goals in priority areas—such as transport and energy, climate-smart agriculture and manufacturing, and land and water systems—can all boost long-term growth, while also enhancing EMDE resilience to future natural disasters, especially in small states (chapter 4; figure 1.16.D; Agrawala, Dussaux, and Monti 2020; IEA 2020; World Bank 2021a). While green transitions need to be carefully managed, sustainable investments, including from the private sector, offer significant opportunities.

---

[3] Other factors beyond investment that also drive long term growth—such as productivity, governance and institutions, gender equality, human capital and labor force participation—are discussed in previous editions of the *Global Economic Prospects* report; please see World Bank (2021b; 2021c; 2022e).

FIGURE 1.16 Structural policy challenges in emerging market and developing economies

The negative shocks of the past three years have led to large cumulative losses, especially for output and investment in emerging market and developing economies (EMDEs), highlighting the need for structural policy responses. Substantial investments are needed to close SDG-related infrastructure gaps and enhance EMDE resilience to natural disasters. A persistent gender gap in labor participation and higher food insecurity, particularly in low-income countries, also require decisive policy action.

A. Cumulative output losses, 2020-24

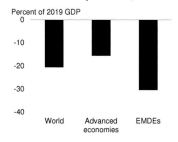

B. Investment in EMDEs

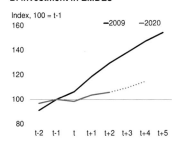

C. Infrastructure investment needs, by region

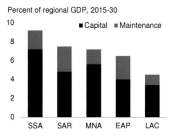

D. Damages and losses from natural disasters, 1990-2021

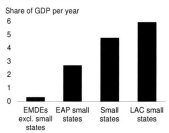

E. Ratio of female to male labor force participation in EMDEs

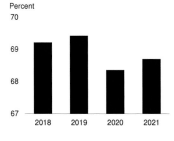

F. Food insecurity in LICs

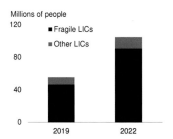

Sources: Consensus Economics; EM-DAT (database); FSIN and GNAFC (2022); GNAFC (2022); Guénette, Kose, and Sugawara (2022); Kose et al. (2017b); Rozenberg and Fay (2019); WDI (database); World Bank.

Note: EMDEs = emerging market and developing economies; LICs = low-income countries; Fragile LICs = LICs with fragile and conflict affected situations; EAP = East Asia and Pacific, LAC = Latin America and the Caribbean; MNA = Middle East and North Africa, SAR = South Asia, SSA = Sub-Saharan Africa. SDG = sustainable development goals. Small states are EMDEs with a population of less than 1.5 million. Unless otherwise indicated, aggregate growth rates are calculated using real U.S. dollar GDP weights at average 2010-19 prices and market exchange rates.

A. Figure shows total output losses, relative to the pre-pandemic trend, over 2020-24, in percent of GDP in 2019. The pre-pandemic trend is based on the January 2020 baseline, which is extended using projected growth for 2022.

B. Investment refers to gross fixed capital formation. Sample includes 69 EMDEs. Year "t" on the horizontal axis refers to the year of global recessions in 2009 and 2020. Dotted portion of the line is a forecast.

C. Bars show average annual spending needs during 2015-30, as estimated by Rozenberg and Fay (2019). Estimates are generated using policy assumptions that cap investment needs at 4.5 percent of GDP per year.

D. Aggregates are calculated using nominal GDP weights.

E. Figure shows the ratio of female to male labor force participation rate for 142 EMDEs.

F. Bars show the number of people in food crisis as classified by the Integrated Food Security Phase Classification (IPC/CH) Phase 3, that is, in acute food insecurity crisis or worse. Data for 2022 are estimates adapted from GNAFC (2022).

Alongside their broader benefits, green investments may represent an important engine for job creation as they tend to be more labor-intensive (Jaeger et al. 2021).

Improving governance frameworks can bolster private investment and investor confidence. This can be accomplished through regulatory and governance reforms that improve the investment climate (World Bank forthcoming). Investment can also be boosted by establishing appropriate and predictable rules for investment decisions. For public-private partnerships and state-owned enterprises, this includes strengthening governance arrangements and harmonizing public investment management frameworks (Engel, Fischer, and Galetovic 2020; Herrera Dappe, Melecky, and Turkgulu 2022). In relation to green investments, policy makers need to incentivize the adoption of low-carbon technologies through carbon taxes and emission trading schemes, as well as reform fuel subsidies. In addition, clear and credible climate change commitments can reduce the perceived risks and financing costs of green technologies (World Bank 2022l).

Reforms to strengthen the business climate are also critical for attracting private investment. Depending on country circumstances, policy makers need to strengthen property rights, improve access to finance, and broaden financial inclusion, all of which have been found to stimulate private investment in EMDEs (Sahay et al. 2015; World Bank forthcoming). These measures can be complemented by labor and product market policies that promote investment. In addition, eliminating unnecessary duties and simplifying trade facilitation and cross-border procedures can help countries bolster trade and benefit from the higher investment flows, given the strong interdependencies between trade and foreign direct investment (Brenton, Ferrantino, and Maliszewska 2022).

Promoting resilience

The overlapping shocks of the past three years have disproportionately hurt women and vulnerable groups—notably children, disabled people, and the elderly. The pandemic worsened health and education outcomes, with the largest losses among the poor (Schady et al. forthcoming). The war in Ukraine and conflicts elsewhere have increased the number of refugees, eroded social conditions, and upended gains in human development. The recent surge in energy and food prices, combined with a sharp deceleration in global activity, are increasing hunger, malnutrition and poverty in many EMDEs. These shocks have pushed out of reach the global goal of ending extreme poverty by 2030 (World Bank. 2022c).

Policy makers need to foster social protection systems that are pro-growth, agile, and sufficiently broad-based to prepare vulnerable groups for major shocks (World Bank 2022m). These measures can be complemented with policies to improve financial inclusion and credit access and reduce the cost of remittance flows, which provide vulnerable populations with short-term buffers to mitigate the effects of crises. In the medium term, EMDEs need to prioritize human capital investment—which came under pressure during the pandemic—to bolster capacity and better harness technology for improved service delivery (Bashir et al. 2021; World Bank and UNESCO 2022). Measures are needed to improve early childhood development and nutrition, as well as to accelerate efforts to achieve universal health coverage and access to quality education. Improving education programs at all levels, and promoting youth employment and entrepreneurship, can help recover learning losses caused by the pandemic, reduce education inequalities, and enhance resilience to labor market shocks (Schady et al. forthcoming). These may include measures that accelerate the teaching of fundamentals, promote catch-up learning, and improve the well-being of children (World Bank et al. 2022).

Progress in gender equality in EMDEs is stalling and is at risk of reversal. The pandemic had a disproportionate economic impact on women, as they were more likely to stop working than men, and subsequently returned to the labor market more slowly (De Paz, Gaddis, and Muller 2021; ILO 2022). More women-led businesses closed due to the pandemic, and they received less government support (Torres et al. 2021). As a result, women have lost ground in the workforce, as reflected by high female unemployment rates and a persistent gap in labor force participation relative to men (figure 1.16.E; Braunstein 2021; Djankov, Goldberg, and Hyland 2021). Policy makers in EMDEs can implement a wide range of policies to close existing gaps and enhance women's ability to prepare for future shocks. These include policies that increase female labor force participation and productivity, such as promoting childcare services (Cali et al. 2022). They also encompass active labor market programs addressing social norms and gender-based violence, while promoting girls' aspirations and socio-emotional skills (Halim, O'Sullivan and Sahay 2022). Ensuring that women have equal access to key financial products, especially those with lower collateral requirements, can enhance their productive and entrepreneurial capacity, including in times of crisis (Hess, Klapper, and Beegle 2021; Ubfal 2022).

Fostering food security requires policy action at both the global and national policy level. Hunger and food insecurity have increased in many of the world's poorest regions because of pandemic-related supply disruptions, higher input costs, and shortages, partly due to Russia's invasion of Ukraine (figure 1.16.F; World Bank 2022d). Extreme weather events such as droughts and floods, localized pest outbreaks, and conflict have also played a role. Food insecurity can also be worsened by market distortions from domestic policy responses to rising food and fertilizer prices, such as food export bans and price controls (Guénette 2020; Laborde, Lakatos, and Martin 2019). In the near term, targeted interventions, such as nutrition programs and direct income support, can help the most in need. In the longer term, well-targeted investments in agricultural R&D, green innovations, measures that improve the uptake of new technology, and diversification of food sources and food supply chain systems are all key to boosting food production and building resilient food systems in EMDEs (Gautam et al. 2022; World Bank 2022c).

TABLE 1.2 Emerging market and developing economies[1]

Commodity exporters[2]		Commodity importers[3]	
Algeria*	Kyrgyz Republic	Afghanistan	Samoa
Angola*	Lao PDR	Albania	Serbia
Argentina	Liberia	Antigua and Barbuda	Sri Lanka
Armenia	Libya*	Bahamas, The	St. Kitts and Nevis
Azerbaijan*	Madagascar	Bangladesh	St. Lucia
Bahrain*	Malawi	Barbados	St. Vincent and the Grenadines
Belize	Mali	Belarus	Thailand
Benin	Mauritania	Bosnia and Herzegovina	Tonga
Bhutan*	Mongolia	Bulgaria	Tunisia
Bolivia*	Mozambique	Cambodia	Türkiye
Botswana	Myanmar*	China	Tuvalu
Brazil	Namibia	Djibouti	Vanuatu
Burkina Faso	Nicaragua	Dominica	Vietnam
Burundi	Niger	Dominican Republic	
Cabo Verde	Nigeria*	Egypt, Arab Rep.	
Cameroon*	Oman*	El Salvador	
Central African Republic	Papua New Guinea	Eswatini	
Chad*	Paraguay	Georgia	
Chile	Peru	Grenada	
Colombia*	Qatar*	Haiti	
Comoros	Russian Federation*	Hungary	
Congo, Dem. Rep.	Rwanda	India	
Congo, Rep.*	São Tomé and Príncipe	Jamaica	
Costa Rica	Saudi Arabia*	Jordan	
Côte d'Ivoire	Senegal	Kiribati	
Ecuador*	Seychelles	Lebanon	
Equatorial Guinea*	Sierra Leone	Lesotho	
Eritrea	Solomon Islands	Malaysia	
Ethiopia	South Africa	Maldives	
Fiji	South Sudan*	Marshall Islands	
Gabon*	Sudan	Mauritius	
Gambia, The	Suriname	Mexico	
Ghana*	Tajikistan	Micronesia, Fed. Sts.	
Guatemala	Tanzania	Moldova	
Guinea	Timor-Leste*	Montenegro	
Guinea-Bissau	Togo	Morocco	
Guyana*	Uganda	Nauru	
Honduras	Ukraine	Nepal	
Indonesia*	United Arab Emirates*	North Macedonia	
Iran, Islamic Rep.*	Uruguay	Pakistan	
Iraq*	Uzbekistan	Palau	
Kazakhstan*	West Bank and Gaza	Panama	
Kenya	Zambia	Philippines	
Kosovo	Zimbabwe	Poland	
Kuwait*		Romania	

* Energy exporters.

1. Emerging market and developing economies (EMDEs) include all those that are not classified as advanced economies and for which a forecast is published for this report. Dependent territories are excluded. Advanced economies include Australia; Austria; Belgium; Canada; Cyprus; Czechia; Denmark; Estonia; Finland; France; Germany; Greece; Hong Kong SAR, China; Iceland; Ireland; Israel; Italy; Japan; the Republic of Korea; Latvia; Lithuania; Luxembourg; Malta; the Netherlands; New Zealand; Norway; Portugal; Singapore; the Slovak Republic; Slovenia; Spain; Sweden; Switzerland; the United Kingdom; and the United States. Since Croatia became a member of the euro area on January 1, 2023, it has been removed from the list of EMDEs, and related growth aggregates, to avoid double counting.

2. An economy is defined as commodity exporter when, on average in 2017-19, either (1) total commodities exports accounted for 30 percent or more of total exports or (2) exports of any single commodity accounted for 20 percent or more of total exports. Economies for which these thresholds were met as a result of re-exports were excluded. When data were not available, judgment was used. This taxonomy results in the classification of some well-diversified economies as importers, even if they are exporters of certain commodities (for example, Mexico).

3. Commodity importers are EMDEs not classified as commodity exporters.

References

Agrawala, S., D. Dussaux, and N. Monti. 2020. "What Policies for Greening the Crisis Response and Economic Recovery? Lessons Learned from Past Green Stimulus Measures and Implications for the Covid-19 Crisis." OECD Environment Working Paper 164, OECD, Paris.

Ahmed, S., R. Correa, D. A. Dias, N. Gornemann, J. Hoek, A. Jain, E. Liu, and A. Wong. 2019. "Global Spillovers of a China Hard Landing." International Finance Discussion Papers 1260, Board of Governors of the Federal Reserve System, Washington, DC.

Amaglobeli, D., E. Hanedar, G. H. Hong, C. Thevenot. 2022. "Fiscal Policy for Mitigating the Social Impact of High Energy and Food Prices." International Monetary Fund, Washington, DC.

Argente, D., and M. Lee. 2021. "Cost of Living Inequality During the Great Recession." *Journal of the European Economic Association* 19 (2): 913-52.

Arteta, C., S. Kamin, F. U. Ruch. 2022. "How Do Rising U.S. Interest Rates Affect Emerging and Developing Economies? It Depends." Policy Research Working Paper 10258, World Bank, Washington, DC.

Arteta, C., M. A. Kose, F. Ohnsorge, and M. Stocker. 2015. "The Coming U.S. Interest Rate Tightening Cycle: Smooth Sailing or Stormy Waters?" Policy Research Note, World Bank, Washington, DC.

Avdjiev, S., E. Eren, and P. McGuire. 2020. "Dollar funding costs during the COVID-19 crisis through the lens of the FX swap market." BIS Bulletin 1, Basel, Switzerland.

Ball, L., D. Leigh, P. Mishra. 2022. "Understanding U.S. Inflation During the COVID Era." BPEA Conference Drafts, Brookings Paper on Economic Activity, Washington, DC.

Bashir, S., C. J. Dahlman, N. Kanehira, K. Tilmes. 2021. *The Converging Technology Revolution and Human Capital: Potential and Implications for South Asia. South Asia Development Forum*. Washington, DC: World Bank.

Baumeister, C., G. Verduzco-Bustos, F. Ohnsorge. 2022. "Special Focus: Pandemic, War, Recession: Drivers of Aluminum and Copper Prices" In *Commodity Markets Outlook*, October. Washington, DC: World Bank.

Bems, R., R. C. Johnson, and K. M. Yi. 2010. "Demand Spillovers and the Collapse of Trade in the Global Recession." *IMF Economic Review* 58 (2): 295-326.

BIS (database). Bank for International Settlements. Accessed on November 20, 2022. https://www.bis.org/statistics/.

Braunstein, E. 2021. "Gender and The Future of Industrialization in a Post- Pandemic World." Inclusive and Sustainable Industrial Development Working Paper Series 10/2021, United Nations Industrial Development Organization, Vienna.

Brenton, P., M. J. Ferrantino, M. Maliszewska. 2022. *Reshaping Global Value Chains in Light of COVID-19: Implications for Trade and Poverty Reduction in Developing Countries*. Washington, DC: World Bank.

Bridle, R., L. Merrill, M. Halonen, A. Zinecker, and P. Tommila. 2018. "Swapping Fossil Fuel Subsidies for Sustainable Energy." Nordic Council of Ministers, Denmark.

Caldara, D., and M. Iacoviello. 2022. "Measuring Geopolitical Risk." *American Economic Review* 112 (4): 1194-1225.

Caldara, D., M. Iacoviello, P. Molligo, A. Prestipino, and A. Raffo. 2020. "The Economic Effects of Trade Policy Uncertainty." *Journal of Monetary Economics* 109: 38-59.

Cali, M., H. C. Johnson, E. Perova, N. R. Ryandiansyah. 2022. "Caring for Children and Firms: The Impact of Preschool Expansion on Firm Productivity." Policy Research Working Papers10193, World Bank, Washington, DC.

Caselli, F., and A. Roitman. 2016. "Non-Linear Exchange Rate Pass-Through in Emerging Markets." IMF Working Paper 16/1, International Monetary Fund, Washington, DC.

Comtrade (database). United Nations. Accessed on December 15, 2022. https://comtrade.un.org.

Davoodi, H. R., P. Elger, A. Fotiou, D. Garcia-Macia, X. Han, A. Lagerborg, W. R. Lam et al. 2022. "Fiscal Rules and Fiscal Councils: Recent Trends and Performance during the COVID-19 Pandemic." International Monetary Fund, Washington, DC.

De Paz, N. C., I. Gaddis, and M. Muller. 2021. "Gender and COVID-19: What Have We Learnt, One

Year Later. Policy Research Working Paper 9709, World Bank, Washington, DC.

Dieppe, A., ed. 2021. *Global Productivity: Trends, Drivers, and Policies*. Washington, DC: World Bank.

Di Pace, F., L. Juvenal, and I. Petrella. 2020. "Terms-of-Trade Shocks Are Not All Alike." IMF Working Paper 280, International Monetary Fund, Washington, DC.

Djankov, S., P. K. Goldberg, and M. Hyland. 2021. "The Evolving Gender Gap in Labor Force Participation During COVID-19." Policy Brief 21-8, Peterson Institute for International Economics, Washington, DC.

Doh, T., and A. T. Foerster. 2022. "Have Lags in Monetary Policy Transmission Shortened?" Economic Bulletin, Federal Reserve Bank of Kansas City, Kansas City, Missouri.

EM-DAT (database). The International Disaster Database. Accessed on November 20, 2022. https://www.emdat.be/.

Engel, E., R. Fischer, and A. Galetovic. 2020. "When and How to Use Public-Private Partnerships in Infrastructure: Lessons from the International Experience." NBER Working Paper 26766, National Bureau of Economic Research, Cambridge, MA.

European Commission. 2022. "European Economic Forecast." Institutional Paper 187, European Commission, Brussels.

Forbes, K., J. E. Gagnon, and C. G. Collins. 2021. "Low Inflation Bends the Phillips Curve Around the World: Extended Results." PIIE Working Papers 21-15, Peterson Institute for International Economics, Washington, DC.

FSIN (Food Security Information Network), and GNAFC (Global Network Against Food Crises). 2022. "Global Report on Food Crises." Food Security Information Network, Rome.

Gautam, M., D. Laborde, A. Mamun, W. Martin, V. Pineiro, and R. Vos. 2022. "Repurposing Agricultural Policies and Support: Options to Transform Agriculture and Food Systems to Better Serve the Health of People, Economies, and the Planet." World Bank, Washington, DC.

Gill, I., and P. Nagle. 2022. "Inflation Could Wreak Vengence on The World's Poor." *Future Development Blog*. March 18, 2022. https://www.brookings.edu/blog/future-development/2022/03/18/inflation-could-wreak-vengence-on-the-worlds-poor/.

Glennerster, R., C. M. Snyder, and B. J. Tan. 2022. "Calculating the Costs and Benefits of Advance Preparations for Future Pandemics." NBER Working Paper 30565, National Bureau of Economic Research, Cambridge, MA.

GNAFC (Global Network Against Food Crises). 2022. "Financing Flows and Food Crises Report." Food Security Information Network, Rome.

Góes, C., and E. Bekkers. 2022. "The Impact of Geopolitical Conflicts on Trade, Growth, and Innovation." WTO Staff Working Paper ERSD-2022-9, World Trade Organization, Geneva.

Gruss, B., and S. Kebhaj. 2019. "Commodity Terms of Trade: A New Database." IMF Working Paper 2019/021, International Monetary Fund, Washington, DC.

Guénette, J. D. 2020. "Price Controls: Good Intentions, Bad Outcomes." Policy Research Working Paper 9212, World Bank, Washington, DC.

Guénette, J. D., M. A. Kose, and N. Sugawara. 2022. "Is a Global Recession Imminent?" EFI Policy Note 4, World Bank, Washington, DC.

Ha, J., M. A. Kose, and F. Ohnsorge. 2019a. *Inflation in Emerging and Developing Economies: Evolution, Drivers, and Policies*. Washington, DC: World Bank.

Ha, J., M. A. Kose, and F. Ohnsorge. 2019b. "Inflation and Exchange Rate Pass-Through." In *Inflation in Emerging and Developing Economies Evolution, Drivers, and Policies*. Washington, DC.: World Bank.

Ha, J., M. A. Kose, F. Ohnsorge. 2022. "Global Stagflation." Koç University-TUSIAD Economic Research Forum Working Papers 2204, Istanbul, Türkiye.

Halim, D., M. B. O'Sullivan, and A. Sahay. 2022. "Thematic Policy Brief on Increasing Female Labor Force Participation." World Bank, Washington, DC.

Herrera Dappe, M., M. Melecky, and B. Turkgulu. 2022. "Fiscal Risks from Early Termination of Public-Private Partnerships in Infrastructure." Policy Research Working Paper 9972, World Bank, Washington, DC.

Hess, J., L. Klapper, and K. Beegle. 2021. "Financial Inclusion, Women, and Building Back Better." World Bank, Washington, DC.

Hoek, J., S. Kamin, and E. Yoldas. 2022. "Are Higher U.S. Interest Rates Always Bad News for Emerging Markets?" *Journal of International Economics* 137: 103-585.

Hofmann, B., A. Mehrotra, D. Sandri. 2022. "Global Exchange Rate Adjustments: Drivers, Impacts and Policy Implications." BIS Bulletin No. 62, Bank of International Settlement, Basel, Switzerland.

Horn, S., C. M. Reinhart, C. Trebesch. 2021. "China's Overseas Lending." *Journal of International Economics* 133: 103-539.

Hoy, C. A. 2022. "How Does the Progressivity of Taxes and Government Transfers Impact People's Willingness to Pay Tax?" Policy Research Working Paper 10167, World Bank, Washington, DC.

IEA (International Energy Agency). 2020. "Sustainable Recovery." World Energy Outlook Special Report in Collaboration with the International Monetary Fund, International Energy Agency, Paris.

IEA (International Energy Agency). 2022a. "Oil Market Report." November. International Energy Agency, Paris.

IEA (International Energy Agency). 2022b. "Defying Expectations, CO2 Emissions from Global Fossil Fuel Combustion are Set to Grow in 2022 by Only a Fraction of Last Year's Big Increase." International Energy Agency, Paris.

ILO (International Labour Organization). 2022. *World Employment and Social Outlook: Trends 2022*. Geneva, Switzerland: International Labour Organization.

IMF (International Monetary Fund). 2022a. "Debt Sustainability Analysis Low-Income Countries." International Monetary Fund, Washington, DC.

IMF (International Monetary Fund). 2022b. *Fiscal Monitor: Helping People Bounce Back*. Washington, DC: International Monetary Fund.

IMF (International Monetary Fund). 2022c. *Fiscal Policy: From Pandemic to War*. Washington, DC: International Monetary Fund.

IMF (International Monetary Fund). 2022d. "Global Financial Stability Report: Navigating the High-Inflation Environment." International Monetary Fund, Washington, DC.

International Debt Statistics (database). World Bank. Accessed on November 1, 2022. https://databank.worldbank.org/source/international-debt-statistics.

IPCC (Intergovernmental Panel on Climate Change). 2022. "Climate Change 2022: Impacts, Adaptation and Vulnerability." IPCC Sixth Assessment Report, Geneva, Switzerland.

Jaeger, J., G. Walls, E. Clarke, J.C. Altamirano, A. Harsono, H. Mountford, S. Burrow, et al. 2021. "The Green Jobs Advantage: How Climate Friendly Investments Are Better Job Creators." Working Paper, World Resources Institute, Washington, DC.

Kalemli-Özcan, Ş., di Giovanni, J., A. Silva, M. Yildirim. 2022. "Challenges for Monetary Policy in a Rapidly Changing World." ECB Forum on Central Banking, European Central Bank, Frankfurt.

Kose, M. A., L. Csilla, F. Ohnsorge, and M. Stocker. 2017a. "Special Focus: The U.S. Economy and the World." In *Global Economic Prospects*, January. Washington, DC: World Bank.

Kose, M. A., S. Kurlat, F. Ohnsorge, and N. Sugawara. 2022. "A Cross-Country Database of Fiscal Space." World Bank, Washington, DC.

Kose, M. A., P. Nagle, F. Ohnsorge, and N. Sugawara. 2021a. *Global Waves of Debt: Causes and Consequences*. Washington, DC: World Bank.

Kose, M. A., P. Nagle, F. Ohnsorge, and N. Sugawara. 2021b. "What Has Been the Impact of COVID-19 on Debt? Turning a Wave into a Tsunami." Policy Research Working Paper 9871, World Bank, Washington, DC.

Kose, M. A., F. Ohnsorge, L. S. Ye, E. Islamaj. 2017b. "Weakness in Investment Growth: Causes, Implications and Policy Responses." Policy Research Working Paper 7990, World Bank, Washington, DC.

Kose, M. A., N. Sugawara, and M. E. Terrones. 2020. "Global Recessions." Policy Research Working Paper 9172, World Bank, Washington, DC.

Laborde, D., C. Lakatos, and W. J. Martin. 2019. "Poverty Impact of Food Price Shocks and Policies." Policy Research Working Paper 8724, World Bank, Washington, DC.

Laborde, D., and A. Mamun. 2022. "Food Export & Fertilizer Restrictions Tracker." Database funded by USAID and FCDO. https://public.tableau.com/app/profile/laborde6680/viz/ExportRestrictionsTracker/FoodExportRestrictionsTracker.

Laeven, L., and F. Valencia. 2020. "Systemic Banking Crises Database II." *IMF Economic Review* 68: 307-361.

Mahler, D. G., N. Yonzan, and C. Lakner. 2022. "The Impact of COVID-19 on Global Inequality and Poverty." Policy Research Working Papers 10198, World Bank, Washington, DC.

Maino, R., and D. Emrullahu. 2022. "Climate Change in Sub-Saharan Africa Fragile States: Evidence from Panel Estimations." IMF Working Paper 22/54, International Monetary Fund, Washington, DC.

Mallucci, E. 2020. "Natural Disasters, Climate Change, and Sovereign Risk." International Finance Discussion Papers 1291, Board of Governors of the Federal Reserve System, Washington, DC.

McKay, A. D. I., A. Staal, J. F. Abrams, R. Winkelmann, B. Sakschewski, S. Loriani, I. Fetzer, et al. 2022. "Exceeding 1.5°C Global Warming Could Trigger Multiple Climate Tipping Points." *Science* 377 (6611).

Moscoviz, L., and D. Evans. 2022. "Learning Loss and Student Dropouts during the COVID-19 Pandemic: A Review of the Evidence Two Years after Schools Shut Down." Working Paper 609, Center for Global Development, Washington, DC.

Obstfeld, M. 2022a. "Emerging-Market and Developing Economies Need Support Amid Rising Interest Rates." *Peterson Institute for International Economics* (blog). October 6, 2022. https://www.piie.com/blogs/realtime-economics/emerging-market-and-developing-economies-need-support-amid-rising-interest.

Obstfeld, M. 2022b. "Uncoordinated Monetary Policies Risk a Historic Global Slowdown." Peterson Institute for International Economics, Washington, DC.

Obstfeld, M., and H. Zhou. 2022. "The Global Dollar Cycle." Brookings Papers on Economic Activity, BPEA Conference Drafts, Washington, DC.

OECD (Organisation for Economic Co-operation and Development). 2018. "Countries Must Strengthen Tax Systems to Meet Sustainable Development Goals." Organisation for Economic Co-operation and Development, Paris.

Ohnsorge, F. L., M. Stocker, M. Y. Some. 2016. "Quantifying Uncertainties in Global Growth Forecasts." Policy Research Working Paper 7770, World Bank, Washington, DC.

OSCDS (United Nations Office of the Special Coordinator for Development in the Sahel) and UNHCR (United Nations High Commissioner for Refugees). 2022. *Moving from Reaction to Action - Anticipating Vulnerability Hotspots in the Sahel. A synthesis report from the Sahel Predictive Analytics project in support of the United Nations Integrated Strategy for the Sahel (UNISS).* Geneva: United Nations.

Oxford Economics. 2019. "Global Economic Model." July. Oxford Economics, Oxford.

Reis, R. 2022. "What Can Keep Euro Area Inflation High?" 76th Economic Policy Panel Meeting, Federal Ministry of Finance, Berlin, Germany.

Rogoff, K. 2022. "Emerging Market Sovereign Debt in the Aftermath of the Pandemic." *Journal of Economic Perspectives* 36 (4): 147-66.

Rozenberg, J., and M. Fay, eds. 2019. *Beyond the Gap: How Countries Can Afford the Infrastructure They Need While Protecting the Planet.* Washington, DC: World Bank.

Rubínová, S. and M. Sebti. 2021. "The WTO Global Trade Costs Index and Its Determinants." WTO Staff Working Paper ERSD-2021-6, World Trade Organization, Geneva.

Sahay, R. M. Cihak, P. N'Diaye, A. Barajas, S. Mitra, A. Kyobe, Y. N. Mooi, and S. R. Yousefi. 2015. "Financial Inclusion: Can It Meet Multiple Macroeconomic Goals?" Discussion Note, International Monetary Fund, Washington, DC.

Schady, N., A. Holla, S. Sabarwal, J. Silva, A. Y. Chang. Forthcoming. *Collapse and Recovery: How the COVID-19 Pandemic Eroded Human Capital and What to Do about It.* Washington, DC: World Bank.

Shapiro, A. H. 2022. "How Much Do Supply and Demand Drive Inflation?" FRBSF Economic Letter, Federal Reserve Bank of San Francisco, San Francisco.

Torres, J., F. Maduko, I. Gaddis, L. Iacovone, and K. Beegle. 2021. "The Impact of the COVID-19 Pandemic on Women-Led Businesses." Policy Research Working Paper 9817, World Bank, Washington, DC.

Ubfal, D. 2022. "What Works in Supporting Women-led Businesses?" Thematic Policy Brief for Gender Strategy Update 2024-2030, World Bank, Washington, DC.

UNDRR (United Nations Office for Disaster Risk Reduction). 2022. *Global Assessment Report on Disaster Risk Reduction 2022: Our World at Risk: Transforming Governance for a Resilient Future.* Geneva: United Nations Office for Disaster Risk Reduction.

Voegele, J. 2022. "How to Manage the World's Fertilizers to Avoid a Prolonged Food Crisis." *World Bank Blog.* July 22, 2022. https://blogs.worldbank.org/voices/how-manage-worlds-fertilizers-avoid-prolonged-food-crisis.

Vorisek, D., and S. Yu. 2020. "Understanding the Cost of Achieving the Sustainable Development Goals." Policy Research Working Paper 9146, World Bank, Washington, DC.

WDI (database). World Development Indicators. Accessed on November 20, 2022. https:// databank.worldbank.org/source/world-development-indicators.

WEO (database). "World Economic Outlook Databases." Accessed on October 30, 2022. https:// www.imf.org/en/Publications/WEO/weo-database/2022/October.

Wessel, T. 2022. "Terminally Underpriced." July. Rates Special Report, Deutsche Bank Research, Deutsche Bank, Frankfurt.

WFP (World Food Program and Food) and FAO (Agriculture Organization of the United Nations). 2022. "Hunger Hotspots. FAO⊠WFP Early Warnings on Acute Food Insecurity: October 2022 to January 2023 Outlook." Rome.

WMO, UNEP, GCP, UK Met office, IPCC, and UNDRR. 2022. "United in Science 2022." World Meteorological Organization, Geneva, Switzerland.

World Bank. Forthcoming. *Potential Growth*. Washington, DC: World Bank.

World Bank. 2021a. "World Bank Group Climate Change Action Plan 2021-2025: Supporting Green, Resilient, and Inclusive Development." World Bank, Washington, DC.

World Bank. 2021b. *Global Economic Prospects*. January. Washington, DC: World Bank.

World Bank. 2021c. *Global Economic Prospects*. June. Washington, DC: World Bank.

World Bank. 2022a. *Commodity Markets Outlook*. October. Washington, DC: World Bank.

World Bank. 2022b. *Reforms for Recovery*. East Asia and the Pacific Economic Update October. Washington, DC: World Bank.

World Bank. 2022c. *Poverty and Shared Prosperity 2022: Correcting Course*. Washington, DC: World Bank.

World Bank. 2022d. *Food Security Update*. Washington, DC: World Bank.

World Bank. 2022e. *Global Economic Prospects*. June. Washington, DC: World Bank.

World Bank. 2022f. "East Asia and Pacific Sustaining Growth, Restraining Inflation, but Facing Risks Ahead." Press release, World Bank, Washington, DC.

World Bank. 2022g. *Global Economic Prospects*. January. Washington, DC: World Bank.

World Bank. 2022h. "The Food and Energy Crisis - Weathering the Storm." Development Committee Meeting DC2022-0005, Washington, DC.

World Bank. 2022i. "Achieving Climate and Development Goals: The Financing Question." Development Committee Meeting DC2022-0006, Washington, DC.

World Bank. 2022j. "State and Trends of Carbon Pricing 2022." World Bank, Washington DC.

World Bank. 2022k. *MENA Economic Update: A New State of Mind*. October. Washington, DC: World Bank.

World Bank. 2022l. "Consolidating the Recovery: Seizing Green Growth Opportunities." April. LAC Semiannual Report, World Bank, Washington, DC.

World Bank. 2022m. *Social Protection for Recovery*. Europe and Central Asia Economic Update October. Washington, DC: World Bank.

World Bank and UNESCO (United Nations Educational, Scientific and Cultural Organization). 2022. "Education Finance Watch 2022." World Bank, UNESCO, Washington, DC., Paris.

World Bank, the Bill & Melinda Gates Foundation, FCDO, UNESCO, UNICEF, and USAID. 2022. "Guide for Learning Recovery and Acceleration: Using the RAPID Framework to Address COVID-19 Learning Losses and Build Forward Better." World Bank, Washington, DC.

WTO (World Tourism Organization). 2022. *World Tourism Barometer*. Madrid, Spain: World Tourism Organization.

WTTC (World Travel and Tourism Council). 2022. "Travel & Tourism Economic Impact: Global Trends." World Travel and Tourism Council, London.

CHAPTER 2

REGIONAL OUTLOOKS

EAST ASIA and PACIFIC

Growth in the East Asia and Pacific (EAP) region is projected at 4.3 percent in 2023—a pickup from last year's estimated 3.2 percent pace, and almost entirely on account of a projected rebound in China. As mobility restrictions ease, growth in China is forecast to firm from 2.7 percent in 2022 to 4.3 percent this year, still below its potential growth rate owing to continued pandemic-related disruptions. Growth in the rest of the region is expected to slow from 5.6 percent in 2022 to 4.7 percent in 2023, as pent-up demand dissipates and declining goods export growth outweighs recovery in tourism and travel. Downside risks to the outlook predominate, including the possibility of recurrent pandemic-related disruptions and a prolonged drag from the real estate sector in China, additional tightening of financial conditions, weaker-than-expected global growth, and extreme weather events.

Recent developments

After a strong rebound in 2021, growth in the East Asia and Pacific (EAP) region slowed markedly in 2022 to an estimated 3.2 percent, 1.2 percentage point below previous forecasts (figure 2.1.1.A; table 2.1). The slowdown was almost entirely due to China (which accounts for about 85 percent of the region's GDP), where growth slowed sharply to 2.7 percent, 1.6 percentage points lower than projected in June. The country faced recurrent COVID-19 outbreaks and mobility restrictions, unprecedented droughts, and prolonged stress in the property sector, all of which restrained consumption, food and energy production, and residential investment (figures 2.1.1.B and 2.1.1.C). Fiscal and monetary policy support for domestic demand and an easing of restrictions on the real estate sector have only partially offset these headwinds (figure 2.1.1.D).

In the region excluding China, the pace of growth more than doubled, rising to 5.6 percent in 2022 (figure 2.1.2.A). Growth was supported by a release of pent-up demand as many countries continued to lift pandemic-related mobility restrictions and travel bans (figure 2.1.2.B).

Note: This section was prepared by Ekaterine Vashakmadze.

Estimated growth in the region excluding China in 2022 was 0.8 percentage point above the June forecast. This reflects upgrades for Malaysia, the Philippines, Thailand, and Vietnam, most of which benefited from a surge in private consumption and strong growth of goods exports (figure 2.1.2.C). Growth in Fiji was much stronger than expected last year, fueled mainly by a resumption of international tourism in responce to a significant easing of travel restrictions.

The recovery from the pandemic-induced recession has been uneven across the region. Output surpassed pre-pandemic levels last year in Cambodia, the Philippines, and Thailand; in contrast, it is expected to remain below such levels this year in many of the region's economies, including Myanmar and several Pacific Island economies (chapter 4). The regional recovery in tourism, including in many Pacific Island economies, has been generally slower than in the rest of the world because of recurring COVID-19 outbreaks, remaining border restrictions, and lack of Chinese tourists, who represent a large share of visitors in some countries.

Growth in some countries has also suffered from large idiosyncratic shocks. For instance, in the Solomon Islands output contracted by an estimated 4.5 percent in 2022, reflecting the effects of civil unrest and widespread community

FIGURE 2.1.1 **China: Recent developments**

Growth in the East Asia and Pacific region slowed in 2022 due to weaker growth in China, where recurrent COVID-19 outbreaks and mobility restrictions, unprecedented droughts, and ongoing stress in the property sector restrained consumption and residential investment. Fiscal and monetary policy support and an easing of restrictions on the real estate sector only partially offset these headwinds.

A. China and the rest of the world: GDP

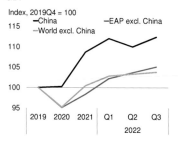

B. China: Components of GDP

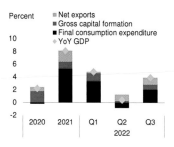

C. China: Fixed-asset investment growth

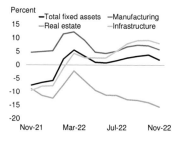

D. China: Change in structural fiscal balance

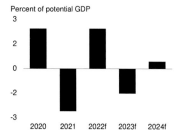

Sources: Haver Analytics; International Monetary Fund; National Bureau of Statistics of China; World Bank.
Note: EAP = East Asia and Pacific.
A. GDP level indexed at 2019Q4 = 100. Last observation is 2022Q3. Aggregates are calculated using average 2010-19 GDP weights and market exchange rates.
B. Figure shows year-over-year GDP growth and contributions of subcomponents. Last observation is 2022Q3.
C. Figure shows 3-month moving average of real growth from one year earlier. Fixed-asset investment deflator is estimated. Last observation is November 2022.
D. f = forecast. World Bank staff calculations. A positive value is consistent with fiscal support.

transmission of COVID-19. A volcanic eruption and subsequent tsunami in early 2022 severely curtailed economic activity in Tonga, until reconstruction efforts gathered momentum in late 2022.

Consumer price inflation increased across the region in 2022. While inflation has remained below the central bank target in China, it has exceeded targets for several months in other countries, including Indonesia, the Philippines and Thailand, mainly reflecting increases in energy and food prices (figure 2.1.2.D). Notwithstanding this increase, price pressures have been generally more muted in EAP than in other regions. This partly reflects remaining negative output gaps due

to a combination of relatively high potential growth and protracted recovery as well as widespread price controls and subsidies (World Bank 2022a). The Chinese renminbi and other major regional currencies depreciated against the U.S. dollar last year, partly reflecting widening interest rate differentials between EAP countries and the United States, but were more stable in trade-weighted terms.

Most central banks in the region have raised policy rates, but financial tightening has generally been less pronounced in the region than in other EMDEs due to comparatively lower price pressures. By contrast, in Mongolia, where price pressures have been strong, rates rose by 6 percentage points last year. These pressures reflect constraints on imports arising from a prolonged border closure with China (associated with its COVID-19 policy) and increased costs of importing through the Russian Federation because of the invasion of Ukraine. In Myanmar, consumer price inflation surged to 19.6 percent by mid-2022 from 6 percent a year earlier, reflecting increasing transport prices and a sharp depreciation of the kyat. In Lao People's Democratic Republic, inflation surpassed 38 percent in November, also fueled by high fuel prices and currency depreciation.

Outlook

Growth in the EAP region is projected to firm to 4.3 percent in 2023 as easing of pandemic-related restrictions allows activity in China to gradually recover (figure 2.1.3.A and 2.1.3.B; table 2.1.2). These projections are below those of last June, where regional growth was expected to surpuss 5 percent in 2023-24. The downward revisions are broad-based and reflect COVID-19 related disruptions and protracted weakness in the real estate sector in China and weaker-than-expected goods export growth across the region. In the face of ongoing monetary tightening, moderating activity, easing supply chain disruptions, and lower prices for many commodities, inflation is expected to ease somewhat after peaking in 2022.

In the region excluding China, growth is projected to moderate to 4.7 percent in 2023 and 2024 as pent-up demand dissipates and declining goods export growth outweighs belated recovery in tourism and travel. While recoveries from the pandemic remain incomplete in many countries, with output in 2023 expected to remain significantly below pre-pandemic trends, elevated prices for food, energy, and other inputs as well as further monetary policy tightening are envisaged to hold back activity this year, especially investment (figure 2.1.3.C). In the region's highly indebted or less creditworthy economies (Lao PDR, Mongolia), tightening global financing conditions are likely to hamper investment particularly sharply amid rising debt servicing costs. In 2024, growth in the region is also likely to be constrained by the effects of accelerated fiscal consolidation on domestic demand. Per capita income growth in EAP is projected to slow to 3.6 percent in 2020-23 from an average of 6.2 percent in the decade before the pandemic.

In Indonesia, GDP is projected to grow by 4.9 percent on average in 2023-24, only slightly slower than in 2022, reflecting softening but still robust private spending. Business confidence is expected to remain solid against the backdrop of sound macroeconomic fundamentals and structural reform implementation momentum, including in tax policy and administration. After the strong rebound in 2022, growth in Malaysia, the Philippines, and Vietnam is expected to moderate as the growth of exports to major markets slows. Growth is projected at 4.0 percent in Malaysia, 5.4 percent in the Philippines, and 6.3 percent in Vietnam. By contrast, growth in Thailand is projected to accelerate to 3.6 percent in 2023, reflecting the delayed recovery of contact-intensive sectors like tourism and transport. Output growth in tourism-dependent Pacific Island economies is also expected to be boosted by the relaxation of border restrictions and increased international tourist arrivals (Palau, Samoa).

Risks

The baseline projection is subject to multiple downside risks, including the possibility of renewed pandemic-related disruptions, more prolonged real estate sector stress in China, sharper tightening of global financial conditions,

FIGURE 2.1.2 **EAP excluding China: Recent developments**

In the region excluding China, growth picked up in 2022, reflecting a release of pent-up demand and a rebound of services exports as many countries continued to lift pandemic-related mobility restrictions and travel bans. Consumer price inflation has increased throughout EAP and exceeded targets for several months in many countries, mainly reflecting higher energy and food prices.

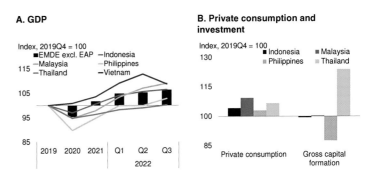

A. GDP

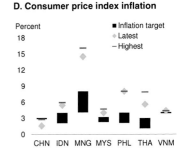

B. Private consumption and investment

C. Exports

D. Consumer price index inflation

Sources: Haver Analytics; national sources; World Bank.
Note: EAP = East Asia and Pacific; CHN = China; IDN = Indonesia; MNG = Mongolia; MYS = Malaysia; PHL = the Philippines; THA = Thailand; VNM = Vietnam.
A. Last observation is 2022Q3. Aggregates are calculated using average 2010-19 GDP weights and market exchange rates.
B.C. Investment is defined as gross capital formation and includes change in inventory. Last observation is 2022Q3.
D. Increase in consumer prices from 12 months earlier. "Highest" refers to the highest inflation rate in 2022. Last observation is November 2022.

weaker global growth, and more frequent disruptive weather events linked to climate change. A prolonged war in Ukraine and intensifying geopolitical uncertainty could further reduce business and consumer confidence globally and lead to a sharper slowdown than projected in the region's export growth.

In China, renewed large-scale COVID-19 outbreaks could lead to further disruptions in both domestic economic activity as well as in regional and global value chains. The impact of pandemic resurgences and associated disruptions could reduce China's growth relative to the baseline by 0.5 percentage point (World Bank 2022b). Pandemic-related disruptions at critical

FIGURE 2.1.3 **EAP: Outlook**

Growth in China is projected to strengthen in 2023 as pandemic-related restrictions ease. In the region excluding China, growth is projected to slow as pent-up demand dissipates and declining goods export growth outweighs belated recovery in tourism and travel. In many countries, recoveries from the pandemic remain incomplete, with output in 2023 significantly below pre-pandemic trends. Per capita income growth in EAP is projected to slow below its pre-pandemic average.

A. GDP growth

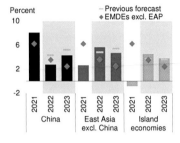

B. GDP growth, China

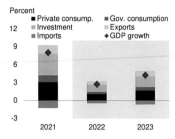

C. Deviation of 2023 GDP from pre-pandemic trends

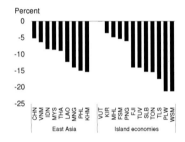

D. Per capita income growth relative to advanced economies

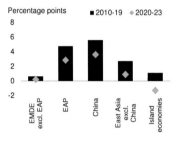

Sources: Haver Analytics; World Bank.
Note: EAP = East Asia and Pacific; EMDEs = emerging market and developing economies. In East Asia, CHN = China, IDN = Indonesia, LAO = Lao PDR, KHM = Cambodia, MMR = Myanmar, MNG = Mongolia, MYS = Malaysia, PHL = the Philippines, THA = Thailand, VNM = Vietnam. In Island economies, FJI = Fiji, FSM = Micronesia, Fed. Sts, KIR = Kiribati, MHL = Marshall Islands, NRU = Nauru, PLW = Palau, PNG = Papua New Guinea, SLB = Solomon Islands, TLS = Timor-Leste, TON = Tonga, TUV = Tuvalu, VUT = Vanuatu, WSM = Samoa.
A. Year-on-year change in real GDP in 2010-19 average prices. Aggregate growth rates are calculated using average 2010-19 GDP weights and market exchange rates. Data in shaded areas are forecasts.
B. Figure shows year-over-year real GDP growth and expenditure contributions. Shaded bar denotes 2022 forecast growth. Last observation is 2021.
C. Figure shows percent deviation between the levels of January 2020 and January 2023 baseline World Bank projections for 2020 to 2023. For 2023, the January 2020 baseline is extended using projected growth for 2022. Growth rates are calculated using GDP weights at average 2010-19 prices and market exchange rates.
D. 2010-19 and 2020-23 growth are simple averages of annual growth rates. Positive value indicates that growth in EMDE sub-groups is faster than that in advanced-economy aggregate. 2022 and 2023 values are projected.

infrastructure facilities like ports could weigh on production and supply chains, dampen investor and consumer confidence, and lower investment and growth across the region.

A more severe downturn in China's real estate sector, which represents about 25 percent of the country's fixed asset investment, could lead to a significant fall in local government revenue and weaker private consumption. Falling house prices

could erode wealth, which is largely concentrated in real estate (60-70 percent). Financial pressure on highly leveraged real estate developers could spill over to the domestic financial sector and affect borrowing costs, especially for riskier companies. A contraction in China's real estate sector would also negatively affect the rest of the region. It is estimated that a 10 percentage point decline in residential investment growth in China could reduce output growth in EAP by 0.3 percentage point (World Bank 2022c).

The baseline projections assume an uneven reopening in China accompanied by recurring COVID-19 outbreaks and economic disruptions. There may be positive surprises to China's economic outlook. This includes an orderly easing of mobility restrictions followed by a strong release of pent-up demand for consumption and services. A quicker-than-expected recovery in the coutnry's real estate sector is another upside possibility.

A prolonged war in Ukraine and intensifying geopolitical uncertainty could further reduce global business and consumer confidence. This could lead to a sharper slowdown than projected in the region's export growth through weaker global demand and trade disruptions. Such disruptions could lead to shortages and higher prices for food, fertilizer, and energy. Further geopolitical fragmentation could also impede global trade and investment and weigh on global and regional growth for a prolonged period. Commodity- and export-dependent economies like Cambodia, Malaysia, Mongolia, and Vietnam are particularly vulnerable to slowing export demand, including from China.

Unexpectedly persistent high global inflation could prompt substantially more monetary tightening than assumed in the baseline in many countries (World Bank 2022a). This could cause a sharper-than-expected slowdown in global growth and trigger significant capital outflows from EMDEs, adding pressure on the region's currencies and exacerbating inflation. Countries would need to raise policy rates more than expected (figure 2.1.4.A). Tighter global financial conditions could also induce debt distress in highly indebted EAP countries (figure 2.1.4.B).

Countries with large external financing needs, reflecting either a reliance on short-term capital (Cambodia, Malaysia), or high overall debt levels (Lao PDR, Mongolia), are particularly vulnerable (figure 2.1.4.C).

The combination of slower growth and tighter financial conditions than assumed in the baseline, amid high levels of debt, would increase the risk of fiscal pressures, rising defaults, and weak investment in many countries in EAP. There are heightened risks of a global recession (chapter 1). Such an event would have severe implications for many EAP economies, particularly those that are heavily exposed to the rest of the world through trade and financial channels, including commodity-exporting countries vulnerable to substantially lower commodity prices.

The region continues to experience an increasing frequency of highly disruptive weather events linked to climate change. Recent severe heat waves in China and cyclones in the Pacific have imposed significant human costs and major infrastructure losses. With global warming, such extreme events are more likely (IPCC 2022). Some countries in the Pacific have also suffered volcanic eruptions followed by tsunamis. Apart from the short-term costs of extreme weather events in terms of human suffering, damaged infrastructure, interruptions to the supply of key commodities, and other disruptions of economic activity, climate change is likely to render some populated areas unin-habitable, reduce productivity and productive capacity, and worsen global poverty. Small island countries, which lost an average of about 1 percent of GDP a year over the past 40 years to damage caused by natural disasters, remain particularly vulnerable to extreme weather events and hence to climate change (figure 2.1.4.D; Scandurra et al. 2018).

FIGURE 2.1.4 **EAP: Risks**

The outlook is subject to multiple downside risks. Persistently high global inflation could prompt substantially more monetary tightening than currently expected. Tighter global financial conditions could lead to debt distress, particularly in countries with high debt levels and large external financing needs. Climate change-related disruptive weather events could lead to costly disasters, especially for small states.

A. Monetary policy interest rates

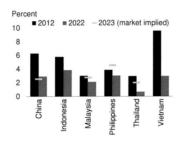

B. External financing needs, 2023

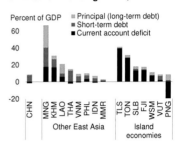

C. Total debt

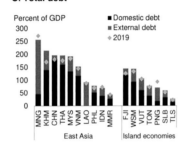

D. Natural disasters, 1980-2022

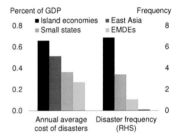

Sources: Bloomberg; EM-DAT; Haver Analytics; International Monetary Fund; World Bank.
Note: EMDEs = emerging market and developing economies. In East Asia, CHN = China, IDN = Indonesia, LAO = Lao PDR, KHM = Cambodia, MMR = Myanmar, MNG = Mongolia, MYS = Malaysia, PHL = the Philippines, THA = Thailand, VNM = Vietnam. In Island economies, FJI = Fiji, FSM = Micronesia, Fed. Sts, KIR = Kiribati, MHL = Marshall Islands, NRU = Nauru, PLW = Palau, PNG = Papua New Guinea, SLB = Solomon Islands, TLS = Timor-Leste, TON = Tonga, TUV = Tuvalu, VUT = Vanuatu, WSM = Samoa.
A. Figure shows the average policy interest rates in 2012 and 2022, respectively. 2023 refers to one-year ahead market implied policy interest rate. Last observation is November 2022.
B. Figure shows the current account balance and debt obligations coming due in 2023. Debt obligations coming due are the sum of short-term and long-term debt principal payments and interest payments (the latter being within the current account). Short-term external debt in 2022 and 2023 are estimates. GDP and current account balances in 2022 and 2023 are an estimation and projection, respectively.
C. Chart shows estimated stock of the domestic and external debt of public and private nonfinancial sectors. Domestic debt stock data are based on World Development Indicators. Last observation is end-2020. External debt stock data for Cambodia, China, Fiji, Indonesia, Malaysia, Mongolia, Papua New Guinea, the Philippines, the Solomon Islands, Thailand, and Tonga are calculated based on Quarterly External Debt Statistics. Last observation is 2022Q2. External debt stock data for Lao PDR, Myanmar, Samoa, Timor-Leste, Vanuatu, and Vietnam are based on World Development Indicators. Last observation is end-2020. Revised GDP methodology is used for measuring Vietnam's debt-to-GDP ratio.
D. East Asia = Cambodia, China, Indonesia, Lao PDR, Malaysia, Mongolia, Myanmar, the Philippines, Thailand, and Vietnam. Island economies = Fiji, Kiribati, Marshall Islands, Micronesia, Nauru, Palau, Papua New Guinea, Samoa, Solomon Islands, Timor-Leste, Tonga, Tuvalu, and Vanuatu. Disaster frequency is calculated based on the annual average number of natural disaster incidents from 1980-2022 per 10,000 square kilometers of land area.

TABLE 2.1.1 **East Asia and Pacific forecast summary**

(Real GDP growth at market prices in percent, unless indicated otherwise)

	2020	2021	2022e	2023f	2024f	Percentage point differences from June 2022 projections 2022e	2023f	2024f
EMDE EAP, GDP[1]	**1.2**	**7.2**	**3.2**	**4.3**	**4.9**	**-1.2**	**-0.9**	**-0.2**
GDP per capita (U.S. dollars)	0.7	6.8	2.9	4.1	4.6	-1.2	-0.9	-0.3
(Average including countries that report expenditure components in national accounts)[2]								
EMDE EAP, GDP[2]	1.2	7.3	3.2	4.4	4.9	-1.2	-0.8	-0.2
PPP GDP	0.8	7.0	3.4	4.4	4.9	-1.1	-0.8	-0.2
Private consumption	-2.1	10.1	2.8	5.3	6.1	-1.1	-0.9	-0.1
Public consumption	3.3	4.0	4.5	4.5	4.0	-2.0	1.4	0.6
Fixed investment	1.9	2.5	1.8	4.0	4.5	-2.6	-1.3	-0.5
Exports, GNFS[3]	-1.8	16.1	4.6	3.1	3.7	0.0	-1.8	-1.0
Imports, GNFS[3]	-4.3	11.9	2.2	4.7	5.0	-3.6	-1.3	-1.0
Net exports, contribution to growth	0.5	1.1	0.6	-0.2	-0.1	0.7	-0.1	0.1
Memo items: GDP								
China	2.2	8.1	2.7	4.3	5.0	-1.6	-0.9	-0.1
East Asia and Pacific excl. China	-3.7	2.6	5.6	4.7	4.7	0.8	-0.7	-0.7
Indonesia	-2.1	3.7	5.2	4.8	4.9	0.1	-0.5	-0.4
Thailand	-6.2	1.5	3.4	3.6	3.7	0.5	-0.7	-0.2
Commodity exporters	-1.8	2.0	5.0	4.7	4.6	0.2	-1.2	-1.4
Commodity importers excl. China	-5.3	3.1	6.1	4.7	4.8	1.3	-0.4	-0.1
Pacific Island economies[4]	-5.3	-1.0	4.5	3.8	3.3	0.8	0.2	0.2

Source: World Bank.
Note: e = estimate; f = forecast; PPP = purchasing power parity; EMDE = emerging market and developing economy. World Bank forecasts are frequently updated based on new information and changing (global) circumstances. Consequently, projections presented here may differ from those contained in other Bank documents, even if basic assessments of countries' prospects do not differ at any given moment in time.
1. GDP and expenditure components are measured in average 2010-19 prices and market exchange rates. Excludes the Democratic People's Republic of Korea and dependent territories.
2. Subregion aggregate excludes the Democratic People's Republic of Korea, dependent territories, Fiji, Kiribati, the Marshall Islands, the Federated States of Micronesia, Myanmar, Palau, Papua New Guinea, Samoa, Timor-Leste, Tonga, and Tuvalu, for which data limitations prevent the forecasting of GDP components.
3. Exports and imports of goods and nonfactor services (GNFS).
4. Includes Fiji, Kiribati, the Marshall Islands, the Federated States of Micronesia, Nauru, Palau, Papua New Guinea, Samoa, the Solomon Islands, Tonga, Tuvalu, and Vanuatu.

TABLE 2.1.2 **East Asia and Pacific country forecasts**[1]

(Real GDP growth at market prices in percent, unless indicated otherwise)

	2020	2021	2022e	2023f	2024f	Percentage point differences from June 2022 projections 2022e	2023f	2024f
Cambodia	-3.1	3.0	4.8	5.2	6.3	0.3	-0.6	-0.3
China	2.2	8.1	2.7	4.3	5.0	-1.6	-0.9	-0.1
Fiji	-17.0	-5.1	15.1	5.4	3.4	8.8	-2.3	-2.2
Indonesia	-2.1	3.7	5.2	4.8	4.9	0.1	-0.5	-0.4
Kiribati	-0.5	1.5	1.5	2.3	2.1	-0.3	-0.2	-0.2
Lao PDR	0.5	2.5	2.5	3.8	4.2	-1.3	-0.2	0.0
Malaysia	-5.5	3.1	7.8	4.0	3.9	2.3	-0.5	-0.5
Marshall Islands	-2.2	1.1	1.5	2.2	2.5	-1.5	-0.2	-0.1
Micronesia, Fed. Sts.	-1.8	-3.2	-0.5	3.0	2.5	-0.9	-0.2	0.6
Mongolia	-4.4	1.6	4.0	5.3	6.4	1.5	-0.5	-0.4
Myanmar[2]	3.2	-18.0	3.0	3.0	..	..	..	..
Nauru	0.7	1.5	0.9	1.9	2.8	0.0	-0.7	0.4
Palau	-9.7	-17.1	-2.5	18.2	4.5	-9.7	2.0	0.0
Papua New Guinea	-3.2	0.1	4.0	3.5	3.3	0.0	0.8	0.8
Philippines	-9.5	5.7	7.2	5.4	5.9	1.5	-0.2	0.3
Samoa	-3.1	-7.1	-6.0	4.0	3.5	-5.7	1.5	-0.3
Solomon Islands	-3.4	-0.2	-4.5	2.6	2.4	-1.6	-2.7	-1.4
Thailand	-6.2	1.5	3.4	3.6	3.7	0.5	-0.7	-0.2
Timor-Leste	-8.6	2.9	3.0	3.0	3.0	0.6	0.2	0.0
Tonga	0.5	-2.7	-1.6	3.3	3.2	0.0	0.1	0.0
Tuvalu	-4.9	0.3	3.0	3.5	4.0	-0.5	-0.3	0.0
Vanuatu	-5.4	0.5	2.2	3.4	3.5	0.2	-0.7	-0.2
Vietnam	2.9	2.6	7.2	6.3	6.5	1.4	-0.2	0.0

Source: World Bank.
Note: e = estimate; f = forecast. World Bank forecasts are frequently updated based on new information and changing (global) circumstances. Consequently, projections presented here may differ from those contained in other Bank documents, even if basic assessments of countries' prospects do not significantly differ at any given moment in time.
1. Data are based on GDP measured in average 2010-19 prices and market exchange rates. Values for Timor-Leste represent non-oil GDP. For the following countries, values correspond to fiscal years: the Marshall Islands, the Federated States of Micronesia, Myanmar, and Palau (October 1– September 30); Nauru, Samoa, and Tonga (July 1–June 30).
2. Forecasts for Myanmar beyond 2023 are excluded because of a high degree of uncertainty.

EUROPE and CENTRAL ASIA

Growth in Europe and Central Asia (ECA) is estimated to have sharply decelerated in 2022, to 0.2 percent, and is projected to remain essentially unchanged at 0.1 percent in 2023. This weakness largely reflects contraction in the Russian Federation in both years and a deep recession in Ukraine in 2022. Excluding these two economies, output in ECA is forecast to grow by a modest 2.1 percent in 2023. Disruptions to the supply of energy in Europe, related to the Russian invasion of Ukraine, and synchronous monetary policy tightening have dampened economic activity, affecting ECA's economies both directly and through spillovers from the euro area. The near-term economic outlook remains especially uncertain, with risks to the baseline forecast tilted to the downside. These risks include an additional tightening of global financial conditions, financial turmoil, and worsening energy shortages.

Recent developments

As a result of the Russian Federation's invasion of Ukraine, growth in Europe and Central Asia (ECA) is estimated to have slowed sharply in 2022, to 0.2 percent (figure 2.2.1.A). This reflects contraction in Russia and a deep recession in Ukraine. Excluding these two countries, growth in ECA nearly halved in 2022, to an estimated 4.2 percent, with broad-based deceleration across the region.

The economic slowdown in ECA was less pronounced than initially anticipated. Instead of contracting in 2022, output grew at a meager pace. In many economies, an upward revision for 2022 reflected stronger-than-projected growth in the euro area in the first half of the year, a quicker-than-expected rebound in international travel as economies reopened, and additional government measures that helped shield households and firms from sharp increases in food and energy prices. The improvement, however, varied across ECA. A surge in capital and migrants from Russia, as well as a possible rerouting of some trade and financial flows, helped fuel domestic demand and services exports in several economies, particularly in the

South Caucasus. In energy exporters, higher energy prices supported activity and fiscal balances. In other economies, however, upward revisions for 2022 were more modest amid large spillovers from the invasion of Ukraine. The slowdown in 2022, while smaller than expected, still left regional output 3.2 percent below pre-pandemic trends after the gap was almost closed at the start of the year.

The Russian economy contracted by an estimated 3.5 percent in 2022—steeper than the pandemic-related recession of 2020—as falling real wages eroded consumer spending and investment was dampened by international sanctions as a result of the invasion of Ukraine. Voluntary withdrawals by foreign businesses and intense uncertainty further weighed on activity. The estimated fall in output is much smaller than previously projected, however, partly owing to larger than expected fiscal support packages. Oil production was also higher than expected, with exports diverted at discounted prices to purchasers outside Europe. Financial market conditions stabilized faster than previously assumed due to a combination of rapidly enacted and extensive capital controls and liquidity operations. Maintenance of the ruble's exchange rate helped to contain inflation and losses in real income. The partial mobilization of troops in September and October, however,

Note: This section was prepared by Collette Mari Wheeler.

FIGURE 2.2.1 **ECA: Recent developments**

Growth in Europe and Central Asia sharply fell in 2022, with much of the weakness reflecting declines in output in the Russian Federation and Ukraine. Despite early monetary policy tightening, inflation accelerated to multidecade highs in 2022, driven in large part by supply-side disruptions from the invasion. In the near term, inflation is likely to continue to exceed central bank targets, weigh on activity, and erode incomes, particularly for poorer households.

A. ECA growth in 2022

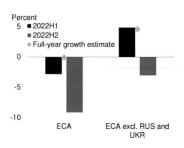

B. Composition of median headline CPI inflation in ECA

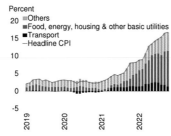

C. Total budget shares for energy products in ECA EU countries

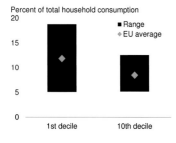

D. Survey-based ECA inflation expectations and target

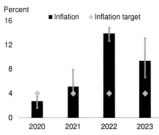

Sources: Ari et al. (2022); Consensus Economics; Haver Analytics; International Monetary Fund; World Bank.

Note: ECA = Europe and Central Asia; RUS = Russian Federation; UKR = Ukraine.

A. Growth for 2022H1 (2022H2) is calculated taking the period average of 2022Q1 and 2022Q2 (2022Q3 and 2022Q4). Quarterly growth rates are seasonally adjusted annual rates. Balanced sample includes 10 ECA economies given data availability, and thus may differ from aggregates presented in table 2.2.1.

B. Contributions to year-on-year headline CPI inflation. Line shows year-on-year headline CPI inflation. Sample size includes 19 ECA economies. Last observation is October 2022.

C. International Monetary Fund staff estimates using the Carbon Pricing Assessment Tool based on Ari et al. (2022). Energy products include coal, electricity, natural gas, oil, gasoline, diesel, kerosene, and liquefied petroleum gas. The budget share is calculated based on household budget surveys and is assumed to be constant over time.

D. Consensus forecast median headline CPI inflation for 2022-23 based on December 2022 surveys of 16 ECA economies. Inflation target is a median of 13 ECA economies. Whiskers show 25th and 75th percentile.

weighed on domestic demand and is likely to lead to rising labor market pressures due to the uptick in emigration.

In Ukraine, economic activity has been seriously disrupted by Russia's invasion, with output estimated to have contracted by 35 percent in 2022. This is an upward revision from the 45 percent decline projected last June, reflecting a partial resumption of grain exports through the Black Sea, some improvement in economic

activity after the liberation of northern regions, and a swifter containment of the conflict to eastern Ukraine. The positive net effect of these developments, however, has likely diminished following Russia's partial annexation of regions in eastern and southern Ukraine and continued shelling and destruction of energy infrastructure. Moreover, the war has led to the largest human displacement crisis in the world, with one-third of Ukraine's population of 44 million people estimated to have been displaced (UNHCR 2022).

In Türkiye, last year's growth exceeded expectations, with output expanding by an estimated 4.7 percent. A tripling of the minimum wage between December 2021 and January 2023 and a rebound in tourism helped support activity and offset drags from multidecade-high inflation, significant currency depreciation, and swelling external liabilities amid rising net errors and omissions. Although the rate of nonperforming loans (NPLs) remained stable, the overall level of distressed debt (NPLs plus debt at risk of default) rose sharply in 2022. The central bank lowered its policy rate further, to 9 percent in November, even as inflation remained about 85 percent, driving the lira to new record lows. Although cuts to the policy interest rate have totaled 1,000 basis points since mid-2021, interest rates for bank loans have risen, with interest rates on consumer and commercial loans about triple and less than double, respectively, the official policy interest rate.

Median headline inflation in ECA surged in 2022—more sharply than in any year since 1998—as rising commodity prices, particularly for energy and food, and currency depreciations passed through to consumers in many economies (figure 2.2.1.B). High energy and food prices carved into incomes, especially for the poorest households (figure 2.2.1.C). Inflation continued to significantly exceed central bank targets throughout the region (figure 2.2.1.D). Moreover, core inflation accelerated rapidly, raising concerns that higher inflation could become embedded into wage and price-setting behavior. Although more than 80 percent of the region's central banks raised their policy rates in 2022, real interest rates remained negative in most ECA countries.

Higher energy prices have translated directly into larger import bills and wider current account deficits in energy-importing economies. They have also generated sizable fiscal costs in several countries because of fossil fuel subsidies, price caps, and support to households and firms. In Central Europe and the Western Balkans, the costs of fiscal support measures in response to high energy prices are estimated to have exceeded 1.5 percent of GDP, on average, in the year to mid-2022, ranging from less than 1 percent of GDP in Serbia to about 3 percent in Bulgaria, mostly reflecting price controls and subsidies (Ari et al. 2022).

Outlook

Output in ECA is projected to remain virtually flat in 2023, with growth of only 0.1 percent—a downward revision of 1.4 percentage points since June 2022 (table 2.2.1). Although much of the projected weakness in regional growth this year emanates from a further output decline in Russia, forecasts for 2023 growth have been downgraded for over 80 percent of ECA's economies (figures 2.2.2.A and 2.2.2.B; table 2.2.2). This deterioration in the near-term outlook mainly reflects the impact from Russia's cutoff of energy supplies to the European Union (EU) and additional monetary policy tightening in the euro area. These developments have adversely affected ECA's economies, particularly in Central Europe, through high energy costs and weaker external demand for ECA goods and services (figure 2.2.2.C; chapter 1). Recession in Russia and subdued growth in China are anticipated to weigh on activity, especially in the South Caucasus and Central Asia. Regional activity is also expected to continue to be dampened by tightening financing conditions as central banks grapple with above-target inflation. In all, output in 2023 is expected to fall 5.7 percent below pre-pandemic trends (figure 2.2.2.D).

The baseline projections for ECA growth assume that the war in Ukraine persists in the near term, with no further escalation in the intensity of warfare. The projections also assume that sanctions on Belarus and Russia remain in place through the forecast period. Energy prices are

FIGURE 2.2.2 **ECA: Outlook**

Growth in Europe and Central Asia is projected to remain relatively flat in 2023, owing in large part to ongoing recession in the Russian Federation. Growth forecasts for 2023 have been downgraded in most countries, but especially in Central Europe due to energy disruptions and the slowdown in the euro area. As a result of the invasion, output in ECA in 2023 is expected to fall 5.7 percent below pre-pandemic trends.

A. Forecast revisions to 2023 growth projections since June 2022

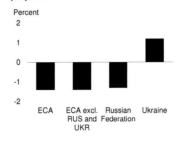

B. Contributions to ECA growth

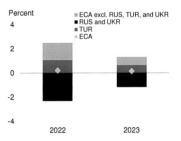

C. ECA growth in 2023, by subregion

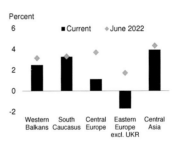

D. Percent deviations of ECA output from pre-pandemic trends

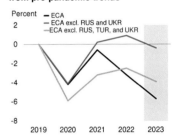

Source: World Bank.
Note: ECA = Europe and Central Asia; RUS = Russian Federation; TUR = Türkiye; UKR = Ukraine. Unless otherwise indicated, aggregates are calculated using real U.S. dollar GDP weights at average 2010-19 prices and market exchange rates.
A. The figure shows the percentage point difference between the latest projections and forecasts released in the June 2022 edition of the *Global Economic Prospects* report (World Bank 2022b).
B. Figure shows the contributions to ECA growth.
C. Figure shows the current growth forecasts and the forecasts in the *Global Economic Prospects* report published in June 2022.
D. Figure shows the percent deviation between the latest estimates and forecasts relative to the January 2020 edition of the *Global Economic Prospects* report. For 2023, the January 2020 baseline is extended using projected growth for 2022.

assumed to moderate from 2022 averages (chapter 1). Although the price of European natural gas has fallen back toward its pre-invasion level, energy prices remain high for consumers and firms, which will continue to weigh on household spending and production (World Bank 2022d). Further energy price spikes are possible, however, due to Russian energy supply disruptions and global supply constraints. Recent increases in core inflation suggest that headline inflation is unlikely to return to central bank targets in the near term in many ECA economies. The regional outlook is subject to unusually high uncertainty related to the war and its repercussions inside and outside the region, including the possibility of worsening energy supply disruptions.

Output in *Russia* in 2023 is projected to decline again, by 3.3 percent, as EU oil embargos are fully implemented and natural gas exports are reduced by Russia's shutoff of deliveries to the EU via the Nord Stream 1 pipeline. Growth is projected to resume in 2024, at a rate of 1.6 percent, with modest consumption growth and a marginal recovery in exports as Russia reorientates its trading relationships. Over the long term, the invasion of Ukraine and its repercussions are likely to reduce Russia's potential growth rate. The ruptures to trade and investment networks are likely to limit technology transfer, slowing productivity growth; fixed investment is likely to be further discouraged by reduced access to international financial markets and increased economic and political uncertainty; and emigration is likely to be a drain on human capital.

In *Ukraine*, growth is projected to resume in 2023, at a subdued rate of 3.3 percent, assuming that the war does not escalate further. Growth forecasts, however, are subject to significant uncertainty because of the ongoing invasion. Targeted attacks on critical infrastructure over the last few months have damaged one-half of Ukraine's power grid, with the country facing a sharp deficit in electricity and blackouts. Recovery and reconstruction needs are estimated to total $349 billion—more than 1.5 times 2021 GDP—but have likely grown larger since June 1, 2022 (World Bank 2022g). Repercussions of the war are expected to be long-lasting, with economic activity dampened by the destruction of infrastructure and productive capacity, damage to arable land, reduced human capital and productivity, and lower labor supply—especially if refugees do not return, which becomes increasingly likely with the passage of time (Dieppe, Kilic-Celik, and Okou 2020).

Growth in *Türkiye* continues to face considerable headwinds and risks, with high inflation and growing external vulnerabilities amid a sharp widening of the current account deficit. Growth is projected to moderate somewhat in 2023, to 2.7 percent, as increased government spending ahead of the June 2023 elections counteracts slowing exports and domestic demand amid persistent inflation and heightened policy uncertainty.

In *Central Europe*, growth is expected to slow sharply in 2023, to 1.1 percent, as these EU economies face significant spillovers from energy supply disruptions and tight financing conditions. High energy costs and elevated inflation are expected to continue to dampen household spending and raise production costs. The deceleration is expected to be exacerbated by weakening external demand, particularly from the slowdown in the euro area. Growth is projected to strengthen over the medium term, assuming that reform milestones under NextGenerationEU plans are met, allowing the disbursement of sizable EU investment funds. Meaningful reforms alongside effective absorption of multiple EU investment funds will be crucial to ensure that the subregion's potential growth is boosted in the remainder of the decade (World Bank 2022f).

In the *Western Balkans*, growth is projected to slow to a modest 2.5 percent in 2023, as EU accession reforms and investment mitigate the negative effects of high energy and food prices, disruptions to trade and investment flows, and spillovers from the slowdown in the euro area. However, there is significant political uncertainty, with a risk that parliamentary impasses create delays in the implementation of reforms and thus prevent efficient absorption of related funds (Bosnia and Herzegovina, Montenegro, North Macedonia).

In *Eastern Europe (excluding Ukraine)*, surging inflation, higher borrowing costs, lower remittances (Moldova), and additional sanctions (Belarus) are expected to continue to depress domestic demand. As a result, output (excluding Ukraine) in 2023 is expected to contract for the third time since 2020, to -1.7 percent. The forecast is subject to significant downside risks, relating particularly to energy supplies. Unfavorable weather conditions could also reduce agricultural yields in the subregion, further exacerbating inflationary pressures and food insecurity.

In the *South Caucasus*, growth in 2023 is projected to halve to 3.3 percent. The forecast deceleration reflects weakening momentum after the strong rebound in 2021-22, the slowdown in the euro area, ongoing border tensions between Armenia and Azerbaijan, and the ongoing contraction of output in Russia, one of the South Caucasus's closest economic partners.

Growth in *Central Asia* is projected to remain flat at 3.9 percent in 2023, with activity held back by weak external demand, especially from Russia and China. Although growth in both the Kyrgyz Republic and Tajikistan is expected to exceed previous projections, renewed border tensions between the two countries pose headwinds to the outlook.

Risks

Risks to the baseline projections for ECA's growth remain skewed to the downside. Above all, a more prolonged or more intense war in Ukraine than assumed in the baseline could, apart from its humanitarian costs, cause significantly larger economic and environmental damage and greater potential for fragmentation of international trade and investment. A further rerouting of trade and investment could partially mitigate the negative effects of the invasion and current account pressures for some regional economies.

Output in ECA could shrink in 2023 if the energy crisis deepens and triggers an economic downturn in the euro area or a steeper recession in Russia (figure 2.2.3.A). Since June, downside risks associated with war-driven disruptions to energy imports from Russia have materialized and worsened the growth outlook, especially for Russia and the euro area, ECA's largest trading partner. Although the EU met its natural gas storage target ahead of schedule for this winter, this is unlikely to be the case next winter given the cutoff of Nord Stream 1 deliveries and lack of needed infrastructure to diversify supply. Even this winter, unusually low temperatures could force an accelerated drawdown of supplies, creating a situation in which countries would have to purchase additional natural gas at high prices, or enforce severe rationing. Either option would place a significant drag on activity, as higher prices or rationing translates into lower firm activity and

FIGURE 2.2.3 ECA: Risks

Risks remain tilted to the downside. A further disruption to energy supplies could tip regional output into contraction in 2023. Meanwhile, the sharp rise in financing conditions leaves ECA economies vulnerable to rollover and exchange rate risks, especially in countries with high debt loads. Tighter financing conditions also make funding critical investment needs more costly.

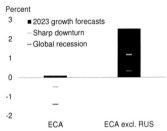

A. ECA growth in 2023: Current forecasts vs. downside scenario

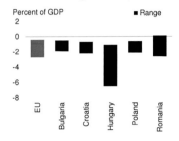

B. EU output loss estimates from Russian natural gas shutoff, 2023

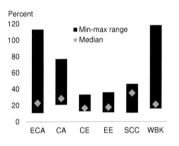

C. ECA debt service costs

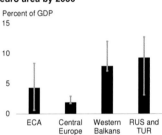

D. Estimated annual infrastructure costs to close half the gap with the euro area by 2030

Sources: Di Bella et al. (2022); Oxford Economics; Kose et al. (2022); World Bank.
Note: ECA = Europe and Central Asia; CA = Central Asia; CE = Central Europe and Baltic Countries; EE = Eastern Europe; EU = European Union; RUS = Russian Federation; SCC = South Caucasus; TUR = Türkiye; WBK = Western Balkans. Unless otherwise indicated, aggregates are calculated using real U.S. dollar GDP weights at average 2010-19 prices and market exchange rates.
A. Figure shows the baseline 2023 growth forecast from table 2.2.1 and growth scenarios using the Oxford Economics Global Economic Model (see chapter 1; Oxford Economics 2019). Sample includes 7 ECA economies for the scenarios.
B. Estimates are calculated as in Di Bella et al. (2022) using two models to estimate the impact of a Russian natural gas shutoff: 1) A multisector partial equilibrium model with demand spillovers, which illustrates the economic impact when gas markets are fragmented, outright physical shortages exist, and the gas market cannot adjust to prices; and 2) A multisector open-economy general equilibrium model, which illustrates the economic impact when markets are integrated and there is complete price-pass through.
C. Figure shows median debt service as a percent of exports of goods, services, and primary income in 2020. Sample includes 20 ECA economies.
D. Data as of 2020.

household consumption (figure 2.2.3.B; Di Bella et al. 2022; World Bank 2022g).

Russia's export earnings could fall further over the next year or so if Europe's expansion of natural gas infrastructure allows it to rapidly reduce reliance on Russian gas. Earlier completion of these EU projects would reduce Russia's fiscal resources, while much of the gas infrastructure in Russia could become effectively obsolete. More broadly,

Russia's isolation from major international financial markets and the freezing of about half of Russia's foreign exchange reserves have left the economy more susceptible to external shocks. A significant decline in energy prices would likely weaken the ruble and thus add upward pressure to inflation in Russia. The fiscal balance, having slipped into deficit in 2022, could then worsen more quickly. The G7 cap on Russia's oil export prices could have similar effects. In such circumstances, financial sector instability could re-emerge in Russia, especially given eroded bank buffers and the weak growth outlook, further damaging consumer and business confidence.

Tighter global financial conditions and the recent general appreciation of the U.S. dollar pose significant risks to financial stability in ECA, particularly for more indebted countries. Türkiye also faces risks arising from its high inflation, as it deploys a mix of loose monetary policy and targeted fiscal support to counter slowing growth. Pandemic- and war-related increases in debt—combined with tightening global financing conditions—have sharply reduced fiscal space and amplified debt vulnerabilities, including from public debt rollovers and currency mismatches. By dampening growth, the war has dented the ability of several economies in ECA to meet external debt obligations, eroded confidence, added to currency depreciation pressures, and increased borrowing costs (figure 2.2.3.C). More broadly, the sharp rise in borrowing costs has prompted some countries to scale back debt issuance, making wide investment gaps harder to close (figure 2.2.3.D).

Substantial currency depreciations have weakened corporate and public balance sheets. Moreover, public sector balance sheet risks could be larger than is apparent: the proliferation of debt-like instruments and commodity-based lending, together with the opaque financial arrangements of some state-owned enterprises, may well be obscuring total public debt levels.

The sharp rise in commodity prices has heightened concerns for the food and energy security of vulnerable households in ECA, especially as these items represent a significant portion of their spending (Ari et al. 2022; Artuc et al. 2022; World Bank 2022d, World Bank 2022h). As a result of the overlapping shocks of the pandemic and war in Ukraine, the poverty headcount at the $6.85 per person per day (in 2017 PPP) threshold is forecast to be almost 20 percent, or 2 million people, higher by 2030 in ECA than indicated by pre-pandemic trends (Ari et al. 2022).

TABLE 2.2.1 Europe and Central Asia forecast summary

(Real GDP growth at market prices in percent, unless indicated otherwise)

Percentage point differences from June 2022 projections

	2020	2021	2022e	2023f	2024f	2022e	2023f	2024f
EMDE ECA, GDP [1]	**-1.7**	**6.7**	**0.2**	**0.1**	**2.8**	**3.2**	**-1.4**	**-0.5**
GDP per capita (U.S. dollars)	-1.9	6.7	0.3	0.2	2.6	3.2	-1.3	-0.5
EMDE ECA excl. Russian Federation, Türkiye, and Ukraine, GDP	-2.7	6.2	3.9	1.7	3.1	0.9	-2.0	-0.5
EMDE ECA excl. Russian Federation and Ukraine, GDP	-1.0	8.2	4.2	2.1	3.4	1.5	-1.4	-0.4
EMDE ECA excl. Türkiye, GDP	-2.7	5.4	-1.1	-0.7	2.4	3.5	-1.6	-0.6
(Average including countries that report expenditure components in national accounts) [2]								
EMDE ECA, GDP [2]	-1.7	6.8	-0.2	-0.2	2.7	3.4	-1.4	-0.5
PPP GDP	-1.7	6.8	-0.9	-0.1	2.7	3.6	-1.3	-0.6
Private consumption	-3.1	9.9	2.6	0.9	3.2	7.0	-1.5	0.4
Public consumption	2.5	2.8	3.7	2.4	2.0	1.0	0.2	0.3
Fixed investment	-1.4	5.6	-3.2	-1.6	4.1	6.6	-1.7	-4.7
Exports, GNFS [3]	-6.5	10.3	-1.5	-0.2	4.4	7.0	-4.6	-0.4
Imports, GNFS [3]	-4.6	12.2	-3.1	4.6	6.7	1.9	-0.7	0.7
Net exports, contribution to growth	-0.9	-0.2	0.5	-1.6	-0.7	2.0	-1.4	-0.4
Memo items: GDP								
Commodity exporters [4]	-2.6	4.8	-4.0	-1.8	2.2	5.0	-1.1	-0.5
Commodity exporters excl. Russian Federation and Ukraine	-2.1	5.3	4.2	3.8	4.1	1.7	-0.2	0.3
Commodity importers [5]	-0.8	8.6	4.2	1.9	3.3	1.4	-1.5	-0.5
Central Europe [6]	-2.9	6.5	4.5	1.1	2.7	0.8	-2.6	-1.0
Western Balkans [7]	-3.1	7.6	3.1	2.5	3.1	0.0	-0.6	-0.1
Eastern Europe [8]	-3.1	3.6	-24.2	1.1	3.5	6.4	-0.8	-0.4
South Caucasus [9]	-5.3	6.6	6.5	3.3	3.5	3.1	0.0	0.2
Central Asia [10]	-1.3	5.1	3.9	3.9	4.3	1.5	-0.4	0.2
Russian Federation	-2.7	4.8	-3.5	-3.3	1.6	5.4	-1.3	-0.6
Türkiye	1.9	11.4	4.7	2.7	4.0	2.4	-0.5	0.0
Poland	-2.0	6.8	4.4	0.7	2.2	0.5	-2.9	-1.5

Source: World Bank.

Note: e = estimate; f = forecast; PPP = purchasing power parity; EMDE = emerging market and developing economy. World Bank forecasts are frequently updated based on new information and changing (global) circumstances. Consequently, projections presented here may differ from those contained in other Bank documents, even if basic assessments of countries' prospects do not differ at any given moment in time. The World Bank is currently not publishing economic output, income, or growth data for Turkmenistan owing to a lack of reliable data of adequate quality. Turkmenistan is excluded from cross-country macroeconomic aggregates. Since Croatia became a member of the euro area on January 1, 2023, it has been added to the euro area aggregate and removed from the ECA aggregate in all tables to avoid double counting.

1. GDP and expenditure components are measured in average 2010-19 prices and market exchange rates, thus aggregates presented here may differ from other World Bank documents.

2. Aggregates presented here exclude Azerbaijan, Bosnia and Herzegovina, Kazakhstan, Kosovo, the Kyrgyz Republic, Montenegro, Serbia, Tajikistan, Turkmenistan, and Uzbekistan, for which data limitations prevent the forecasting of GDP components.

3. Exports and imports of goods and nonfactor services (GNFS).

4. Includes Armenia, Azerbaijan, Kazakhstan, the Kyrgyz Republic, Kosovo, the Russian Federation, Tajikistan, Ukraine, and Uzbekistan.

5. Includes Albania, Belarus, Bosnia and Herzegovina, Bulgaria, Georgia, Hungary, Moldova, Montenegro, North Macedonia, Poland, Romania, Serbia, and Türkiye.

6. Includes Bulgaria, Hungary, Poland, and Romania.

7. Includes Albania, Bosnia and Herzegovina, Kosovo, Montenegro, North Macedonia, and Serbia.

8. Includes Belarus, Moldova, and Ukraine.

9. Includes Armenia, Azerbaijan, and Georgia.

10. Includes Kazakhstan, the Kyrgyz Republic, Tajikistan, and Uzbekistan.

TABLE 2.2.2 Europe and Central Asia country forecasts [1]

(Real GDP growth at market prices in percent, unless indicated otherwise)

Percentage point differences
from June 2022 projections

	2020	2021	2022e	2023f	2024f	2022e	2023f	2024f
Albania	-3.5	8.5	3.5	2.2	3.4	0.3	-1.3	-0.1
Armenia	-7.2	5.7	10.8	4.1	4.8	7.3	-0.5	-0.1
Azerbaijan	-4.3	5.6	4.2	2.8	2.6	1.5	0.6	0.3
Belarus	-0.9	2.6	-6.2	-2.3	2.5	0.3	-3.8	0.9
Bosnia and Herzegovina[2]	-3.1	7.5	4.0	2.5	3.0	1.3	-0.6	-0.5
Bulgaria	-4.0	7.6	3.1	1.7	3.3	0.5	-2.6	-0.4
Croatia	-8.6	13.1	6.6	0.8	3.1	2.8	-2.6	0.0
Georgia	-6.8	10.4	10.0	4.0	5.0	4.5	-1.5	0.0
Hungary	-4.5	7.1	5.1	0.5	2.2	0.5	-3.3	-1.2
Kazakhstan	-2.5	4.1	3.0	3.5	4.0	1.0	-0.5	0.5
Kosovo	-5.3	10.7	3.1	3.7	4.2	-0.8	-0.6	0.0
Kyrgyz Republic	-8.4	3.6	5.5	3.5	4.0	7.5	0.1	0.0
Moldova	-7.4	13.9	-1.5	1.6	4.2	-1.1	-1.1	0.0
Montenegro	-15.3	13.0	5.9	3.4	3.1	2.3	-1.3	-0.6
North Macedonia	-4.7	3.9	2.1	2.4	2.7	-0.6	-0.7	-0.5
Poland	-2.0	6.8	4.4	0.7	2.2	0.5	-2.9	-1.5
Romania	-3.7	5.1	4.6	2.6	4.2	1.7	-1.1	0.3
Russian Federation	-2.7	4.8	-3.5	-3.3	1.6	5.4	-1.3	-0.6
Serbia	-0.9	7.5	2.5	2.3	3.0	-0.7	-0.4	0.2
Tajikistan	4.4	9.2	7.0	5.0	4.0	7.4	1.7	-0.3
Türkiye	1.9	11.4	4.7	2.7	4.0	2.4	-0.5	0.0
Ukraine	-3.8	3.4	-35.0	3.3	4.1	10.1	1.2	-1.7
Uzbekistan	1.9	7.4	5.7	4.9	5.1	1.4	-0.4	-0.4

Source: World Bank.

Note: e = estimate; f = forecast. World Bank forecasts are frequently updated based on new information and changing (global) circumstances. Consequently, projections presented here may differ from those contained in other Bank documents, even if basic assessments of countries' prospects do not significantly differ at any given moment in time. The World Bank is currently not publishing economic output, income, or growth data for Turkmenistan owing to a lack of reliable data of adequate quality. Turkmenistan is excluded from cross-country macroeconomic aggregates.

1. Data are based on GDP measured in average 2010-19 prices and market exchange rates, unless indicated otherwise.

2. GDP growth rate at constant prices is based on production approach.

LATIN AMERICA and THE CARIBBEAN

Growth in Latin America and the Caribbean is forecast to slow to a meager 1.3 percent in 2023 before recovering somewhat to 2.4 percent in 2024. Decelerating global demand will dampen the external drivers of near-term growth in the region, while domestic demand will be curbed by monetary policy tightening and persistent policy uncertainty in some countries. The main downside risks to the outlook are external: tightening global financial conditions could precipitate capital outflows and currency depreciations, and the global economy could slow more than predicted, leading to sharp falls in commodity export prices. These or other adverse shocks could reduce growth further, which could catalyze social unrest, given stagnating living standards. Climate-related disasters also remain an ever-present threat, especially for the region's small states.

Recent developments

Latin America and the Caribbean (LAC) is estimated to have grown 3.6 percent in 2022, 1.1 percentage point above last June's forecast. The upward revision was the result of robust expansion in the first half of the year, driven by buoyant consumer spending, which was supported by steady labor market recoveries and the lagged effects of sizeable fiscal transfers in many countries (figure 2.3.1.A; World Bank 2022i). However, activity weakened late in 2022 across most large LAC economies, as a global economic slowdown spilled into the region (figure 2.3.1.B). Subdued industrial production contributed to the economic deceleration, as rising domestic and global interest rates tightened financial conditions.

Terms-of-trade developments have varied across LAC. Energy exporters have continued to benefit from high fossil fuels prices, while slowing external growth, particularly in China, has weighed on metal prices and the export earnings of metal producers (Baumeister, Verduzco-Bustos, and Ohnsorge 2022). Agricultural commodity prices remain elevated compared to the pre-pandemic period. However, differing climatic conditions have seen some exporters benefit more than

others. Conditions have been favorable for Brazil's soy harvest, but Argentine wheat production was curbed by extended drought.

Consumer prices surged in 2022, with many countries experiencing inflation at multi-decade highs. In most of the region, inflation peaked far above central bank targets in Q2 or Q3, before starting to decline gradually. Food prices rose particularly rapidly, in part due to the Russian Federation's invasion of Ukraine, registering double digit annual increases in most countries. Yet price pressures also broadened over the year (figure 2.3.1.C). To combat persistently high and broad-based inflation, central banks continued to hike already elevated policy rates in the second half of 2022, leading to sizeable increases in real short-term interest rates (figure 2.3.1.D).

Regional financial conditions tightened materially over 2022, in line with global conditions and domestic monetary policies, though riskier assets showed some resilience. This likely reflected both commodity export-related tailwinds in South America, and favorable investor responses to early and rapid monetary tightening in many LAC economies, which established sizable interest rate differentials with advanced economies. Domestic bond yields followed U.S. yields higher, but equity markets across the region held up over the second half of the year. Sovereign borrowing spreads also

Note: This section was prepared by Phil Kenworthy.

FIGURE 2.3.1 LAC: Recent developments

Labor market recoveries helped to support buoyant consumption for most of 2022, but output growth decelerated late in the year as global weakness spilled into the region. Price pressures have broadened markedly in the last two years, driving inflation to multi-decade highs in many economies and prompting continued monetary tightening. Higher real interest rates have contributed to slowing investment growth, but also helped limit currency depreciation. Though financial conditions have tightened, sovereign spreads for most countries remain contained.

A. Changes in unemployment

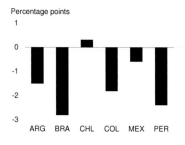

B. GDP growth

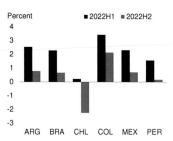

C. Consumption basket components with above-target inflation

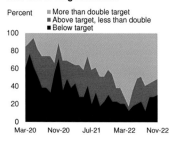

D. Changes in interest rates and U.S. dollar exchange rates since June 2022

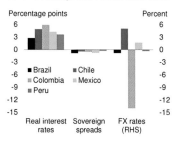

Sources: Consensus Economics; Haver Analytics; J.P. Morgan; World Bank.
Note: ARG = Argentina, BRA = Brazil, CHL = Chile, COL = Colombia, MEX = Mexico, PER = Peru; FX = foreign exchange.
A. Unemployment rates are seasonally adjusted. Change is between December 2021 (2021Q4 for Argentina) and October 2022 (2022Q2 for Argentina). A negative change indicates a fall (that is, an improvement) in the unemployment rate.
B. Annualized growth rates. 2022H1 is seasonally adjusted GDP growth in the first half of 2022 compared to the second half of 2021. 2022H2 is expected GDP growth in the second half of 2022 compared to seasonally adjusted growth in the first half of 2022.
C. Proportion of major component indices within consumer inflation baskets growing faster than the inflation target on a monthly basis. Data for Brazil, Chile, Colombia, and Mexico. Last observation is November 2022.
D. Real interest rate is the policy rate minus the one-year-ahead inflation expectation from Consensus Economics, transformed to a constant time horizon using a weighted average of expectations from 2022 and 2023. The change in real interest rates is the change compared to real interest rates reported in the June 2022 *Global Economic Prospects*. Changes in sovereign spread are J.P. Morgan's Emerging Market Bond Index Global spreads, and nominal exchange rate changes are versus the U.S. dollar. Both reflect changes since end-June 2022, with the last observation on December 16, 2022.

remained largely constant, suggesting limited sovereign stress risks. Currencies in LAC were mostly resilient to a generally strong U.S. dollar in the latter half of 2022 and appreciated in trade-weighted terms in several countries. Colombia was the only large inflation-targeting economy in LAC to see sharp currency depreciation.

Outlook

Growth in Latin America and the Caribbean is projected to slow from an estimated 3.6 percent in 2022 to 1.3 percent in 2023, before recovering somewhat to 2.4 percent in 2024 (figure 2.3.2.A). The forecast for 2023 has been downgraded since June by 0.6 percentage point. The sharp deceleration of growth this year reflects efforts by the region's monetary authorities to tame inflation, and spillovers from weakening global growth. Per capita GDP growth is expected to be just 0.6 percent in 2023.

A sluggish growth outlook in the United States and China will curtail export demand in 2023, while the increase in U.S. interest rates is likely to also keep global financial conditions restrictive. The boon for South American incomes from recently elevated commodity prices is expected to unwind over the next two years, except in a small number of fossil fuel exporters. Meanwhile, weakening global growth is expected to reduce export growth in LAC from 5.9 percent in 2022 to 3.6 percent in 2023.

Domestic sources of growth appear similarly lacking. Investment is the primary driver of forecast downgrades, with negative regionwide investment growth projected in 2023 in the context of softening business confidence and increased financing costs (chapter 3). Elevated levels of domestic policy uncertainty in most of the region's largest economies present a further headwind to investment, especially in key export industries such as mining. The recovery in services following the lifting of pandemic-related restrictions has also largely run its course. With prices rising faster than wages in much of the region, lower real incomes are expected to constrain consumption growth.

The cycle of policy rate increases is likely coming to an end across inflation targeting economies, with solidly positive interest rates in real terms (that is, adjusted for anticipated future inflation). Policy rates in the largest economies are expected to remain fairly stable this year, meaning inflation-adjusted policy rates will increase in some economies if inflation recedes as projected (figure

2.3.2.B). This should help central banks keep medium-term inflation expectations close to targets, but is likely to hold back activity in 2024. The costs of servicing elevated household and corporate debt, the legacy of years of weak growth, will also squeeze spending as borrowing costs rise (figure 2.3.2.C). Fiscal policy is expected to be neutral for regional growth in 2023 and mildly contractionary in 2024, reflecting continued fiscal consolidation in most of the region (figure 2.3.2.D).

In *Brazil*, a steep growth slowdown is underway. The economy is expected to expand by just 0.8 percent in 2023, unchanged from June's forecast, following growth of 3 percent in 2022. Investment is expected to contract sharply in 2023 following a nearly 12-percentage point increase in the central bank policy interest rate since early 2021. Uncertainty regarding the fiscal policy outlook poses a further headwind to business confidence and investment. Exports are likely to grow more slowly than in recent years because of slowing demand growth for non-energy commodities. Consumer spending in 2023 will be supported somewhat by increased fiscal transfers and tax cuts legislated last year to offset soaring food and fuel prices. Growth is expected to pick up to 2 percent in 2024. The decline in investment is expected to abate, while consumption accelerates somewhat, and improving global demand supports export growth.

Mexico's economy is projected to grow 0.9 percent in 2023—1 percentage point below the June forecast, following higher than forecast growth of 2.6 percent in 2022. The expansion is expected to firm again in 2024, with growth of 2.3 percent. Domestic demand for services should continue to gradually recover in 2023, but a sharply weaker U.S. outlook is likely to curtail growth of exports and inward remittances. In view of stubborn price pressures—core inflation is at its highest level in more than two decades—monetary policy is anticipated to remain tight, with the policy rate in double digits for some time. More restrictive monetary conditions are expected to weigh on cyclical components of growth, with investment stagnating below its 2019 level throughout the forecast period. Consumption and export growth

FIGURE 2.3.2 **LAC: Outlook**

Growth in LAC is forecast to slow sharply in 2023, with investment set to contract as financial conditions tighten and global growth falters. Though nominal tightening cycles in LAC's major inflation-targeting economies are concluding, short-term real interest rates are expected to further increase in some countries in 2023. Rising debt service costs on the region's large debt stock—a legacy of a decade of weak growth—will squeeze private sector spending. Fiscal policy is projected to be about neutral for regionwide growth in 2023 and 2024.

A. GDP growth

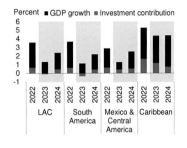

B. Market-implied real policy rates

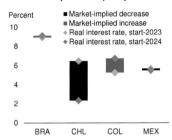

C. Debt stock

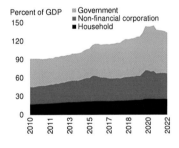

D. Fiscal impulse in LAC

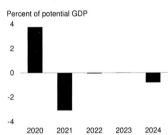

Sources: Bloomberg; Consensus Economics; Institute of International Finance; International Monetary Fund; World Bank.
Note: BRA = Brazil, CHL = Chile, COL = Colombia, MEX = Mexico.
A. Aggregate growth rates are calculated using GDP weights at average 2010-19 prices and market exchange rates. South America includes Argentina, Bolivia, Brazil, Chile, Colombia, Ecuador, Paraguay, Peru, and Uruguay. Mexico and Central America includes Costa Rica, El Salvador, Guatemala, Honduras, Mexico, Nicaragua, and Panama. Caribbean includes The Bahamas, Belize, the Dominican Republic, and Jamaica (growth rates differ to those reported in table 2.3.1 due to the exclusion of Haiti and several Caribbean small states for which GDP expenditure components are not separately forecast).
B. Real interest rate is as described in 2.3.1.D (above). Market-implied change is the one-year-ahead policy rate implied by interest rate swap markets, minus the Bloomberg private forecasters median 2024 consumer price inflation forecast. Last observation is December 20, 2022.
C. GDP-weighted averages. Sample includes Argentina, Brazil, Chile, Colombia, Costa Rica, Dominican Republic, Ecuador, El Salvador, Grenada, Jamaica, Mexico, and Peru. Last observation is 2022Q2.
D. Figure shows the negative of the regionwide GDP-weighted change in the structural primary balance (calculated as the structural balance net of projected interest costs). A positive value therefore indicates a positive impulse to GDP growth.

are expected to pick up in 2024, as inflation subsides and external conditions improve.

Argentina's GDP is forecast to expand 2 percent in 2023 and 2024, following stronger than expected growth of 5.2 percent last year. The deceleration in growth reflects external headwinds, and constraints on domestic activity related to the high inflation environment. Weakening foreign demand is likely to weigh on export growth, while capital, import, and price controls continue to complicate the business environment. Planned investments to operationalize the domestic "Nestor Kirchner" gas pipeline should benefit fiscal and current accounts by lowering energy imports. Exposure to financial cross-border spillovers is limited by reliance on official external financing. The context is nonetheless highly challenging given the need to reduce inflation from recent rates of above 80 percent (year-on-year), while also allowing the peso to depreciate and reforming energy subsidies.

Growth in *Colombia* is projected to weaken markedly to 1.3 percent in 2023, from 8 percent in 2022, before recovering somewhat to 2.8 percent in 2024. The economy is expected to slow as the surge in activity that accompanied reopening from pandemic restrictions abates, and as monetary policy remains tight amid high inflation. Investment growth is also forecast to decelerate. More restrictive monetary and fiscal conditions should help to moderate import growth and narrow the current account deficit, which is estimated to have remained above 5 percent of GDP in 2022, despite favorable terms of trade.

In *Chile*, output is projected to contract by 0.9 percent in 2023, before rebounding by 2.3 percent in 2024. Reduced real incomes due to high inflation, twinned with a softening labor market, are expected to erode near-term consumption. Despite weak activity, monetary policy is likely to remain tight early in the year. This should help mitigate potential capital flow pressures associated with softer copper prices and a sizeable current account deficit. However, tighter financial conditions will also weigh on investment, which is expected to contract this year, and raise financing costs for a heavily indebted private sector. Considerable policy uncertainty remains, linked to the constitutional reform process and ongoing pension and tax reforms efforts.

In *Peru*, steady growth of 2.6 percent a year is expected in 2023 and 2024. Exports are forecast to remain a key driver of growth, reflecting expanding copper output, though terms of trade are expected to weaken as metal prices decline. Expanding consumption will be supported by

mass early pension withdrawals and government stimulus measures intended to help maintain living standards despite high inflation. Political uncertainty and concerns about the consequences of social unrest (such as mine closures) are likely to weigh on investment.

In *Central America*, growth is projected to moderate, from 4.4 percent in 2022 to 3.2 percent in 2023 and 3.5 percent in 2024. Weaker near-term growth in the United States will weigh on remittances, exports, and foreign direct investment. Inflation reached record highs in the sub-region in 2022 but is expected to slow. This reflects commodity price developments, as well as monetary tightening (which in Panama and El Salvador is a consequence of full dollarization). A modest growth outlook implies slow progress on poverty reduction, especially in Honduras and Nicaragua, the sub-region's poorest countries. At 4.5 percent a year in 2023 and 2024, Panama is expected to be the sub-region's fastest growing economy, underpinned by mining and public investment.

Growth in the *Caribbean* is expected to slow to 5.6 percent in 2023 and 5.7 percent 2024, from 7.7 percent last year. Aside from Guyana, which remains in a natural resources-fueled growth boom, the sub-region faces renewed headwinds (chapter 4). Though 2022 saw resurgent tourism, a sharp downturn in advanced-economy growth is likely to slow the recovery. Tighter financing conditions will squeeze investment, and make it harder for many islands to roll over debt and finance large fiscal and current account deficits. Among the Caribbean's larger economies, growth in the Dominican Republic is expected to average a solid 4.9 percent in 2023 and 2024. In contrast, Haiti's economy is expected to contract for the fifth consecutive year in 2023. It remains beset by violence and instability, with nearly one-in-five children chronically malnourished (WFP 2022a).

Risks

The possibility of a sharper-than-projected global slowdown—or outright global recession—represents a significant downside risks for the region, particularly commodity exporters (figure

2.3.3.A). Slowing global growth and weak demand from China has already caused metal prices to fall substantially since mid-2022. Should growth decline more than expected in 2023, energy and agricultural commodity prices could also weaken more significantly, resulting in deteriorating terms of trade across much of South America. Terms of trade in LAC are closely correlated with investment growth, which could turn deeply negative due to reduced investment in commodity-production, and because lower export earnings would dampen domestic demand generally (de la Torre, Filippini, and Ize 2016). As in the mid-2010s, the result could be a drawn-out period of weak growth, potentially reinforced by a tendency toward fiscal pro-cyclicality in commodity exporters (Arroyo Marioli and Vegh, forthcoming).

There is also a serious risk that unexpectedly persistent inflation and additional interest rate increases in advanced economies result in a severe external financing shock. More monetary tightening than assumed in the United States, in particular, could precipitate a sudden acceleration of capital outflows. This could lead to widening borrowing spreads and depreciating currencies, or further depletion of reserves in countries intervening to stabilize exchange rates. Some large regional economies (Chile, Colombia) currently have outsized current account deficits, and could become vulnerable to shifts in market sentiment. Among smaller LAC economies, especially some in the Caribbean and Central America that are highly indebted, external financing needs appear large relative to GDP (figure 2.3.3.B). Further tightening of global financial conditions could result in balance of payments stresses in these economies, which could trigger financial crises (Claessens and Kose 2013).

Similar risks from tighter financial conditions could prevail if inflation in LAC does not fall as expected. Medium-term inflation expectations have risen materially, and several factors could cause further increases (figure 2.3.3.C). Recent price rises could become embedded through explicit or tacit wage indexation. Pass-through from currency depreciations to prices could cause inflation and inflation expectations to increase

FIGURE 2.3.3 LAC: Risks

Elevated commodity prices have supported growth in LAC, but they could decline rapidly in a sharper-than-expected global slowdown or recession, leading to deteriorating economic activity. High external financing needs could presage financial stress in some Caribbean and Central American countries, given rising advanced economy interest rates and diminished investor risk appetite. Rapid inflation in LAC may prove more stubborn than projected; rising inflation expectations could then necessitate further domestic monetary tightening. In the context of high inequality, a projected half-decade of feeble per capita income growth could increase the risk of episodes of disruptive social unrest.

A. LAC commodity export prices during global recessions

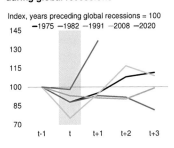

B. External financing needs in 2023

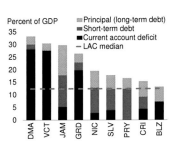

C. Two-year-ahead inflation expectations in LAC

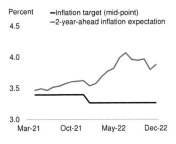

D. Per capita income growth, 2020-24, and income inequality

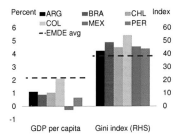

Sources: Haver Analytics; International Monetary Fund; national sources; World Bank; WTO Stats (database).
Note: ARG = Argentina, BLZ = Belize, BRA = Brazil, CHL = Chile, COL = Colombia, CRI = Costa Rica, DMA = Dominica, GRD = Grenada, JAM = Jamaica, MEX = Mexico, NIC = Nicaragua; PER = Peru, PRY = Paraguay, SLV = El Salvador, VCT = St. Vincent and Grenadines; EMDE avg = emerging market and developing economy average.
A. Index is composed of nominal annual price changes for energy, agricultural commodities, and metals (excluding precious metals), weighted by nominal export values for the seven largest economies in LAC (Argentina, Brazil, Chile, Colombia, Ecuador, Mexico, and Peru) by year. Global recessions as defined in Kose, Sugawara, and Terrones (2020). Year t is the year of the global recession indicated in the legend. For the 1975 global recession series, export weights for the 1982 series are used.
B. Figure shows the current account balance and debt obligations coming due in 2023. Debt obligations coming due are the sum of short-term and long-term debt principal payments and interest payments (the latter being within the current account). Short-term external debt in 2023 is estimated. GDP and current account balance in 2023 are projections. Blue dashed line denotes the regional median.
C. GDP-weighted average of median survey expectations for annual inflation in 24 months. Sample includes Brazil, Chile, Colombia, and Mexico. Last observation is December 2022. Inflation target declines in 2022 due to a reduction in Brazil's inflation target.
D. Left bars denote the annual average growth of GDP per capita from 2020 to 2024 (inclusive). Right bars refer to Gini index, with higher values indicating greater income inequality. Observations for Gini index are the most recent available for each country since 2015. Sample includes 96 EMDEs.

(IMF 2016). Memory of past hyper-inflations could influence the public to revise inflation expectations upwards more rapidly (Malmendier and Nagel 2016). Facing such challenges, the region's central banks could be forced into necessary but costly additional tightening to re-anchor expectations, resulting in a more severe and protracted slowdown than the baseline forecast. In countries with substantial stocks of interest rate-sensitive public debt (Brazil, Jamaica), this would cause debt interest burdens to increase quickly, potentially requiring governments to tighten fiscal policy to reinforce commitments to stability (Kehoe and Nicolini 2021).

LAC has long been afflicted by low productivity and per capita income growth, and higher income inequality than other EMDE regions (World Bank 2022e). These trends are set to persist, with elevated prices for essential goods endangering poverty reduction, and per capita GDP growth forecast to average just 0.6 percent per year over 2020-24 (figure 2.3.3.D). Regressive effects of high food prices may prove especially pronounced

because poverty is concentrated in urban communities, where incomes do not rise with agricultural prices (World Bank 2022j). These factors, and the stagnating living standards they imply, may heighten the risk of episodes of disruptive social unrest. Work stoppages could curtail production, while protests or other disturbances could undermine consumer and business confidence. The perception of limited economic opportunity for many could also make it harder for some countries to combat elevated levels of violence and corruption, which create enduring headwinds to inclusive growth (de Paulo, de Andrade Lima, and Tigre 2022). Economic losses from climate-related disasters add to these challenges, especially in the region's small states, where progress toward advanced economy income levels has stalled for two decades (chapter 4).

TABLE 2.3.1 Latin America and the Caribbean forecast summary

(Real GDP growth at market prices in percent, unless indicated otherwise)

	2020	2021	2022e	2023f	2024f	Percentage point differences from June 2022 projections		
						2022e	2023f	2024f
EMDE LAC, GDP [1]	-6.2	6.8	3.6	1.3	2.4	1.1	-0.6	0.0
GDP per capita (U.S. dollars)	-7.0	6.0	2.9	0.6	1.7	1.1	-0.6	0.1
(Average including countries that report expenditure components in national accounts)[2]								
EMDE LAC, GDP [2]	-6.2	6.8	3.5	1.2	2.3	1.1	-0.6	-0.1
PPP GDP	-6.5	7.0	3.5	1.3	2.4	1.0	-0.6	0.0
Private consumption	-7.5	7.6	4.1	1.7	2.7	1.3	-0.4	0.3
Public consumption	-1.9	4.3	1.6	0.6	0.9	0.8	0.1	0.4
Fixed investment	-11.5	16.8	3.4	-0.5	2.4	1.2	-2.1	-1.1
Exports, GNFS [3]	-9.1	8.0	5.9	3.6	4.7	1.0	-1.1	0.5
Imports, GNFS [3]	-13.9	17.3	5.5	2.8	4.4	1.2	-1.5	0.2
Net exports, contribution to growth	1.2	-2.0	0.0	0.1	0.0	-0.1	0.1	0.0
Memo items: GDP								
South America [4]	-5.4	7.2	3.7	1.1	2.2	1.2	-0.5	-0.1
Central America [5]	-7.6	10.3	4.4	3.2	3.5	0.5	-0.3	-0.1
Caribbean [6]	-7.5	9.7	7.7	5.6	5.7	0.8	-0.9	1.7
Brazil	-3.3	5.0	3.0	0.8	2.0	1.5	0.0	0.0
Mexico	-8.0	4.7	2.6	0.9	2.3	0.9	-1.0	0.3
Argentina	-9.9	10.4	5.2	2.0	2.0	0.7	-0.5	-0.5

Source: World Bank.

Note: e = estimate; f = forecast; PPP = purchasing power parity; EMDE = emerging market and developing economy. World Bank forecasts are frequently updated based on new information and changing (global) circumstances. Consequently, projections presented here may differ from those contained in other Bank documents, even if basic assessments of countries' prospects do not differ at any given moment in time. The World Bank is currently not publishing economic output, income, or growth data for República Bolivariana de Venezuela owing to a lack of reliable data of adequate quality. República Bolivariana de Venezuela is excluded from cross-country macroeconomic aggregates.

1. GDP and expenditure components are measured in average 2010-19 prices and market exchange rates.

2. Aggregate includes all countries in notes 4, 5, and 6, plus Mexico, except Antigua and Barbuda, Barbados, Dominica, Grenada, Guyana, Haiti, St. Kitts and Nevis, St. Lucia, St. Vincent and the Grenadines, and Suriname.

3. Exports and imports of goods and nonfactor services (GNFS).

4. Includes Argentina, Bolivia, Brazil, Chile, Colombia, Ecuador, Paraguay, Peru, and Uruguay.

5. Includes Costa Rica, El Salvador, Guatemala, Honduras, Nicaragua, and Panama.

6. Includes Antigua and Barbuda, The Bahamas, Barbados, Belize, Dominica, the Dominican Republic, Grenada, Guyana, Haiti, Jamaica, St. Kitts and Nevis, St. Lucia, St. Vincent and the Grenadines, and Suriname.

TABLE 2.3.2 **Latin America and the Caribbean country forecasts** [1]

(Real GDP growth at market prices in percent, unless indicated otherwise)

Percentage point differences from
June 2022 projections

	2020	2021	2022e	2023f	2024f	2022e	2023f	2024f
Argentina	-9.9	10.4	5.2	2.0	2.0	0.7	-0.5	-0.5
Bahamas, The	-23.8	13.7	8.0	4.1	3.0	2.0	0.0	0.0
Barbados	-13.7	0.7	10.0	4.8	3.9	-1.2	-0.1	0.9
Belize	-13.7	16.3	3.5	2.0	2.0	-2.2	-1.4	0.0
Bolivia	-8.7	6.1	3.3	3.1	2.7	-0.6	0.3	0.0
Brazil	-3.3	5.0	3.0	0.8	2.0	1.5	0.0	0.0
Chile	-6.0	11.7	2.1	-0.9	2.3	0.4	-1.7	0.3
Colombia	-7.0	10.7	8.0	1.3	2.8	2.6	-1.9	-0.5
Costa Rica	-4.1	7.8	4.1	2.9	3.1	0.7	-0.3	-0.1
Dominica	-16.6	6.5	5.8	4.6	4.6	-1.0	-0.4	0.0
Dominican Republic	-6.7	12.3	5.3	4.8	5.0	0.3	-0.2	0.0
Ecuador	-7.8	4.2	2.7	3.1	2.8	-1.0	0.0	-0.1
El Salvador	-8.1	10.2	2.4	2.0	2.0	-0.3	0.1	0.0
Grenada	-13.8	4.7	5.8	3.2	3.0	2.0	-0.2	-0.1
Guatemala	-1.8	8.0	3.4	3.1	3.5	0.0	-0.3	0.0
Guyana	43.5	20.0	57.8	25.2	21.2	9.9	-9.1	17.4
Haiti [2]	-3.3	-1.8	-1.5	-1.1	2.0	-1.1	-2.5	0.0
Honduras	-9.0	12.5	3.5	3.1	3.7	0.4	-0.5	0.0
Jamaica	-10.0	4.6	3.2	2.0	1.2	0.0	-0.3	0.0
Mexico	-8.0	4.7	2.6	0.9	2.3	0.9	-1.0	0.3
Nicaragua	-1.8	10.3	4.1	2.0	2.5	1.2	-0.3	0.0
Panama	-18.0	15.3	7.2	4.5	4.5	0.9	-0.5	-0.5
Paraguay	-0.8	4.1	-0.3	5.2	4.2	-1.0	0.5	0.4
Peru	-11.0	13.3	2.7	2.6	2.6	-0.4	-0.3	-0.4
St. Lucia	-24.4	11.9	8.9	4.4	3.2	2.5	-0.8	-0.1
St. Vincent and the Grenadines	-5.3	0.7	5.0	6.0	4.8	1.3	-0.4	1.6
Suriname	-16.0	-2.7	1.3	2.3	3.0	-0.5	0.2	0.3
Uruguay	-6.1	4.4	5.0	2.7	2.5	1.7	0.1	0.0

Source: World Bank.
Note: e = estimate; f = forecast. World Bank forecasts are frequently updated based on new information and changing (global) circumstances. Consequently, projections presented here may differ from those contained in other Bank documents, even if basic assessments of countries' prospects do not significantly differ at any given moment in time.
1. Data are based on GDP measured in average 2010-19 prices and market exchange rates.
2. GDP is based on fiscal year, which runs from October to September of next year.

MIDDLE EAST and NORTH AFRICA

Growth in the Middle East and North Africa region is projected to slow to 3.5 percent in 2023, as the boost from the earlier increase in oil production and the recovery in services following reopening from the pandemic fade. Prospects vary substantially across the region, with some economies facing macroeconomic instability and conflict while others grow above their potential. Spillovers from further weakness in key trading partners, tighter global financial conditions, increasing climate-related risks, rising social tensions, and political instability highlight the possibility of further economic contractions and increasing poverty. A further deterioration in global and domestic financial or economic conditions could see economies with large macroeconomic imbalances fall into crisis.

Recent developments

Output in the Middle East and North Africa (MNA) region rebounded in 2022, expanding by an estimated 5.7 percent—the region's highest growth rate in a decade—as oil exporters enjoyed windfalls from increased oil and gas prices and rising production. The rebound also reflected the ongoing recovery in services from their pandemic slump. Nonetheless, the region is still characterized by widely divergent economic conditions and growth paths, high levels of poverty and unemployment in many countries, low labor productivity growth, elevated vulnerabilities, and fragile political and social contexts. Rising inflation and tightening financing conditions have weighed on consumer spending, which stagnated across the region in the first half of the year. Authorities in many countries stepped in to help stabilize economic activity by raising spending (figure 2.4.1.A). In Saudi Arabia, for example, activity was supported by a government relief package, equivalent to 0.5 percent of GDP, to help households cope with the rising cost of living.

Among net oil exporters, the rise in oil prices and expansion of oil production led to a rapid increase in goods export earnings of 35 percent in the year

to August 2022 (figure 2.4.1.B; World Bank 2022d). The region's oil production in 2022 to November, at an average of 34.1 million barrels a day, was 10.4 percent higher than the same period a year earlier, with close to 80 percent of the increase being accounted for by the member countries of the Gulf Cooperation Council (GCC) and half by *Saudi Arabia* alone. Most of Saudi Arabia's 8.3 percent growth in 2022—the fastest in a decade—was due to increasing oil production. In *Iraq*, output grew by an estimated 8.7 percent last year, also driven by rising oil production; however, activity in other economic sectors has been more subdued owing to continued policy uncertainty. In *Libya*, oil output fell in June to about one-half of its recent peak as violence between political factions undermined production.

Economic conditions for net oil importers are starkly different from those for oil exporters. In the *Arab Republic of Egypt* output slowed significantly in the first half of 2022. *Morocco's* economy also decelerated sharply in the first half of 2022 due to the drought and rising energy prices, partially compensated by a recovery of services boosted by the tourism sector. MNA's oil-importing economies have been adversely affected by the growth slowdown in the European Union (EU)—the destination for almost half of their goods exports in 2021, and accounting for about 7.4 percent of GDP (figure 2.4.1.C). With weak

---

Note: This section was prepared by Franz Ulrich Ruch.

FIGURE 2.4.1 MNA: Recent developments

Higher inflation and tighter financial conditions, stemming partly from the war in Ukraine, have curbed growth in private consumption. Governments have ramped up spending to support demand, and higher oil prices have lifted investment among net oil exporters. Goods exports in late-2022 were below levels at the start of the year in net oil importers but 35 percent higher in oil exporters. Oil importers are heavily dependent on exports to Europe, where growth is weakening. Inflation has continued to rise, with food prices reaching double-digit annual increases in oil importers.

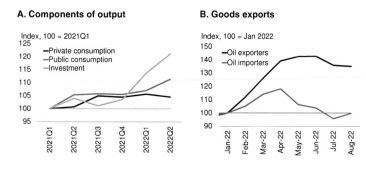

A. Components of output | B. Goods exports

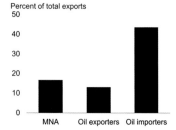 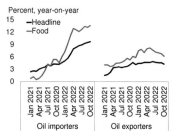

C. Exports to European Union | D. Consumer price index inflation

Sources: Haver Analytics; International Monetary Fund; World Bank.
Note: MNA = Middle East and North Africa.
A. Based on seasonally adjusted data for the Arab Republic of Egypt, the Islamic Republic of Iran, Morocco, Saudi Arabia, and West Bank and Gaza. GDP-weighted average. Investment refers to gross fixed capital formation except in Egypt and Morocco, where it is gross capital formation.
B. Based on goods exports in US$ for five oil importers and five oil exporters in MNA.
C. Based on total value of goods exports in US$ for 2021. Sample includes 11 oil exporters and 7 oil importers.
D. Unweighted average of four oil importers and seven oil exporters. Figure excludes the Islamic Republic of Iran and Lebanon.

export growth and rising import bills, current account deficits have widened or remained elevated in several oil importers, including Egypt (3.5 percent of GDP in 2022), Jordan (7.0 percent), Morocco (4.9 percent), and Tunisia (10.3 percent).

Inflation developments have also diverged between oil exporters and importers. In oil importers, consumer price inflation, on a year-on-year basis, increased last year to double-digit rates in many countries, mainly on account of rising food and energy prices (figure 2.4.1.D). In Egypt, urban inflation reached 18.7 percent on a year-on-year basis in November, well above the central

bank's target band of 5-9 percent. Inflation in Morocco in the same month reached over 8 percent, its highest level since the 1990s. In contrast, inflation in the GCC economies remained lower than the global average, benefiting from fixed exchange rates and fuel subsidies (World Bank 2022k). In Saudi Arabia, consumer prices rose by 2.9 percent. There was wide variation among oil exporters, however, with inflation at 52 percent in the Islamic Republic of Iran and at 8.1 percent in Algeria.

Financial conditions have tightened in the region in line with global developments but have shifted particularly sharply in several oil-importing economies. In *Tunisia*, adverse terms of trade shocks, a stalled economic recovery, unsustainable public finances, and political and policy uncertainty saw the sovereign spread vis-à-vis the United States widen to 16 percentage points in December, and the currency depreciate by 8 percent from a year earlier against the U.S. dollar. The dinar, however, has only depreciated by 2 percent against the euro with about four-tenths of its debt in euros. In *Egypt*, pressures from rising food and energy prices contributed to a widening of sovereign spreads, which about doubled from their 2019 levels to reach 8 percentage points, with the pound 57 percent lower from a year earlier against the U.S. dollar; exchange rate flexibility was an important step toward securing an IMF arrangement. In *Morocco*, sovereign risk spreads have widened but remain manageable, while the dirham has depreciated by about 6 percent against the U.S. dollar and against the euro between June and December.

Outlook

Growth in MNA is projected to decelerate from 5.7 percent last year to 3.5 percent in 2023 and to 2.7 percent in 2024 (figure 2.4.2.A; table 2.4.1). This pace of expansion over the forecast period is set to be notably below the region's average rate in 2000-19 of 4.0 percent a year, reflecting domestic structural impediments as well as spillovers from the ongoing global slowdown. The projected deceleration of regional growth is accounted for by the unwinding of the recent pickup in oil exporters (figure 2.4.2.B).

Growth in oil exporters is expected to slow from 6.1 percent in 2022 to 3.3 percent in 2023 and 2.3 percent in 2024. While the estimated rebound in 2022 in *Saudi Arabia* was well above last June's forecast, projections for growth for 2023 and 2024 have been revised down, to 3.7 percent and 2.3 percent, respectively (table 2.4.2). This reflects the expected deceleration in major trading partners, new oil production cuts, and lagged effects of domestic monetary policy tightening (Saudi Arabia generally tracks U.S. interest rates because of its pegged exchange rate regime). Growth in 2023 is envisaged to be supported by continuing recovery in religious tourism and the government's capital spending drive.

In the *Islamic Republic of Iran,* growth in FY2023/24 has been revised down by 0.5 percentage point, to 2.2 percent, on account of slower growth in key trading partners and new export competition from discounted Russian oil. Domestic demand is also likely to be curbed by the effects of high inflation on real incomes, which is expected to average 44 percent in FY2023/24. Growth is projected to slow further, to 1.9 percent, in FY2024/25. Growth in *Iraq* is forecast to slow to a downwardly revised 4.0 percent in 2023 and 2.9 percent in 2024, below its pre-pandemic pace. Water and electricity shortages, as well as political instability and violence, are set to prevent a stronger expansion. In contrast, growth in *Algeria* has been revised up to 2.3 percent in 2023, supported by higher public spending.

In the region's oil importers, growth is projected to be steady over 2023-24, at slightly above 4 percent a year. Growth in *Egypt*, while continuing to benefit from earlier reforms, is expected to slow to 4.5 percent in FY2022/23, as high inflation erodes real wages, weighing on domestic consumption. Weakening growth of external demand is also likely to limit activity in the manufacturing and tourism sectors. Fiscal and monetary policy tightening to rein in high inflation and a large current account deficit are expected to further restrain growth (figure 2.4.2.C). Meanwhile, authorities are gradually dismantling new import rules to contain balance of payment pressures, but continued trade disruptions may still occur from, for example, rules governing sourcing of foreign currency.

FIGURE 2.4.2 MNA: Outlook

Growth is forecast to slow markedly in 2023-24 as the boost from earlier increases in oil prices and production unwinds in net oil exporters. While growth in net oil importers is projected to remain close to its long-run average, growth in oil exporters is expected to slow below it. Rising monetary policy interest rates to rein in inflation will temper activity. Labor productivity growth in the region is expected to remain weak.

A. Growth

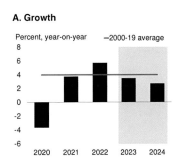

B. Growth, subregions

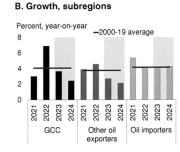

C. Monetary policy interest rates

D. Labor productivity growth

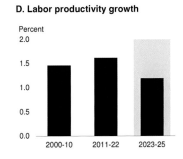

Sources: Haver Analytics; United Nations; World Bank.
Note: EMDEs = emerging market and developing economies; GCC = Gulf Cooperation Council; MNA = Middle East and North Africa.
B. "Other oil exporters" include Algeria, Iraq, and the Islamic Republic of Iran.
C. Unweighted average. Based on data for four oil importers and eight oil exporters.
D. Real GDP per worker. Period averages of annual GDP-weighted averages. Forecast assumes unchanged employment to population ratio from 2021 levels.

Growth in *Morocco* is projected to pick up to 3.5 percent in 2023—below previous projections—and to 3.7 percent in 2024 as its agriculture sector recovers gradually from last year's drought. Government spending is expected to partially offset weakness in private consumption stemming from high inflation. The global commodity price rally and inadequate progress in implementing structural reforms have dampened an already anemic recovery in *Tunisia*, which is saddled with growing fiscal and current account deficits. Growth is expected to pick-up to only 3.3 percent in 2023 and 3.6 percent in 2024. As a result, Tunisia is expected to be one of the last economies in the region to regain pre-pandemic output levels.

The region continues to struggle with weaker labor productivity growth than most other EMDE

FIGURE 2.4.3 **MNA: Risks**

Policy buffers have dwindled, particularly among net oil-importing econo-mies, as external current account deficits have widened and foreign ex-change reserves have fallen. Sovereign spreads have risen significantly in several economies, reflecting large government debts and other domestic vulnerabilities. The share of the region's population without sufficient food has increased. Economic and financial fragilities point to heightened risks of social unrest and violence that could further undermine growth.

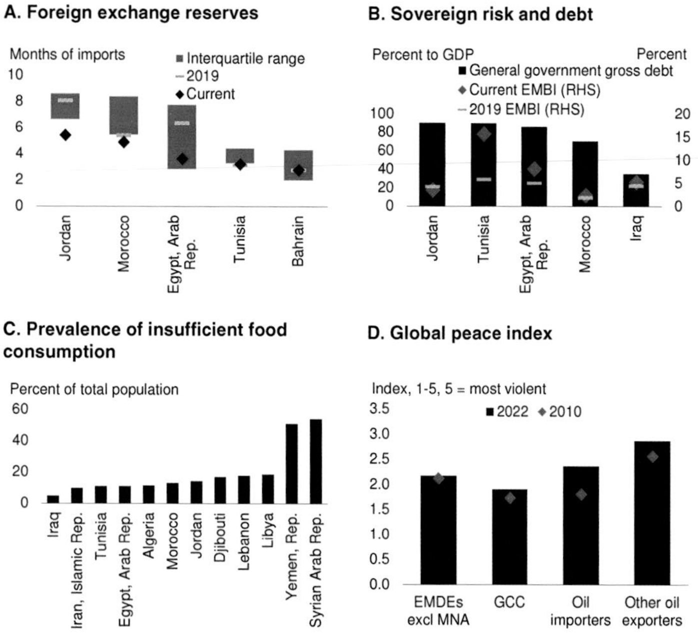

A. Foreign exchange reserves

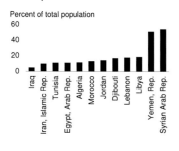

B. Sovereign risk and debt

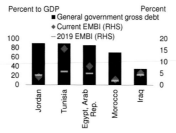

C. Prevalence of insufficient food consumption

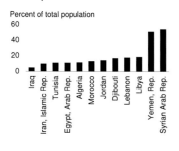

D. Global peace index

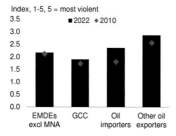

Sources: Haver Analytics; J.P. Morgan; Institute of Economics and Peace; International Monetary Fund; World Bank; World Food Programme.
Note: EMBI = emerging market bond index; EMDEs = emerging market and developing economies; GCC = Gulf Cooperation Council; MNA = Middle East and North Africa.
A. Interquartile ranges refer to monthly data from January 2000 to October 2022 or latest available. "2019" refers to the average of monthly data for the year.
B. Estimated gross government debt in 2023 as a ratio of GDP. "Current EMBI" is average of December 2022 observations to the 16th.
C. Based on World Food Programme's Hunger Map from December 15, 2022. "Insufficient food consumption" refers to households that are not consuming staples and vegetables every day and never or very seldom consume protein-rich food such as meat and dairy (poor food consumption) or households that consume staples and vegetables every day, accompanied by oil and pulses a few times a week (borderline food consumption).
D. Overall scores for Global Peaceful Index. Sample includes 127 EMDEs, 6 GCC countries, 8 oil importers, and 5 other oil exporters. "Other oil exporters" include Algeria, Iraq, the Islamic Republic of Iran, Libya, and the Republic of Yemen.

regions (figure 2.4.2.D; Vorisek et al. 2021). Labor productivity gains are limited by substantial structural challenges, including large gender gaps in work and education, low returns to education, limited economic diversification, excessive state involvement in economic activity, and prolonged armed conflicts (Montenegro and Patrinos 2014).

Risks

Risks to the baseline growth projections remain tilted to the downside. They include the possibility of adverse changes in global and domestic financing conditions, further weakness in growth in the EU (a vital export market), and rising violence and social tensions. Economies with weak policy buffers, and large fiscal and current account deficits, face elevated risks of financial crisis. The region is also at risk in the event of a global recession, which would undermine export demand and oil production. Climate change can damage economies in the short run and remains an existential threat in the long-run.

The vulnerability of many of the region's economies, particularly oil importers, to external financial pressures that could arise from capital outflows has increased as a result of widening current account deficits and dwindling foreign exchange reserves (figure 2.4.3.A). If sentiment continues to deteriorate, or global interest rates rise further than assumed, for example because of persistent inflation, oil importers could face even more adverse credit conditions as they seek to finance growing deficits. This could lead to severe difficulties meeting food and energy needs and servicing external debt. High government debt in several economies (Bahrain, Djibouti, Egypt, Jordan, Lebanon, Morocco, Tunisia) further complicate the outlook. Sovereign risk spreads have widened in several economies in recent years (figure 2.4.3.B). In *Tunisia*, for example, the sovereign spread vis-à-vis the United States increased rapidly in the last three years, reflecting growing concerns on the sustainability of public debt given increased pressures from public sector wages and food and energy subsidies (World Bank 2022l). Across the region more broadly, energy subsidies averaged 13 percent of government revenues in 2022. With continued high food and energy prices and weakening income growth, calls for expanded subsidies may mount.

Spillovers from the rest of the world are a major risk to the region's forecast as the global economy faces a heightened possibility of falling into recession (chapter 1). Oil exporters may face slower growth by implementing OPEC+ produc-tion cuts to stabilize oil prices at higher levels despite weakening demand. A deep recession in Europe would undermine growth among oil importing economies. The worsening of stagflation pressures, which include high energy and consumer prices and slowing global growth, could also harm the travel and tourism sectors that many economies in the region rely on heavily. Inbound tourism expenditure averaged 6 percent of GDP in 2019, and it was equivalent to 10 percent or more of GDP in Bahrain, Jordan, and Lebanon.

Much of the region has faced social unrest, violence, and armed conflict in the past, undermining economic growth and social stability. The recovery from such events is usually protracted, leaving several countries prone to safety and security challenges (figure 2.4.3.D). Current conditions, including elevated food and energy prices, limited policy space to support social protection, and increasing financial crisis risks could exacerbate safety and security vulnerabilities. Food insecurity has risen in the region because of the war in Ukraine, especially in economies that depend on imported food and energy and already face fragility and conflict (World Bank 2022h). In the *Republic of Yemen*, for example, where 19 million people (of a population of 30 million) have insufficient food, an end to a negotiated ceasefire raises the risk of renewed conflict, the knock-on effects of which could plunge even more of the population into acute food insecurity (WFP 2022b). Should conflicts reemerge, growth and development in the region would suffer.

Climate-related disasters are becoming more frequent in the region and threaten access to potable water, crop productivity, and populations that live along the coast. Agriculture-dependent economies are particularly at risk as rising temperatures reduce growing areas for agriculture and yields, and exacerbate already-scarce water resources. This could undermine food security, force migration, lower labor productivity, and raise the likelihood of conflict. In Morocco, for example, where droughts already constitute a major source of macroeconomic vulnerability, a continuation of recent trends could result in a rationing of water to various sectors. The water shortage could cause the loss of up to 6.5 percent of GDP by 2050 (only partially offset by new infrastructure and improved efficiency) and prompt the migration of up to 5.4 percent of the population (World Bank 2022m). For the region, crop yields could decline by up to 30 percent if temperatures were to rise by 1.5-2 degrees Celsius relative to pre-industrial times (World Bank 2014).

TABLE 2.4.1 Middle East and North Africa forecast summary

(Real GDP growth at market prices in percent, unless indicated otherwise)

Percentage point differences from June 2022 projections

	2020	2021	2022e	2023f	2024f	2022e	2023f	2024f
EMDE MNA, GDP[1]	-3.6	3.7	5.7	3.5	2.7	0.4	-0.1	-0.5
GDP per capita (U.S. dollars)	-4.9	2.5	4.3	2.1	1.4	0.4	-0.2	-0.5
(Average including countries that report expenditure components in national accounts)[2]								
EMDE MNA, GDP[2]	-2.9	4.0	5.6	3.5	2.7	0.6	0.0	-0.4
PPP GDP	-2.0	4.1	5.3	3.5	2.8	0.3	0.0	-0.4
Private consumption	-2.1	6.0	3.4	3.1	3.0	-0.2	-0.2	-0.1
Public consumption	1.6	2.0	2.7	2.2	2.5	0.7	0.4	0.9
Fixed investment	-6.5	5.3	5.4	5.3	3.7	0.0	0.2	-0.6
Exports, GNFS[3]	-11.1	5.3	10.3	5.2	4.1	0.6	-0.9	-1.3
Imports, GNFS[3]	-12.6	7.4	6.9	5.1	4.7	-0.4	-0.6	-0.2
Net exports, contribution to growth	-0.5	-0.2	2.1	0.6	0.2	0.3	-0.2	-0.6
Memo items: GDP								
Oil exporters[4]	-4.3	3.3	6.1	3.3	2.3	0.5	-0.1	-0.6
GCC countries[5]	-4.7	3.0	6.9	3.7	2.4	1.0	0.0	-0.8
Saudi Arabia	-4.1	3.2	8.3	3.7	2.3	1.3	-0.1	-0.7
Iran, Islamic Rep.[6]	1.9	4.7	2.9	2.2	1.9	-0.8	-0.5	-0.4
Oil importers[7]	-0.8	5.4	4.1	4.1	4.3	0.0	-0.3	0.0
Egypt, Arab Rep.[6]	3.6	3.3	6.6	4.5	4.8	0.5	-0.3	-0.2

Source: World Bank.

Note: e = estimate; f = forecast; PPP = purchasing power parity; EMDE = emerging market and developing economy. World Bank forecasts are frequently updated based on new information and changing (global) circumstances. Consequently, projections presented here may differ from those contained in other Bank documents, even if basic assessments of countries' prospects do not differ at any given moment in time.

1. GDP and expenditure components are measured in average 2010-19 prices and market exchange rates. Excludes Lebanon, Libya, the Syrian Arab Republic, and the Republic of Yemen as a result of the high degree of uncertainty.

2. Aggregate includes all economies in notes 4 and 7 except Djibouti, Iraq, Qatar, and West Bank and Gaza, for which data limitations prevent the forecasting of GDP components.

3. Exports and imports of goods and nonfactor services (GNFS).

4. Oil exporters include Algeria, Bahrain, the Islamic Republic of Iran, Iraq, Kuwait, Oman, Qatar, Saudi Arabia, and the United Arab Emirates.

5. The Gulf Cooperation Council (GCC) includes Bahrain, Kuwait, Oman, Qatar, Saudi Arabia, and the United Arab Emirates.

6. Fiscal year-based numbers. The fiscal year runs from July 1 to June 30 in the Arab Republic of Egypt, with 2020 reflecting FY2019/20. For the Islamic Republic of Iran, it runs from March 21 through March 20, with 2020 reflecting FY2020/21.

7. Oil importers include Djibouti, the Arab Republic of Egypt, Jordan, Morocco, Tunisia, and West Bank and Gaza.

TABLE 2.4.2 **Middle East and North Africa economy forecasts**[1]

(Real GDP growth at market prices in percent, unless indicated otherwise)

Percentage point differences from June 2022 projections

	2020	2021	2022e	2023f	2024f	2022e	2023f	2024f
Algeria	-5.1	3.5	3.7	2.3	1.8	0.5	1.0	0.4
Bahrain	-4.9	2.2	3.8	3.2	3.2	0.3	0.1	0.1
Djibouti	1.2	4.3	3.6	5.3	6.2	0.3	0.1	0.0
Egypt, Arab Rep.[2]	3.6	3.3	6.6	4.5	4.8	0.5	-0.3	-0.2
Iran, Islamic Rep.[2]	1.9	4.7	2.9	2.2	1.9	-0.8	-0.5	-0.4
Iraq	-11.3	2.8	8.7	4.0	2.9	-0.1	-0.5	-0.1
Jordan	-1.6	2.2	2.5	2.4	2.4	0.4	0.1	0.1
Kuwait	-8.9	1.3	8.5	2.5	2.5	2.8	-1.1	0.0
Lebanon[3]	-21.4	-7.0	-5.4	..	..	1.1	..	..
Libya[3]	-31.3	99.3	1.1	..	..	..	..	..
Morocco	-7.2	7.9	1.2	3.5	3.7	0.1	-0.8	0.1
Oman	-3.4	3.1	4.5	3.9	2.4	-1.1	1.1	-0.2
Qatar	-3.6	1.5	4.0	3.4	2.9	-0.9	-1.1	-1.5
Saudi Arabia	-4.1	3.2	8.3	3.7	2.3	1.3	-0.1	-0.7
Syrian Arab Republic[3]	-3.9	-2.9	-3.5	-3.2	..	-0.9	..	..
Tunisia	-8.8	4.4	2.5	3.3	3.6	-0.5	-0.2	0.3
United Arab Emirates	-5.0	3.9	5.9	4.1	2.3	1.2	0.7	-1.3
West Bank and Gaza	-11.3	7.1	3.5	3.0	3.0	-0.2	-0.2	-0.1
Yemen, Rep.[3]	-8.5	-1.0	1.0	1.0	..	0.2	-1.5	..

Source: World Bank.

Note: e = estimate; f = forecast. World Bank forecasts are frequently updated based on new information and changing (global) circumstances. Consequently, projections presented here may differ from those contained in other Bank documents, even if basic assessments of economies' prospects do not significantly differ at any given moment in time.

1. Data are based on GDP measured in average 2010-19 prices and market exchange rates.

2. Fiscal-year based numbers. The fiscal year runs from July 1 to June 30 in the Arab Republic of Egypt, with 2020 reflecting FY2019/20. For the Islamic Republic of Iran, it runs from March 21 through March 20, with 2020 reflecting FY2020/21.

3. Forecasts beyond 2022 are excluded for Lebanon and Libya because of a high degree of uncertainty. Forecast beyond 2023 are excluded for the Republic of Yemen and the Syrian Arab Republic because of a high degree of uncertainty.

SOUTH ASIA

South Asia continues to be adversely affected by spillovers from the invasion of Ukraine, rising global interest rates, and weakening growth in key trading partners. Regional growth is estimated to have slowed to 6.1 percent in 2022 and is projected to slow further to 5.5 percent in 2023—below previous projections on global spillovers—before picking up to 5.8 percent in 2024. Risks to the outlook continue to be tilted to the downside, including further pressure from tightening global financial conditions; higher-than-projected inflation leading to lower real incomes and spending; and the reemergence of financial sector stress. Dwindling international reserves and rising sovereign spreads increase the risk of more economies falling into crisis.

Recent developments

The economies of the South Asia region (SAR) continue to be adversely affected by shocks emanating from the Russian Federation's invasion of Ukraine, including higher food and energy prices, and by the tightening of global financial conditions as central banks in the region and elsewhere act to fight high inflation. The repercussions of these developments led to contractions in trade, hospitality, and manufacturing in SAR, as household's real incomes came under pressure (figure 2.5.1.A).

In some economies, the deterioration in economic conditions has led to a substantial rise in poverty (Afghanistan, Pakistan, Sri Lanka; World Bank 2022j). Many households are consuming less nutritious food, and rolling electricity blackouts have become common as fuel has been rationed (World Bank 2022h). The combination of limited foreign exchange buffers and widening external current account deficits encouraged several countries (Bangladesh, Pakistan) to approach the International Monetary Fund (IMF) for help in bolstering foreign exchange reserves and mitigating external financing pressures. In parallel, governments have tightened fiscal policies and, in

some cases, imposed import controls and food-export bans.[1]

In *India*, which accounts for three-fourths of the region's output, growth expanded by 9.7 percent on an annual basis in the first half of fiscal year 2022/23, reflecting strong private consumption and fixed investment growth (World Bank 2022o). Consumer inflation spent most of last year above the Reserve Bank's upper tolerance limit of 6 percent, prompting the policy rate to be raised by 2.25 percentage points between May and December. India's goods trade deficit has more than doubled since 2019, and was $24 billion in November, with deficits for crude petroleum and petroleum products ($7.6 billion) and other commodities (for example, ores and minerals at $4.2 billion) accounting for the widening (figure 2.5.1.B).

Bangladesh was hard hit by spillovers from the changing global environment. The country was priced out of global energy markets and unable to meet the energy needs of households and businesses. Rising energy costs and supply constraints saw industrial production contract in September from its peak in March. The rising cost of imports about doubled the trade deficit since 2019. The deficit could have been even larger had

---

Note: This section was prepared by Franz Ulrich Ruch.

[1] See tables 1.2 and 1.3 in World Bank (2022n) for details on policy interventions.

FIGURE 2.5.1 SAR: Recent developments

Rapidly rising inflation and tightening financial conditions have undermined activity in retail trade, hospitality, and manufacturing. Trade deficits have doubled since 2019 in some countries as food and energy prices have soared and export growth has slowed. International arrivals are yet to recover in the region, although country experiences vary. The region's currencies have depreciated further since June as capital outflows have increased, international reserves have collapsed, and current account deficits have widened. Inflation expectations have shifted further away from inflation targets. Sovereign spreads are rising rapidly in vulnerable economies.

A. Economic activity

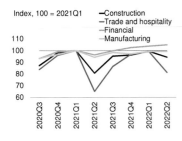

B. Goods trade balance

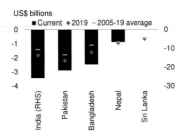

C. International tourist arrivals

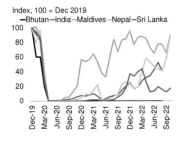

D. Exchange rate and international reserves

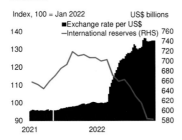

E. Consumer price index inflation

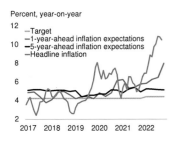

F. Sovereign risk spreads, change since June

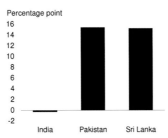

Sources: Bloomberg; Consensus Economics; Haver Analytics; J.P. Morgan; World Bank; World Tourism Organization.
A. GDP-weighted average. Based on data for India, Sri Lanka, and the Maldives.
D. Average exchange rate against the US$ for Bangladesh, India, Pakistan, and Sri Lanka. Total foreign exchange reserves including gold for all economies except Afghanistan and Nepal.
E. GDP-weighted averages. "One-year-ahead inflation expectations" are fixed horizon forecasts based on Consensus Economics for Bangladesh, India, Pakistan, and Sri Lanka, while the five-year-ahead is based on forecasts for Bangladesh, India, and Pakistan. "Headline inflation" is based on data for all SAR economies excluding Afghanistan.
F. Based on the Emerging Market Bond Index plus spread. Latest observation is December 16, 2022.

it not been for robust growth in demand for its ready-made garments and a growing share of the global market. The government responded to high global energy prices with blackouts and factory closures to reduce energy consumption, stopped purchasing vehicles, and made it harder to purchase luxury goods, among other measures to preserve international reserves.

In *Pakistan*, an already precarious economic situation, with low foreign exchange reserves and large fiscal and current account deficits, was exacerbated last August by severe flooding, which cost many lives. About one-third of the country's land area was affected, damaging infrastructure, and directly affecting about 15 percent of the population (Benhassine et al. 2022; World Bank 2022p). Recovery and reconstruction needs are expected to be 1.6 times the FY2022/23 national development budget (Government of Pakistan et al. 2022). The flooding is likely to have seriously damaged agricultural production—which accounts for 23 percent of GDP and 37 percent of employment—by disrupting the current and up-coming planting seasons and pushed between 5.8 and 9 million people into poverty (World Bank 2022p). Policy uncertainty further complicates the economic outlook.

In *Sri Lanka*, output is estimated to have fallen by 9.2 percent in 2022 as the government ran out of the foreign exchange needed to cover food and fuel imports, and to service external debt. The rupee plummeted, and imports contracted sharply. While the authorities are now implementing a stabilization program, the country faces con-tinuing shortages of food, energy, and medical supplies. The crisis and its repercussions have increased poverty and reversed much of the country's income gains over the past decade. Tourist arrivals, an important source of foreign exchange, continue to be depressed with interna-tional arrivals last October about one-third of their 2019 level (figure 2.5.1.C). *Nepal* also saw international arrivals drop, particularly from Chinese tourists affected by COVID-related restrictions. In contrast, tourism in *Maldives* rebounded robustly in 2022, returning its GDP to its pre-pandemic level more quickly than pre-viously expected; growth for the year is expected to be 12.4 percent.

Between June and December, the region's currencies have depreciated against the U.S. dollar by an average of 10 percent, above the EMDE average (figure 2.5.1.D). In conjunction with rising global commodity prices, consumer price inflation has continued to rise, and one-year-ahead inflation expectations remain well above central bank targets (figure 2.5.1.E). Since early June, the Bangladeshi taka has depreciated by 18 percent and foreign exchange reserves have declined by $8 billion, pushing inflation to 8.7 percent (year-on-year) in December. Pakistan, with low foreign exchange reserves and rising sovereign risk, saw its currency depreciate by 14 percent between June and December and its country risk premium rise by 15 percentage points over this same period (figure 2.5.1.F). Pakistan's consumer price inflation reached 24.5 percent in December on an annual basis, recently coming off its highest rate since the 1970s. India used its international reserves (at $550 billion in November, or 16 percent of GDP) to curb excess exchange rate volatility helping to limit Rupee depreciation, and its sovereign spread has remained broadly stable at 1.4 percent in December, similar to average levels in the five years before the pandemic.

Outlook

Growth in SAR is projected to slow to 5.5 percent in 2023 on slowing external demand and tightening financial conditions before picking up slightly to 5.8 percent in 2024 (table 2.5.1). Growth is revised lower over the forecast horizon and is below the region's 2000-19 average growth of 6.5 percent (figure 2.5.2.A and 2.5.2.B). This pace reflects still robust growth in India, Maldives, and Nepal offsetting the effects of the floods in Pakistan and the economic and political crises in Afghanistan and Sri Lanka. The deteriorating global environment, however, will weigh on investment in the region (figure 2.5.2.C).

Growth in India is projected to slow from 8.7 percent in FY2021/22 to 6.9 percent in FY2022/23, the latter revised 0.6 percentage point lower since June (table 2.5.2). The slowdown in the global economy and rising uncertainty will weigh on export and investment growth. Governments increased infrastructure spending and various business facilitation measures, however,

FIGURE 2.5.2 **SAR: Outlook**

Domestic crises, global growth spillovers, and tightening financing conditions continue to buffet economies, contributing to a downgrade in growth prospects. Fixed investment is likely to be set back further by recent developments. Monetary and fiscal policy has tightened significantly in Pakistan and Sri Lanka to address domestic vulnerabilities in the former, and the ongoing economic crisis in the latter.

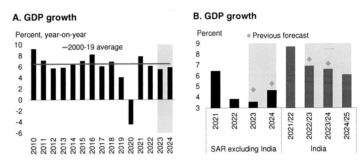

A. GDP growth

B. GDP growth

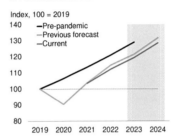

C. Fixed investment

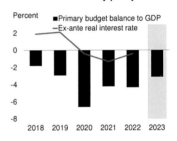

D. Fiscal and monetary policy stances

Sources: Consensus Economics; Haver Analytics; International Monetary Fund; World Bank.
Note: SAR = South Asia.
B.C. "Previous forecast" reflects June 2022 *Global Economic Prospects* report.
C. "Pre-pandemic" based on the January 2020 *Global Economic Prospects* report.
D. GDP-weighted average. "Ex-ante real interest rate" is the difference between policy rates and one-year-ahead inflation forecasts at fixed horizons based on Consensus Economics for Bangladesh, India, Pakistan, and Sri Lanka.

will crowd-in private investment and support the expansion of manufacturing capacity. Growth is projected to slow, to 6.6 percent in FY2023/24 before falling back toward its potential rate of just above 6 percent. India is expected to be the fastest growing economy of the seven largest EMDEs.

In the region excluding India, growth in 2023 and 2024—at 3.6 percent and 4.6 percent, respectively—is expected to underperform its average 2000-19 pre-pandemic rate. This is mainly due to weak growth in *Pakistan*, which is projected at 2.0 percent in FY2022/23, half the pace that was anticipated last June. Pakistan faces challenging economic conditions, including the repercussions of the recent flooding and continued policy and political uncertainty. As the country implements policy measures to stabilize macroeconomic conditions, inflationary pressures dissipate, and rebuilding begins following the floods, growth is expected to pick up to 3.2 percent in FY2023/24, still below previous projections. In Bangladesh, growth is expected to slow to 5.2 percent in FY2022/23 due to rising inflation and its negative impact on household incomes and firms' input costs, as well as energy shortages, import restrictions, and monetary policy tightening. This is down from 7.2 percent growth in the previous year, but is expected to pick up again and return towards its potential pace in FY2023/24. In *Maldives*, growth is expected to moderate to 8.2 percent in 2023, which is below previous projections, as the post-pandemic boost fades. Nonetheless, Maldives is expected to remain the fastest growing economy in the region, benefiting from an increase in tourist arrivals and infrastructure investments. *Bhutan* is forecast to grow by 4.1 percent in FY2022/23 helped by the opening of its borders in September, which will support growth in the industry and services sectors.

Sri Lanka and *Afghanistan* remain in crisis, albeit of different kinds. In Sri Lanka, output is expected to contract again in 2023, by 4.2 percent (World Bank 2022q). The forecast for growth in 2023, like the estimate for 2022, has been revised down owing to ongoing foreign currency shortages, the effects of higher inflation, and policy measures designed to restore macroeconomic stability. In Afghanistan, the sudden pause of international aid in August 2021—the foundation of economic activity for much of the preceding two decades—is estimated to have an accumulated contraction of output between 2021 and 2022 of about one-third, leading to a large increase in poverty. Over the next two years, growth is expected to stabilize at low-single-digit annual rates, with reduced international on-budget support and an economic and policy environment still precarious for households and businesses (World Bank 2022r). This projected output path will be insufficient to arrest widespread food deprivation.

The turn to more restrictive fiscal and monetary policies in several countries to address rising domestic and external imbalances and financing pressures is occurring at a time when growth is already slowing globally and output gaps are widening in several regional economies (figure 2.5.2.D). In India, monetary and fiscal tightening over the forecast horizon is expected to be less

pronounced than in much of the rest of the region, as adequate policy buffers have provided breathing room to support the ongoing recovery and boost public investment. Pakistan and Sri Lanka have had to tighten policies more rapidly in pursuit of macroeconomic stability.

Risks

Risks to the outlook remain predominantly to the downside, including those related to the repercussions of the invasion of Ukraine, tightening global financing conditions, legacies from the pandemic, and country-specific vulnerabilities of several regional economies. The potential for crises in more countries is also rising but varies based on the availability of adequate policy buffers, and institutional and macroeconomic management strengths and weaknesses, among other factors. The projections for several economies are predicated on their ability to secure foreign exchange funding and implement policies to resolve balance of payments pressures. Other downside risks include a deeper-than-projected global economic slowdown, a more persistent period of elevated inflation, and financial sector stress. Additional deceleration in growth in China (and any additional mobility restrictions), Europe, and the United States would undermine many countries' exports as well as the tourism earnings of SAR's tourism-dependent economies (Maldives, Sri Lanka).

More persistent high inflation in advanced economies would require additional increases in their policy rates, which could lead to financial stress in the region and further exchange rate pressures (chapter 1). Addressing rising macroeconomic imbalances, which requires fiscal and monetary policy consolidation, is challenging when growth is slowing and human deprivation is rising. The complexities of such an environment can amplify the risk of policy mistakes that undermine economic activity, especially in circumstances of high domestic debt and dwindling foreign exchange reserves (figure 2.5.3.A).

External financing needs increased significantly in several SAR economies in 2022. External current account deficits widened and are forecast to average 7 percent of GDP in 2023, while short-term external debt has also been elevated in recent years in some countries (figure 2.5.3.B). Several factors heighten the risk that countries may be unable to secure adequate financing at manageable costs. Apart from increases in interest rates, a rise in global risk aversion could see a repricing of debt as investors shift toward safer assets. This could lead to capital outflows from SAR economies, currency depreciations, and increases in financing costs. Domestic factors could aggravate this risk, including policy uncertainty.

Food prices have risen rapidly in SAR, especially in Pakistan and Sri Lanka, increasing the incidence of food insecurity in the region (figure 2.5.3.C). In Sri Lanka, for example, more than one-third of the population are food insecure, up from less than one-tenth in 2019 (WFP 2022c). Although global food price inflation appears to have subsided, risks of increased deprivation and inadequate nutrition remain elevated. High fertilizer and petroleum prices are likely to affect upcoming planting seasons, increasing the persistence of high food prices and threatening households' ability to cope by depleting savings. Several countries in SAR have taken steps to try to insulate people from the effects of rising food and energy prices; however, some of these may prove unsustainable and could lead to unintended and costly consequences (Espitia, Rocha, and Ruta 2022). For example, import controls have now been implemented in several economies, worsening the business environment. Export bans on food, also increasingly prevalent, could have unintended consequences and exacerbate increases in global food prices. Afghanistan, Bangladesh, India, and Pakistan implemented export restrictions on food in 2022 including in rice, wheat, and sugar.

Climate change is a significant threat in the region. Increasingly frequent extreme weather events have already imposed substantial costs, with droughts and floods damaging livelihoods and increasing the volatility of food prices. Natural disasters have increased in frequency since 2000, and the average annual costs of damage in 2001-20 were double those in 1980-2000 (figure 2.5.3.D). The recent floods in Pakistan are estimated to have caused damage equivalent to about 4.8 percent of GDP (Government of Pakistan et al. 2022). Extreme weather events can

FIGURE 2.5.3 SAR: Risks

Limited foreign exchange reserve cover in some economies raises the likelihood of balance of payments stress, especially if large existing external financing needs worsen. Food price increases and pressure on incomes is raising food insecurity in the region. Natural disasters events are becoming more frequent and more costly, increasing human and economic risks.

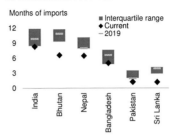

A. International reserves

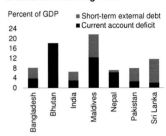

B. External financing needs

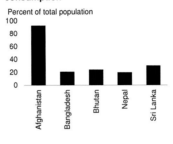

C. Prevalence of insufficient food consumption

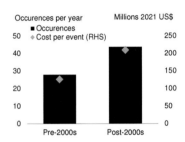

D. Natural disasters

Sources: CEIC; EM-DAT; Haver Analytics; International Monetary Fund; Kose et al. (2022); World Bank; World Food Programme.
A. Based on monthly data from January 2000 to October 2022 or where available. "2019" reflects an average for the year.
B. Current account deficit based on forecasts for 2023 and reflected as a positive number. Short-term external debt based on data for 2021 from Kose et al. (2022).
C. Based on WFP Hunger Map from December 15, 2022. "Insufficient food consumption" refers to households that are not consuming staples and vegetables every day and never or very seldom consume protein-rich food such as meat and dairy (poor food consumption) or households that consume staples and vegetables every day, accompanied by oil and pulses a few times a week (borderline food consumption).
D. Based on data from 1980-2021. "Cost per event" in current 2021 US dollars.

exacerbate food deprivation, cut the region off from essential supplies, destroy infrastructure, and directly impede agricultural production. Estimates for Bangladesh suggest that current climate trends will see rice, vegatables, and wheat yields decline by 5-6 percent by 2050 compared to a no-climate-change scenario (World Bank 2022s). Extreme weather can also complicate the implementation of macroeconomic policies. For example, in India, more erratic monsoon rains have translated into more volatile food prices, destabilizing households' inflation expectations, undermining the ability to forecast inflation, and muddling the formulation of monetary policy (Singh, Mishra and Shaw 2022; Dilip and Kundu 2020).

TABLE 2.5.1 **South Asia forecast summary**

(Real GDP growth at market prices in percent, unless indicated otherwise)

Percentage point differences from June 2022 projections

	2020	2021	2022e	2023f	2024f	2022e	2023f	2024f
EMDE South Asia, GDP[1,2]	-4.5	7.9	6.1	5.5	5.8	-0.7	-0.3	-0.7
GDP per capita (U.S. dollars)	-5.5	6.8	5.2	4.5	4.7	-0.6	-0.3	-0.7
EMDE South Asia excluding India, GDP	2.7	6.4	3.8	3.6	4.6	-0.2	-1.1	-0.7
(Average including countries that report expenditure components in national accounts)[3]								
EMDE South Asia, GDP[3]	-4.4	7.8	6.1	5.5	5.8	-0.7	-0.3	-0.7
PPP GDP	-4.5	7.8	6.1	5.5	5.8	-0.7	-0.3	-0.7
Private consumption	-4.1	9.1	7.9	4.8	6.1	2.1	-0.8	0.0
Public consumption	0.0	6.7	2.5	6.7	4.7	-8.0	2.0	-1.5
Fixed investment	-10.3	15.3	8.4	6.3	7.6	-2.1	0.4	-0.7
Exports, GNFS[4]	-10.4	19.1	12.4	7.5	7.7	3.5	-0.8	-0.2
Imports, GNFS[4]	-10.5	28.0	17.0	6.3	9.4	5.7	-0.6	0.9
Net exports, contribution to growth	0.9	-3.8	-2.7	-0.5	-1.5	-0.7	0.2	-0.2
Memo items: GDP[2]	2019/20	2020/21	2021/22e	2022/23f	2023/24f	2021/22e	2022/23f	2023/24f
India	3.7	-6.6	8.7	6.9	6.6	0.0	-0.6	-0.5
Pakistan (factor cost)	-0.9	5.7	6.0	2.0	3.2	1.7	-2.0	-1.0
Bangladesh	3.4	6.9	7.2	5.2	6.2	0.8	-1.5	-0.7

Source: World Bank.

Note: e = estimate; f = forecast; PPP = purchasing power parity; EMDE = emerging market and developing economy. World Bank forecasts are frequently updated based on new information and changing (global) circumstances. Consequently, projections presented here may differ from those contained in other Bank documents, even if basic assessments of countries' prospects do not differ at any given moment in time.

1. GDP and expenditure components are measured in average 2010-19 prices and market exchange rates. Excludes Afghanistan because of the high degree of uncertainty.

2. National income and product account data refer to fiscal years (FY) while aggregates are presented in calendar year (CY) terms. (For example, aggregate under 2020/21 refers to CY 2020). The fiscal year runs from July 1 through June 30 in Bangladesh, Bhutan, and Pakistan; from July 16 through July 15 in Nepal; and April 1 through March 31 in India.

3. Subregion aggregate excludes Afghanistan, Bhutan, and Maldives, for which data limitations prevent the forecasting of GDP components.

4. Exports and imports of goods and nonfactor services (GNFS).

TABLE 2.5.2 **South Asia country forecasts**

(Real GDP growth at market prices in percent, unless indicated otherwise)

Percentage point differences from June 2022 projections

	2020	2021	2022e	2023f	2024f	2022e	2023f	2024f
Calendar year basis[1]								
Afghanistan[2]	-2.4	-20.7	..	..	..	..	..	..
Maldives	-33.5	41.7	12.4	8.2	8.1	4.8	-2.0	1.0
Sri Lanka	-3.5	3.3	-9.2	-4.2	1.0	-1.4	-0.5	0.0
Fiscal year basis[1]	2019/20	2020/21	2021/22e	2022/23f	2023/24f	2021/22e	2022/23f	2023/24f
Bangladesh	3.4	6.9	7.2	5.2	6.2	0.8	-1.5	-0.7
Bhutan	-2.3	-3.3	4.6	4.1	3.7	0.2	-0.6	-3.0
India	3.7	-6.6	8.7	6.9	6.6	0.0	-0.6	-0.5
Nepal	-2.4	4.2	5.8	5.1	4.9	2.1	1.0	-0.9
Pakistan (factor cost)	-0.9	5.7	6.0	2.0	3.2	1.7	-2.0	-1.0

Source: World Bank.

Note: e = estimate; f = forecast. World Bank forecasts are frequently updated based on new information and changing (global) circumstances. Consequently, projections presented here may differ from those contained in other Bank documents, even if basic assessments of countries' prospects do not significantly differ at any given moment in time.

1. Historical data is reported on a market price basis. National income and product account data refer to fiscal years (FY) with the exception of Afghanistan, Maldives, and Sri Lanka, which report in calendar year. The fiscal year runs from July 1 through June 30 in Bangladesh, Bhutan, and Pakistan; from July 16 through July 15 in Nepal; and April 1 through March 31 in India.

2. Data for Afghanistan beyond 2021 are excluded because of a high degree of uncertainty.

SUB-SAHARAN AFRICA

Growth in Sub-Saharan Africa (SSA) slowed to an estimated 3.4 percent in 2022, as weakening external demand, high inflation, and tightening global financial conditions dampened regional activity. Soaring food and energy prices, stemming partly from the war in Ukraine, triggered sharp cost-of-living increases across the region, leading to millions more people falling into food insecurity and poverty. Global demand for many non-energy commodities softened, adversely affecting the region's exporters of industrial metals. Fiscal space needed to protect the poor has been depleted in many countries, while rising borrowing costs and muted growth prospects have sharply worsened debt dynamics. The regional outlook for 2023-24 is for only a modest pickup in growth and a slow rise in per capita incomes, dimming prospects for a rapid reversal of recent increases in poverty. Risks are tilted to the downside. A more pronounced weakness in major economies, further increases in global interest rates, higher and persistent inflation, fragility, and increased frequency and intensity of adverse weather events could further slow growth across the region, exacerbating poverty and leading to debt distress in some countries.

Recent developments

Growth in Sub-Saharan Africa (SSA) decelerated to an estimated 3.4 percent last year—0.3 percentage point below previous forecasts (table 2.6.1). The downgrade masks diverse circumstances and the uneven impact of terms-of-trade and cost-of-living developments across the region. Growth estimates were revised down for over 60 percent of countries as a marked weakening of the global economy combined with tightening financial conditions and rising inflation dampened already fragile recoveries and amplified domestic vulnerabilities (figure 2.6.1.A; table 2.6.2).

The cost-of-living increases, intensified by the effects of the war in Ukraine, have reduced food affordability and domestic demand across the region, especially in countries lacking policy space to protect the poor (Rother et al. 2022). Almost 60 percent of the world's extreme poor, who spend a substantial share of their income on food, live in SSA (World Bank 2022j). In 2022, the estimated number of people experiencing acute food insecurity or worse in SSA surpassed 140 million, up nearly 24 million since 2021

(FSIN and GNAFC 2022). Soaring food prices are, therefore, having grave repercussions on food security, poverty alleviation, social cohesion, and growth in many countries. Food price increases, which accounted for more than half of overall inflation, pushed average inflation in SSA to 13 percent—almost three times above its pre-pandemic rate (figure 2.6.1.B; World Bank 2022h). Annual inflation in some countries surpassed 30 percent (Ghana, Rwanda) with food price inflation exceeding 20 percent in over a quarter of all SSA economies. Currency depreciations resulting from unfavorable terms-of-trade shocks, the loss of foreign exchange reserves, capital outflows, and elevated debt levels exacerbated inflationary pressures (Ethiopia, Ghana, Malawi).

A sharp slowdown in global growth, especially in China, and weakness in many non-energy commodity prices, have weighed on activity across SSA, particularly in metal exporters. The recent moderation of global energy and food prices has provided some relief, but many countries are still facing a less favorable external environment as import costs remain elevated (figure 2.6.1.C).

Growth in *Nigeria*—the region's largest economy—weakened to 3.1 percent in 2022, a 0.3

Note: This section was prepared by Sergiy Kasyanenko.

FIGURE 2.6.1 SSA: Recent developments

Growth in SSA slowed in 2022 as surging inflation and weaker external demand weighed on regional activity. Inflation rose sharply across the region amid soaring global prices of staple foods and energy, and depreciating currencies. A moderation of global prices of metals, such as copper and gold, exacerbated headwinds for many SSA commodity exporters. Elevated prices of imported fuel, food, and fertilizers led to a deterioration of external balances in non-oil exporting economies.

A. GDP growth, 2022: revisions since June

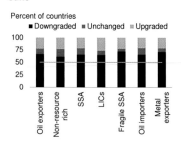

B. Consumer price index inflation

C. Commodity terms of trade

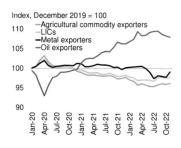

D. Current account balances

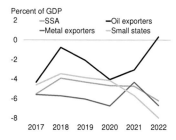

Sources: Comtrade (database); Haver Analytics; International Monetary Fund; World Bank.
Note: LICs = low-income countries; SSA = Sub-Saharan Africa.
A. Fragile SSA = SSA countries with fragile and conflict affected situations. Figure shows revisions between latest forecasts and those of the June 2022 *Global Economic Prospects* report.
B. Change in prices from 12 months earlier. Unweighted averages for the sample of 22 SSA EMDEs. Last observation is October 2022.
C. Median across each group. Commodity terms of trade is calculated as changes in real commodity prices weighted by each commodity's net exports share in GDP. An increase indicates improving terms of trade—that is, export prices rising relative to import prices. Last observation is November 2022.
D. Median across each group.

percentage point downgrade from the June projection. Oil output dropped to 1 million barrels per day, down by over 40 percent compared to its 2019 level, reflecting technical problems, insecurity, rising production costs, theft, lack of payment discipline in joint ventures, and persistent underinvestment, partly because of the diversion of oil revenues to petrol subsidies, estimated at over 2 percent of GDP in 2022 (NEITI 2022; World Bank 2022t). A strong recovery in non-oil sectors moderated in the second half of the year as floods and surging consumer prices (annual inflation surpassed 21 percent for the first time in 17 years) disrupted

activity and depressed consumer demand. Persistent fuel and foreign exchange shortages, with the naira depreciating by over 30 percent last year in the parallel market, further dampened economic activity.

Oil production stabilized in *Angola*, supporting 3.1 percent growth last year. The currency strengthened by almost 10 percent against the US dollar amid surging oil exports, reducing the country's debt-to-GDP ratio and lessening the impact of higher global prices on domestic inflation.

In *South Africa*, growth in 2022 slowed markedly to an estimated 1.9 percent. The 0.2 percentage point downgrade from the June projection reflects the impact of rising cost of living and weakening of the terms of trade due to falling global metal prices. Power outages have also tempered growth in the region's second largest economy. Capital outflows and shrinking trade surpluses contributed to a depreciation of the rand against the U.S. dollar by nearly 10 percent in 2022, further adding to price pressures. Annual inflation reached its highest level in over a decade, prompting more policy tightening.

Elsewhere, the region's metal exporters suffered from softening metal prices. Excluding oil-exporting countries, current account deficits widened last year because of surging spending on imports as terms of trade generally deteriorated (figure 2.6.1.D). In nonresource-rich countries (Senegal, members of the West African Economic and Monetary Union), monetary policy tightening, costlier imports, currency depreciations, and high public debt all contributed to slower growth in 2022. Several large agricultural commodity exporters (Ethiopia, Kenya) endured prolonged droughts, which further lowered agricultural output—a sector already stressed by high production costs. Activity in the region's small states, which have been struggling with rising import prices, was dragged down by slower inflows of remittances (Cabo Verde, Comoros, The Gambia). In contrast, growth in some tourism-reliant economies (Mauritius, the Seychelles) picked up last year, benefiting from the recovery of global tourism (chapter 4).

Pandemic-related deteriorations in fiscal positions lingered in 2022, with government debt remaining above 60 percent of GDP in almost half of SSA economies. Diverging global prices of energy and metals have, however, led to varying fiscal dynamics across the region. Among SSA's oil-producing countries, government debt fell by nearly 10 percent of GDP on average, due to fiscal surpluses and stronger exchange rates. In contrast, debt sustainability and investor sentiment deteriorated further in many other countries, leading to rising borrowing costs (credit spreads widened markedly in several countries, for example, in Ghana and Zambia), capital outflows, credit rating downgrades (Ghana, Nigeria), and large currency depreciations. Financing deficits also became increasingly challenging, with international bond issuance by governments in the region stalling in the second half of last year.

Outlook

Growth in SSA is projected to edge up in 2023 to 3.6 percent—a 0.2 percentage point downward revision from the June forecast—before picking up to 3.9 percent, in 2024 (figure 2.6.2.A). Even though an expected moderation of global commodity prices should temper cost-of-living increases, tighter policy stances to address elevated inflation and public debt will weigh on domestic demand. Meanwhile, weakening growth in advanced economies and China is expected to pose headwinds for external demand, particularly among exporters of industrial commodities. Constrained access to external financing, tight fiscal space, and high borrowing costs are expected to markedly limit many governments' ability to spur faster growth.

The modest downward revision to regional growth this year primarily reflects small downgrades for the largest economies. Forecast revisions for individual countries are mixed, with downward revisions for almost 60 percent of countries. This includes downward revisions for over 70 percent of metal exporters, which are expected to be affected by the further easing of global metal prices. In more diversified economies, lower prices of imports are expected to have a stronger positive effect by boosting activity in services and

FIGURE 2.6.2 SSA: Outlook

Growth in 2023-24 is projected to remain below long-term averages in several economies as cost-of-living increases and tighter policies continue to dent domestic demand. Subdued growth will make it difficult to reverse increases in food insecurity and poverty. Many commodity producers, particularly of metals, face weakening global demand and lower export prices. Tight global financial conditions are raising borrowing costs across the region, heightening debt vulnerabilities.

A. GDP growth

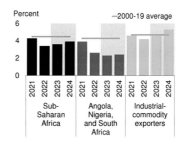

B. Food insecurity in SSA

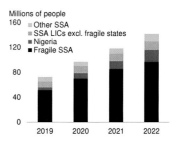

C. Commodity prices

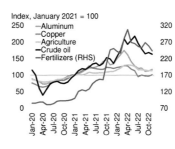

D. Change in 10-year government bond yields in 2022

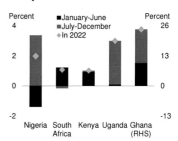

Sources: FSIN and GNAFC (2022); Haver Analytics; World Bank.
Note: EMDEs = emerging market and developing economies; Fragile SSA = SSA countries with fragile and conflict affected situations; LICs = low income countries; SSA = Sub-Saharan Africa.
A. Aggregate growth rates calculated using constant GDP weights at average 2010-19 prices and market exchange rates. Other SSA excludes Angola, Nigeria, and South Africa.
B. Bars show the number of people in food crisis as classified by the Integrated Food Security Phase Classification (IPC/CH) Phase 3, that is, in acute food insecurity crisis or worse. Data for 2022 are estimates as of September 2022.
C. Last observation is November 2022.
D. Last observation is December 8, 2022.

agriculture; nevertheless, for one in three SSA economies, the growth projection for 2023 has been revised down for the second time in a year. This mainly reflects larger-than-expected and more persistent damage to consumer demand from sharp cost-of-living increases, amplified by other vulnerabilities, such as unfavorable weather, high debt, and insecurity.

The ongoing cost-of-living increases are expected to temper the growth of real incomes and domestic demand across the region—especially in LICs, where the number of vulnerable people increased sharply in 2022 (WFP and FAO 2022).

Increased insecurity has worsened fragility and is expected to reduce access to food for many more people across the region (figure 2.6.2.B). The resulting increases in the number of poor, especially in countries where many people were already experiencing acute food insecurity because of violence and conflict (Nigeria, South Sudan) are expected to weigh on economic recoveries.

Per capita income in the region as a whole is expected to grow by only 1.2 percent a year on average in 2023-24, half a percentage point below its trend rate before the pandemic. Such meagre growth is especially concerning in those countries where poverty increased significantly because of pandemic and worsened fragility. Per capita incomes in almost half of the region are forecast to remain below 2019 levels this year.

In *Nigeria*, growth is projected to decelerate to 2.9 percent in 2023 and remain at that pace in 2024—barely above population growth. A growth momentum in the non-oil sector is likely to be restrained by continued weakness in the oil sector. Existing production and security challenges, and a moderation in oil prices are expected to hinder a recovery in oil output. Policy uncertainty, sustained high inflation, and rising incidence of violence are anticipated to temper growth. Growth in agriculture is expected to soften because of the damage from last year's floods. The fiscal position is expected to remain weak because of high borrowing costs, lower energy prices, a sluggish growth of oil production, and a subdued activity in the non-oil sectors.

Growth in *South Africa* is forecast to weaken further to 1.4 percent this year before picking up to a still sluggish 1.8 percent in 2024. Weak activity in major trading partners (China, the euro area, the United Kingdom, and the United States account for over 40 percent of exports), tight global financial conditions, political and policy uncertainty will constrain growth and widen external vulnerabilities. Further domestic policy tightening is bound to temper domestic demand and investment, while high unemployment and worsening power cuts will also weigh on growth. Implementation of much-needed reforms to remove structural bottlenecks has remained slow.

Recent improvements in public finances are expected to provide some room for policy support, for example, the extension of COVID-19 relief grants. Nevertheless, fiscal policy is expected to remain a drag on growth as further consolidation measures are required to lower elevated debt burdens, especially given the possibility that the government may take on a large portion of the debt of the state power company Eskom.

Growth in *Angola* is projected to slow to 2.8 percent on average in 2023-24, a downward revision of 0.4 percentage point from the June forecasts. More stable oil production and revenues are expected to support activity in the non-oil economy and help improve the fiscal position, but lower oil prices along with fiscal consolidation measures to reduce public debt are expected to weigh on government spending and constrain growth.

Elsewhere in the region, growth is anticipated to strengthen to 5.0 percent on average in 2023-24, slightly below the June forecast. A delayed recovery from the COVID-19 pandemic is expected to pick up steam in many countries as the easing of the cost-of-living pressures boosts domestic demand. Some energy producers are expected to benefit from increasing exports of oil and natural gas (Mozambique, Niger, Senegal). The external environment, however, is anticipated to remain challenging for some countries, with further declines in several global commodity prices dampening export revenues and growth. Most countries are also expected to continue to face elevated prices for imported fertilizers and fuel, albeit somewhat off the highs reached last year (figure 2.6.2.C). Large current account deficits are likely to keep currencies under pressure in several countries, adding to inflation and external vulnerabilities (The Gambia, Ghana). In some agricultural commodity producers unfavorable weather conditions (for example, below-average rainfall in East Africa) are expected to persist, exacerbating the adverse impact of costlier farming inputs on agricultural production. Elevated levels of violence and conflict in many fragile countries are expected to dampen growth, especially among the region's LICs (Burkina Faso, Mali, South Sudan).

Over 60 percent of countries in SSA already in, or at high risk of, debt distress, and with tighter access to external financing, fiscal efforts to support demand and activity are likely to be heavily constrained. Capital flows to SSA are expected to remain weak amid sharply increased credit risks, as soaring borrowing costs exacerbate debt sustainability concerns across the region (figure 2.6.2.D).

Risks

The baseline projections remain subject to multiple downside risks amid continuing uncertainty about the war in Ukraine, the Black Sea Grain Initiative, the degree of global and domestic monetary tightening that will be needed to subdue inflation, and the extent of deceleration of the world economy. Commodity prices may drop further than assumed if growth in major economies falls short of projections (World Bank 2022d). Policy tightening across SSA may have to pick up pace if price pressures persist or if risks of debt distress are increased by higher global interest rates and currency depreciations (figure 2.6.3.A).

If global inflationary pressures intensify further or persist longer than expected, global interest rates may rise by more than assumed, leading to an even greater deterioration of financial conditions in SSA and increased difficulty in regaining access to international borrowing markets. This could trigger financial distress and government debt defaults. Government debt distress would have large adverse spillovers on growth and financial stability in many countries, especially where banks are heavily exposed to sovereign debt (Ghana, Kenya, Sierra Leone). Increased reliance on non-concessional borrowing in SSA could cause a sharp rise in debt service costs if global interest rates keep rising (figure 2.6.3.B).

Despite the expected moderation of global food price inflation, a sudden disruption in global or local supplies of staple foods could trigger bouts of substantial price rises across the region (Okou, Spray, and Unsal 2022). SSA food markets remain tight because of declines in stocks, limited imports, weather-induced disruptions to production (droughts in Kenya, Somalia; floods in

FIGURE 2.6.3 SSA: Risks

Inflationary pressures that are more intense or persistent than assumed could trigger additional policy tightening both globally and within SSA, further constraining growth. A surge in violence and insecurity could cause substantial disruptions to activity. Greater-than-expected policy tightening across the world could sharply increase borrowing costs in the region. Low vaccination rates and constrained fiscal space highlight a limited ability to respond to future public health emergencies.

A. Changes in policy interest rates since January 2020

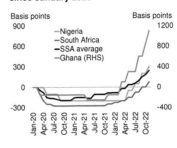

B. SSA credit spreads in 2022

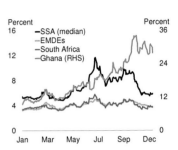

C. Violence in SSA

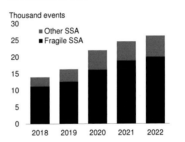

D. COVID-19 vaccinations

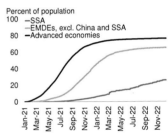

Sources: Armed Conflict Location & Event Data Project (ACLED), https://www.acleddata.com; J.P. Morgan; Ritchie et al. 2022; World Bank.
Note: EMDEs = emerging market and developing economies; Fragile SSA = SSA countries with fragile and conflict affected situations; SSA = Sub-Saharan Africa.
A. Change in policy rates since January 2002. SSA average is the unweighted average for 8 SSA EMDEs. Last observation is November 2022.
B. SSA (median) is a median for 9 SSA EMDEs. Last observation is December 13, 2022.
C. Cumulative number of reported violent events during the first 11 months of each year; violent events include battles, explosions, violence against civilians, riots and protests. Last observation is December 2, 2022.
D. Total number of people who are fully vaccinated. Last observation is December 15, 2022.

Nigeria, South Sudan), high prices of farming inputs, and the negative impact of insecurity on farming and suppliers' ability to access food markets (Burkina Faso, Mali). These conditions make food systems in SSA particularly vulnerable to various shocks, including volatility of global food prices and climate change (Baptista et al. 2022; Jafino et al. 2020). Costlier farming inputs, a decline in fertilizer use, and persistent droughts could also lead to lasting damage to production of staple crops in SSA, further depleting stocks and worsening poverty and food insecurity (IFA 2022). The current La Niña climate episode is expected to last for an unusual third consecutive year likely prolonging severe drought conditions in the Horn of Africa. In some affected countries (Somalia, South Sudan) half of population is already acutely food insecure. As a result, even more people could be at high risk of starvation and famine.

Though a ceasefire agreement was reached in Ethiopia last November after two years of war, the incidence of violence and conflict in SSA remains elevated, particularly in the Sahel region, but also elsewhere, such as in Mozambique and Nigeria (figure 2.6.3.C). Such violence—a major driver of food insecurity and poverty—could further disrupt farming activities and the flow of human-itarian aid, as well as trigger delays of large-scale investment projects in extractive sectors in some countries. Increased fragility, which is often associ-ated with a severely reduced institutional capacity to address environmental and climate vulnera-bilities, could also significantly amplify the impact of climate change on poverty and food insecurity (Maino and Emrullahu 2022).

Although the COVID-19 pandemic is in retreat across the region, vaccination rates in SSA remain very low, while public health systems are still inadequately prepared to mount an effective response to future outbreaks of infectious diseases. As of end-December, just 28 percent of the population in SSA has been fully vaccinated, compared to 65 percent in EMDEs as a whole (figure 2.6.3.D). This is especially concerning considering that the fiscal space needed to address public health emergencies is largely depleted in many countries.

TABLE 2.6.1 Sub-Saharan Africa forecast summary

(Real GDP growth at market prices in percent, unless indicated otherwise)

Percentage point differences from
June 2022 projections

	2020	2021	2022e	2023f	2024f	2022e	2023f	2024f
EMDE SSA, GDP [1]	**-2.0**	**4.3**	**3.4**	**3.6**	**3.9**	**-0.3**	**-0.2**	**-0.1**
GDP per capita (U.S. dollars)	-4.5	1.7	0.9	1.0	1.4	-0.2	-0.3	-0.1
(Average including countries that report expenditure components in national accounts) [2]								
EMDE SSA, GDP [2,3]	-2.0	4.3	3.4	3.6	3.9	-0.3	-0.2	-0.1
PPP GDP	-1.8	4.2	3.4	3.6	4.0	-0.3	-0.3	-0.1
Private consumption	-1.6	10.1	3.7	3.1	3.4	0.4	-0.5	-0.2
Public consumption	9.0	-2.1	0.7	0.7	2.8	-2.3	-0.2	0.1
Fixed investment	-2.0	6.0	6.8	7.0	7.3	1.4	-0.2	-0.8
Exports, GNFS [4]	-15.7	2.7	6.0	6.6	6.3	0.0	0.4	0.5
Imports, GNFS [4]	-19.5	15.5	8.7	7.2	7.4	2.2	1.0	1.2
Net exports, contribution to growth	1.5	-3.0	-0.9	-0.5	-0.6	-0.6	-0.3	-0.3
Memo items: GDP								
Eastern and Southern Africa	-2.9	4.6	3.3	3.5	3.9	-0.1	-0.1	0.1
Western and Central Africa	-0.8	4.0	3.5	3.7	4.0	-0.5	-0.4	-0.3
SSA excluding Nigeria, South Africa, and Angola	0.2	4.6	4.2	4.8	5.3	-0.3	-0.3	-0.1
Oil exporters [5]	-2.0	3.1	3.1	2.9	3.0	-0.5	-0.5	-0.4
CFA countries [6]	0.5	4.1	4.3	5.2	5.7	-0.2	-0.1	-0.1
CEMAC	-1.8	1.2	3.2	3.0	3.2	-0.2	0.1	-0.2
WAEMU	1.8	5.9	4.9	6.4	7.0	-0.2	-0.3	-0.2
SSA3	-4.1	3.9	2.6	2.3	2.4	-0.2	-0.2	-0.3
Nigeria	-1.8	3.6	3.1	2.9	2.9	-0.3	-0.3	-0.3
South Africa	-6.3	4.9	1.9	1.4	1.8	-0.2	-0.1	0.0
Angola	-5.8	0.8	3.1	2.8	2.9	0.0	-0.5	-0.3

Source: World Bank.

Note: e = estimate; f = forecast; PPP = purchasing power parity; EMDE = emerging market and developing economy. World Bank forecasts are frequently updated based on new information and changing (global) circumstances. Consequently, projections presented here may differ from those contained in other Bank documents, even if basic assessments of countries' prospects do not differ at any given moment in time.

1. GDP and expenditure components are measured in average 2010-19 prices and market exchange rates.

2. Subregion aggregate excludes the Central African Republic, Eritrea, Guinea, São Tomé and Príncipe, Somalia, and South Sudan, for which data limitations prevent the forecasting of GDP components.

3. Subregion growth rates may differ from the most recent edition of Africa's Pulse (https://www.worldbank.org/en/region/afr/publication/africas-pulse) because of data revisions and the inclusion of the Central African Republic and São Tomé and Príncipe in the subregion aggregate of that publication.

4. Exports and imports of goods and nonfactor services (GNFS).

5. Includes Angola, Cameroon, Chad, the Republic of Congo, Equatorial Guinea, Gabon, Ghana, Nigeria, and South Sudan.

6. The Financial Community of Africa (CFA) franc zone consists of 14 countries in Sub-Saharan Africa, each affiliated with one of two monetary unions. The Central African Economic and Monetary Union (CEMAC) comprises Cameroon, the Central African Republic, Chad, the Republic of Congo, Equatorial Guinea, and Gabon; the West African Economic and Monetary Union (WAEMU) comprises Benin, Burkina Faso, Côte d'Ivoire, Guinea-Bissau, Mali, Niger, Senegal, and Togo.

TABLE 2.6.2 Sub-Saharan Africa country forecasts[1]

(Real GDP growth at market prices in percent, unless indicated otherwise)

Percentage point differences from June 2022 projections

	2020	2021	2022e	2023f	2024f	2022e	2023f	2024f
Angola	-5.8	0.8	3.1	2.8	2.9	0.0	-0.5	-0.3
Benin	3.8	7.2	5.7	6.2	6.0	-0.2	0.1	0.0
Botswana	-8.7	11.4	4.1	4.0	4.0	0.0	0.0	0.0
Burkina Faso	1.9	6.9	4.3	5.0	5.3	-0.5	-0.4	0.0
Burundi	0.3	1.8	2.1	3.0	4.0	-0.4	-0.3	-0.1
Central African Republic	1.0	1.0	1.5	3.0	3.8	-1.7	-0.4	-0.2
Cabo Verde	-14.8	7.0	4.0	4.8	5.7	-1.5	-1.3	-0.3
Cameroon	0.3	3.6	3.8	4.3	4.6	-0.2	0.0	0.2
Chad	-1.6	-1.2	3.1	3.3	3.3	0.3	-0.2	-0.6
Comoros	-0.3	2.2	1.4	3.3	3.8	-1.4	0.2	0.1
Congo, Dem. Rep.	1.7	6.2	6.1	6.4	6.6	0.1	0.0	0.5
Congo, Rep.	-6.2	-2.2	1.9	3.7	4.5	-1.6	0.7	0.0
Côte d'Ivoire	2.0	7.0	5.7	6.8	6.6	0.0	0.0	0.0
Equatorial Guinea	-4.9	-1.6	3.2	-2.6	-3.4	1.4	0.0	-1.3
Eritrea	-0.5	2.9	2.5	2.7	2.9	-2.2	-0.9	-0.8
Eswatini	-1.6	7.9	1.1	2.6	2.7	-0.9	0.8	0.9
Ethiopia[2]	6.1	6.3	3.5	5.3	6.1	0.2	0.1	0.2
Gabon	-1.8	1.5	2.7	3.0	2.9	-0.6	0.4	-0.1
Gambia, The	0.6	4.3	3.5	4.0	5.5	-2.1	-2.2	-1.0
Ghana	0.5	5.4	3.5	2.7	3.5	-2.0	-2.5	-1.5
Guinea	4.9	3.9	4.6	5.3	5.6	0.3	-0.6	-0.2
Guinea-Bissau	1.5	5.0	3.5	4.5	4.5	0.0	0.0	0.0
Kenya	-0.3	7.5	5.5	5.0	5.3	0.0	0.0	0.0
Lesotho	-8.4	1.3	2.6	2.3	2.9	0.3	0.2	0.9
Liberia	-3.0	5.0	3.7	4.7	5.7	-0.7	-0.1	0.5
Madagascar	-7.1	4.4	2.6	4.2	4.6	0.0	0.0	0.0
Malawi	0.8	2.8	1.5	3.0	3.4	-0.6	-1.3	-0.8
Mali	-1.2	3.1	1.8	4.0	4.0	-1.5	-1.3	-1.0
Mauritania	-0.9	2.4	4.0	5.1	7.9	-0.5	-0.2	0.2
Mauritius	-14.6	3.6	5.8	5.5	4.2	-0.1	-0.5	0.3
Mozambique	-1.2	2.3	3.7	5.0	8.0	0.1	-1.0	2.2
Namibia	-8.0	2.7	2.8	2.0	1.9	-0.1	-0.1	-0.1
Niger	3.6	1.4	5.0	7.1	10.1	-0.2	0.0	-0.3
Nigeria	-1.8	3.6	3.1	2.9	2.9	-0.3	-0.3	-0.3
Rwanda	-3.4	10.9	6.0	6.7	7.0	-0.8	-0.5	-0.4
São Tomé and Príncipe	3.1	1.8	1.1	2.1	2.4	-1.7	-0.9	-0.9
Senegal	1.3	6.1	4.8	8.0	10.5	0.4	-0.5	-0.1
Seychelles	-7.7	7.9	11.0	5.2	4.8	6.4	-0.5	-0.2
Sierra Leone	-2.0	4.1	3.7	3.7	4.4	-0.2	-0.7	-0.4
South Africa	-6.3	4.9	1.9	1.4	1.8	-0.2	-0.1	0.0
Sudan	-3.6	-1.9	0.3	2.0	2.5	-0.4	0.0	0.0
South Sudan[2]	9.5	-5.1	-2.8	-0.8	2.1	-2.0	-3.3	-1.9
Tanzania	2.0	4.3	4.6	5.3	6.1	-0.7	-0.4	0.0
Togo[3]	1.8	5.3	4.8	5.6	6.4	-0.2	-0.2	0.0
Uganda[2]	3.0	3.5	4.7	5.5	6.1	1.0	0.4	-0.4
Zambia	-3.0	3.6	3.0	3.9	4.1	-0.3	0.3	0.1
Zimbabwe	-5.3	5.8	3.4	3.6	3.6	-0.3	0.0	0.0

Source: World Bank.

Note: e = estimate; f = forecast. World Bank forecasts are frequently updated based on new information and changing (global) circumstances. Consequently, projections presented here may differ from those contained in other Bank documents, even if basic assessments of countries' prospects do not significantly differ at any given moment in time.

1. Data are based on GDP measured in average 2010-19 prices and market exchange rates.
2. Fiscal-year based numbers.
3. For Togo, growth figure in 2019 is based on pre-2020 rebasing GDP estimates.

References

Ari, A., N. Arregui, S. Black, O. Celasun, D. Iakova, A. Mineshima, V. Mylonas, et al. 2022. "Surging Energy Prices in Europe in the Aftermath of the War: How to Support the Vulnerable and Speed up the Transition Away from Fossil Fuels." IMF Working Paper 22/152, International Monetary Fund, Washington, DC.

Arroyo Marioli, F., and C. A. Vegh. Forthcoming. "Fiscal Procyclicality in Commodity Exporting Countries: How Much Does It Pour and Why." World Bank, Washington, DC.

Artuc, E., G. Falcone, G. Porto, and B. Rijkers. 2022. "War-Induced Food Price Inflation Imperils the Poor." VoxEU.org, CEPR Policy Portal, April 1. https:// voxeu.org/article/war-induced-food-price-inflation-imp erils-poor.

Baptista, D., M. Farid, D. Fayad, L. Kemoe, L. Lanci, P. Mitra, T. Muehlschlegel, C. Okou, J. Spray, K. Tuitoek, and F. Unsal. 2022. "Climate Change and Chronic Food Insecurity in Sub-Saharan Africa." Departmental Paper 2022/16, International Monetary Fund, Washington, DC.

Baumeister, C., G. Verduzco-Bustos, F. Ohnsorge. 2022. "Special Focus: Pandemic, War, Recession: Drivers of Aluminum and Copper Prices" In *Commodity Markets Outlook*, October. Washington, DC: World Bank.

Benhassine, N., Z. Kherous, S.S.A Mohibi; M.M. Do Rosario Francisco. 2022. *From Swimming in Sand to High and Sustainable Growth—A Roadmap to Reduce Distortions in the Allocation of Resources and Talent in the Pakistani Economy.* Pakistan Economic Memorandum. Washington, DC: World Bank.

Claessens, S., and M. A. Kose. 2013. "Financial Crises: Explanations, Types, and Implications." IMF Working Paper 13/28, International Monetary Fund, Washington, DC.

Comtrade (database). United Nations. Accessed on November 30, 2022. https://comtrade.un.org.

de Paulo, L. D., R. C. de Andrade Lima, and R. Tigre. 2022. "Corruption and Economic Growth in Latin America and the Caribbean." *Review of Development Economics* 26 (2): 756-73.

de la Torre, A., F. Filippini, and A. Ize. 2016. *The Commodity Cycle in Latin America: Mirages and Dilemmas.* April. Washington, DC: World Bank.

Di Bella, G., M. J. Flanagan, K. Foda, S. Maslova, A. Pienkowski, M. Stuermer, and F. G, Toscani. 2022. "Natural Gas in Europe: The Potential Impact of Disruptions to Supply." IMF Working Paper 22/145, International Monetary Fund, Washington, DC.

Dieppe, A., S. Kilic-Celik, and C. Okou. 2020. "Implications of Major Adverse Events on Productivity." Policy Research Working Paper, World Bank, Washington, DC.

Dilip, A. and S. Kundu. 2020. "Climate Change: Macroeconomic Impact and Policy Options for Mitigating Risks." *RBI Bulletin*, April. Reserve Bank of India, New Delhi.

Espitia, A., N. Rocha, and M. Ruta. 2022. "How Export Restrictions Are Impacting Global Food Prices." *Private Sector Development Blog.* July 6, 2022. https:// blogs.worldbank.org/psd/how-export-restrictions-are-impacting-global-food-prices.

FSIN (Food Security Information Network) and GNAFC (Global Network Against Food Crises). 2022. *Global Report on Food Crises. Mid-Year Update.* Rome: Food Security Information Network.

Government of Pakistan, Asian Development Bank, European Union, United Nations Development Programme, and World Bank. 2022. *Pakistan Floods 2022: Post-Disaster Needs Assessment.* Islamabad: Ministry of Planning Development and Special Initiatives.

IFA (International Fertilizer Association). 2022. *Medium-Term Fertilizer Outlook 2022-2026.* Paris,: International Fertilizer Association.

IMF (International Monetary Fund). 2016. *Regional Economic Outlook: Western Hemisphere.* April. Washington, DC: International Monetary Fund.

IPCC (Intergovernmental Panel on Climate Change). 2022. "Climate Change 2022: Impacts, Adaptation and Vulnerability." IPCC Sixth Assessment Report, Geneva, Switzerland.

Jafino, B., B. Walsh, J. Rozenberg, and S. Hallegatte. 2020. "Revised Estimates of the Impact of Climate Change on Extreme Poverty by 2030." Policy Research Working Paper 9417, World Bank, Washington, DC.

Kehoe, T. J., and J. P. Nicolini. 2021. *A Monetary and Fiscal History of Latin America, 1960-2017.* Minneapolis, MN: University of Minnesota Press.

Kose, M. A., S. Kurlat, F. Ohnsorge, and N. Sugawara. 2022. "A Cross-Country Database of Fiscal Space."

Journal of International Money and Finance 128 (November): 102682.

Maino, R., and D. Emrullahu. 2022. "Climate Change in Sub-Saharan Africa Fragile States: Evidence from Panel Estimations." IMF Working Paper 22/54, International Monetary Fund, Washington, DC.

Malmendier, U., and S. Nagel. 2016. "Learning from Inflation Experiences." *The Quarterly Journal of Economics* 131 (1): 53-87.

Montenegro, C. E., and H. A. Patrinos. 2014. "Comparable Estimates of Returns to Schooling around the World." Policy Research Working Paper 7020, World Bank, Washington, DC.

NEITI (Nigeria Extractive Industries Transparency Initiative). 2022. *NEITI 2020 Oil and Gas Industry Report.* Abuja, Nigeria: Nigeria Extractive Industries Transparency Initiative.

Okou, C., J. Spray, and F. Unsal. 2022. "Staple Food Prices in Sub-Saharan Africa: An Empirical Assessment." Working Paper 22/135, International Monetary Fund, Washington, DC.

Oxford Economics. 2019. "Global Economic Model." July, Oxford Economics, Oxford, UK.

Ritchie, H., E. Mathieu, L. Rodés-Guirao, C. Appel, C. Giattino, E. Ortiz-Ospina, J. Hasell, B. Macdonald, D. Beltekian, and M. Roser. 2022. "Coronavirus Pandemic (COVID-19)". Published online at *OurWorldInData.org.* Accessed November 30, 2022. Available at https://ourworldindata.org/coronavirus.

Rother, B., S. Sosa, D. Kim, L. Kohler, G. Pierre, N. Kato, M. Debbich, et al. 2022. "Tackling the Global Food Crisis: Impact, Policy Response, and the Role of the IMF." Note 2022/004, International Monetary Fund, Washington, DC.

Scandurra, G., A. A. Romano, M. Ronghia, and A. Carforab. 2018. "On the Vulnerability of Small Island Developing States: A Dynamic Analysis." *Ecological Indicators* 84 (January): 382-392.

Singh, D. P., A. Mishra, and P. Shaw. 2022. "Taking Cognisance of Households' Inflation Expectations in India." RBI Working Paper 02, Reserve Bank of India, New Delhi.

UNHCR (United Nations High Commissioner for Refugees). 2022. "Ukraine Situation: Flash Update #8." UNHCR Regional Bureau for Europe. April 13. https://data2.unhcr.org/en/documents/details/92011.

Vorisek, D., G. Kindberg-Hanlon, R. Steinbach, T. Taskin, E. Vashakmadze, C. M. Wheeler, and L. S. Ye, L.S., 2021. "Regional Productivity: Trends, Explanations, and Policies." In *Global Productivity: Trends, Drivers and Policies*, edited by A. Dieppe, 213-310. Washington, DC: World Bank.

WFP (World Food Programme). 2022a. "Haiti Country Brief." August. World Food Programme, Rome.

WFP (World Food Programme). 2022b. *WFP Yemen Situation Report #11.* November. Rome: World Food Programme.

WFP (World Food Programme). 2022c. *Sri Lanka: Remote Household Food and Security Survey Brief.* November. Rome: World Food Programme.

WFP (World Food Programme) and FAO (The Food and Agriculture Organization of the United Nations). 2022. *Hunger Hotspots. FAO-WFP Early Warnings on Acute Food Insecurity: October 2022 to January 2023 Outlook.* Rome: Food and Agriculture Organization of the United Nations.

World Bank. 2014. *Turn Down the Heat: Confronting the New Climate Normal.* Washington, DC: World Bank.

World Bank. 2022a. *Reform for Recovery.* East Asia and the Pacific Economic Update October. Washington, DC: World Bank.

World Bank. 2022b. *Global Economic Prospects.* June. Washington, DC: World Bank.

World Bank. 2022c. *Braving the Storms.* East Asia and the Pacific Economic Update April. Washington, DC: World Bank.

World Bank. 2022d. *Commodity Markets Outlook: Pandemic, War, Recession: Drivers of Alminum and Copper Prices.* October. Washington, DC: World Bank.

World Bank. 2022e. *Global Economic Prospects.* January. Washington, DC: World Bank.

World Bank. 2022f. "EU Regular Economic Report: Living Up to Potential in the Wake of Adverse Shocks." Issue 8, World Bank, Washington, DC.

World Bank. 2022g. *Social Protection for Recovery.* Europe and Central Asia Economic Update October. Washington, DC: World Bank.

World Bank. 2022h. *Food Security Update.* November 10. Washington, DC: World Bank.

World Bank. 2022i. *New Approaches to Closing the Fiscal Gap.* Latin America and the Caribbean Economic Review. Washington, DC: World Bank.

World Bank. 2022j. *Poverty and Shared Prosperity 2022: Correcting Course.* Washington, DC: World Bank.

World Bank. 2022k. *MENA Economic Update: A New State of Mind.* October. Washington, DC: World Bank.

World Bank. 2022l. *Tunisia Economic Monitor: Navigating the Crisis during Uncertain Times.* October. Washington, DC: World Bank.

World Bank. 2022m. *Morocco Country Climate and Development Report.* CCDR Series. Washington, DC: World Bank.

World Bank. 2022n. *South Asia Economic Focus: Coping with Shocks: Migration and the Road to Resilience.* October. Washington, DC: World Bank.

World Bank. 2022o. *India Development Update: Navigating the Storm.* November. Washington, DC: World Bank.

World Bank. 2022p. *Pakistan Development Update: Inflation and the Poor.* October. Washington, DC: World Bank.

World Bank. 2022q. *Sri Lanka Development Update: Protecting the Poor and Vulnerable in a Time of Crisis.* October. Washington, DC: World Bank.

World Bank. 2022r. *Afghanistan Development Update: Adjusting to the New Realities.* October. Washington, DC: World Bank.

World Bank. 2022s. *Bangladesh Country Climate and Development Report.* CCDR Series. Washington, DC: World Bank.

World Bank. 2022t. *Nigeria Development Update. June 2022. The Continuing Urgency of Business Unusual.* Washington, DC: World Bank.

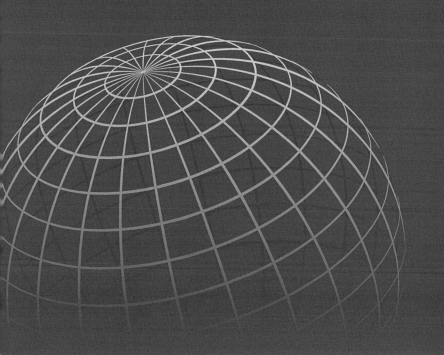

CHAPTER 3

INVESTMENT GROWTH
AFTER THE PANDEMIC

Investment growth in emerging market and developing economies (EMDEs) is expected to remain below its average rate of the past two decades through the medium term. This subdued outlook follows a decade-long, geographically widespread investment growth slowdown before the COVID-19 pandemic. An empirical analysis covering 2000-21 finds that periods of strong investment growth were associated with strong real output growth, robust real credit growth, terms of trade improvements, growth in capital inflows, and investment climate reform spurts. Each of these factors has been decreasingly supportive of investment growth since the 2007-09 global financial crisis. Weak investment growth is a concern because it dampens potential growth, is associated with weak trade, and makes achieving the development and climate-related goals more difficult. Policies to boost investment growth need to be tailored to country circumstances, but include comprehensive fiscal and structural reforms, including repurposing of expenditure on inefficient subsidies. Given EMDEs' limited fiscal space, the international community will need to significantly increase international cooperation, official financing and grants, and leverage private sector financing for adequate investment to materialize.

Introduction

As the COVID-19 pandemic began, emerging market and developing economies (EMDEs) had experienced a slowdown in real investment growth for most of the previous decade, from nearly 11 percent in 2010 to 3.4 percent in 2019. In EMDEs excluding China, investment growth tumbled more sharply: from 9 percent in 2010 to a mere 0.9 percent in 2019. The slowdown during the 2010s occurred in all EMDE regions, in both commodity-importing and commodity-exporting country groups, and in a large share of individual economies. In advanced economies, by contrast, investment growth was more sluggish but also more stable, hovering around its long-term average of 2 percent per year.

The pandemic triggered a severe investment contraction in EMDEs excluding China in 2020—a far deeper decline than in the 2009 global recession caused by the global financial crisis. EMDEs including China did not avoid an investment contraction in 2020, as they had in 2009 (figure 3.1.A). In advanced economies, however, investment shrank by less in 2020 than in 2009, thanks to large fiscal support packages and steep monetary easing. After a sharp rebound in 2021, investment growth in EMDEs is projected to revert to a pace still below the average during the previous two decades. The medium-term investment growth outlook remains subdued and has been downgraded substantially, along

with the GDP growth outlook, due to the effects of the Russian Federation's invasion of Ukraine on commodity markets and supply chains, and because of historically high debt-to-GDP ratios and the sharp tightening of financing conditions as monetary policy responds to rising inflation.

Slowing investment growth is a concern because investment is critical to sustaining long-term growth of potential output and per capita income. Capital accumulation raises labor productivity, the key driver of the long-term growth of real wages and household incomes through capital deepening—equipping workers with more capital—and by incorporating productivity-enhancing technological advances. Despite large unmet investment needs, investment growth has weakened in most EMDEs.

Partly because of these unmet investment needs, slowing investment growth has held back progress on meeting the Sustainable Development Goals (SDGs) and fulfilling commitments made under the Paris Agreement. Meeting these goals will require filling substantial unmet infrastructure needs, including growing needs for climate-resilient infrastructure and infrastructure that reduces net greenhouse gas emissions. Given limited fiscal space in EMDEs, scaling up investment will require additional financing from the international community and the private sector.

Against this backdrop, this chapter addresses four questions:

- How has investment growth evolved over the past decade?

Note: This chapter was prepared by Kersten Stamm and Dana Vorisek.

FIGURE 3.1 Investment growth

EMDEs experienced a broad-based slowdown in investment growth in the period between the 2007-09 global financial crisis and the COVID-19 pandemic. The pandemic-induced investment contraction in EMDEs excluding China in 2020 was historically large and much sharper than in advanced economies. The investment growth slowdown in EMDEs during the 2010s reflected underlying trends in both commodity-exporting and commodity-importing economies and in the three largest EMDEs, especially China.

A. Investment growth

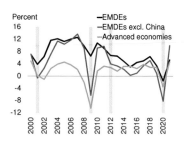

B. Investment growth relative to long-term average

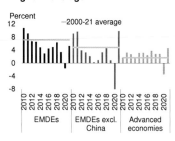

C. Contribution to EMDE investment growth, by commodity exporter status

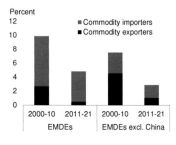

D. Contribution to EMDE investment growth, by country

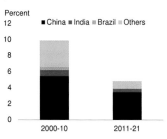

Sources: Haver Analytics; World Bank; World Development Indicators database.
Note: EMDEs = emerging market and developing economies. Investment refers to gross fixed capital formation. Investment growth is calculated with countries' real annual investment in constant U.S. dollars as weights. Shaded areas indicate global recessions (in 2009 and 2020) and slowdowns (in 2001 and 2012).
A.B. Sample includes 69 EMDEs and 35 advanced economies.
C.D. Bars show the percentage point contribution of each country or country group to EMDE investment growth during the indicated years. Height of the bars is average EMDE investment growth during the indicated years. Sample includes 69 EMDEs.

- What are the key factors associated with investment growth?

- What are the implications of weak investment growth for development prospects?

- Which policies can help promote investment growth?

Contributions. The chapter makes several contributions to the literature on investment. First, this is the first study to examine investment growth since the pandemic in a large sample of EMDEs. Previous studies analyzing investment in EMDEs have tended to be based on pre-global

financial crisis data, confined to analysis of the global financial crisis, or focused on specific regions.[1] Second, the chapter examines the likely medium- and long-term consequences of the damage to investment in EMDEs from the pandemic and the war in Ukraine, focusing on the effects on productivity, potential output growth, trade, and the ability to achieve the SDGs and climate-related goals. Third, the chapter provides a broad set of policy recommendations to revive investment growth, including new priorities created by the pandemic and climate change.

Main findings. The chapter presents four main findings.

First, compared to the years following the global financial crisis, the investment recovery following the COVID-19 pandemic is proceeding more slowly. The slow recovery partly reflects the widespread impact of the pandemic on investment, which shrank in nearly three-quarters of EMDEs during the pandemic. The effects of the pandemic and the war in Ukraine are expected to extend the prolonged and broad-based slowdown in investment growth seen in the 2010s. Both private and public investment growth were more sluggish during the 2010s than in the previous decade.

Second, investment growth in EMDEs over the past two decades reflects in large part the path of output, changes in the capital flow-to-GDP ratio, and low private sector real credit growth. The empirical analysis in the chapter also finds that terms of trade improvements and investment climate reform spurts are associated with strengthening real investment growth.

Third, investment growth in EMDEs in 2022 remained about 5 percentage points below the 2000-21 average, and nearly 0.5 percentage points below in EMDEs excluding China. For all

---

[1] Macroeconomic studies of investment include Anand and Tulin (2014); Bahal, Raissi, and Tulin (2018); Caselli, Pagano, and Schivardi (2003); Cerra et al. (2016); and Qureshi, Diaz-Sanchez, and Varoudakis (2015); Firm-level studies include Li, Magud, and Valencia (2015) and Magud and Sosa (2015). Kose et al. (2017) and World Bank (2019) examine investment trends and correlates in a large sample of EMDEs.

EMDEs, projected investment growth through 2024 will be insufficient to return investment to the level suggested by the pre-pandemic (2010-19) trend. Investment weakness dampens long-term output growth and productivity, is associated with weak global trade growth, and makes meeting the development and climate goals more challenging.

Fourth, a sustained improvement in investment growth in EMDEs requires the use of policy tools and international financial support, with appropriate prescriptions dependent on country circumstances. Macroeconomic policy can support investment in EMDEs in a variety of ways, including through preserving macroeconomic stability. Even with constrained fiscal space, spending on public investment can be boosted by reallocating expenditures, freeing resources by moving away from distorting subsidies, improving the effectiveness of public investment, and strengthening revenue collection. Structural policies also play a key role in creating conditions conducive to attracting investment. Institutional reforms could address a range of impediments and inefficiencies, such as high business startup costs, weak property rights, inefficient labor and product market policies, weak corporate governance, costly trade regulation, and shallow financial sectors. Setting appropriate, predictable rules governing investment, including for public-private partnerships (PPPs), is also important.

Data and definitions. In this chapter, investment refers to real gross fixed capital accumulation, including both private and public investment. Gross fixed capital formation includes produced tangible (for example, buildings, machinery, and equipment) and intangible assets (for example, computer software, mineral exploration, entertainment, and original writing or art) used for more than one year in the production of goods and services. Investment growth is calculated with countries' real annual investment at average 2010-19 prices and constant 2019 U.S. dollars as weights for 69 EMDEs and 35 advanced economies (table 3.1). These economies have represented about 97 percent of global GDP since the mid-2000s. A decomposition of investment into type of use, such as buildings, transport equipment, and information and communications technology (ICT) equipment, is not possible due

to limited comparable data for EMDEs. Data availability also prevents an econometric exploration of private and public investment.

Evolution of investment growth

Several key features of investment growth in EMDEs during the pre-pandemic decade are evident. There was a pronounced slowdown between 2010 and 2015, followed by a moderate recovery until 2018 (figure 3.1.B). The slowdown over the course of the decade was unmistakable, however. Investment growth in EMDEs fell from nearly 11 percent in 2010 to 3.4 percent in 2019. In EMDEs excluding China, investment growth tumbled more sharply: from 9 percent in 2010 to a mere 0.9 percent in 2019.

The slowdown in EMDEs in the 2010s occurred alongside broadly stable, albeit more sluggish, investment growth in advanced economies. Although investment growth in EMDEs remained above that in advanced economies, the difference in investment growth rates between EMDEs and advanced economies, especially in the second half of the decade, was far smaller than in the 2000s.

Weak investment growth during the 2010s was widespread across EMDEs. In each year between 2012 and 2020, investment growth was well below the pre-global financial crisis (2000-08) average in well over half of EMDEs. The slowdown during the 2010s occurred in both commodity-exporting and commodity-importing EMDEs, and in all EMDE regions (Vashakmadze et al. 2018; figure 3.1.C). Slowing investment growth in China made a large contribution to the aggregate EMDE slowdown (figure 3.1.D). In low-income countries (LICs), investment growth slowed sharply after a decade of solid investment growth that contributed to modest per capita income gains in the early 2000s. The slowdown was also observed in private and public investment growth, which grew at a slower pace in the 2010s than in the previous decade (figures 3.2.A, 3.2.B).

As business operations were disrupted and uncertainty spiked in 2020 due to the COVID-19 pandemic, aggregate investment in EMDEs

FIGURE 3.2 Private and public investment growth

Private and public investment growth in EMDEs excluding China were both weaker in the decade before the COVID-19 pandemic than during the years prior to the global financial crisis.

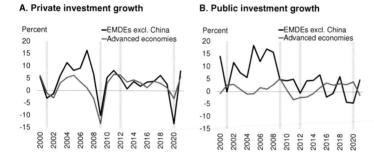

A. Private investment growth

B. Public investment growth

Sources: Haver Analytics; World Bank; World Development Indicators database.
A.B. Investment growth is calculated with countries' real annual investment in constant U.S. dollars as weights. Shaded areas indicate global recessions (in 2009 and 2020) and slowdowns (in 2001 and 2012). Sample includes 32 EMDEs excluding China and 11 advanced economies.

FIGURE 3.3 Investment around global recessions

Investment in EMDEs excluding China shrank by more than 8 percent during the global recession in the first year of the COVID-19 pandemic in 2020, about 2 percentage points more than the drop during the global financial crisis. Due to the large number of EMDEs impacted by the 2020 global recession, the investment recovery is proceeding more slowly than the recovery after the 2009 global recession.

A. Investment in EMDEs

B. Investment growth in EMDEs, excluding China

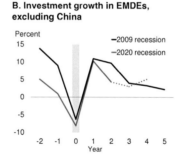

C. Investment in EMDEs, excluding China

D. Share of EMDEs with an investment contraction

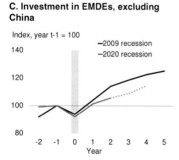

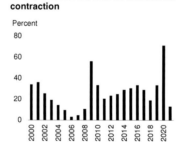

Sources: Haver Analytics; World Bank; World Development Indicators database.
Note: EMDEs = emerging market and developing economies. Investment refers to gross fixed capital formation. Investment growth is calculated with countries' real annual investment in constant U.S. dollars as weights.
A.-C. On the x-axis, year zero refers to the year of global recessions in 2009 and 2020. Dotted portions of lines are forecasts.
A.-D. Sample includes 69 EMDEs.

shrank, after avoiding a contraction in 2009, when the global financial crisis triggered a global recession (figure 3.3.A). EMDEs excluding China suffered an especially sharp investment contraction of more than 8 percent, a deeper decline than in 2009 (figures 3.3B, 3.3.C). A key difference between 2009 and 2020 is the number of affected EMDEs. About 70 percent of EMDEs experienced an investment contraction in 2020, well above the 55 percent of EMDEs in 2009 (figure 3.3.D). Regionally, the investment contraction in 2020 was sharpest in Latin America and the Caribbean and South Asia, the regions where output also declined the most.

Macroeconomic backdrop

Slowing investment growth in EMDEs in the decade or so before the pandemic occurred in the context of a worsening global macroeconomic environment. Compared to 2002-07, the global economy was characterized in 2010-19 by slower output growth, lower commodity prices, lower and more volatile capital inflows to EMDEs, higher economic and geopolitical uncertainty, and a substantial buildup of public and private debt (Kose and Ohnsorge 2020).

Weak activity. Investment tends to respond, and respond more than proportionately, to economic activity, a phenomenon dubbed the accelerator effect (Shapiro, Blanchard, and Lovell 1986). EMDE per capita output growth slowed sharply in the decade following the global financial crisis, from 7.5 percent in 2010 to a trough of 3.9 percent in 2019. There was a roughly parallel growth slowdown in EMDEs excluding China—from 5 percent in 2010 to 1.6 percent in 2019. To the extent that the slowing of output growth in EMDEs was structural rather than cyclical or otherwise transitory, the slowing of investment growth may also be expected to persist (Didier et al. 2015; World Bank 2022a). The sources of the slowdown in output growth varied across EMDEs, but they included lower commodity prices, spillovers from weak growth in major economies, weakening productivity growth, tightening financial conditions, and a maturing of supply chains that slowed global trade growth. A 1 percentage point decline in U.S. or euro area output growth has been found to reduce aggregate EMDE investment growth by more than 2 percentage points (World Bank 2017).

In China, growth rates slowed gradually as the economy was rebalanced from investment- and export-driven growth in manufacturing to consumption-driven growth in services. This transition reduced commodity demand and prices, with adverse spillovers to commodity-exporting EMDEs (Huidrom et al. 2020; World Bank 2016a). A 1 percentage point decline in China's output growth has been estimated to slow output growth in commodity-exporting EMDEs by about 1 percentage point after one year, with associated effects on investment growth (World Bank 2017).

Adverse terms of trade shocks. Almost two-thirds of EMDEs are reliant on exports of energy, metals, or agricultural commodities. Most commodity prices (in U.S. dollar terms) fell sharply from early-2011 peaks, with metals and energy prices plunging by more than 40 percent to troughs in 2016, followed by moderate recoveries in the following three years (figure 3.4.A). Surging U.S. oil production and a shift in OPEC policy in mid-2014 triggered an oil price plunge during 2014-16 that caused large disruptions in oil-exporting economies. At end-2019, energy prices were 21 percent below 2010 levels, and industrial metal and agricultural prices 19 percent and 13 percent below, respectively. As a result, the terms of trade of commodity exporters deteriorated by 6.5 percent between 2011 and 2019, and those of oil exporters by 27 percent. EMDEs with lower terms of trade growth experienced lower investment growth over 2000-21 (figure 3.4.B).

Rapid private sector credit growth and debt overhang. After rising continuously between 2001 and 2007, from close to zero to a peak above 30 percent, annual growth of real credit to the private sector (from domestic and foreign financial institutions) in EMDEs retreated during the 2008-09 global financial crisis. It subsequently slowed further, from 11.5 percent in 2011 to a trough of 4.8 percent in 2016, before stabilizing at about 6 percent in 2019-21 (figure 3.5.A). Average credit growth in 2011-19 was highly uneven across EMDEs, with some countries

FIGURE 3.4 Terms of trade and investment growth

The terms of trade of commodity exporters deteriorated between 2010 and 2019, reflecting steady declines in global energy, metals, and agricultural commodity prices between 2011 and 2016. EMDEs with higher terms of trade growth experienced higher investment growth over 2000-21.

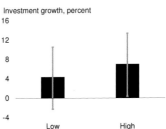

Source: Haver Analytics; World Bank; World Development Indicators database.
Note: EMDEs = emerging market and developing economies.
A. Energy index includes crude oil (85 percent weight), coal, and natural gas. Agriculture index includes 21 agricultural commodities. Metals and minerals index includes the six metals traded on the London Metal Exchange (aluminum, copper, lead, nickel, tin, zinc) plus iron ore. Prices indexes are calculated using commodity prices in nominal U.S. dollars. Last observation is December 2022.
B. Bars show group medians; vertical lines show interquartile ranges. "Low" and "high" indicate annual terms of trade growth in the top and bottom third of the distribution, respectively. Difference in medians between "low" and "high" subsamples is significant at the 1 percent level. Sample includes 69 EMDEs.

experiencing credit surges despite an overall downward trend. In contrast to the three decades before the global financial crisis, when around 40 percent of credit booms were accompanied or followed by investment surges within one or two years, credit booms since 2010 have been unusually "investment-less." Virtually none of the credit booms in EMDEs since the global financial crisis have been accompanied or followed by investment surges (World Bank 2017). In several countries, rapid credit growth instead fueled above-average consumption growth.

Despite declining credit growth since the global financial crisis, the ratio of outstanding credit to GDP in EMDEs has risen to record highs (figure 3.5.B). In the median EMDE, private credit as a share of GDP rose by 20 percentage points of GDP from 2000 to 2021, and by 27 percentage points in commodity-importing EMDEs. About four in ten EMDEs had private credit-to-GDP ratios exceeding 60 percent in 2021, up from one in ten in 2000. High leverage can lead to financial stress, restrict future access to credit, and divert resources from productive investment (Banerjee and Duflo 2005; World Bank 2022b). EMDEs

FIGURE 3.5 Credit growth, debt, and investment growth

Since 2011, weakening investment growth in EMDEs has been accompanied by slowing real credit growth to the private sector. EMDEs with higher credit growth experienced higher investment growth during 2000-21. Private sector debt has risen steadily, relative to GDP, in EMDEs over the past two decades. EMDEs with larger private debt-to-GDP ratios experienced slower investment growth during 2000-21.

A. Private credit growth in EMDEs

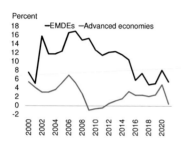

B. Private debt in EMDEs

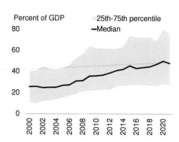

C. Investment growth in EMDEs with high and low credit growth, 2000-21

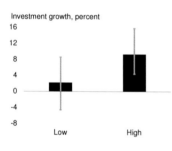

D. Investment growth in EMDEs with high and low private debt-to-GDP ratios, 2000-21

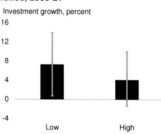

Sources: Bank for International Settlements; Haver Analytics; IMF International Financial Statistics database; World Bank; World Development Indicators database.
Note: EMDEs = emerging market and developing economies. Private debt refers to domestic credit to the private sector as a percent of GDP.
A. Private credit refers to real annual credit growth to the private sector. Lines show weighted averages with countries' real annual investment in constant U.S. dollars as weights. Sample includes 69 EMDEs and 35 advanced economies. Last observation is 2021.
B. Sample includes 71 EMDEs. Last observation is 2021.
C. D. Bars show group medians; vertical lines show interquartile ranges. "Low" and "high" indicate years when annual credit growth (C) and private debt-to-GDP ratios (D) were in the bottom and top third of the distribution, respectively, during 2000-21. Difference in medians between "low" and "high" and subsamples is significant at the 1 percent level.
C. Sample includes 69 EMDEs.
D. Sample includes 68 EMDEs.

with lower credit growth and higher private debt-to-GDP ratios experienced slower investment growth during 2000-21 (figures 3.5.C, 3.5.D).

Subdued and volatile capital inflows. Foreign direct investment (FDI) inflows to EMDEs more than tripled during 2000-19, accounting for about 40 percent of global capital inflows in 2015 and 62 percent in 2019. Since 2010, however, growth in FDI inflows to EMDEs has slowed,

partly due to weak activity in advanced economies. Growth of non-FDI inflows has shown more resilience and volatility, reflecting investors' search for higher yields amid low interest rates in advanced economies, a shift from bank to nonbank flows, and increased interest from institutional investors. (Cole et al. 2020; McQuade and Schmitz 2016). While the cost of capital is higher in EMDEs, the global financial crisis has led to a significant decrease in the average interest cost of outstanding government debt in advanced economies. In contrast, the average interest cost of outstanding government debt in EMDEs has barely decreased due to persistently high risk premia and increased reliance on international borrowing, particularly in foreign currency and on nonconcessional terms (United Nations 2022). Nevertheless, compared to the period leading up to the global financial crisis, 2000-07, there were twice as many sudden stop events in EMDEs in the years prior to the COVID-19 pandemic, 2011-19. During sudden stops, non-FDI inflows tend to decline much more sharply and for longer than FDI flows (Eichengreen, Gupta, and Masetti 2018).[2]

Heightened uncertainty. Policy uncertainty increased in many EMDEs after the global financial crisis, owing to geopolitical tensions in Eastern Europe, security challenges and conflicts in the Middle East, and acute domestic political tensions in several EMDEs. While the effects of uncertainty on investment and output growth are clearly negative, their scale depends on the context; they have been found to be more pronounced in countries that have a lower tolerance for uncertainty or where uncertainty interacts with other constraints such as access to credit (Carrière-Swallow and Céspedes 2013; Hofstede 2001; Inklaar and Yang 2012).

---

[2] The literature has produced mixed findings on the link between FDI and investment. Although there is evidence that FDI has a positive relationship with economic growth and investment, mainly in countries with well-developed financial markets, the literature has not found a consistent and significantly positive effect (Alfaro et al. 2004; OECD 2015). One possible explanation for the mixed evidence is that FDI crowds out domestic investment (Farla, de Crombrugghe, and Verspagen 2016).

Empirical analysis of investment growth

A panel regression analysis formalizes the role of macroeconomic factors in driving the investment weakness. Investment growth is estimated for 57 EMDEs covering 2000-21 as the dependent variable in a system generalized method of moments (GMM) panel regression, similar to Nabar and Joyce (2009). Drivers of investment growth, such as the marginal return to capital and risk-adjusted cost of capital, are proxied by real output growth, terms of trade growth, real private credit growth, the capital flow-to-GDP ratio, and a dummy variable for large improvements in the investment climate.

Real annual investment growth in EMDEs is found to be positively associated with real output growth, real credit growth, terms of trade improvements, increasing capital flow-to-GDP ratios, and investment climate reform spurts (annex 3.1; annex tables 3.1.1 and 3.1.2). These results are consistent with other studies finding multiple drivers of investment growth (G20 2016; IMF 2015; Libman, Montecito, and Razmi 2019). The importance of corporate borrowing as a driver of investment growth has also been found in other studies (Garcia-Escribano and Han 2015). The finding of a positive link between institutional quality, financial development, and investment growth is also in line with previous work (Lim 2014). While the coefficient of reform spurts is large and statistically significant, these events do not explain much of the variation in EMDE investment growth during 2000-21. On average, there were 0.8 investment profile reform spurts per year in the sample.

Using the results of the main regression to predict the contribution of the explanatory variables to investment growth shows that between 2000 and 2021, investment growth was primarily correlated with real output growth, followed by real credit growth (figure 3.6.A). Declining capital flow-to-GDP ratios contributed negatively to investment growth in commodity importers in multiple years since 2011, while energy exporting EMDEs experienced particularly low credit growth after 2015 (figures 3.6.B, 3.6.C, and 3.6.D).

FIGURE 3.6 Estimated contribution of explanatory variables to predicted investment growth

The investment growth slowdown in EMDEs in 2011-19 reflected, on average, declining output growth and real credit growth. In commodity importers, worsening real credit growth and several years of falling capital flow-to-GDP ratios weighed on investment growth. In energy exporting EMDEs, terms of trade growth has been highly correlated with investment growth, for example during the fall in commodity prices in 2015-16 and 2020 and the subsequent recoveries in 2017-18 and 2021.

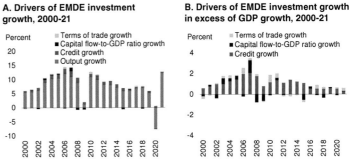

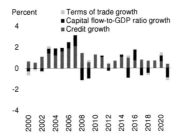

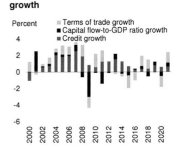

Source: World Bank.
Note: EMDEs = emerging market and developing economies.
A.-D. Estimated impact of explanatory variables on investment growth in 57 EMDEs during 2000-21, based on the system generalized method of moments (GMM) estimation presented in the chapter. Bars show the contribution of each explanatory variable to predicted investment growth (defined, for each variable, as the coefficient shown in the regression results in column 1 of annex table 3.1.1 multiplied by the actual value of the variable). For presentational clarity, the charts show only the four explanatory variables with the largest contributions to predicted investment growth. Panels B, C, and D highlight the smaller but still significant contribution to investment growth after accounting for output growth.

The contribution of terms of trade was more volatile and comoved strongly with investment growth in energy exporting EMDEs, particularly during periods of falling or rising oil prices in 2015-16, 2020, 2017-18, and 2021 (Stocker et al. 2018). The negative shock to the terms of trade of energy-commodity exporters may be viewed as having lowered investment growth by reducing the expected return to capital in the exporting sector (Bleaney and Greenaway 2001). In contrast, improving terms of trade did not significantly offset the factors that slowed investment growth in

FIGURE 3.7 Investment growth outlook

Investment growth in EMDEs is projected to be below its 2000-21 average rate in 2023 and 2024. The war in Ukraine adds to downside risks relating to the pandemic and could further hold back investment growth.

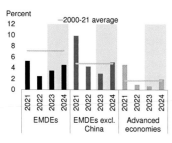

A. Investment growth: short-term forecasts

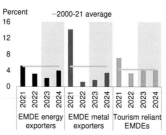

B. Investment growth: short-term forecasts, by EMDE subgroup

Sources: Haver Analytics; United Nations World Tourism Organization; World Bank; World Development Indicators database.
Note: EMDEs = emerging market and developing economies. Investment refers to gross fixed capital formation.
A.B. Investment growth is calculated with countries' real annual investment in constant U.S. dollars as weights. Sample includes 69 EMDEs and 35 advanced economies.
B. Sample includes 15 EMDE energy exporters, 9 EMDE metals exporters, and 14 tourism-reliant EMDEs.

commodity importers, in part because the improvement was less pronounced than the deterioration experienced by commodity exporters.

In 2020-21, the output growth collapse and rebound generated even larger swings in investment growth. In energy exporters, these were amplified by terms of trade swings in the same direction. Low real credit growth did not compensate for the collapse in output in 2020 and then held back the recovery in 2021 in both commodity exporters and importers alike.

Investment prospects

After a robust rebound in 2021, investment growth is projected to average 3.5 percent per year in EMDEs and 4.1 percent in EMDEs excluding China in 2022-24, below the long-term (2000-21) average rates for both country groups (figure 3.7.A). Commodity-exporting EMDEs are projected to have lower investment growth rates than tourism-reliant EMDEs (figure 3.7.B). Investment growth is projected to be below the individual country trend of the past 20 years for about three-fifths of EMDEs for 2023 and 2024. For all EMDEs, projected investment growth through 2024 will be insufficient to return investment to the level suggested by the pre-

pandemic trend from 2010-19 (the period between the highly disruptive 2009 and 2020 global recessions), in part due to slowing investment growth in China (figure 3.8.B). Investment in EMDEs excluding China, however, is projected to return to pre-pandemic trend by 2024, with the recovery after the global recession in 2020 taking a year longer than after the global financial crisis (figure 3.8.A).

The weak outlook for investment reflects several factors, and may deteriorate further if the global economy tips into recession (Guénette, Kose, and Sugawara 2022). Uncertainties about the post-pandemic economic landscape, the war in Ukraine, and high inflation may discourage investment for some time. Tighter financial conditions are limiting the fiscal support governments can provide to stimulate public investment (World Bank 2022c). At the same time, the legacy of high corporate debt may constrain investment growth after the pandemic (Caballero and Simsek 2020; Stiglitz 2020). In China, investment growth is projected to remain well below the average of the past two decades: regulatory curbs on the property and financial sectors and continuing mobility restrictions related to the pandemic will both be restraining factors, in an environment of slower economic growth.

Implications of weak investment growth

Weakening investment growth has lasting implications for global trade as well as for long-term output growth and EMDEs' ability to reach key development and climate-related goals. The slowing of capital accumulation in EMDEs, and consequently of technological progress embedded in investment, implies slowing productivity growth and potential output, with adverse implications for their ability to catch up with advanced economy per capita incomes.

Slower trade growth. In part because investment is more import intensive than other components of demand, weakening investment growth contributed to the slowdown in trade growth prior to the pandemic (figures 3.9.A and 3.9.B; Bobasu et al. 2020; IMF 2016; World Bank 2021b). The investment weakness was further accompanied by a pullback in cross-border investment by multi-national companies, which account for one-third of global trade (Lakatos and Ohnsorge 2017).

Global trade also propagates a pickup or slowdown in investment growth across countries (Freund 2016). Trade can facilitate more efficient allocation of capital goods, in turn improving overall productivity and rates of return on capital, thus encouraging investment (Mutreja, Ravikumar, and Sposi 2014). Countries engaged in deepening trade integration saw the price of investment goods fall relative to the prices of consumption goods, especially between 2005 and 2011, thus boosting investment rates (Lian et al. 2019). Indeed, trade openness has been found to be positively correlated with capital accumulation (Alvarez 2017; Irwin 2019; Sposi 2019; Wacziarg and Welch 2008).

Slower potential output growth. The prospect that investment growth will remain weak in the medium term raises fundamental concerns about the economic health of EMDEs, and about meeting the infrastructure needs of expanding and urbanizing populations in many EMDEs. Before the COVID-19 pandemic, potential output growth—the rate of growth achievable at full capacity utilization and full employment—had already slowed in EMDEs (Kilic Celik, Kose, and Ohnsorge 2020; World Bank 2018). Low investment growth in the medium term will further weaken potential output growth and result in capital accumulation contributing on average 0.6 percentage points per year less to EMDE potential growth in 2022-30 than in 2011-19. (figure 3.10.A; World Bank 2021a).

In addition to lowering capital accumulation, weak investment growth leads to weaker potential output growth partly by lowering total factor productivity (TFP) growth. Weaker investment and TFP growth can also be a symptom of market distortions that subsidize investment by less productive firms (Restuccia and Rogerson 2008). In contrast, increased investment often involves the adoption of productivity-enhancing tech-nologies, including in the investment goods sector itself (Colecchia and Schreyer 2002; Hsieh and Klenow 2007; OECD 2016a).

FIGURE 3.8 Investment compared to trend

After the COVID-19 pandemic, China is expected to be a source of weakness for EMDE investment. In EMDEs excluding China, investment is projected to return to the level of investment suggested by the pre-pandemic trend by 2024. Including China, EMDE investment will not return to trend.

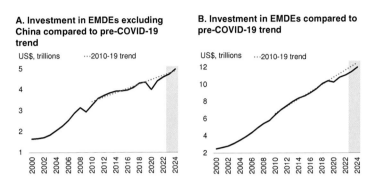

A. Investment in EMDEs excluding China compared to pre-COVID-19 trend

B. Investment in EMDEs compared to pre-COVID-19 trend

Sources: Haver Analytics; World Bank; World Development Indicators database.
Note: EMDEs = emerging market and developing economies. Investment refers to gross fixed capital formation. Investment levels after 2022 are forecast. Trendlines are calculated using linear regression on investment levels during 2010-19. Gray shading indicates forecasts. Sample includes 69 EMDEs.

FIGURE 3.9 Slowdown in growth of investment and trade

The investment growth slowdown in EMDEs after the global financial crisis was accompanied by a downturn in the growth of imports. Both imports and investment fell below their 2000-10 trend, and were further lowered by the COVID-19 pandemic.

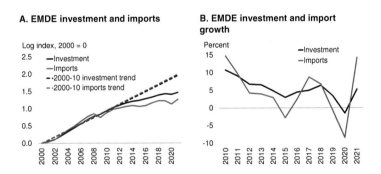

A. EMDE investment and imports

B. EMDE investment and import growth

Sources: Haver Analytics; World Bank; World Development Indicators database.
Note: EMDEs = emerging market and developing economies. Investment refers to gross fixed capital formation.
A. Levels of real gross fixed capital formation and imports.
B. Aggregate investment growth is calculated using real annual investment in constant U.S. dollars as weights.

Alongside slowing investment growth, TFP growth in EMDEs slowed in the decade prior to the pandemic, to 1.2 percent per year in 2010-19, on average, from 2.3 percent per year in 2000-08 (figures 3.10.B, 3.10.C). EMDEs with low investment growth tend to also have low TFP growth (figure 3.10.D). TFP growth weakened

FIGURE 3.10 Growth of investment, productivity, and potential output

EMDEs with low investment growth also tend to have low total factor productivity (TFP) growth. Fluctuations in investment growth in EMDEs between 2000 and 2020 are mirrored in fluctuations in TFP growth. Slowing investment and TFP growth have lowered potential growth in EMDEs, especially in commodity-importing EMDEs, among which China has an outsize weight.

A. Potential output growth

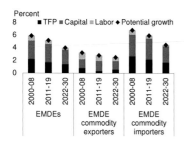

B. EMDE investment and total factor productivity

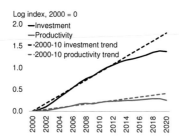

C. EMDE investment and total factor productivity growth

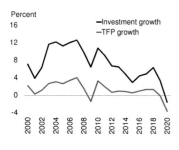

D. Total factor productivity growth in EMDEs with high and low investment growth, 2000-20

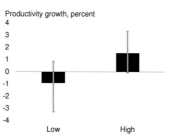

Sources: Dieppe (2021); Haver Analytics; International Labor Organization; Penn World Tables; UN World Population Prospects; World Bank; World Development Indicators database.
Note: EMDEs = emerging market and developing economies.
A. Potential output growth based on production function estimates. Sample includes 53 EMDEs.
B.C. Total factor productivity is derived from labor productivity (output per worker) by adjusting for human capital and capital deepening; see Dieppe (2021). Investment refers to gross fixed capital formation. Investment growth and TFP growth are calculated with countries' real annual investment in constant U.S. dollars as weights. Sample includes 69 EMDEs.
D. Bars show group medians; vertical lines show interquartile ranges. "Low" and "high" indicate years when annual investment growth was in the bottom and top third of the distribution, respectively, during 2000-20. Difference in medians between "high" and "low" subsamples is significant at the 1 percent level. Sample includes 69 EMDEs.

despite evidence of somewhat faster cross-country technology absorption from countries at the productivity frontier (Comin and Ferrer 2013; Moelders 2016). Weaker TFP growth would also be reflected in slower labor productivity growth—the key long-term driver of growth in real incomes (Blanchard and Katz 1999; Feldstein 2008).

Slower progress toward the SDGs and climate goals. Achieving the SDGs and climate-related goals requires increasing investment in EMDEs. Raising infrastructure investment is especially

important, following several years of subdued public infrastructure investment growth before the pandemic (Foster, Rana, and Gorgulu 2022; Vorisek and Yu 2020). Meeting greenhouse gas emissions reduction commitments, advancing the clean energy transition, and capping the rise in temperature is expected to require infrastructure investment and other adaptations of several trillion U.S. dollars per year (Black et al. 2022; IEA 2021; IPCC 2022; Songwe, Stern, and Bhattacharya 2022). For a partial set of EMDEs, building resilience to climate change and putting countries on track to reduce emissions by 70 percent compared to current levels by 2050 will require investment of 1 to 10 percent of GDP annually between 2022-30, with higher investment needed in LICs (World Bank 2022d). Similarly, the increase in spending needed to achieve the SDGs (relative to GDP) will be much larger for LICs than for the average EMDE (Gaspar et al. 2019). Substantial additional financing from the global community and the private sector will be needed to close investment gaps.

To achieve the SDGs related to infrastructure (electricity, transport, water supply and sanitation) and infrastructure-related climate change preparation (flood protection, irrigation) in low- and middle-income countries, an estimated investment of $1.5-$2.7 trillion per year is required on average during 2015-30, mostly for transport and electricity (Rozenberg and Fay 2019). This is equivalent to 4.5-8.2 percent of these countries' combined annual GDP, depending on policy choices and the quality and infrastructure service quality (figures 3.11.A, 3.11.B). The 4.5 percent of GDP estimate anticipates investment in renewable energy; transport and land-use planning that result in denser cities and more affordable, reliable public transport; as well as deployment of decentralized technologies such as minigrids and water purifications systems in rural areas.

Gaps in investment relative to the levels needed to reach the health-related SDGs also remain substantial (Stenberg et al. 2017; UNCTAD 2014). Likewise, investment in education is vital to achieving schooling-related SDGs, closing education achievement gaps created by the pandemic, and supporting long-term income growth (Barro 2013; Psacharopoulos et al. 2021).

Investment in infrastructure has multiple potential benefits. For one, it appears to be inversely correlated with income inequality in EMDEs. The channels through which infrastructure investment lowers income inequality and poverty can be direct, for example by employing low-income households or providing services at lower cost and better quality, or indirect, for example by lowering trade costs in stimulating economic growth.[3] Investment in climate-related resilience, adaptation, and mitigation is central to eliminating extreme poverty and achieving the SDGs. Such investment is perhaps most crucial in low-income and high-poverty countries, which are particularly vulnerable to the impacts of climate change and increasingly frequent adverse weather events on agriculture, energy generation and usage, water availability (World Bank 2022d). Green infrastructure and the adoption of environmentally sustainable technologies can support faster growth in the long term, while mitigating climate change (OECD 2020; Strand and Toman 2010). Improving and expanding access to infrastructure can enhance productivity (Bizimana et al. 2021; Calderón, Moral-Benito, and Servén 2015; Perez Sebastian and Steinbuks 2017). Public investment in infrastructure has also been found to create jobs, especially in LICs (Moszoro 2021).

Policies to promote investment growth

EMDEs' investment needs—to bolster resilience to climate change, improve social conditions, smooth the transition away from growth driven by natural resources, and support long-term growth of output and per capita incomes—are substantial. At the same time, investment growth prospects are weak, fiscal space is constrained, and macroeconomic conditions are uncertain. The urgent need to ramp up investment in EMDEs is clear. However, mobilization of sufficient financing to

---

FIGURE 3.11 Infrastructure spending needs related to the Sustainable Development Goals (SDGs)

Substantial gaps in infrastructure investment remain across EMDEs. Continued weak investment growth will make filling these large gaps more challenging.

A. Average annual investment needs in infrastructure sectors related to SDGs

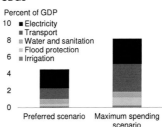

B. Average annual investment needs in infrastructure sectors related to SDGs, by region

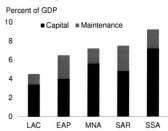

Sources: Rozenberg and Fay (2019); World Bank.
Note: EAP = East Asia and Pacific, LAC = Latin America and the Caribbean, MNA = Middle East and North Africa, SAR = South Asia, SSA = Sub-Saharan Africa, SDGs = Sustainable Development Goals.
A. Bars show average annual spending needs on capital (not including maintenance) during 2015-30. "Preferred scenario" is constructed using ambitious goals and high spending efficiency, and "maximum spending scenario" using ambitious goals and low spending efficiency. Country sample includes low- and middle-income countries, as defined in the technical appendix of Rozenberg and Fay (2019).
B. Bars show average annual spending needs during 2015-30.

---

close development-related investment gaps—from domestic resources, international assistance, borrowing from multilateral development banks, and foreign private sector investment—will be challenging (Bhattacharya and Stern 2021; United Nations 2019).

It is critical to design policy that can stimulate investment with lasting benefits while discouraging opportunistic behavior such as rent seeking, and to focus on high-quality investment projects (G20 2019). The challenges demand a multipronged strategy featuring a variety of fiscal and structural measures to boost public and private investment, with specific priorities driven by country circumstances.

Two areas with strong growth potential are investment in digital capabilities and the clean energy transition. The pandemic created new opportunities for the adoption of digital infrastructure in commerce and governance, while energy market volatility due to Russia's invasion of Ukraine and an increasingly urgent need to meet climate goals have made the development of clean, renewable, and affordable energy sources a priority. The pandemic also underscored the

---

[3] Calderón and Servén (2014) reviews multiple channels through which infrastructure investment affects the poor; Ferreira (1995) and Getachew (2010) discuss the role of public infrastructure investment and Madeiros, Ribeiro, and do Amaral (2021) the role of infrastructure investment; and Maliszewska and van der Mensbrugghe (2019) examine the role of infrastructure investment in lowering trade cost and generating opportunities for the poor.

potential for digital approaches to education in EMDEs, not to only to make up for the effect of lost schooling on future earnings, but also to help reduce inequality in education, provided that the necessary infrastructure and other appropriate underlying conditions are in place (Bashir et al. 2021; Muñoz-Najar et al. 2021; Wilichowski et al. 2021). In the long term, investment in education is needed to spur research and development, and ultimately, innovation.

Fiscal policy

Public investment in infrastructure, education, and health systems can be paid for in three main ways. First, funding can be raised through government borrowing, including through counter-cyclical fiscal stimulus programs during economic downturns. The extended low interest rate environment in the decade or more before 2022 offered an opportunity for many governments to borrow for investment projects, with limited risks to long-term fiscal sustainability (OECD 2016b). With debt burdens now at historically high levels and financing costs rising with global interest rates, however, EMDEs have limited capacity for expansionary fiscal policy financed by increased borrowing. Countries that are in or near debt distress can focus on fiscal sustainability in the short term to free fiscal resources for investment (World Bank 2022b).

Second, increased public investment can be financed by increasing revenues or cutting other expenditures. Revenues could be increased by strengthening tax administrations, broadening tax bases, or raising tax rates. Revenue-to-GDP ratios are particularly low in South Asia and Sub-Saharan Africa (World Bank 2015, 2016b). Even without tax rate increases, efforts to remove exemptions, tighten tax administration, and broaden tax bases could yield revenue gains that increase resources to finance public investment projects. Measures that have proven successful include the adoption of digital payments, taxpayer and property regis-tration, and monitoring compliance (Okunogbe and Santoro 2021). Expenditures could also be reallocated toward welfare-improving investment. For example, eliminating distortive agriculture and fossil fuel subsidies would free sizable funds for investment

in renewable energy, health, education, and targeted social safety net programs, even in fiscally constrained EMDEs (World Bank 2022e). For commodity-exporting economies, well-imple-mented fiscal rules and stabilization funds allow governments to use windfall gains earned when commodity prices are high to smooth public investment and expenditures during economic downturns or when commodity prices are low. Pro-cyclical fiscal policy in commodity-exporting countries has been found to worsen the depth of economic downturns (World Bank 2022a).

Third, within an existing envelope of public investment spending, it may be possible to improve spending efficiency and increase the benefits to growth (Buffie et al. 2012). For example, medium-term budget frameworks can improve spending predictability while greater transparency of expenditures and independent spending evaluations can generate incentives to improve efficiency. Better coordination between different levels of government can reduce duplication and inconsistencies (Mandl, Dierx, and Ilzkovitz 2008; St. Aubyn et al. 2009). Limiting contractual and institutional risks related to public-private partnerships in infrastructure can reduce contingent liabilities, while careful monitoring of state-owned enterprises can limit the need to inject fiscal resources in these companies (Dappe, Melecky, and Turkgulu 2022; Dappe et al. 2022). In some countries, there is also capacity to improve budget execution of planned public investment (World Bank 2022f).

For EMDEs, boosting public investment can have large benefits in terms of output because multipliers tend to be large (Izquierdo et al. 2019). Few studies estimate the fiscal multipliers of infrastructure investment in EMDEs, but the existing literature suggests that investment in green and digital infrastructure may have high multipliers (Vagliasindi and Gorgulu 2021). And in the right conditions, public investment can boost private investment. A positive effect on private investment from public investment is more likely in the presence of falling trade barriers and privatization efforts especially if the stock of infrastructure is low and if access to credit is not constrained (Bahal, Raissi, and Tulin 2018; Erden and Holcombe 2005).

Fiscal policy can also support private investment indirectly. Prospects for growth of demand and output play a major role in private investment decisions. To the extent that a growth slowdown in EMDEs is cyclical, counter-cyclical fiscal stimulus can help raise private investment during and after a downturn, where there is policy space (Cerra, Hakamada, and Lama 2021; Huidrom, Kose, and Ohnsorge 2016). Yet expansionary fiscal policy can also crowd out private investment and thus hinder economic growth. If increased government borrowing, through the pressure it puts on credit markets or through reactions of the central bank, leads to increases in interest rates and domestic currency appreciation, the cost of financing will increase and reduce the country's international competitiveness. For example, high levels of public investment in China after the global financial crisis boosted economic growth but also saddled cities with large amounts of public government debt (Huang, Pagano, and Panizza 2020). Increases in local public debt in China tightened financial conditions and lowered private investment by local manufacturing firms. Conversely, reducing fiscal deficits can, in some circumstances, boost private investment (Essl et al. 2019).

Monetary policy also has a role in supporting the growth of private investment, primarily by ensuring low and stable inflation over the medium term. Monetary policy can also play a countercyclical role through management of interest rates and credit growth, thereby support-ing investment growth when activity is weak and inflation is low and helping to contain investment when the economy is overheating.

Structural policy

Structural reforms, including regulatory and governance reforms that improve the investment climate, can boost investment growth. Compared to advanced economies, banks extend less credit to the private sector as a share of GDP in EMDEs. This access gap to credit is largest for loans with long maturities (United Nations 2022). The empirical results in this chapter suggest that investment climate reform spurts and higher real credit growth have been associated with stronger

FIGURE 3.12 Investment growth around reform spurts and setbacks in EMDEs

In EMDEs, investment growth increased around reform spurts before returning to trend growth. Reform setbacks were associated with a significant decrease in investment growth.

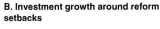
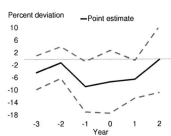
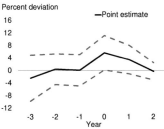

A. Investment growth around reform spurts

B. Investment growth around reform setbacks

Sources: International Country Risk Guide; World Bank.
Note: EMDEs = emerging market and developing economies. Sample includes 60 EMDEs from 1984-2022. Reform spurts and setbacks are defined in annex 3.2.
A.B. Solid lines show the increase in investment growth around a reform spurt (panel A) or setback (panel B) at t=0 relative to the countries not experiencing a reform spurt or setback. Dashed lines show the 95 percent confidence interval.

investment growth (annex 3.1). This positive impact is also apparent in a panel regression of investment growth on large spurts and setbacks in investment climate reforms among 60 EMDEs during 1984-2022 (figure 3.12.A). Reform spurts are associated with significantly higher investment growth—by about 6 percentage points, on average (annex 3.2). The impact of reform setbacks is more mixed (figure 3.12.B).

Reforms that improve the business climate can stimulate private investment directly and amplify the positive effects of investment, such as less informality and more job creation.[4] Informal firms are both less productive and capital intensive than formal firms (IMF 2019; Ohnsorge and Yu 2021). Structural reforms that encourage entry of informal firms into the formal sector can therefore raise investment and potential output growth, particularly in countries where informal firms are prevalent. Reducing business startup costs has been linked to higher profitability of incumbent

---

[4] For the linkages between reform measures and investment growth, see Andrews, Criscuolo, and Gal (2015); Calcagnini, Ferrando, and Giombini (2015); Corcoran and Gillanders (2015); Field (2005); Munemo (2014); Reinikka and Svensson (2002); Schivardi and Viviano (2011); and Wacziarg and Welch (2008).

firms and greater investment in information ICT. Stronger property rights can encourage business and real estate investment. Labor and product market reforms that increase firm profitability can also encourage investment. In countries where access to finance is constrained, measures to promote financial deepening could boost investment, although risk indicators must be monitored to avoid financial instability (Kiyotaki and Moore 2005; Sahay et al. 2015).

Developing digital and technological infrastructure can be an important driver of investment growth. Policies to stimulate private and public investment include closing the rural access gap to broadband networks, aligning regulations with international standards, implementing regulation that encourages competition, ensuring price affordability for consumers, and educating the workforce in ICT-relevant skills (OECD and IDB 2016). Between 2003 and 2018, new high-speed undersea internet connections to Africa, in the presence of a reliable electricity supply, increased FDI flows into the technology and financial sectors and expanded the size of investment projects (Mensah and Traore 2022). In Nigeria, the expansion of mobile broadband internet led to an increase of consumption by covered households, lower poverty rates, and higher labor market participation (Bahia et al. 2020).

Addressing climate change and building reliable energy infrastructure requires structural reforms that encourage private investment participation and lower barriers to access for the private sector. In many EMDEs, governance and institutional reforms are necessary to improve and unify the often fragmented regulatory and institutional environment, including regional cooperation in, for example, electricity trade. Unpredictable regulatory and policy risk is one of the reasons that the cost of capital for solar energy producers is two to three times higher in EMDEs (excluding China) than in advanced economies (IEA 2022).

EMDEs have made progress in establishing policy frameworks for renewable energy and energy efficiency since 2010, but the gap with regulatory frameworks of advanced economies is still large, especially for LICs (ESMAP 2020). Medium-term

policy targets and development plans can lower policy uncertainty holding back private investment (World Bank 2022b). For energy-importing EMDEs, Russia's invasion of Ukraine has underscored the energy security benefits of relying on a diversified mix of energy inputs, transitioning to clean energy sources, and improving the energy efficiency of buildings and production processes (World Bank 2022g).

Setting appropriate, predictable rules relating to investment decisions can boost investment but also help avoid potential pitfalls. Using firm-level data, Gutierrez and Philippon (2017) find that when firms invest less than would be expected based on their market performance, two-thirds of this shortfall is explained by corporate governance and industry concentration. Improvements in the planning and allocation of investment and in the implementation of public investment management systems, including reforms that resolve problems of asymmetric information and moral hazard, can enhance the benefits of infrastructure investment—for instance, through the establishment of a sound legal and institutional setting, robust appraisal systems, and effective procurement and monitoring systems (Gardner and Henry 2021; Kim, Fallov, and Groom 2020). For EMDEs where PPPs for infrastructure investment are common, a robust PPP governance structure can limit fiscal risks and avoid opportunistic renegotiations (Dappe, Melecky, and Turkgulu 2022; Engel, Fischer, and Galetovic 2020). A robust PPP regulatory framework is especially critical in LICs, where related reforms are lagging (World Bank 2020a).

Trade-related reforms, such as simplifying border procedures, eliminating unnecessary duties and improving trade-related transport infrastructure, could help increase trade flows, with associated benefits for investment (Brenton, Farrantino, and Maliszewska 2022). Lowering uncertainty related to at-the-border trade costs and committing to current or reduced tariff levels as well as other non-tariff barriers will decrease trade costs and encourage investment. These reforms should be accompanied by high-quality and well-maintained infrastructure, such as ports and airports (World Bank 2021b). In some EMDEs, lower barriers to cross-border trade finance are needed to help close the trade finance gap and further support trade growth (IFC and WTO 2022).

Membership in trade and integration agreements, such as the most recent African Continental Free Trade Area, solidifies reforms, which should benefit a country's investment climate, particularly if such agreements boost integration into global value chains and help lower the cost of tradable investment goods (machinery and equipment), for which EMDEs still face significantly higher costs than advanced economies (Lian et al. 2019). These reforms should include standardization of inspection and labeling requirements, which add significant costs to trade even if tariffs are low (Moïsé and Le Bris 2013). Lower trade barriers can integrate participating economies in regional and global value chains, while investment, intellectual property rights, and competition protocols aim to increase cross-border investment (Echandi, Maliszewska, and Steenbergen 2022; World Bank 2020b).

In the long term, many commodity-exporting EMDEs need to diversify so that terms of trade shocks are less likely to impact investment decisions. This can be done by, for instance, moving production up the value chain or building infrastructure that promotes activity outside the natural resource sector. EMDEs will also increasingly need to develop policies to offset the investment-dampening effects of population aging (Aksoy et al. 2019; Zhang, Zhang, and Lee 2003).

Conclusion

Investment growth slowed during the decade prior to the pandemic. On an aggregate level, the investment collapse in EMDEs in 2020 (including or excluding China) was larger than in the global recession in 2009 and the return to the pre-recession trend is expected to take longer.

The empirical analysis in this chapter finds that strong real output growth, robust real credit growth, terms of trade improvements, growth in capital inflows as a share of GDP, and investment climate reform spurs are associated with strengthening real investment growth.

At a time when investment growth is projected to be sluggish in most EMDEs, fiscal space for expansion of public investment is limited, and borrowing conditions are much tighter than during the long period of easy credit in the decade prior to the pandemic. Policy makers will need to identify innovative ways to fill unmet investment needs. Meeting climate goals and SDG targets, and supporting long-term growth, requires sound fiscal policies, including debt sustainability, as well as targeted investment and reforms.

These reforms should be carefully sequenced and implemented and should reflect country-specific circumstances. For example, in countries in acute fiscal stress, the priority may be to improve spending efficiency in public investment; in countries with anemic private investment, the priority may be business climate reforms, including robust competition policy, to foster private investment; in countries with large foreign direct investment, the priority may be to improve human capital to ensure that such foreign direct investment is growth enhancing.

Fiscal policies include increasing spending efficiency; implementing counter-cyclical fiscal rules; and strengthening tax administration and revenue collection. Counter-cyclical fiscal rules and improved tax administration and revenue collection are equally important. Fiscal policy to boost investment will need to be complemented by additional financing from the international community and the private sector. Structural reforms are needed to crowd in private investment, such as lowering tariffs and nontariff barriers to trade, improving the business climate, and putting in place predictable rules such as governance structures that enable PPPs. Public and private investment can both play important roles in supporting long-term growth prospects by supporting productive sectors or expanding infrastructure (including digital, transportation, and electricity infrastructure), improving health sector outcomes, and improving and expanding education.

TABLE 3.1 Investment sample

Emerging market and developing economies (EMDEs)			Advanced economies
East Asia and Pacific	**Latin America and the Caribbean**	**South Asia**	Australia
Cambodia *	Argentina	India *	Austria
China *	Belize	Nepal *	Belgium
Indonesia	Bolivia	Sri Lanka *	Canada
Malaysia *	Brazil		Croatia
Mongolia	Chile	**Sub-Saharan Africa**	Cyprus
Philippines *	Colombia	Benin	Czech Republic
Thailand *	Costa Rica	Botswana	Denmark
Vietnam *	Dominican Republic *	Burkina Faso	Estonia
	Ecuador	Côte d'Ivoire	Finland
Europe and Central Asia	El Salvador *	Equatorial Guinea	France
Albania *	Guatemala	Ghana	Germany
Armenia	Honduras	Kenya	Greece
Belarus *	Jamaica *	Mali	Hong Kong SAR, China
Bulgaria *	Mexico *	Mauritius *	Iceland
Hungary *	Nicaragua	Mozambique	Ireland
North Macedonia *	Panama *	Namibia	Israel
Poland *	Paraguay	Niger	Italy
Romania *	Peru	Nigeria	Japan
Russian Federation	Uruguay	Rwanda	Korea, Rep.
Türkiye *		Senegal	Latvia
Ukraine	**Middle East and North Africa**	South Africa	Lithuania
	Algeria	Tanzania	Malta
	Bahrain	Togo	Netherlands
	Iran, Islamic Rep.	Uganda	New Zealand
	Kuwait		Norway
	Lebanon *		Portugal
	Morocco *		Singapore
	Oman		Slovak Republic
	Saudi Arabia		Slovenia
	United Arab Emirates		Spain
			Sweden
			Switzerland
			United Kingdom
			United States

Source: World Bank.

Note: * = EMDE commodity importers. Each EMDE is classified as a commodity importer or commodity exporter. An economy is defined as commodity exporter when, on average in 2017-19, either (1) total commodity exports accounted for 30 percent or more of total exports or (2) exports of any single commodity accounted for 20 percent or more of total exports. Economies for which these thresholds were met due to reexports were excluded. When data were not available, judgment was used. This taxonomy results in the classification of some well-diversified economies as importers, even if they are exporters of certain commodities (for example, Mexico). Pakistan and Bangladesh are not included in the sample because these countries report annual investment data for their fiscal year which does not align with the calendar year.

ANNEX 3.1 Determinants of investment growth: Empirical framework

Framework. Investment decisions are based on the expected marginal return of capital and the risk-adjusted cost of financing the investment. While public investment decisions may also involve other considerations, private investment accounts for the majority of investment in EMDEs, about three-quarters of total gross fixed capital formation.

Therefore, investment is modelled as the level of investment *I* chosen such that the marginal return on capital (*MPK*) equals the cost of capital, which is the sum of the risk-adjusted real interest rate *r* and the rate of depreciation of capital (δ), absent binding constraints:

$$MPK = r + \delta$$

As a result, investment *I* also depends on the determinants of the marginal product of capital—especially total factor productivity *TFP* and the existing stock of capital *K*. Since investment decisions are about the expected future returns to capital, the cost of capital also includes a risk premium π:

$$I = I(TFP, K, r, \pi, \delta)$$

A higher cost of capital—whether due to higher risk premia or higher risk-free real interest rates—would reduce investment, whereas higher productivity, lower depreciation, or a low capital stock would raise it.

To proxy these factors, the regression includes real output growth, terms of trade growth, real credit growth, change in capital flows as a percent of GDP, and a dummy for investment reform spurts. As exports are included in GDP, output growth also captures trade growth beyond the impact through terms of trade.

Data sources. Real investment growth is calculated from real gross fixed capitation formation taken primarily from Haver Analytics and, for countries or years not available in Haver Analytics, from the World Bank's World Development Indicators

(WDI) or *Global Economic Prospects* (GEP) for 2021. Real output growth is taken from the World Bank's GEP. Real credit growth to the private sector and the credit-to-GDP ratio in the robustness section are taken from the Bank for International Settlements and supplemented with data from the International Financial Statistics (IFS) published by the International Monetary Fund (IMF). Credit growth proxies both depth of the financial sector as well as the cost of financing investment, since data on comparable financing cost for a sufficiently large number of countries over the past two decades is not available . Terms of trade are from WDI and, for 2021, from the GEP. Capital flows are calculated using data on the sum of FDI, portfolio flows, and changes in external bank liabilities from the IMF's IFS. Missing data for all three flow variables are imputed by taking the average of adjacent years. This imputation is limited to at most two consecutive missing observations per economy. Reform spurts are calculated using the Investment Profile Index taken from the PRS Group's International Country Risk Guide (ICRG). Reform spurts are defined as a two-year increase in the index above two times the standard deviation of the country-specific index. The data set includes a panel of 57 EMDEs and 31 advanced economies and covers the period from 1999 to 2021. The regression starts in 2000 and allows for lagged variables.

Methodology. The analysis estimates the correlates of investment growth in 57 EMDEs for the period 2000-21 in a system generalized method of moments (GMM) framework, with the third to sixth lag used to instrument the differenced equation and second lags for the level equation. These GMM-type instruments are used for output growth, real credit growth, growth in capital flows, and terms of trade growth. The econometric framework is similar to that of Nabar and Joyce (2009). However, the focus in this chapter is on investment growth—a critical component of overall output growth (ultimately, the source of rising living standards)—rather than changes in the investment-to-GDP ratio, which would only capture changes in investment growth relative to output growth. Use of investment growth is in line with recent studies on advanced economies and individual EMDEs.[5] The results are shown in annex table 3.1.1. The sample is unweighted to avoid a small number of EMDEs dominating the results (China and India, for example, account for a large share of total EMDE investment). Lastly, the terms of trade, real credit growth, and capital flow variables exclude the top and bottom 1 percent of observations in the entire sample to deal with outliers. Standard errors are clustered at the country level.

Robustness. Annex table 3.1.2 details a range of robustness checks. The regressions are robust to using OLS with fixed effects instead of system GMM (to account for the initial level of capital, for example). Further, when dividing capital flows into its components, the change of FDI flows is not significant, but the changes in portfolio and bank flows are. The credit-to-GDP ratio is not significant once China is excluded from the sample, and credit growth does not exhibit non-linear behavior. The regression is also robust to adding advanced economies to the sample (excluding Ireland, Malta, and Singapore, as these countries are large outliers for capital flows). Further robustness checks in the system GMM specification include controlling for various institutional quality variables from ICRG, time fixed effects, as well as the relative price of capital from Penn World Table 10. These additional variables were not significant while the main results are generally robust. Only the coefficient on terms of trade becomes insignificant when global trend variables are included. The subsamples of commodity-importing EMDEs and commodity-exporting EMDEs are too small to generate significant results.

TABLE A3.1.1 Correlates of investment growth

Dependent variable: real investment growth (percent)	(1) EMDEs
Real GDP growth (percent)	1.807***
	(13.66)
Real credit growth (percent)	0.132***
	(3.22)
Terms of trade growth (percent)	0.095*
	(1.95)
Investment climate reform spurt	6.970*
	(1.78)
Change in capital flows (percent of GDP)	0.218**
	(2.15)
Constant	-2.854***
	(-5.30)
Observations	1024
Number of economies	57

Source: World Bank.
Note: Results of a panel system GMM regression for 57 EMDEs during 2000-21. Column (1) denotes the baseline regression for EMDEs. Real GDP growth, real credit growth, terms of trade growth, as well as change in capital flows are treated as endogenous. Standard errors are clustered at the country level. *t*-statistics in parentheses. *** $p<0.01$, ** $p<0.05$, * $p<0.1$.

---

[5] Banerjee, Kearns, and Lombardi (2015); Barkbu et al. (2015); Bussière, Ferrara, and Milovich (2016); and Kothari, Lewellen, and Warner (2015) cover advanced economies. Anand and Tulin (2014) covers India.

TABLE A3.1.2 **Correlates of investment growth robustness**

Dependent variable: real investment growth (percent)	(1) EMDE excl. China	(2) Split capital flows	(3) Credit to GDP ratio excl. China	(4) Real credit growth squared	(5) Nominal credit growth	(6) Global
Real GDP growth (percent)	1.839***	1.840***	1.979***	1.855***	1.854***	1.743***
	(14.04)	(12.73)	(17.58)	(14.06)	(13.85)	(19.29)
Real credit growth (percent)	0.132***	0.148***		0.102		0.102***
	(3.28)	(3.32)		(1.60)		(3.16)
Terms of trade growth (percent)	0.084*	0.092*	0.116**	0.084*	0.086*	0.091*
	(1.75)	(1.78)	(2.25)	(1.87)	(1.75)	(1.85)
Investment climate reform spurt	7.834*	3.165*	8.173**	6.384*	7.701*	4.375*
	(1.87)	(1.83)	(2.01)	(1.82)	(1.99)	(1.80)
Change in capital flows (percent of GDP)	0.219**		0.195**	0.226**	0.203**	0.132***
	(2.16)		(2.05)	(2.14)	(2.17)	(3.55)
Change in FDI flows (percent of GDP)		0.102				
		(0.91)				
Change in portfolio flows (percent of GDP)		0.343**				
		(2.60)				
Change in net liabilities of financial corporations (percent of GDP)		0.076***				
		(2.90)				
Change in credit-to-GDP ratio (percent of GDP)			0.123			
			(1.38)			
Real credit growth squared				-0.000		
				(-0.20)		
Nominal credit growth					0.089**	
					(2.32)	
Constant	-2.861***	-3.049***	-2.509***	-2.719***	-3.221***	-2.056***
	(-5.34)	(-5.79)	(-4.72)	(-5.46)	(-5.23)	(-6.15)
Observations	1002	948	1022	1024	1037	1649
Number of economies	56	57	56	57	57	88

Source: World Bank.

Note: Results of a panel regression for 56-57 EMDEs and 31 advanced economies during 2000-21. Number of economies varies based on data availability. Columns (1) to (5) are variations of the system GMM regression in column (1) of table 3.1.1 Column (1) excludes China from the sample. Column (2) separates capital flows into the three components. Column (3) replaces real credit growth with the change in the credit to GDP ratio, excluding China. Column (4) tests for nonlinearity of real credit growth. Column (5) replaces real credit growth with nominal credit growth. Column (6) estimates the baseline for a global sample of 57 EMDEs and 31 advanced economies (the sample excludes Ireland, Malta, and Singapore, as these economies are large outliers for capital flows). All additional control variables in columns (1) to (5) are assumed to be endogenous. Standard errors are clustered at the country level. t-statistics in parentheses. *** $p<0.01$, ** $p<0.05$, * $p<0.1$.

ANNEX 3.2 Investment growth and reforms

Values in figure 3.12 are based on a panel data regression in which the dependent variable is real investment growth. A spurt (setback) is defined as a two-year increase (decrease) above (below) two times the country-specific standard deviation of the investment profile index, a component of the International Country Risk Guide (ICRG) published by the PRS Group. The sample spans 60 EMDEs over 1984-2022. Overall, there are 44 reform spurt events and 10 reform setback events.

In the regression, t denotes the end of a two-year spurt, and s the end of a two-year setback. The coefficients are dummy variables for spurts and setbacks over the $[t$-3, t+2] or $[s$-3, s+2] window around these episodes (annex table 3.2.1). In figure 3.12, "reform" at time t refers to the two-year change from t-2 to t. All coefficients show the investment growth differential of economies during an episode compared to those that experienced neither improvements nor setbacks. All estimates include time fixed effects to control for global common shocks and country fixed effects to control for time-invariant heterogeneity at the country level.

TABLE A3.2.1 Investment growth around investment climate reform spurts and setbacks

Dependent variable: real investment growth (percent)	(1) EMDEs
t-3	-2.460
	(3.752)
t-2	0.385
	(2.501)
t-1	0.014
	(2.550)
Period *t* of reform spurt	5.577**
	(2.815)
t+1	3.417
	(2.320)
t+2	-0.393
	(1.403)
s-3	-4.395
	(2.772)
s-2	-1.163
	(2.592)
s-1	-8.891**
	(4.129)
Period *s* of reform setback	-7.323
	(5.137)
s+1	-6.490**
	(3.108)
s+2	-0.098
	(5.438)
Observations	1,854

Source: World Bank.
Note: The regression includes time and country fixed effects. *t* indicates the period of the significant reform spurt, and *s* the period of the significant reform setback. Robust standard errors are in parentheses. *** $p<0.01$, ** $p<0.05$, * $p<0.1$.

References

Aksoy, Y., H. S. Basso, R. P. Smith, and T. Grasl. 2019. "Demographic Structure and Macroeconomic Trends." *American Economic Journal: Macroeconomics* 11 (1): 193-222.

Alfaro, L., A. Chanda, S. Kalemli-Ozcan, and S. Sayek. 2004. "FDI and Economic Growth: The Role of Local Financial Markets." *Journal of International Economics* 64 (1): 89-112

Alvarez, F. 2017. "Capital Accumulation and International Trade." *Journal of Monetary Economics* 91 (C): 1-18.

Anand, R., and V. Tulin. 2014. "Disentangling India's Investment Slowdown." IMF Working Paper 14/47, International Monetary Fund, Washington, DC.

Andrews, D., C. Criscuolo, and P. N. Gal. 2015. "Frontier Firms, Technology Diffusion and Public Policy: Micro Evidence from OECD Countries." Productivity Working Paper 2015-02, Organisation for Economic Co-operation and Development, Paris.

Bahal, G., M. Raissi, and V. Tulin. 2018. "Crowding-Out or Crowding-In? Public and Private Investment in India." *World Development* 109 (September): 323-333.

Bahia, K., P. Castells, G. Cruz, T. Masaki, X. Pedrós, T. Pfutze, C. Rodríguez-Castelán, and H. Winkler. 2020. "The Welfare Effects of Mobile Broadband. Evidence from Nigeria." Policy Research Working Paper 9230, World Bank, Washington, DC.

Banerjee, A. V., and E. Duflo. 2005. "Growth Theory through the Lens of Development Economics." In *Handbook of Economic Growth, Volume 1A*, edited by P. Aghion and S. Durlauf, 473-552. Amsterdam: Elsevier.

Banerjee, R., J. Kearns, and M. Lombardi. 2015. "(Why) Is Investment Weak?" BIS Quarterly Review, March. Bank for International Settlements, Geneva.

Barkbu, B., S. P. Berkmen, P. Lukyantsau, S. Saksonovs, and H. Schoelermann. 2015. "Investment in the Euro Area: Why Has It Been Weak?" IMF Working Paper 15/32, International Monetary Fund, Washington, DC.

Bashir, S., C. J. Dahlman, N. Kanehira, and K. Tilmes. 2021. *The Converging Technology Revolution and Human Capital: Potential and Implications for South Asia.* Washington, DC: World Bank.

Bhattacharya, A., and N. Stern. 2021. "Beyond the $100 Billion: Financing a Sustainable and Resilient Future." Policy Note, Grantham Research Institute on Climate Change and the Environment, London School of Economics and Political Science, London.

Bizimana, O., L. Jaramillo, S. Thomas, and J. Yoo. 2021. "Scaling Up Quality Infrastructure Investment." IMF Working Paper 21/117, International Monetary Fund, Washington, DC.

Black, S., J. Chateau, F. Jaumotte, I. W. H. Parry, G. Schwerhoff, S. D. Thube, and K. Zhunussova. 2021. "Getting on Track to Net Zero: Accelerating a Global Just Transition in This Decade." Staff Climate Note

2022/010, International Monetary Fund, Washington, DC.

Blanchard, O. J., and L. Katz. 1999. "Wage Dynamics: Reconciling Theory and Evidence." NBER Working Paper 6924, National Bureau of Economic Research, Cambridge, MA.

Bleaney, M., and D. Greenaway. 2001. "The Impact of Terms of Trade and Real Exchange Rate Volatility on Investment and Growth in Sub-Saharan Africa." *Journal of Development Economics* 65: 491-500.

Bobasu, A., A. Geis, L. Quaglietti, and M. Ricci. 2020. "Tracking Global Economic Uncertainty: Implications for Global Investment and Trade." ECB Economic Bulletin 1/2020, European Central Bank, Frankfurt.

Brenton, P., M. J. Ferrantino, and M. Maliszewska. 2022. *Reshaping Global Value Chains in Light of COVID-19.* Washington, DC: World Bank.

Buffie, E. F., A. Berg, C. Pattillo, R. Portillo, and L.-F. Zanna. 2012. "Public Investment, Growth, and Debt Sustainability: Putting Together the Pieces." IMF Working Paper 12/144, International Monetary Fund, Washington, DC.

Bussière, M., L. Ferrara, and J. Milovich. 2016. "Explaining the Recent Slump in Investment: The Role of Expected Demand and Uncertainty." *IMF Research Bulletin* 17 (1): 1-3.

Caballero, R. J., and A. Simsek. 2020. "Asset Prices and Aggregate Demand in a 'Covid-19' Shock: A Model of Endogenous Risk Intolerance and LSAPs." NBER Working Paper 27044, National Bureau of Economic Research, Cambridge, MA.

Calcagnini, G., A. Ferrando, and G. Giombini. 2015. "Multiple Market Imperfections, Firm Profitability and Investment." *European Journal of Law and Economics* 40 (1): 95-120.

Calderón, C., E. Moral-Benito, and L. Servén. 2015. "Is Infrastructure Capital Productive? A Dynamic Heterogeneous Approach." *Journal of Applied Econometrics* 30 (20): 177-198.

Calderón, C., and L. Servén. 2014. "Infrastructure, Growth, and Inequality: An Overview." Policy Research Working Paper 7034, World Bank, Washington, DC.

Carrière-Swallow, Y., and L. F. Céspedes. 2013. "The Impact of Uncertainty Shocks in Emerging Economies." *Journal of International Economics* 90 (2): 316-325.

Caselli, F., P. Pagano, and F. Schivardi. 2003. "Uncertainty and the Slowdown in Capital Accumulation in Europe." *Applied Economics* 35 (1): 79-89.

Cerra, V., A. Cuevas, C. Goes, I. Karpowicz, T. Matheson, I. Samake, and S. Vtyurina. 2016. "Highways to Heaven: Infrastructure Determinants and Trends in Latin America and the Caribbean." IMF Working Paper 16/185, International Monetary Fund, Washington, DC.

Cerra, V., M. Hakamada, and R. Lama. 2021. "Financial Crises, Investment Slumps, and Slow Recoveries." IMF Working Paper 21/170, International Monetary Fund, Washington, DC.

Cole, S., M. Melecky, F. Moelders, and T. Reed. 2020. "Long-Run Returns to Impact Investing in Emerging Markets and Developing Economies." NBER Working Paper 27870, National Bureau of Economic Research, Cambridge, MA.

Colecchia, A., and P. Schreyer. 2002. "ICT Investment and Economic Growth in the 1990s: Is the United States a Unique Case? A Comparative Study of Nine OECD Countries." *Review of Economics Dynamics* 5 (2): 408-442.

Comin, D., and M. M. Ferrer. 2013. "If Technology Has Arrived Everywhere, Why Has Income Diverged?" NBER Working Paper 19010, National Bureau of Economic Research, Cambridge, MA.

Corcoran, A., and R. Gillanders. 2015. "Foreign Direct Investment and the Ease of Doing Business." *Review of World Economics* 151 (1): 103-126.

Dappe, M. H., M. Melecky, and B. Turkgulu. 2022. "Fiscal Risks from Early Termination of Public-Private Partnerships in Infrastructure." Policy Research Working Paper 9972, World Bank, Washington, DC.

Dappe, M. H., A. Musacchio, C. Pan, Y. V. Semikolenova, B. Turkgulu, and J. Barboza. 2022. "Smoke and Mirrors: Infrastructure State-Owned Enterprises and Fiscal Risks." Policy Research Working Paper 9970, World Bank, Washington, DC:.

Didier, T., M. A. Kose, F. Ohnsorge, and L. S. Ye. 2015. "Slowdown in Emerging Markets: Rough Patch or Prolonged Weakness?" Policy Research Note 4, World Bank, Washington, DC.

Echandi, R., M. Maliszewska, and V. Steenbergen. 2022. *Making the Most of the African Continental Free Trade Area.* Washington, DC: World Bank.

Eichengreen, B., P. Gupta, and O. Masetti. 2018. "Are Capital Flows Fickle? Increasingly? And Does the Answer Still Depend on Type?" *Asian Economic Papers* 17 (1): 22-41.

Engel, E., R. Fischer, and A. Galetovic. 2020. "When and How to Use Public-Private Partnerships in Infrastructure: Lessons from the International Experience." NBER Working Paper 26766, National Bureau of Economic Research, Cambridge, MA.

Erden, L., and R. G. Holcombe. 2005. "The Effects of Public Investment on Private Investment in Developing Countries." *Public Finance Review* 33 (5): 575-602.

ESMAP (Energy Sector Management Assistance Program). 2020. "Regulatory Indicators for Sustainable Energy (RISE) 2020: Sustaining the Momentum." World Bank, Washington, DC.

Essl, S., S. K. Celik, P. Kirby, and A. Proite. 2019. "Debt in Low-Income Countries." Policy Research Working Paper 8794, World Bank, Washington, DC.

Farla, K., D. de Crombrugghe, and B. Verspagen. 2016. "Institutions, Foreign Direct Investment and Domestic Investment: Crowding Out or Crowding In?" *World Development* 88 (December): 1-9.

Feldstein, M. 2008. "Did Wages Reflect Growth in Productivity?" NBER Working Paper 13953, National Bureau of Economic Research, Cambridge, MA.

Ferreira, F. H. G. 1995. "Wealth Distribution Dynamics with Public-Private Capital Complementarity." Discussion Paper TE/95/286. London School of Economics and Political Science, London.

Field, E. 2005. "Property Rights and Investment in Urban Slums." *Journal of the European Economic Association* 3 (2-3): 279-290.

Foster, V., A. Rana, and N. Gorgulu. 2022. "Understanding Public Spending Trends for Infrastructure in Developing Countries." Policy Research Working Paper 9903, World Bank, Washington, DC.

Freund, C. 2016. "The Global Trade Slowdown and Secular Stagnation." *Trade and Investment Policy Watch* (blog), April 20, 2016. https://www.piie.com/blogs/trade-and-investment-policy-watch/global-trade-slowdown-and-secular-stagnation.

G20 (Group of 20). 2016. "Developments in Investment and Policy Challenges." Paper for G-20, June. Organisation for Economic Co-operation and Development, Paris.

G20 (Group of 20). 2019. "G20 Principles for Quality Infrastructure Investment." Annex 6.1. G20 Finance and Central Bank Meeting June 2019. Fukuoka, Japan.

Garcia-Escribano, M., and F. Han. 2015. "Credit Expansion in Emerging Markets: Propellor of Growth?" IMF Working Paper 15/212, International Monetary Fund, Washington, DC.

Gardner, C., and P. B. Henry. 2021. "The Global Infrastructure Gap: Potential, Perils, and a Framework for Distinction." Working Paper, New York University, New York.

Gaspar, V., D. Amaglobali, M. Garcia-Escribano, D. Prady, and M. Soto. 2019. "Fiscal Policy and Development: Human, Social, and Physical Investments for the SDGs." Staff Discussion Note 2019/003, International Monetary Fund, Washington, DC.

Getachew, Y. Y. 2010. "Public Capital and Distributional Dynamics in a Two-Sector Growth Model." *Journal of Macroeconomics* 32 (2): 606-616.

Guénette, J. D., M. A. Kose, and N. Sugawara. 2022. "Is a Global Recession Imminent?" EFI Policy Note 4, World Bank, Washington, DC.

Gutierrez, G., and T., Philippon 2017. "Investmentless Growth: An Empirical Investigation." *Brookings Papers on Economic Activity* (Fall): 89-169.

Hofstede, G. H. 2001. *Culture's Consequences: Comparing Values, Behaviors, Institutions, and Organizations across Nations.* Thousand Oaks, CA: Sage.

Hsieh, C.-T., and P. Klenow. 2007. "Relative Prices and Relative Prosperity." *American Economic Review* 97 (3): 562-585.

Huang, Y., M. Pagano, and U. Panizza. 2020. "Local Crowding-Out in China." *The Journal of Finance* 75 (6): 2855-2898.

Huidrom, R., M. A. Kose, and F. Ohnsorge. 2016. "A Ride in Rough Waters." *Finance & Development* 53 (3): 1-4.

Huidrom R., M. A. Kose, H. Matsuoka, and F. Ohnsorge. 2020. "How Important Are Spillovers from Major Emerging Markets?" *International Finance* 23 (1): 47-63.

IEA (International Energy Agency). 2022. "World Energy Outlook 2022." Paris: International Energy Agency.

IEA (International Energy Agency). 2021. "Net Zero by 2050 A Roadmap for the Global Energy Sector." International Energy Agency, Paris.

IFC (International Finance Corporation), and WTO (World Trade Organization). 2022. "Trade Finance in West Africa." Geneva: World Trade Organization and Washington, DC: International Finance Corporation.

IMF (International Monetary Fund). 2015. "Private Investment: What's the Holdup?" Chapter 4, *World Economic Outlook*, April. Washington, DC: International Monetary Fund.

IMF (International Monetary Fund). 2016. "Global Trade: What's Behind the Slowdown?" In *World Economic Outlook—Subdued Demand: Symptoms and Remedies*, Chapter 2. October. Washington, DC: International Monetary Fund.

IMF (International Monetary Fund). 2019. "Reigniting Growth in Low-Income and Emerging Market Economies: What Role can Structural Reforms Play?" In *World Economic Outlook: Global Manufacturing Downturn, Rising Trade Barriers*, Chapter 3. October. Washington, DC: International Monetary Fund.

Inklaar, R., and J. Yang. 2012. "The Impact of Financial Crises and Tolerance for Uncertainty." *Journal of Development Economics* 97 (2): 466-80.

IPCC (Intergovernmental Panel on Climate Change). 2022. "Climate Change 2022: Mitigation of Climate Change." IPCC Sixth Assessment Report. Cambridge, U.K. and New York: Cambridge University Press.

Irwin, D. A. 2019. "Does Trade Reform Promote Economic Growth? A Review of Recent Evidence." Working Paper 19-9, Peterson Institute for International Economics, Washington, DC.

Izquierdo, A., R. Lama, J. P. Medina, J. Puig, D. Riera-Crichton, C. Vegh, and G. Vuletin. 2019. "Is the Public Investment Multiplier Higher in Developing Countries? An Empirical Exploration." Working Paper 19/289, International Monetary Fund, Washington, DC.

Kilic Celik, S., M. A. Kose, and F. Ohnsorge. 2020. "Subdued Potential Growth: Sources and Remedies." In *Growth in a Time of Change: Global and Country Perspectives on a New Agenda*, edited by H.-W. Kim

and Z. Qureshi, 25-73. Washington, DC: Brookings Institution.

Kim, J.-H., J. A. Fallov, and S. Groom. 2020. *Public Investment Management Reference Guide*. Washington, DC: World Bank.

Kiyotaki, N., and J. Moore 2005. "Financial Deepening." *Journal of the European Economic Association* 3 (2/3): 701-713.

Kose, M. A., and F. Ohnsorge, eds. 2020. *A Decade after the Global Recession: Lessons and Challenges for Emerging and Developing Economies*. Washington, DC: World Bank.

Kose, M. A., F. Ohnsorge, L. S. Ye, and E. Islamaj. 2017. "Weakness in Investment Growth: Causes, Implications and Policy Responses." Policy Research Working Paper 7990, World Bank, Washington, DC.

Kothari, S. P., J. Lewellen, and J. B. Warner. 2015. "The Behavior of Aggregate Corporate Investment." MIT Sloan Research Paper 5112-14, Massachusetts Institute of Technology, Cambridge.

Lakatos, C., and F. Ohnsorge 2017. "Arm's-Length Trade: A Source of Post-Crisis Trade Weakness." Policy Research Working Paper 8144, World Bank, Washington, DC.

Li, D., N. Magud, and F. Valencia. 2015. "Corporate Investment in Emerging Markets: Financing vs. Real Options Channel." Working Paper 15/285, International Monetary Fund, Washington, DC.

Lian, W., N. Novta, E. Pugacheva, Y. Timmer, and P. Topalova. 2019. "The Price of Capital Goods: A Driver of Investment Under Threat." IMF Working Paper WP/19/134, International Monetary Fund, Washington, DC.

Libman, E., J. A. Montecino, and A. Razmi. 2019. "Sustained Investment Surges." *Oxford Economic Papers* 71 (4): 1071-1095.

Lim, J. J. 2014. "Institutional and Structural Determinants of Investment Worldwide." *Journal of Macroeconomics* 41 (September): 160-77.

Magud, N., and S. Sosa. 2015. "Investment in Emerging Markets. We Are Not in Kansas Anymore...Or Are We?" IMF Working Paper 15/77, International Monetary Fund, Washington, DC.

Maliszewska, M., and D. van der Mensbrugghe. 2019. "The Belt and Road Initiative: Economic, Poverty and

Environmental Impacts." Policy Research Working Paper 8814, World Bank, Washington, DC.

Mandl, U., A. Dierx, and F. Ilzkovitz. 2008. "The Effectiveness and Efficiency of Public Spending." *Economic Papers* 301, European Commission, Brussels.

McQuade, P., and M. Schmitz. 2016. "The Great Moderation in International Capital Flows: A Global Phenomenon?" ECB Working Paper 1952, European Central Bank, Frankfurt.

Medeiros, V., R. S. M. Ribeiro, and P. V. M. do Amaral. 2021. "Infrastructure and Household Poverty in Brazil: A regional Approach Using Multilevel Models." *World Development* 137 (January): 105118.

Mensah, J., and N. Traore. 2022. "Infrastructure Quality and FDI inflows. Evidence from the Arrival of High-Speed Internet in Africa." Policy Research Working Paper 9946, World Bank, Washington, DC.

Moelders, F. 2016. "Global Productivity Slowdown and the Role of Technology Adoption in Emerging Markets." International Finance Corporation, Washington, DC.

Moïsé, E., and F. Le Bris. 2013. "Trade Costs—What Have We Learned?: A Synthesis Report." OECD Trade Policy Papers 150, Organisation for Economic Co-operation and Development, Paris.

Moszoro, M. 2021. "The Direct Employment Impact of Public Investment." IMF Working Paper 21/131, International Monetary Fund, Washington, DC.

Munemo, J. 2014. "Business Start-Up Regulations and the Complementarity Between Foreign and Domestic Investment." *Review of World Economics* 150 (4): 745-61.

Muñoz-Najar, A., A. Gilberto, A. Hasan, C. Cobo, J. P. Azevedo, and M. Akmal. 2021. "Remote Learning during COVID-19: Lessons from Today, Principles for Tomorrow." World Bank, Washington, DC.

Mutreja, P., B. Ravikumar, and M. J. Sposi. 2014. "Capital Goods Trade and Economic Development." Working Paper 2014-012B, Federal Reserve Bank of St. Louis.

Nabar, N., and J. Joyce. 2009. "Sudden Stops, Banking Crises, and Investment Collapses." *Journal of Development Economics* 90 (2): 163-189.

OECD (Organisation for Economic Co-operation and Development). 2015. "Lifting Investment for Higher Sustainable Growth." In *OECD Economic Outlook* 1, Chapter 3. Paris: OECD Publishing.

OECD (Organisation for Economic Co-operation and Development). 2016a. *Compendium of Productivity Indicators 2016*. Paris: OECD Publishing.

OECD (Organisation for Economic Co-operation and Development). 2016b. "Using the Fiscal Levers to Escape the Low-Growth Trap." In *OECD Economic Outlook*, Chapter 2. Paris: OECD Publishing.

OECD (Organisation for Economic Co-operation and Development). 2020. "Building Back Better: A Sustainable, Resilient Recovery After COVID-19." OECD Policy Responses to Coronavirus (COVID-19), OECD, Paris.

OECD (Organisation for Economic Co-operation and Development) and IDB (Inter-American Development Bank). 2016. "Broadband Policies for Latin America and the Caribbean: A Digital Economy Toolkit." Paris: OECD Publishing.

Ohnsorge, F., and S. Yu. 2021. *The Long Shadow of Informality: Challenges and Policies*. Washington, DC: World Bank.

Okunogbe, O. M., and F. Santoro. 2021. "The Promise and Limitations of Information Technology for Tax Mobilization." Policy Research Working Paper 9848, World Bank, Washington, DC.

Perez Sebastian, F., and J. Steinbuks. 2017. "Public Infrastructure and Structural Transformation." Policy Research Working Paper 8285, World Bank, Washington, DC.

Psacharopoulos, G., V. Collis, H.A. Patrinos, and E. Vegas. 2021. "The COVID-19 Cost of School Closures in Earnings and Income across the World." *Comparative Education Review* 65 (2): 271–87.

Qureshi, Z., J. L. Diaz-Sanchez, and A. Varoudakis. 2015. "The Post-Crisis Growth Slowdown in Emerging Economies and the Role of Structural Reforms." *Global Journal of Emerging Market Economies* 7 (2): 179-200.

Reinikka, R., and J. Svensson. 2002. "Coping with Poor Public Capital." *Journal of Development Economics* 69 (1): 51-69.

Restuccia, D., and R. Rogerson. 2008. "Policy Distortions and Aggregate Productivity with Heterogeneous Establishments." *Review of Economic Dynamics* 11 (4): 707-720.

Rozenberg, J., and M. Fay, eds. 2019. *Beyond the Gap: How Countries Can Afford the Infrastructure They Need While Protecting the Planet.* Washington, DC: World Bank.

Sahay, R., M. Čihák, P. N'Diaye, A. Barajas, R. Bi, D. Ayala, Y Gao, et al. 2015. "Rethinking Financial Deepening: Stability and Growth in Emerging Markets." IMF Staff Discussion Note 15/08, International Monetary Fund, Washington, DC.

Schivardi, F., and E. Viviano. 2011. "Entry Barriers in Retail Trade." *The Economic Journal* 121 (551): 145-170.

Shapiro, M. D., O. J. Blanchard, and M. C. Lovell. 1986. "Investment, Output, and the Cost of Capital." *Brookings Papers on Economic Activity* 1986 (1): 111-64.

Songwe, V., N. Stern, and A. Bhattacharya. 2022. "Finance for Climate Action: Scaling Up Investment for Climate and Development." Grantham Research Institute on Climate Change and the Environment, London School of Economics and Political Science, London.

Sposi, M., K.-M. Yi, and J. Zhang. 2021. "Trade Integration, Global Value Chains and Capital Accumulation." *IMF Economic Review* 69 (3): 505-539.

St. Aubyn, M., A. Pina, F. Garcia, and J. Pais. 2009. "Study on the Efficiency and Effectiveness of Public Spending on Tertiary Education." *Economic Papers* 390, European Commission, Brussels.

Stenberg, K., O. Hanssen, T. Edejer, M. Bertram, C. Brindley. A. Meshreky, J. E. Rosen, J. Stover, P. Verboom, R. Sanders, and A. Soucat. 2017. "Financing Transformative Health Systems Towards Achievement of the Health Sustainable Development Goals: A Model for Projected Resource Needs in 67 Low-Income and Middle-Income Countries." *Lancet Global Health* 5: e875-887.

Stiglitz, J. E. 2020. "The Pandemic Economic Crisis, Precautionary Behavior, and Mobility Constraints: An Application of the Dynamic Disequilibrium Model with Randomness." NBER Working Paper 27992, National Bureau of Economic Research, Cambridge, MA.

Stocker, M., J. Baffes, M. Some, D. Vorisek, and C. Wheeler. 2018. "The 2014-16 Oil Price Collapse in Retrospect: Sources and Implications." Policy Research Working Paper 8419, World Bank, Washington, DC.

Strand, J., and M. Toman. 2010. "Green Stimulus, Economic Recovery, and Long-Term Sustainable Development." Policy Research Working Paper 5163, World Bank, Washington, DC.

UNCTAD (United Nations Conference on Trade and Development). 2014. "Investment in SDGs: An Action Plan." *World Investment Report.* New York: United Nations.

United Nations. 2019. *Financing for Sustainable Development Report 2019.* New York: United Nations.

United Nations. 2022. *Financing for Sustainable Development Report 2022: Bridging the Finance Divide.* New York: United Nations.

Vagliasindi, M., and N. Gorgulu. 2021. "What Have We Learned about the Effectiveness of Infrastructure Investment as a Fiscal Stimulus?" Policy Research Working Paper 9796, World Bank, Washington, DC.

Vashakmadze, E., G. Kambou, D. Chen, B. Nandwa, Y. Okawa, and D. Vorisek. 2018. "Regional Dimensions of Recent Weakness in Investment: Drivers, Investment Needs and Policy Responses." *Journal of Infrastructure, Policy and Development* 2(1): 37-66.

Vorisek, D., and S. Yu. 2020. "Understanding the Cost of Achieving the Sustainable Development Goals." Policy Research Working Paper 9146, World Bank, Washington, DC.

Wacziarg, R., and K. H. Welch. 2008. "Trade Liberalization and Growth: New Evidence." *The World Bank Economic Review* 22 (2): 187-231.

Wilichowski, T., C. Cobo, A. Patil, and M. Quota. 2021. "How to Enhance Teacher Professional Development Through Technology: Takeaways from Innovations Across the Globe." Blog. *Education for Global Development* (blog). September 23, 2021. https://blogs.worldbank.org/education/how-enhance-teacher-professional-development-through-technology-takeaways-innovations.

World Bank. 2015. *Global Economic Prospects: Having Fiscal Space and Using It.* January. Washington, DC: World Bank.

World Bank. 2016a. *Global Economic Prospects: Spillovers amid Weak Growth.* January. Washington, DC: World Bank.

World Bank. 2016b. *South Asia Economic Focus: Investment Reality Check.* World Bank, Washington, DC.

World Bank. 2017. *Global Economic Prospects: Weak Investment in Uncertain Times.* January. Washington, DC: World Bank.

World Bank. 2018. *Global Economic Prospects: Broad-Based Upturn, but for How Long?* January. Washington, DC: World Bank.

World Bank. 2019. *Global Economic Prospects: Heightened Tensions, Subdued Investment.* June. Washington, DC: World Bank

World Bank. 2020a. *Benchmarking Infrastructure Development 2020: Assessing Regulatory Quality to Prepare, Procure, and Manage PPPs and Traditional Public Investment in Infrastructure Projects.* Washington, DC: World Bank.

World Bank. 2020b. The African Continental Free Trade Area: Economic and Distributional Effects. Washington, DC: World Bank.

World Bank. 2021a. *Global Economic Prospects.* January. Washington, DC: World Bank.

World Bank. 2021b. *Global Economic Prospects.* June 2021. Washington, DC: World Bank.

World Bank. 2022a. *Global Economic Prospects.* January. Washington, DC: World Bank.

World Bank. 2022b. *World Development Report 2022: Finance for an Equitable Recovery.* Washington, DC: World Bank.

World Bank. 2022c. *Global Economic Prospects.* June. Washington, DC: World Bank.

World Bank. 2022d. "Climate and Development: An Agenda for Action - Emerging Insights from World Bank Group 2021-22 Country Climate and Development Reports." World Bank, Washington, DC.

World Bank. 2022e. "The Food and Energy Crisis - Weathering the Storm." Development Committee Paper October. Washington, DC: World Bank.

World Bank. 2022f. *South Asia Economic Focus: Coping with Shocks: Migration and the Road to Resilience.* October. Washington, DC: World Bank.

World Bank. 2022g. "Vietnam Country Climate and Development Report." CCDR Series. Washington, DC: World Bank.

Zhang J., J. Zhang, and R. Lee. 2003. "Rising Longevity, Education, Savings, and Growth." *Journal of Development Economics* 70 (1): 83-101.

CHAPTER 4

SMALL STATES

Overlapping Crises, Multiple Challenges

Small states' economies were hit particularly hard by COVID-19, largely due to prolonged disruptions to global tourism. Now facing spillovers from the Russian Federation's invasion of Ukraine and the global monetary tightening cycle, small states are expected to have weak recoveries with large and possibly permanent losses to the level of output. Small states are diverse in their economic features, but they share attributes that make them especially vulnerable to shocks, including dependence on imports of essential goods, highly concentrated economies, elevated levels of debt, reliance on external financing, and susceptibility to natural disasters and climate change. Policy makers in small states can improve long-term growth prospects by building fiscal space, fostering effective economic diversification, and improving resilience to climate change. There is a need for intensified international cooperation to support small states in addressing their challenges. The global community can assist small states in these efforts by maintaining the flow of official assistance, helping restore and preserve debt sustainability, facilitating trade, and supporting climate change adaptation.

Introduction

Small states—countries with a population of 1.5 million or less—were hit particularly hard by the COVID-19 pandemic (World Bank 2022a). They suffered a far more severe recession and a much weaker initial rebound than other emerging market and developing economies (EMDEs; figure 4.1.A). Their recoveries are being slowed by spillovers from the Russian Federation's invasion of Ukraine and synchronized global monetary policy tightening. Most small states are not expected to regain their pre-pandemic level of per capita output until after 2023 (figure 4.1.B).

Against this backdrop, this chapter addresses the following questions:

- What are the key economic features of small states?

- How have overlapping global crises—the COVID-19 pandemic, Russia's invasion of Ukraine, and sharp monetary tightening to offset global inflation—affected small states?

- What are the near-term economic prospects for small states?

- What policy measures can boost growth and improve resilience in small states?

Contributions. This chapter presents a comprehensive analysis of recent economic developments in, and growth prospects for, small

states as a group. First, it discusses how current global economic conditions, such as rising financing costs and weak tourism, affect small states. Second, it examines how the typical features of small states amplified the effects of the global recession triggered by the pandemic, and of Russia's invasion of Ukraine, and may now hold back the recovery. Third, the chapter presents a broad set of policy priorities that can help small states build resilience to future shocks and improve long-term growth prospects. In combining analysis of structural features of small states with a discussion of short-term growth prospects and deriving policy priorities for the whole group of small states, this chapter goes beyond the existing literature that focused on narrower topics.[1]

Main findings. The chapter reviews the key features of small states and how recent global crises have impacted these countries. It presents the growth outlook for small states, examines the risks to the outlook, and discusses how policy actions can support growth and improve resilience.

- *Key features.* Small states are a heterogeneous group, but tend to have high levels of economic concentration, and many are challenged by remoteness and lack of connectivity. They have very high levels of

---

Note: This chapter was prepared by Philip Kenworthy, Patrick Kirby, and Dana Vorisek.

[1] Some recent studies provide economic updates for regional groupings of small states, such as those in the Pacific or the Caribbean (IMF 2022; World Bank 2022b). Other studies examine small states through the lens of their recovery from the pandemic (FAO 2020; OECD 2021) or program effectiveness (Rustomjee et al. 2022), or through a description of characteristics of small states with little reference to recent developments (Briguglio 2022; Piemonte 2021). Other recent work has examined exchange rate regimes in small states and the risks of currency and banking crises (Al-Sadiq, Bejar, and Ötker 2021; Pizzinelli, Khan, and Ishi 2021).

FIGURE 4.1 Growth and income in small states

Small states entered the pandemic with already weak growth prospects, and have been hit particularly hard by the economic effects of the pandemic and the war in Ukraine. They suffered far deeper recessions in 2020 than other EMDEs and the recovery has been slower than in other EMDEs.

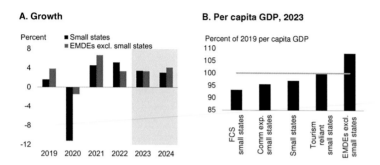

A. Growth

B. Per capita GDP, 2023

Source: World Bank.
Note: EMDEs = emerging market and developing economies; FCS = fragile and conflict-affected states. Country groups are GDP weighted at average 2010-19 prices and market exchange rates.
A. Grey area indicates forecast. Sample includes 34 EMDE small states and 115 EMDEs excluding small states. Guyana is excluded.
B. Descriptions of small state subgroups are in table 4.1. Horizontal line indicates 100. Sample includes 34 small states (of which 11 are commodity-exporters, 6 are FCS, and 22 are tourism-reliant) and 115 EMDEs excluding small states. Guyana is excluded.

trade openness, importing large proportions of their food and fuel, and are three times more reliant on shipping than the world average. Their exports are concentrated in tourism and the production of primary commodities (but in most cases not energy, metals, meat, or grain). As a group, small states tend to run fiscal deficits and depend on a mixture of aid and foreign direct investment to finance large current account deficits. On average, small states have higher public debt levels than other EMDEs. Nearly all small states have fixed exchange rates.

- *Overlapping crises.* The 2020 global recession was especially severe for small states, primarily due to their reliance on tourism. Output contracted by more than 11 percent in small states, seven times as much as in other EMDEs. The recession was even deeper in the three-fifths of small states classified as tourism reliant, which contracted by nearly 13 percent. Recoveries remained weak in 2021 and at least part of 2022, amid new COVID-19 variants and ongoing travel restrictions. In parallel, soaring global prices and supply chain disruptions brought into focus the risks of

depending on imported essentials. From 2 percent in January 2020, inflation in the median small state increased to 7.5 percent in September 2022, even as domestic demand remained weak. With small state debt levels well above the EMDE average, global monetary policy tightening raises debt servicing costs and threatens to further slow small state recoveries.

- *Risks and structural barriers to growth.* The outlook is subject to a range of risks. Food, energy, and shipping prices could surge again, dealing a further blow to real incomes in small states. New COVID-19 variants and virus waves remain a serious risk, particularly given many small states' dependence on tourism. Most small states entered the global tightening cycle with adequate reserve buffers, but an external financing shock could nonetheless prompt financial stress, particularly in small states with highly indebted private sectors. In the long term, small states face structural headwinds that weaken their prospects. Damages from climate and natural disasters, equivalent to nearly 5 percent of GDP annually, on average, are increasing. Remoteness, lack of scale, and limited connectivity raise costs and constrain diversification efforts.

- *Policy priorities.* Policy makers in small states, with support from the global community, can take steps to limit pandemic-related losses and reduce vulnerability to future crises. Improved infrastructure could support diversification into higher value-added sectors and reduce disaster-related losses and the effects of climate change. Curbing public debt would increase fiscal space, enhancing capacity to respond to future shocks. Reducing trade costs and strengthening domestic institutions should help raise productivity. The global community can also help small states through capacity building and financial support as well as actions at the international level: fostering open trade and investment networks, augmenting the institutional architecture for dealing with excessive debt, maintaining the flow of official assistance, and supporting climate change mitigation and adaptation at the global level.

Characteristics of small states

Small states share many characteristics, while also differing in important ways. Many small states are prosperous and have moved up the per capita income spectrum over the past two decades. As of 2022, 24 percent of small states were classified as high income, up from 9 percent in 2000, and no small states are currently classified as low income, compared to 12 percent in 2000.[2] This chapter covers the 37 small states that are also EMDEs, which have per capita incomes ranging from about $1,100 (Timor-Leste) to more than $30,000 (Brunei Darussalam) in 2021.

According to the available data, about one-quarter of the population in the median small state lives on an income below the lower-middle-income country poverty threshold of $3.65 per day, and another quarter has an income below the upper-middle-income country poverty threshold of $6.85 per day (these shares are similar to those of South Africa and Indonesia).[3] Median poverty at the $3.65 threshold declined by about 15 percentage points between the 2000s and the 2010s. There is disparity across small states, however. About 70 percent of the population of Eswatini lives on less than $3.65 per day, compared to close to 0 percent in Mauritius. Bhutan has achieved especially swift poverty reduction, with the lower-middle-income poverty rate declining by more than three-quarters between the 2000s and 2010s.

Regionally, small states are concentrated in East Asia and the Pacific (EAP), Latin America and the Caribbean (LAC), and to a lesser degree Sub-Saharan Africa (SSA), although there are several in the other three EMDE regions (table 4.1). Three-

---

quarters of small states are islands, a much larger share than among other EMDEs, and many of the island small states in EAP are dispersed across large areas. Two small states (Bhutan and Eswatini) are landlocked. Three-fifths are commodity importers, compared to one-third of other EMDEs, and most commodity-importing small states are also reliant on tourism. Of the two-fifths of small states classified as commodity exporters, most produce agricultural and marine products such as fish, fruit, sugar, cocoa, and wood, but six are energy exporters, and two are metal exporters (Bhutan and Suriname). Nine small states, mostly in EAP, are among the most reliant on remittances of all EMDEs. Six small states are considered by the World Bank to be experiencing fragile and conflict-affected situations (FCS, all due to institutional and social fragility rather than conflict), all in EAP. This is equivalent to one-sixth of small states, while one out of four other EMDEs are FCS countries.

Despite their diversity, several features are common across small states: remoteness, economic concentration, vulnerability to the effects of climate change, openness, large public sectors with limited capacity, indebtedness, and reliance on external financing. These features, together with other country-specific challenges, make small states especially vulnerable to shocks.

Remoteness and economic concentration. Remoteness and economic concentration present structural challenges that make it harder for small states to adapt when faced with external shocks. Long distances to potential trading partners, especially when combined with weak transport and digital connectivity, present a barrier to trade and global value chain integration for many small states in EAP and SSA (figures 4.2.A and 4.2.B; Armstrong and Read 2006). Small domestic markets make generating domestic economies of scale and economic diversification challenging. High fixed costs to establish and operate businesses (relative to market size), together with labor market rigidity, can dampen competitiveness and disincentivize diversification.

At the macroeconomic level, small states tend to concentrate output and exports in a limited set of

---

[2] Based on gross national income per capita using the World Bank Atlas method. The last small state to transition from low income to middle income, the Comoros, did so in 2018.

[3] The collection of poverty data around the world was disrupted during the pandemic, worsening the sparseness of data for small states (World Bank 2022c). Data using international poverty lines does not exist for any country in the Caribbean, for example, and most countries only have one or two observations per decade. The discussion of poverty here reflects available data for 16 small states collected between 2000 and 2019.

FIGURE 4.2 **Features of small states**

Remoteness and weak digital connectivity are challenges for small states, particularly those in EAP and SSA.

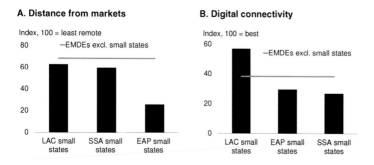

A. Distance from markets

Index, 100 = least remote

—EMDEs excl. small states

B. Digital connectivity

Index, 100 = best

—EMDEs excl. small states

Sources: Cantu-Bazaldua 2021; World Bank.
Note: EAP = East Asia and Pacific; LAC = Latin America and the Caribbean; SSA = Sub-Saharan Africa. Bars and line show medians of country groups. Sample includes 13 EAP small states, 12 LAC small states, and 7 SSA small states.
A. The index is a composite measure of distance to nearest neighbor, distance to economic centers, and distance to trading partners.
B. Digital connectivity is a composite measure of Internet access of the population, international bandwidth per Internet user, and latency rate (a measure of network performance).

industries in which they have inherent advantages (for example, primary commodities and tourism). About one-fourth of output is derived from a single economic sector in both tourism-reliant and commodity-exporting small states, and about two-fifths from two sectors (figures 4.3.A and 4.3.B). In some commodity-exporting small states, export product concentration rose between the late 1990s and late 2010s (for example, Cabo Verde, Guyana, the Solomon Islands, and Suriname; figure 4.3.C).

A high degree of economic concentration has contributed to more volatile business cycles in small countries than in larger countries, with deeper cyclical contractions, shorter expansions, and more procyclical exports and inflation (Blanco et al. 2020). Other indicators, such as investment, the current account balance, and government consumption, also tend to be more volatile in small states than in other economies (Hnatkovska and Koehler-Geib 2018). The very large contraction of tourism-reliant economies during the pandemic is the most recent example of the downside of heavy reliance on a particular sector.

Vulnerability to natural disasters and climate change. Being mostly islands, many small states are heavily exposed to the effects of rising sea levels, floods, and coastal erosion. Damages from individual disasters can be multiples of GDP,

while the return needed to compensate for the risk of disaster raises the cost of commercial financing. The need to support populations and rebuild after disasters puts pressure on fiscal resources. The mounting costs of long-term climate change adaptation make it difficult for small states to maintain the fiscal buffers needed to respond to periodic disasters.

Openness. Small states have very high levels of trade openness and are unusually reliant on trade to obtain essential goods, importing most of their food and fuel (figure 4.3.D; FAO 2020). Shipping intensity of GDP (defined as the ratio of port container traffic to real GDP) in small states is more than three times higher than the world level (figure 4.3.E). Many small states are especially reliant on tourism. Tourism expenditures were equivalent to an average of 18 percent of economic activity in small states prior to the pandemic, and substantially more in several of the 22 tourism-reliant small states (figure 4.3.F). Dependence on tourism does not lend itself to rapid productivity growth, due to the labor-intensive nature of the sector, but it provides a key source of income (Arezki, Cherif, and Piotrowski 2009).

The combination of trade openness, reliance on imported essentials, and economic concentration leaves small states particularly exposed to global developments (Easterly and Kraay 2000). These vulnerabilities are further magnified by the fact that most small states lack two important mechanisms for buffering shocks: floating exchange rates and independent monetary policy. All except two small states (Mauritius and the Seychelles) operate under some form of fixed exchange rate—including conventional pegs, pegs within horizontal bands, crawling pegs, managed arrangements, stabilized arrangements, and currency boards (27 small states, including several that peg to a basket of currencies)—or use the currency of another country (eight small states, most of which use the U.S. dollar or the Australian dollar). The prevalence of fixed exchange rates suggests that reducing exchange rate volatility is more valuable to small states than the loss in monetary policy autonomy, possible because they allow small states to effectively import the credibility of the anchor currency's institutions, which can help maintain low inflation (Airaudo, Buffie, and Zanna 2016; Imam 2012).

Openness in small states also manifests in the movement of people, with high levels of temporary and permanent emigration. Between 2015 and 2020, the median island small state lost about 1 percent of its population to emigration. The emigration of highly skilled workers has long prompted concerns about the impact of brain drain on small state economies, with evidence that skilled emigration has more adverse impacts on total factor productivity in small states than in other EMDEs (Schiff and Wang 2008). Yet temporary emigration can give individuals the opportunity to boost their education and skills, benefiting home countries if emigrants can be enticed to return, and the promise of skills premia overseas can incentivize the pursuit of more education domestically (Ha, Yi, and Zhang 2016). Remittance inflows provided by emigrants are also a key source of external financing in some countries (Wenner 2016).

Large governments with limited capacity, persistent deficits, and high debt. As a share of GDP, governments in small states tend to be larger than in other EMDEs. Both average annual current government spending and tax revenues were about 8 percentage points of GDP higher than in other EMDEs, with public sector wages accounting for a disproportionate share of these funds (figures 4.4.A and 4.4.B). This is partly a reflection that the fixed costs of public administration are high relative to small economies and populations. Frequent natural disasters contribute to periods of reduced revenues and increased expenditures. State-owned enterprises are also prevalent in small states, operating in sectors such as energy generation, transport, and water, and comprise significant shares of GDP in some countries (for example, Cabo Verde, Maldives, Mauritius, the Federated States of Micronesia, the Seychelles, and St. Kitts and Nevis; Heller 2022).

In absolute terms, however, small state governments are often too small to achieve economies of scale and effectively provide many public services, as human resource and institutional constraints

FIGURE 4.3 Output and trade characteristics of small states

Output remains highly concentrated in a small number of sectors, although commodity-exporting small states have made some progress at diversification. Small states exhibit higher export concentration than other EMDEs, making them susceptible to shocks to their main industries. Export concentration has increased in some small states. Small states are highly open to trade, and many rely heavily on tourism.

A. Output concentration in small states

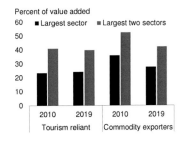

B. Goods export concentration, 2016-20

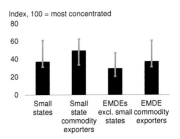

C. Goods export concentration among commodity-exporting small states

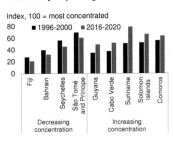

D. Trade openness

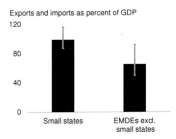

E. Shipping intensity of GDP

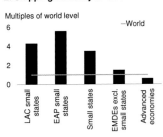

F. Inbound tourism expenditure

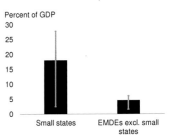

Sources: national sources; UN Conference on Trade and Development; UN World Tourism Organization; World Development Indicators; World Bank.

Note: EMDEs = emerging market and developing economies; EAP = East Asia and Pacific; LAC = Latin America and the Caribbean.

A. Bars show averages of country groups. Based on data for 12 sectors. Sample includes 15 tourism-reliant and 10 commodity-exporting small states in 2019 and 9 tourism-reliant and 6 commodity-exporting small states in 2010.

B.C. Export concentration is measured as a Herfindahl-Hirschmann index of export product concentration (includes only goods exports).

B. Bars show group medians of indicated country groups. Vertical lines show interquartile ranges within groups. Sample includes 37 EMDE small states, 14 commodity-exporting small states, 115 EMDEs excluding small states, and 97 commodity-exporting EMDEs.

C. Bars show averages in each country during the indicated years. Commodity-exporting small states where the change in the index between the two-year spans is less than 5 points (Belize, Brunei Darussalam, Equatorial Guinea, and Trinidad and Tobago) are omitted.

D. Bars show medians of indicated country groups. Vertical lines show interquartile ranges within groups. Sample includes 37 EMDE small states and 107 EMDEs excluding small states.

E. Ratios of port container traffic (20-foot equivalent units) to real 2019 GDP, indexed to world ratio. Data for 2019. Sample includes 36 advanced economies and 155 EMDEs, of which 37 are EMDE small states (12 Pacific Ocean islands and 12 Caribbean small states).

F. Bars show averages of indicated country groups. Vertical lines show interquartile ranges within groups. Data for 2019. Sample includes 22 EMDE small states and 81 EMDEs excluding small states.

FIGURE 4.4 Fiscal positions of small states

Small states tend to have proportionally larger governments than other EMDEs. They typically run fiscal deficits, which have become substantially larger in recent years. Public, private, and external debt levels in small states have increased during the past decade.

A. Government expenditures

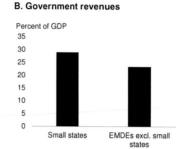

B. Government revenues

C. Fiscal balances

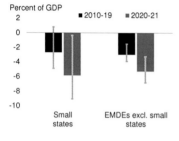

D. Government debt

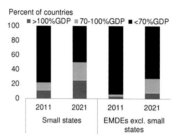

E. External debt

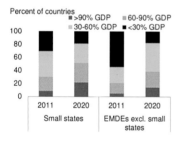

F. Private debt

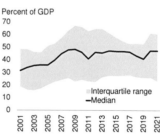

Sources: International Monetary Fund; World Bank.
Note: EMDEs = emerging market and developing economies.
A.B. Bars show medians of simple average values for country groups during 2010-19 period. Sample includes 37 EMDE small states, and 110 EMDEs excluding small states for panel A and 115 for B.
C. Bars show medians. Orange whiskers show interquartile range within groups. Sample includes 37 EMDE small states and 116 EMDEs excluding small states.
D. Sample includes 36 EMDE small states and 113 EMDEs excluding small states.
E. Sample includes 27 EMDE small states and 110 EMDEs excluding small states.
F. Sample includes 31 EMDE small states.

may limit their ability to, for example, collect and monitor statistical and supervisory data, or implement reforms (Rustomjee et al. 2022).

In the decade prior to the pandemic, most small states regularly ran fiscal deficits. The average annual fiscal balance was a deficit of 2.1 percent of GDP, compared to an average deficit of 2.8 per-

cent in other EMDEs (figure 4.4.C). Revenue sources in small states differ from those in other EMDEs in important ways, with a much greater reliance on taxes on trade and lower reliance on taxes on capital in small states. Non-tax revenues (for example, aid and royalties) provide important sources of government revenue in many small states, with those in EAP in particular receiving large proportions of GDP in grants. Sovereign rents also account for an important share of small state revenues in some cases, for example, in Kiribati (fishing licensing fees), Tuvalu (domain names) and Nauru (fees for hosting Australia's Regional Processing Centre for refugees).

As in other EMDEs, fiscal positions worsened markedly in small states during the pandemic. Some small states were already in the midst of a prolonged government debt buildup prior to the pandemic, and debt levels jumped further due to a plunge in revenues and a continued rise in expenditures during the pandemic (Kose et al. 2021; World Bank 2019a). Between 2011 and 2021, the share of small states with government debt above 100 percent of GDP rose from one-tenth to one-third (figure 4.4.D). Much of this debt was on concessional terms, such that, in the pre-pandemic decade, the average small state spent about 1 percent of GDP per year servicing debt, compared to 1.5 percent in other EMDEs.

There are notable regional differences in public debt profiles across small states, with LAC and SSA small state governments much more indebted, on average, than those in EAP, some of which receive unusually large proportions of GDP in official development assistance (ODA). In 2021, many small states had public debt above 70 percent of GDP, including about three-quarters of those in LAC, half of those in SSA, and only one (Fiji) in EAP. One of the reasons for the increase in debt has been the costs associated with the increased frequency of natural disasters. Nearly half of small states had external debt of more than 60 percent of GDP as of 2020, compared to 30 percent in 2010 (figure 4.4.E). Most government debt in small states is external, reflecting limited pools of domestic savings.

Private sectors in some small states are also increasingly leveraged. On average, private debt in small states was equivalent to 50 percent of GDP as of 2020 (figure 4.4.F), virtually identical to the average in other EMDEs. Private debt stocks rose by more than 10 percentage points of GDP between 2010 and 2020 in some small states (for example, Cabo Verde, Mauritius, and Samoa), and by more than 20 percentage points in others (for example, Bhutan, Fiji, and the Seychelles), increasing these countries' vulnerability to rising financing costs.

Dependence on external financing. Most small states run sizeable and persistent current account deficits, which widened considerably during the pandemic. In the pre-pandemic decade, the median current account balance among small states was 5.4 percent of GDP, compared to 3.5 percent of GDP among other EMDEs. Small state current account deficits are mostly financed by a combination of ODA, in the form of capital grants and official lending and, in small states with successful tourism and commodity sectors, foreign direct investment (figure 4.5.A). Some small states, particularly those in the EAP region, are also among the most dependent in the world on remittances, which provide a stable source of foreign income, allowing for consumption smoothing (figure 4.5.B). Net portfolio flows, which tend to be more volatile, comprise a limited part of most small state current account financing. The scale of external financial flows relative to GDP means that even a moderate reduction in foreign exchange inflows (for example, lower tourism earnings, weaker remittances, or diminished aid flows) can result in sizeable financing gaps.

Some small states are, relative to the size of their economies, significant intermediaries for financial flows between other countries. Relative to GDP, gross external assets and liabilities in the median small state were nearly twice as large as in the median EMDE in the years 2015-19. Mauritius, the Marshall Islands, and The Bahamas, in particular, host prominent specialized financial sectors that principally serve non-residents (Pogliani, von Peter, and Wooldridge 2022). Nonetheless, the depth and breadth of domestic financial sectors generally remains limited, and a lack of domestic lending capacity means small

FIGURE 4.5 External financing of small states

Small states finance substantial current account deficits mostly through direct investment and official financing. Small states, particularly those in EAP, tend to be far more reliant on official development assistance than other EMDEs.

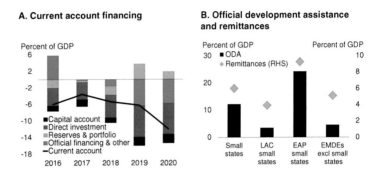

A. Current account financing

B. Official development assistance and remittances

Sources: International Monetary Fund; World Bank.
Note: EMDEs = emerging market and developing economies; EAP = East Asia and Pacific; LAC = Latin America and the Caribbean.
A. Positive and negative bars do not net to current account total due to errors and omissions. Sample includes 35 EMDE small states.
B. Simple averages for 2019. For ODA, sample includes 30 EMDE small states, 8 LAC small states, 12 EAP small states, and 101 EMDEs excluding small states. For remittances, sample includes 18 EMDE small states, 7 EAP small states, 4 LAC small states, and 80 EMDEs excluding small states.

states must rely heavily on external borrowing, often in foreign currencies.

Over the past two decades, private creditors have accounted for a growing share of small state external debt. External debt (relative to GDP) increased in about two-fifths of small states in the decade prior to the pandemic, with particularly sharp increases in Cabo Verde, Mauritius, Montenegro, and Trinidad and Tobago. Some small states have experienced slowing aid flows as donor countries prioritize low-income or conflict-affected countries, and as a result have increased their reliance on private creditors.

The use of currency pegs helps to shield small states from exchange rate shocks that could lead to significant and unpredictable changes in the valuation of foreign-denominated assets and liabilities (Calvo and Reinhart 2000). Historically, small states have been less prone to banking, currency, or debt crises than other EMDEs. For example, between 1950 and 2019 the average small state was in crisis in 14 percent of years, compared to 29 percent for other EMDEs (Nguyen, Castro, and Wood 2022). However, record high debt levels among some small states

FIGURE 4.6 Growth in small states during the past two decades

Since 2000, growth in small states has been lower and more volatile than in other EMDEs. After some making gains toward advanced economy per capita GDP in the 2000s, most small states stagnated or lost ground during the 2010s and were set back further during the pandemic.

A. Average annual growth

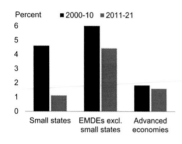

B. Volatility of growth in small states, 2000-21

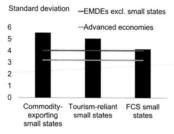

C. Average per capita GDP growth, 2000-21

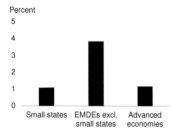

D. Per capita GDP relative to advanced economies

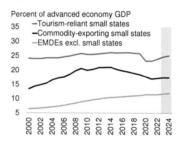

Source: World Bank.
Note: EMDEs = emerging market and developing economies; FCS = fragile and conflict-affected states.
A.C. Average annual growth of aggregate GDP and GDP per capita for groups of countries. Sample includes 35 EMDE small states, 113 EMDEs excluding small states, and 36 advanced economies.
B. Average of standard deviations of growth from 2000-21 for countries in each group. Sample contains 12 commodity-exporting, 22 tourism-reliant, and 6 FCS small states. Sample contains 113 EMDEs excluding small states. Extreme outliers are excluded.
D. Sample includes 34 EMDE small states and 114 EMDEs excluding small states. Guyana is excluded. Grey area indicates forecast.

increase the likelihood that pegs do eventually come under pressure.

Economic impact of overlapping crises

Since 2000, average growth in small states has been slower and more volatile than in other EMDEs (figures 4.6.A, 4.6.B, and 4.6.C). In the decade prior to the pandemic, growth in small states decelerated to just 1.8 percent per year, in part due to the outsized effects of natural disasters and spillovers from slower global growth, but also due to markedly weak growth in energy exporting

small states following the 2014 commodity price bust. Overall, small states have made no relative gains toward advanced economy per capita GDP levels for an extended period (figure 4.6.D). This lack of convergence was broad-based across small states in all regions. The knock-on impacts of the war in Ukraine and the ongoing global tightening cycle have further set back the recovery to pre-pandemic output levels.

The COVID-19 pandemic

The COVID-19 pandemic decimated global demand for tourism, small states' largest export and a major source of employment. The extent of the tourism collapse in many small states was compounded by extensive pandemic-related restrictions that were implemented to protect public health in contexts of limited health system capacity. Restrictions in small states generally remained tighter for longer than in other EMDEs, but converged to the EMDE average by mid-2022, with some outliers (figure 4.7.A). Most small states avoided large COVID-19 outbreaks at the beginning of the pandemic, but in the second half of 2021 average case numbers and deaths rose toward the EMDE average as more transmissible variants of the virus became dominant (figure 4.7.B). The pandemic worsened health and education outcomes, with the largest losses among the poor (Schady et al. forthcoming).

As the pandemic progressed, disruptions to global supply chains manifested as a terms of trade shock in small states, contributing to weak economic recoveries. The sharp rise in shipping costs was a particular headwind for small states, and unusual in the aftermath of a global recession. Indeed, in the other two global recessions since 1990 (in 2009 and 2012), shipping costs were substantially lower in the first year of recovery than in the pre-slowdown year. In contrast, in 2021 shipping costs were more than twice their level in 2019.

The economic costs of the pandemic were much more severe for small states than other EMDEs, with activity shrinking more than 11 percent in 2020, compared with less than 2 percent in other EMDEs (figure 4.7.C). The collapse of global travel had a disproportionate impact on the three-fifths of small states that rely on tourism, as their aggregate output contracted by nearly 13 percent in 2020. During the four global recessions prior to 2020, the largest annual decline in global tourist arrivals was about 4 percent, between 2008 and 2009. In 2020, arrivals fell by more than 70 percent (figure 4.7.D).

Aggregate growth in small states rebounded to an estimated 4.6 percent in 2021. Growth remained weak, in part because an initial recovery in tourism was interrupted by the spread of the Omicron variant of COVID-19 (figure 4.7.E). In all, small state aggregate output in 2021 was about 12 percent below what was projected just before the pandemic. In line with global trends, remittances to small states proved resilient, providing a crucial source of external finance during the early stages of the pandemic, with some small states such as Samoa and Tonga even seeing increases of close to 10 percentage points of GDP (figure 4.7.F). (The increase in recorded remittances in 2020 among most small states with available data was partly because of a shift of remittances from informal to formal channels.) ODA also provides a consistent source of external resources for small states, amounting to 12 percent of small state GDP in 2019, but considerably more for some EAP small states. For example, ODA was equivalent to nearly 80 percent of GDP in Tuvalu and 45 percent of GDP in Nauru. ODA flows strengthened by about 11 percent in 2020-21, according to preliminary donor data, likely implying increased dependence on aid in some small states.

Despite firm remittance inflows, small state current account balances deteriorated markedly between 2019 and 2020 as export performance suffered and government spending responded to the public health emergency. The average small state current account balance weakened by 2.5 percentage points of GDP in 2020, to a deficit of 8.3 percent of GDP, while the average fiscal balance deteriorated by 3 percentage points of GDP, from a deficit of 1.8 to 4.8 percent of GDP. Fiscal balances improved moderately in 2021, to an average deficit of 4.1 percent of GDP, but current accounts deteriorated further as travel remained depressed and the prices of imported commodities began to rise sharply.

FIGURE 4.7 The COVID-19 pandemic in small states

Small states had more prolonged mobility restrictions than other EMDEs, as COVID-19 deaths peaked later. The recession in 2020 was by far the most severe recession for small states in the past four decades and the recovery has been the weakest. The collapse in global travel during the pandemic had a disproportionate impact on small states, though increased remittance inflows partially cushioned the loss.

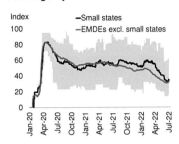

A. Stringency of COVID-19 restrictions

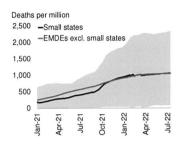

B. Cumulative COVID-19 deaths

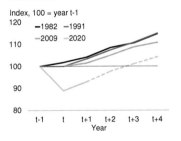

C. GDP in small states in global recessions

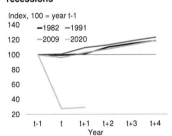

D. Tourist arrivals during global recessions

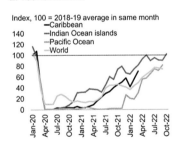

E. Tourist arrivals

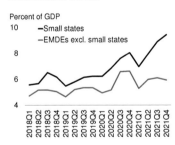

F. Remittance inflows

Sources: Hale et al. (2021); Haver Analytics; International Monetary Fund; national statistical agencies; Our World in Data; UN World Tourism Organization; World Development Indicators; World Bank.
Note: EMDEs = emerging market and developing economies.
A. Lines show simple averages of countries in each group. Grey shading shows the 5th to 95th percentile range in small states. Last observation is July 1, 2022.
B. Simple averages. Sample includes 147 EMDEs, of which 33 are small states. Grey shading shows 5th to 95th percentile range in small states. Last observation is July 12, 2022.
C.D. Lines show one year before (t-1) to four years after (t+4) the year of the recession, except where data are not yet available for the 2020 recession. Dotted lines represent forecasts.
C. Sample includes 35 EMDE small states.
E. Total non-seasonally adjusted visitor arrivals to each country group. Caribbean includes Antigua and Barbuda, The Bahamas, Barbados, Belize, Dominica, Grenada, St. Kitts and Nevis, St. Lucia, and St. Vincent and the Grenadines. Indian Ocean islands include Maldives, Mauritius, and the Seychelles. Pacific Ocean islands include Fiji and Palau. Last observation is March 2022 for the Caribbean, September 2022 for Pacific Ocean islands and the world, and October 2022 for Indian Ocean islands.
F. Simple averages. Sample includes 16 small states and 69 EMDEs excluding small states. Last observation is 2021Q4.

FIGURE 4.8 Economic effects of the war in Ukraine

Imports of food and fuel account for a larger share of GDP in small states than in other EMDEs. Inflation in small states rose sharply in 2022, partly due to the effects of Russia's invasion of Ukraine on commodity prices.

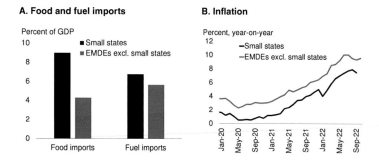

A. Food and fuel imports

B. Inflation

Sources: Haver Analytics; International Monetary Fund; national statistical agencies; UN Comtrade; World Bank; World Development Indicators.

Note: EMDEs = emerging market and developing economies.

A. Bars show simple averages. Data for 2019. Food imports sample includes 22 EMDE small states and 95 EMDEs excluding small states. Fuel imports sample includes 18 EMDE small states and 78 EMDEs excluding small states. Energy exporting EMDEs were dropped from the fuel imports sample.

B. Lines show medians. Sample includes 19 EMDE small states and 45 EMDEs excluding small states. Last observation is September 2022 for small states and October 2022 for EMDEs excluding small states.

Russia's invasion of Ukraine, inflation, and global monetary policy tightening

The war in Ukraine. Even prior to Russia's invasion of Ukraine in February 2022, commodity prices had risen substantially, and global supply chains were strained. The start of the war exacerbated these trends globally, weakening small state terms of trade more than those of other EMDEs.

The additional surge in energy and food prices raised already elevated import costs among small states. Typically, food and fuel imports are equivalent to about one-sixth of GDP in small states, substantially more than in other EMDEs, with some small states spending considerably more than the average (figure 4.8.A). Steep rises in food prices brought on by war-related disruptions to grain, energy, and fertilizer markets have squeezed living standards. In Cabo Verde, the combination of global food price increases and pre-existing local drought conditions sparked an acute food inse-curity crisis expected to severely affect about 10 percent of the population (FAO 2022).

The war-induced energy price shock could prove enduring, with oil prices expected to remain well above their pre-pandemic level throughout the next three years (World Bank 2022d). This contrasts with previous periods of weak global growth, which were generally associated with soft commodity prices (Baffes and Nagle 2022). The terms of trade shock and further damage to small state export prospects have contributed to a renewed deterioration of small state current account balances, to an average estimated deficit of 9.4 percent of GDP in 2022, and more than 15 percent of GDP in nine small states.

Inflation. Across small states, rising import prices quickly pushed up inflation in 2022, despite still weak domestic demand. In a consistent sample of 15 small states with available data, median year-on-year inflation in September 2022 was 7.5 percent, up from 2 percent just prior to the pandemic (figure 4.8.B). Several small states, including Mauritius, Montenegro, Samoa, São Tomé and Príncipe, Suriname, and Tonga, are experiencing double-digit inflation. In contrast, annual inflation in the median small state was below 2 percent for most of the 2010s, anchored by fixed exchange rates during a period of low inflation in advanced economies.

Monetary policy tightening. Rising price pressures have triggered synchronized monetary policy tightening across advanced economies and most EMDEs. The associated tightening of financial conditions has led to worsening perceptions of the sovereign creditworthiness of many EMDEs, especially issuers with lower credit ratings, as illustrated by a large rise in non-investment grade sovereign spreads since the start of the year. The median sovereign credit rating of small states in mid-2022 was six notches below investment grade (B3 by Moody's), and one notch lower than 2019. Consequently, apart from countries that rely mostly on concessional financing (for example, the Comoros, Samoa, and São Tomé and Príncipe), small states are likely to see much-increased spreads on new commercial borrowing compared to recent years.

Rising interest rates will squeeze non-interest spending in small states with sizeable existing stocks of variable rate debt, such as Fiji and Maldives. Diminished access to credit generally will test nascent recoveries in a number of countries where private sectors are heavily indebted, including Mauritius and several Caribbean economies. In parallel, more restrictive macroeconomic policies are expected to dampen global growth, leading to softer external demand for small states.

Prospects for recovery

Following an unprecedented economic contraction in 2020, the return to the level of output prevailing before the pandemic has been slow. Small states are forecast to grow 3.5 percent in 2023, slowing from an estimated 5.2 percent in 2022 (figure 4.9.A; table 4.2). The 2023 growth forecasts for about two-thirds of small states have been downgraded relative to the June forecast. Although small states have limited direct trade and financial linkages with Russia and Ukraine, they have experienced the inflationary impacts of the war and the ongoing global financial tightening cycle. At the projected pace of growth, small states will regain their aggregate 2019 level of activity only in 2023, while other EMDEs exceeded this threshold in 2021 (figure 4.9.B).

In tourism-reliant small states, growth is projected to be above the historical (2000-19) average through 2024. However, these growth rates follow a severe recession of nearly 13 percent in 2020. The return of tourism to pre-pandemic levels is incomplete. An incipient recovery at end-2021 was halted as COVID-19 cases spiked. In mid-2022, global international arrivals were still about one-third below pre-pandemic levels (UNWTO 2022). Yet there are clear signs of pent-up demand—global searches for flights and accommodation are well above pre-pandemic levels, and tourist arrivals in small states are rising (figure 4.7.E). Growth in tourism-reliant small states is projected to cool to 4.3 percent in 2023, from an estimated 6.1 percent in 2022, supported by a continued global tourism recovery. Per capita GDP in this group of countries is expected to regain its pre-pandemic level only by 2023.

Growth in commodity-exporting small states is forecast to soften to 2.4 percent in 2023, down from 4.3 percent in 2022. This growth trajectory would leave aggregate GDP in commodity-

FIGURE 4.9 **Prospects for recovery**

After a deep recession in 2020, the economic recovery in small states is projected to be prolonged. Aggregate GDP in small states is forecast to exceed its 2019 level only in 2023, two years after other EMDEs. By 2023, GDP in small states is projected to be about 7 percent below the pre-pandemic forecast, a much larger gap than for other EMDEs. As in other EMDEs, the pandemic caused large losses in working hours and extended school closures in small states, which may have permanently scarred potential growth.

A. Growth in small states, by sub-group

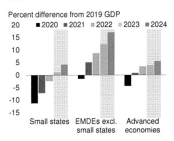

B. GDP compared to pre-pandemic level

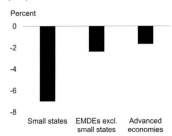

C. GDP compared to pre-pandemic level, by country group

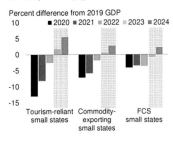

D. Gap in 2023 GDP with pre-pandemic trend

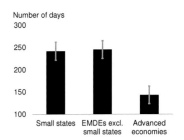

E. Working hours lost due to the pandemic

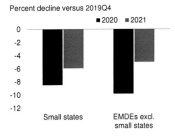

F. Duration of school closures

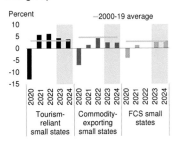

Source: Hale et al. 2021; International Labour Organization; World Bank.
Note: EMDEs = emerging market and developing economies. FCS = fragile and conflict-affected states.
A.-C. Growth rates are calculated using GDP weights at average 2010-19 prices and market exchange rates.
A. Sample includes 22 tourism-reliant, 11 commodity-reliant, and 6 FCS small states. Guyana is excluded. Descriptions of small state sub-groups are included in table 4.1.
B. Sample includes 34 EMDE small states, 115 EMDEs excluding small states, and 37 advanced economies. Guyana is excluded.
C. Sample includes 22 tourism-reliant small states, 11 commodity-exporting small states, and 6 FCS small states.
D. Figure shows percent deviation between levels of GDP in 2023 forecast in the January 2020 and January 2023 *Global Economic Prospects* reports. For 2023, the January 2020 baseline is extended using projected growth for 2022. Aggregate GDP for each group calculated using GDP weights at average 2010-19 prices and market exchange rates.
E. Bars show simple averages of countries in indicated groups. Sample includes 26 small states and 116 EMDEs excluding small states.
F. Simple averages within groups of the duration, in calendar days, of required school closures at all levels between January 1, 2020 and December 4, 2022. Whiskers show interquartile range within groups. Sample includes 23 small states, 113 EMDEs excluding small states, and 38 advanced economies.

exporting small states only slightly below the 2019 level by 2023, and per capita GDP in commodity-exporting small states more than 8 percent below the pre-pandemic level in 2023 (figure 4.9.C). The prices of agricultural commodities exported by small states—such as fish, fruit, sugar, cocoa, and wood—have mostly decreased since early 2022, while prices of commodities directly impacted by the war in Ukraine, such as oil, gas, coal, and wheat, have risen substantially. As commodity-exporting small states are still mostly net importers of food staples and energy, recent changes to their terms of trade remain unfavorable, with inflation increasingly squeezing real incomes.

The growth outlook during 2022-24 for the six small states classified as being in fragile and conflict-affected situations (FCS) is weaker than for most other subgroups, but output in this group of countries also contracted less than other subgroups of small states in 2020, in part due to their lower reliance on tourism. However, continued institutional and structural vulnerabilities, combined with the rising price of fuel and food imports, is expected to keep growth at a relatively low 2.9 percent in 2023, after a slight recession in 2022.

The forecasts for small states are predicated on several assumptions. Global tourism is expected to remain below pre-pandemic levels in 2023, but will continue to regain ground without major reversals due to, for example, new outbreaks of COVID-19 or further geopolitical turmoil. Central banks across the world are expected to tighten monetary policy in the near term in response to still-high inflation. Energy prices are expected to remain higher than previously forecast, but to ease somewhat over the course of the year.

Like other EMDEs, small states face long-term economic damage related to the shocks of the previous three years (figure 4.9.D). Skills and education losses incurred through extended periods of unemployment and school closures have been similar in magnitude to those in other EMDEs, and are likely to weigh on human capital accumulation and potential growth until they are recouped (figures 4.9.E and 4.9.F). The capital

stock is likely to be permanently lower than it would otherwise have been as a result of weaker investment and lapsed infrastructure maintenance. The protracted nature of the tourism downturn prompts further concerns about the future dynamism of small state economies, given that tourism growth and broader economic growth have been found to be mutually reinforcing in small states (Kumar and Stauvermann 2021; Ridderstaat, Croes, and Nijkamp 2013; Seetanah 2011).

Risks

Small states face several major risks. Some are common to all EMDEs with distinct impacts on small states, such as the effects of the pandemic, financing shocks, and the inflationary effects from Russia's invasion of Ukraine. Others are more specific to small states, such as exposure to climate-related and natural disasters, and structural and institutional challenges.

External financing shocks

Small states' high debt burdens and heavy reliance on foreign financing exacerbate the challenges of the current global environment of rising inflation and tightening financing conditions. Historically, financial crises in EMDEs have been more likely when the U.S. Federal Reserve tightens monetary policy, as it is currently doing in tandem with other central banks. The pace of tightening in advanced economies may accelerate further if the current period of persistent and elevated inflation causes inflation expectations to drift upward, requiring central banks to reset expectations to match targets. A credit event in a large EMDE could trigger disruptive, cross-border financial sector dynamics that could spill over to small states, especially those with elevated levels of debt, limited fiscal space, and more tenuous access to capital markets.

Many small states are also vulnerable to the realization of contingent liabilities from state-owned enterprises (SOEs), some of which have faced financial hardship since the beginning of the pandemic. For example, state-owned airlines in several Pacific Islands depend on various forms of government support (for example, direct budget support, guarantees, and lending from pension funds) and have balance sheets that are large relative to GDP (Balasundharam et al. 2021). Borrowing from China represents another distinct debt repayment risk. Data are incomplete, but eight small states (The Bahamas, Djibouti, Dominica, Maldives, Montenegro, Samoa, Tonga, Vanuatu) are among the 20 countries with the highest estimated stocks of debt owed to entities in China as a share of their GDP (Horn, Reinhart, and Trebesch 2019).

If borrowing cost were to rise sharply, refinancing debt would become increasingly burdensome and subject to risks. Interest payments were equivalent to about 15 percent or more of public revenues prior to the pandemic in some countries (The Bahamas, Barbados, St. Lucia). Officially reported government debt service was already above the threshold of 10 percent of exports of goods, services, and other foreign earnings in several countries prior to the pandemic, and far exceeded that threshold in some countries in 2020 (figure 4.10.A). Indeed, of 19 international development assistance-eligible (IDA) small states for which a Debt Sustainability Analysis was conducted by the World Bank and the IMF between 2019 and mid-2022, 13 were deemed to be at high risk of debt distress or already technically considered to be in distress. Twelve small states requested use of the Debt Service Suspension Initiative in 2020 and 2021, which provided temporary liquidity support by reprofiling debt service payments into the future but expired at end-2021 (IMF and World Bank 2021).

The liquidity and solvency risks from rapidly rising private and public debts may be amplified in some small states by heavy banking sector credit exposure to national governments (IMF 2013). This could allow financial stress in any of the corporate, financial and government sectors to spill into the others, which potentially constitutes a hidden risk even in small states where fiscal and external positions appear adequate to cover foreseeable government liabilities.

In the near term, the need to finance large current account deficits will intensify pressure on small state external financial accounts. From 2020 onwards, current account deficits expanded to

FIGURE 4.10 External financing risks

Debt servicing costs are already elevated for some small states and are likely to rise further as global interest rates rise. The large current account deficits of many small states make them vulnerable to external financing shortages. These risks are often mitigated by sufficient reserve coverage.

A. Total debt service

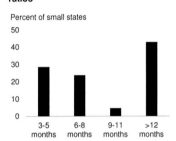

B. Current account balances

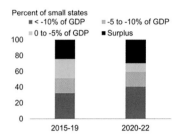

C. Reserves-to-months of imports ratios

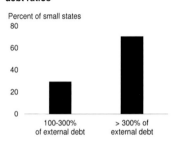

D. Reserves-to-short-term external debt ratios

Sources: International Monetary Fund; World Bank.
A. Horizontal line shows a threshold of 10 percent of goods, services, and primary income. Montenegro is not shown but its debt service-to-export ratio was about 55 percent of GDP in 2017-19, and more than 100 percent in 2020. Sample includes 18 small states.
B. For 2020-22, data are a mix of actuals, estimates, and forecasts. Sample includes 37 EMDE small states.
C. Data is the latest available (either 2020 or 2021), which varies by country. Categories sum to 100 percent. Sample includes 21 EMDE small states.
D. Data from 2020 due to limited data availability for short-term external debt. Most small states (about 80 percent) increased their official reserves from end-2020 to end-2021. Sample includes 17 EMDE small states.

more than 10 percent of GDP for about half of small states (figure 4.10.B). Much of this larger financing requirement has been met through increased official lending and transfers (which has also enabled some small states to strengthen reserve positions somewhat). Portfolio inflows also increased in 2020, representing about 0.5 percentage points of aggregate small state GDP. In the current environment of tighter financial conditions and still large current account deficits, portfolio flows could reverse, requiring a further increase in other funding sources or sharp reductions in spending.

In part reflecting the recent allocation of increased special drawing rights (SDRs), and strong remittance and donor inflows, reserve buffers appear adequate to insulate most small states from shortfalls in the near term (figure 4.10.C). Based on recent data, almost all small states hold reserves worth more than three months of imports, which also appear sufficient to cover total short-term external debt liabilities (figure 4.10.D). Nonetheless, if pressures on reserves were to arise, the sustainability of debt and existing currency pegs could come into question, heightening the risk of financial crisis. In the past, small state banking and currency crises have been particularly associated with lower ratios of reserves to money supply, which can compromise confidence in exchange rate pegs, leading to a run on the currency (Pizzinelli, Khan, and Ishi 2021).

Inflation

Additional disruptions to global energy and food markets could add to inflation, widen current account deficits, and further slow growth in small states. High and rising inflation could stoke social tensions, especially if food insecurity was already present prior to the recent surge in inflation. For example, food insecurity is expected to become even more widespread in Djibouti and Eswatini as food prices rise, adding to the 17 percent and 30 percent of the population, respectively, already in food crisis (World Bank 2022e; World Food Program 2021).

Higher inflation than in trading partners can undermine the fixed exchange rate arrangements used by nearly all small states by generating real appreciation. Persistent real appreciation can widen current account deficits, which have to be financed with unsustainable drawdowns of international reserves. Over time, this may eventually lead to pressure on the peg (MacDonald 2007).

Global downturn

Given their openness to trade and dependence on foreign sources of financing, small states could suffer severe consequences from a sharper-than-expected slowdown in the global economy. Since 1970, global recessions have been more likely when global growth weakens significantly in the previous year, as was the case in 2022. All global recessions since 1970 have coincided with sharp

slowdowns or outright recessions in multiple major economies, such as the United States, euro area, and China (Guénette, Kose, and Sugawara 2022).

Slower activity in major economies impacts the outlook for small states through multiple channels, including trade, confidence, and commodity markets. Small states are also vulnerable to slowing financial inflows in the form of ODA or remittances. The pandemic-induced recession was unusual in that many host countries provided large amounts of social support that helped prevent remittances from declining. This is unlikely to re-occur in the case of a future slowdown given limited fiscal space and the need to unwind pandemic-related fiscal support in many major economies. Strained fiscal positions may also cause donor governments to reduce ODA as budgets are re-allocated toward debt service, programs to buffer against the impact of recent commodity price increases, and restoring fiscal sustainability.

Climate change and natural disasters

In part because of their geography, small states are highly vulnerable to natural disasters such as hurricanes or tropical cyclones, floods, and droughts, as well as earthquakes and volcanic eruptions. The frequency and intensity of weather-related natural disasters in these countries has increased in recent decades, and is expected to rise further as a result of climate change (figure 4.11.A; IPCC 2022). Small states already face severe, in some cases existential, threats from a climate-related rise in sea levels and coastal erosion. In The Bahamas, Bahrain, Kiribati, Maldives, the Marshall Islands, and Tuvalu, for example, more than one-third of the land area and one-quarter of the population is located less than 5 meters above sea level. Other small states are highly vulnerable to drought (Djibouti, Eswatini).

Scaled by land mass, natural disasters in small economies dwarf those in large economies (figure 4.11.B; von Peter, von Dahlen, and Saxena 2012). It is not uncommon for the damages from a single disaster to be equivalent to a substantial portion of a country's GDP, or even multiples of GDP in extreme cases. Estimated damages and losses from Hurricane Maria in 2017 in Dominica and Hurricane Ivan in Grenada in 2004, for instance, amounted to 200 percent or more of GDP (Government of Dominica 2017; OECS 2005). Even averaged over a number of years, the cost of damages can be substantial. A severe natural disaster in a small state typically triggers a shock to productivity and substantial temporary disruption in output, alongside a surge in localized demand for public services (for example, healthcare and housing provision) and a decline in public revenues. Reconstruction costs can be well beyond the reach of the domestic budget and contingency funds, requiring substantial additional borrowing at increased capital costs.

The specific channels by which climate change negatively impacts small state economies are many and varied. Increased vulnerability stems in part from the concentration of economic activity near coastal areas, which is likely to intensify in many small states given urbanization trends (Mycoo and Donovan 2017). Direct effects are via damage to public infrastructure and broader capital stocks, but these in turn impede production and disrupt supply chains, causing further economic losses. For example, the ports of small island states, which are essential for both tourism and goods trade, are assessed to be the most vulnerable globally to operational disruption due to climate change (Izaguirre et al. 2021).

Over the long term, rising sea levels and environmental changes pose a severe risk to tourism. Attractions such as beaches and coral reefs could be degraded, while rising sea levels could submerge prime real estate—a 1 meter sea level rise in the Caribbean has been estimated to damage 49 to 60 percent of tourism resorts (Scott, Simpson, and Sim 2012). For agricultural producers, shifting weather patterns could disrupt ecosystems in unexpected ways, with negative impacts on crop yields due to factors such as the emergence of unfamiliar pests and bacteria (Taylor, McGregor, and Dawson 2016). The compound effects of climate change on small states are likely to exacerbate already substantial emigration pressure and curb labor force growth, and to hinder productivity (Dieppe 2021).

FIGURE 4.11 Climate change and natural disasters

Small states have experienced an increased frequency of climate-related shocks. Damages and losses from disasters have been substantial, averaging 4.8 percent of GDP per year since 1990, and even more in LAC small states.

A. Natural disasters in small states

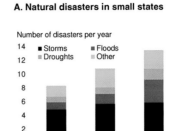

B. Damages and losses from natural disasters, 1990-2021

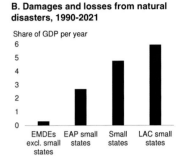

Sources: EM-DAT; World Bank.
Note: EMDEs = emerging market and developing economies.
A. Disasters are counted as the total number in all small states per year. Other disasters include earthquakes, landslides, and volcanic activity. Sample includes 26 EMDE small states.
B. Bars show the sum of damages in each group of countries in each year divided by the sum of nominal GDP in each group of countries, weighted by country-level nominal GDP.

Policy priorities

Policy makers have options to reverse small state losses from the pandemic and to lower their vulnerability to future crises. Achieving sustainably higher and more stable growth than currently projected will require addressing both immediate and more structural challenges, and appropriately sequencing reforms. Since small states, notwithstanding some common features, are highly heterogeneous, reforms have to be tailored to country characteristics and circumstances. By their nature, small states are highly exposed to global developments over which they have little control. Therefore, while many policy options exist for small states, they have fewer policy levers than larger countries, and the global community has a critical role to play in assisting these countries.

Domestic policies

In the short-term, small state policy makers can seek to mitigate the effects of global inflation and position their economies to move past COVID-19 and take advantage of a tourism revival. In the longer term, they can pursue structural reforms that reduce vulnerability to external shocks, increase debt sustainability, foster effective economic diversification, and raise growth prospects.

Inflation. With overwhelmingly fixed exchange rates and open capital accounts, small states have almost no scope for reining in inflation through discretionary monetary policy. Small states can use fiscal policy to diminish the negative distributional impacts of inflation, however. Numerous small states have sought to dampen rising domestic inflation by reducing value added taxes on select basic commodities or introducing subsidies on fuel (for example, Barbados, Dominica, Fiji, Grenada, and St. Lucia), or providing subsidies for essential goods like food (Mauritius). Although such assistance can alleviate price pressures for individuals and businesses in the short term, it does not concentrate help on those most in need and comes at a time when budgets are already strained.

The preferred option for policy makers to offset rising food and fuel prices is to implement more targeted protection programs, as Antigua and Barbuda recently did in offering new subsidies to transport operators, and to take advantage, where possible, of fintech solutions to reach households in geographic areas where banks are sparse. Certain structural reforms could help small states buffer future periods of high inflation. These include converting electricity production from imported fossil fuel sources to renewable sources available domestically, or expanding domestic food production, if permitted by land availability and growing conditions, to reduce reliance on imported products. Measures to facilitate trade could also bring down import costs and inflation, as described below.

Moving past COVID-19. In the short term, progress on COVID-19 vaccination continues to be a priority given its public health benefits and the need to avoid outbreaks that may discourage tourism or inhibit broader commercial activity. For EAP small states, a larger proportion of tourism demand originates in countries that pursued strict policies to prevent viral transmission. In this context, small states like Tonga and Samoa, both of which fully vaccinated their populations by early 2022, were better placed

to benefit from the tourism recovery than Vanuatu or the Marshall Islands, where broad vaccination coverage took longer. In several small states, particularly in the Caribbean, vaccine hesitancy proved a significant barrier (World Bank forthcoming). Providing accessible scientific information and pursuing communication campaigns that combat such misperceptions and resonate with unvaccinated populations are potentially an effective low-cost way to increase vaccine uptake (Taylor 2022; UNICEF 2021).

In addition, as in other EMDEs, learning and job losses from the pandemic have interrupted the accumulation of skills and human capital and are likely to weigh on incomes and potential growth for years to come. Investments in human capital can allow for greater technology use, bolstering productivity and improving service delivery (World Bank and UNESCO 2022). Small states would also benefit from efforts to improve early childhood development and nutrition coverage. Improving education programs at all levels while also promoting youth employment and entrepreneurship could help recover learning losses caused by the pandemic, reduce education inequalities, and enhance resilience to labor market shocks (Schady et al. forthcoming).

Fiscal sustainability. Given the inability of most small states to use exchange rates or monetary policy as a stabilizer, responsibility for counter-cyclical policy rests largely on fiscal policy, making the maintenance of fiscal space especially important. At the country level, medium-term fiscal consolidation in small states, to the extent possible in a challenging global environment, would also help reduce risks from the recent increase in debt burdens. Expenditure restraint—particularly of recurrent spending—would bolster fiscal positions and reduce the need for additional debt. Redesigning subsidy programs in favor of approaches that more precisely target the poor would be one such reform (Heller 2022). Addressing inefficiencies in public sectors could yield substantial fiscal benefits, as could encouraging the transfer of a greater share of the economy from the informal to the formal sector (Ohnsorge and Yu 2021). In some countries, this could be complemented by limiting fiscal risks related to state-owned enterprises (for instance, in Cabo Verde and Maldives; World Bank 2019b, 2021a). Given country-level capacity constraints, proximate small states could consider pooling some administrative functions and commonly needed services (for example, data gathering and potentially some logistical and regulatory services) to generate better economies of scale.

Although revenues in small states are higher as a share of GDP than in other EMDEs, a phaseout of tax exemptions and improvements in the efficiency of tax administration (including by modernizing the technology used, in many countries) could also help improve fiscal positions. In small states in EAP, for instance, tax revenues could be increased by an estimated 3 percent in the medium term through a combination of improvements to VAT systems, rationalizing tax exemptions, closing loopholes, and reforming tax administration (Sy et al. 2022). Small states in EAP also tend to derive a smaller proportion of revenue from taxing income, profits, and capital gains than other EMDEs. Measures to broaden these tax bases could improve fiscal positions without materially constraining activity. In addition to limiting borrowing needs, fiscal reprioritization could free budgetary resources for critical investments in human and physical capital.

Looking ahead, policy makers can put in place and bolster the fiscal and regulatory frameworks necessary to make the best use of the financial inflows resulting from tourism and commodity exports, and help rebuild room to maneuver when hit by negative shocks. Public financial and investment management reforms are underway in several countries (for example, The Bahamas and Bhutan). Improvements in debt transparency—particularly with respect to private and non-Paris club lending—can reduce risks of debt distress and prevent delays in restructuring should it be needed in the future (Rivetti 2021). Historically, a better policy and institutional environment in small states is associated with higher debt carrying capacity and better ability to withstand external shocks (Prasad, Pollock, and Li 2013). Clear medium-term fiscal frameworks, including appropriately designed fiscal rules and anchors, can create macroeconomic policy room and support investor confidence.

In view of the growing effects of climate change in small states, explicitly incorporating climate adaptation costs into domestic budgets has become increasingly urgent. As of 2021, slightly more than one-third of small states had some type of fiscal rule, about the same share as other EMDEs. These were mostly debt rules. For small states in LAC facing high macroeconomic volatility, however, structural balance rules have been found to be the most suitable (Blanco et al. 2020).

The likelihood of adhering to fiscal rules can be increased by the presence of precautionary mechanisms, such as sovereign wealth funds or access to contingent credit. A substantial number of small states have established sovereign wealth funds or trust funds (for example, Bahrain, Brunei Darussalam, Equatorial Guinea, Guyana, Kiribati, the Marshall Islands, the Federated States of Micronesia, Palau, Timor-Leste, Tonga, Trinidad and Tobago, and Tuvalu), which in principle can support debt sustainability in small states by helping to buffer fiscal shocks and stabilize otherwise volatile revenue and expenditure profiles. Given the differing purposes of sovereign funds (for example, budget stabilization, promotion of intergenerational equity, or transitioning away from donor dependence), a range of approaches to risk and liquidity management may be appropriate (Drew 2016). Varied objectives notwithstanding, sovereign wealth funds can be counterproductive if they are managed in a way that introduces budgeting rigidities and distortions, or is insufficiently prudent. Integrating funds into a coherent and holistic medium-term budgeting framework, avoiding off-budget activities, and establishing transparent and professional governance can support the stability of sovereign wealth funds (Le Borgne and Medas 2007).

The rise in public and private debt and the concentrated nature of small state banking sectors has increased the risk that economic shocks are amplified by financial sector stress. To guard against this, in addition to rebuilding fiscal and external positions, small states can build capacity in financial sector supervision, and ensure banking sectors have ample capital buffers. In assessing specific risks to bank balance sheets (for example, in the context of stress-testing) small states can place particular emphasis on integrating an assessment of disaster-related vulnerabilities (IMF 2019). Small states can also benefit from financing innovations and contractual clauses to pre-emptively transfer disaster-related financial risks away from small state balance sheets.

Diversification. Greater economic and export diversification is associated with lower growth volatility and higher long-term average growth in small states (McIntyre, Li, and Wang 2018). Diversification efforts must be calibrated, however, to align with areas where small states can realistically build advantages, and must take into account the limitations of small economic size and government capacity. The appropriate strategies for small states in the Caribbean, with their relative proximity to the United States and Latin America, will differ from other groups of small states. By contrast, the Pacific Islands are spread across a vast geographical area, are far from potential trading partners, and have varied circumstances (Fiji is more than 80 times as populous as Nauru, for example).

Facilitating effective diversification could include the development of blue economy activities in island economies, such as aquaculture, carbon sequestration, renewable energy generation, or commercially oriented research (OECD 2021; Patil et al. 2016). The diversification process could also entail differentiation within important sectors—for example, developing high value-added eco-tourism and cultural tourism. The promotion of activity focused on the rich biodiversity of many small states could help preserve natural capital and unlock new sources of finance (similar to the "rhino bond" recently issued in South Africa; World Bank 2022f). Fisheries and associated activities, such as processing and vessel support, could provide sustainable growth, as long as catch limits that maintain the health of fish stock are enforced.

There may also be niche markets where small states, due to institutional or geographic factors, have particular advantages—for example, some Caribbean islands host internationally oriented medical schools. Agricultural producers could benefit from diversifying into production of higher value products or moving agricultural sector production up the value chain (agro-

processing). Belize, for example, has had some success with the former (World Bank 2017). Mauritius is an example of a small state that succeeded through sustained policy efforts in developing new types of services and manufacturing activity over several decades, with GDP per capita nearly doubling (in U.S. dollar terms) in the two decades prior to the COVID-19 pandemic.

Reforms to support growth. In general, small states can improve long-term prospects by seeking to enhance the competitiveness and resilience of sectors in which they have advantages, improving access to foreign markets, bolstering the skills of the population, and fostering nimbleness and adaptability to quickly embrace new opportunities (Briguglio 2022). More specifically, reducing trade costs, boosting digital connectivity, increasing financial inclusion, and prioritizing the development of sound institutions could all help to sustainably increase growth, while also building resilience to external shocks arising from disruptions in activity to major trading partners or to global supply chains.

There is considerable opportunity to improve the competitiveness of small states by improving digital connectivity. Ensuring connectivity and a baseline of digital skills in the population could, for example, help small businesses access global markets through integration with online platforms. Digital connectivity, augmented with access to essential services (for example, healthcare), could also help partially offset outward emigration by attracting increasing numbers of "digital nomads," especially if cultural shifts toward remote working are sustained (World Bank 2021b). In 2020, Barbados and several other island nations instituted schemes encouraging foreigners to work remotely from their territory, in effect diversifying their services exports. Further, the digitization of public services and records could support more streamlined and responsive public sectors that are better able to facilitate private sector growth, while requiring fewer resources.

Broadly, lack of access to credit for micro and small businesses is a constraint on private sector growth in small states (World Bank 2022g,

2022h, forthcoming). Bolstering small state fintech sectors could help to address this, complementing other efforts to unlock finance for small firms, such as guarantee programs supported by the Eastern Caribbean Partial Credit Guarantees Corporation. Furthering fintech could also have other growth-enhancing benefits, such as reducing remittance fees, improving credit reporting, facilitating more effective social safety nets, enabling better insurance coverage, and reducing inefficiencies associated with high cash usage (Davidovic et al. 2019). In The Bahamas, for instance, the Sand Dollar, a digital currency backed by the central bank's foreign reserves, was launched with the intention of promoting financial inclusion. In addition, greater digitalization of financial systems could facilitate more efficient anti-money laundering and counter-terrorist financing procedures, which could help address perceived risks that have led to a decline in correspondent banking relationships in small states (Alwazir et al. 2017).

Given high levels of trade openness, small states could support long-term productivity growth by reducing trade costs. Across EMDEs, trade costs double the cost of internationally traded goods in comparison to domestic goods, with the bulk of these costs coming from shipping and logistics, as well as cumbersome trade procedures (World Bank 2021c). Trade costs are almost one-half higher in EMDEs than in advanced economies. Data for small states is limited, but it is likely that their trade costs are even more elevated than other EMDEs. Despite being highly reliant on shipping to distribute exports, small states are comparatively poorly integrated into global shipping networks, due to both remoteness and lack of scale. The average efficiency of customs procedures and quality of trade-related infrastructure in small states is broadly comparable to EMDEs but lags substantially behind advanced economies. Import tariffs in small states, at nearly 11 percent, are notably higher than in other EMDEs (figure 4.12.A). Small states could lower trade costs through deeper trade liberalization, streamlining customs procedures, improving port and other infrastructure, and making logistics and transport services more competitive.

FIGURE 4.12 Policies to reduce vulnerability to global price shocks

In the medium term, small states could reduce price pressures and increase living standards through streamlining trade procedures and increased transport connectivity. Increasing the share of renewables in energy consumption could help lessen the vulnerability to global energy price volatility.

A. Trade connectivity and costs

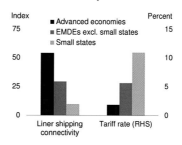

B. Renewable energy consumption

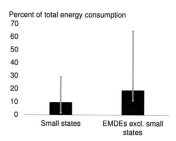

Sources: World Bank; World Development Indicators.
Note: EMDEs = emerging market and developing economies; RHS = right hand side.
A. Simple averages of countries in each group. Liner shipping connectivity is an index based on number of ships, their container-carrying capacity, maximum vessel size, number of services, and number of companies that deploy container ships in a country's ports; data for 2020. Tariff rate is the weighted mean import tariff on all products. Data for 2018.
B. Bars show medians within indicated country groups. Vertical lines show interquartile ranges within groups. Sample includes 37 small states and 111 EMDEs excluding small states. Data for 2019.

Small states could also seek to codify more and deeper free trade agreements, both by negotiating new agreements and by acceding to existing agreements involving larger economies, although in some cases country-level capacity constraints may present an obstacle. Small state participation in free trade agreements is limited. Seven EAP small states have entered, or are about to enter, a trade agreement with Australia. Brunei Darussalam is a member of several free trade agreements, including the Trans-Pacific Partnership. Twelve LAC small states in the Caribbean are part of CARICOM, an intra-Caribbean free trade agreement. The economic benefits of CARICOM could potentially be improved, however, through regional harmonization of investment codes (which has begun, but could be accelerated), and by reducing the common external tariffs on intermediate and capital goods (World Bank forthcoming). More generally, improving regulatory alignment with larger trading partners could encourage companies to expand into small states, helping to boost competition.

Inefficient state-owned enterprises may exert a drag on the broader economy in some small states, given their significant size in the context of small economies. Budget transfers to lossmaking SOEs restrict public resources that could otherwise be made available for productive public investment. SOE wages may also put upward pressure on wages in the broader government sector, contributing to mismatches between pay and productivity (Heller 2022). In some cases, corporate sectors could be made more productive if SOEs were privatized or regulated more effectively. In Fiji, for example, the predominance of SOEs in sectors that are usually private, such as fisheries and agribusiness, may distort competitive dynamics (World Bank 2022g).

Where SOEs are providing essential quasi-public services, it is important that their governance promotes disciplined management. Financial accounts need to be public and subject to rigorous audit, board decision-making needs to be transparent and accountable, and regulatory and commercial functions should be effectively separated. The pricing of SOE goods and services can also be reformed to support efficient use of resources. Offering services at less than cost recovery, for example, is likely to distort private consumption decisions by providing an untargeted subsidy that the government ultimately funds.

Small states are likely to have both advantages and disadvantages in fostering effective public institutions, which are broadly associated with stronger growth in EMDEs (Butkiewicz and Yanikkaya 2006). Smallness may confer challenges in delivering high value-for-money public services, because of indivisible overheads that increase per capita costs and the absence of deep pools of human capital. The risks from administrative missteps may be higher because varied responsibilities may be allocated to relatively few people, and individual projects may represent proportionally large draws on government resources.

On the other hand, smallness means that government is closer to the people, which may promote social cohesion, trust, and resilience, in turn increasing the ability of small states to address coordination problems and local externalities (Brito 2015). While broadly applicable prescri-

ptions to help build stronger institutions—including limiting opportunities for corruption; increasing financial and political transparency; professionalizing public services; curtailing nepotism; and limiting state activities that crowd out private enterprise—are not distinct to small states, the long-term benefits of prioritizing such goals may be greater in small states than in other, comparable EMDEs. Accordingly, small states may be able to benefit disproportionately from leveraging international community assistance in developing sound institutions and governance.

Reducing vulnerability to external shocks. As well as bolstering fiscal and external positions, small states can pursue other measures to increase the flexibility of their economies and reduce vulnerability to external shocks.

Given their generally fixed exchange rates, shocks that would usually be cushioned by real exchange rate depreciations need to be met by other adjustment mechanisms. In this context, developing more flexible product and factor markets, for example through increasing labor market flexibility, encouraging competition, limiting the role of the state in production, and improving the regulation of natural monopolies, can help small state economies become adaptable to changing circumstances. Following the pandemic, increased labor market flexibility could be twinned with active labor market policies to facilitate the upskilling and reallocation of workers. Some small states with underdeveloped financial sectors could also augment their capacity to weather income shocks by deepening integration with international capital markets, though additional financial risk exposures would need to be prudently managed.

Small states could lessen the local impacts of global energy price spikes by expanding electrical grids and accelerating their transitions to renewable energy, making greater use of solar, hydro, geothermal, and wind sources available domestically. For some small states, large increases in cost-effective domestic energy generation could be transformative—Fiji, Palau, and the Seychelles import fuel worth more than 10 percent of GDP annually, while the high cost of electricity constrains the competitiveness of many Caribbean islands (World Bank forthcoming). Recognizing these potential benefits, several small states have committed to dramatically increasing use of renewables. For example, Fiji's national development plan commits to using entirely renewable energy by 2036, while Palau's renewable energy roadmap lays out plans to exclusively use renewables by 2050 (Government of Fiji 2017; IRENA 2022). In Cabo Verde, the recently completed Cabeólica wind farm meets about a quarter of domestic energy requirements and has lowered power generation costs, while reducing the need for fuel imports (InfraCo Africa 2016).

Nonetheless, as a group, small states lag other EMDEs in their share of energy consumption from renewable sources (figure 4.12.B). Low renewable energy shares may reflect challenges securing financing for large up-front capital costs associated with installing renewable energy infrastructure. In this context, it is important for small states to ensure that their energy sector regulatory frameworks are able to attract private investment (World Bank 2022g).

Reducing vulnerability to climate-related and natural disasters. There is no way for small states to entirely offset the disruption that climate-related and natural disasters will bring. However, a holistic, integrated approach to crisis preparedness can reduce the economic and human impact of these events by investing in both ex ante disaster resilience (market insurance, self-insurance, and self-protection) and ex post disaster recovery (Ehrlich and Becker 1972). Successfully boosting resilience to climate change without sacrificing broader development objectives requires policy reforms, reallocating public resources, mobilizing private capital, and financial support from the global community (World Bank 2022i).

Postdisaster recovery and reconstruction can be funded by dedicated savings, in the form of sovereign wealth funds or national recovery funds, or by proceeds from catastrophe bonds, disaster- and weather-based insurance mechanisms, and lending with specialized contingency options in case of a disaster. These latter mechanisms can help to pre-emptively transfer disaster-related financial risks to capital markets, via appropriate contractual clauses. Barbados and Belize have issued "blue bonds," with guarantees from the

international community, to refinance existing debt at lower rates. In the case of Belize, the bonds are linked to marine conservation that includes "catastrophe wrapper" credit insurance in the case of hurricanes. Region-specific disaster risk insurance pools, such as the Caribbean Catastrophe Risk Insurance Facility and the Pacific Catastrophe Risk Assessment and Financing Facility, provide services to numerous small states. Various forms of these mechanisms have been developed with international financial institutions and other development partners.

Regarding ex ante climate change resilience and adaptation, development of a National Adaptation Plan (NAP) is an important step. Some countries have already adopted NAPs (Cabo Verde, Fiji, Grenada, Kiribati, St. Lucia, St. Vincent and the Grenadines, Suriname, Timor-Leste, and Tonga) and others are in the process of developing them (the Marshall Islands). A substantial portion of the needed actions related to resilience involve infrastructure, including constructing and retrofitting infrastructure to be able to withstand the impacts of one-off and long-term disasters; desalinization systems; early warning systems; and adaptations to safeguard certain industries, such as agriculture. Ensuring the resilience of infrastructure has dual benefits, as it both helps avoid large reconstruction costs associated with natural disasters and supports the livelihoods and well-being of people (Hallegatte, Rentschler, and Rozenberg 2019). With limited public resources to dedicate to infrastructure, it is crucial that policy makers in small states prioritize climate-related infrastructure investments in fiscal frameworks and that they take advantage of available sources of climate-related financing (World Bank 2016).

Policy support from the global community

As policy makers in small states seek to accelerate their economic recoveries, the global community is supporting them in a variety of ways (ADB 2022; Rustomjee et al. 2022; World Bank 2022j). In the short term, the international community can help by scaling up nonconcessional official financing, concessional financing, and grants; helping to leverage private sector financing; continuing to support COVID-19 vaccination programs; and upgrading the international architecture for dealing with excessive debt. The global community can also assist small states by providing technical assistance to build institutional capacity; enhancing pandemic preparedness; delivering on commitments to tackle climate change; and promoting open, rules-based global trade and investment networks.

Vaccinations and pandemic preparedness. In some remote or lower-middle-income small states, limited access to vaccines and the health services to deliver them remains a challenge. For example, vaccination rates in Eswatini and the Solomon Islands remain only about 40 percent. The global community can continue to support small states in sourcing adequate vaccine shipments and ensuring that the necessary health sector staff and logistics requirements are in place to utilize vaccines when they are delivered.

The COVID-19 pandemic has illustrated the extreme vulnerability of small states to extended disruptions to international travel. Future pandemics caused by easily transmissible pathogens represent a severe ongoing risk to small state economies. The global community can help mitigate these risks by continuing to upgrade pandemic preparedness and financing. Establishing stronger global epidemiological surveillance, early warning systems, research cooperation, and rapid response architecture (including procurement facilities and vaccine and therapeutic manufacturing and distribution capacity) can help minimize disruptions from future emergencies (World Bank 2022k). Putting in place such systems across groups of small states, where capacity building and market power is limited, is another area where the international community can play a role.

Debt sustainability. The international community has a role to play in addressing the debt burden in small states. This includes the provision of technical assistance on debt management and reduction strategies, as well as identifying and mitigating fiscal risks linked to contingent liabilities. The World Bank Group and the IMF are supporting current initiatives aimed at facilitating effective and comprehensive debt restructuring. In that respect, for eligible small

states, the G20's Common Framework provides a potential route to address debt vulnerabilities that prove unsustainable. The World Bank Group and IMF have advocated for expanding the Common Framework to include middle-income countries (World Bank and IMF 2022). They have also suggested a set of reforms to make the Common Framework process more swift and predictable.

Official assistance. In the last two years, increased financial flows from official sources have helped to bolster small state reserves and broader financial positions, partially offsetting reductions in foreign direct investment and tourism revenues and increases in import costs. Even before the pandemic, small states received substantially more international assistance in per capita terms than LICs as a result of their unique vulnerabilities. While sound macroeconomic policies should help small states transition away from aid dependence in the future, in the near term many small states will be more reliant than usual on official assistance. As many advanced economies pursue fiscal consolidation and resource reprioritization in the aftermath of pandemic-era fiscal expansions, it is crucial to sustain assistance to vulnerable communities in countries that have not yet recovered from the pandemic.

Many small states also depend on technical assistance from the World Bank, the IMF, and their development partners to make up for their generally limited government capacity. The global community helps develop the institutional capacity of small states through training in a variety of areas related to governance and policy analysis. This includes providing technical support on specialized subjects such as procurement, financing, data collection, climate change adaptation, integration with the global financial system, and other topics needed for the implementation of structural reforms. As the challenges of climate change become more pronounced, the need for technical assistance on climate-related budgeting and financing is likely to expand.

Open, rules-based trade, investment, and migration networks. Very high levels of trade openness mean small states are likely to experience magnified negative effects from disruptions to global trade and investment networks. For example, the proliferation in food-related export restrictions since Russia's invasion of Ukraine is likely to have severe consequences for the one-fifth of small states that import food worth more than 10 percent of GDP (Espitia, Rocha, and Ruta 2022). The global community can therefore support the revival of small-state economies by promoting open, rules-based trade and investment frameworks, including intra-regional frameworks among small states. Migration policies can also be tailored to ensure mutually beneficial movement of workers where possible—for example, in circumstances where temporary migration can reduce labor shortages in the host country and support human capital formation and remittance flows for the home country (Gibson and McKenzie 2011).

Climate change. Small states are responsible for a miniscule proportion of global greenhouse gas emissions but bear a disproportionate share of the costs arising from extreme weather events. The greatest contribution the global community can make to small states' long-term prospects is to fully implement climate agreements reached in international fora to limit the rise in global temperatures, sea levels, and other climate-related changes. Nonetheless, more extreme and more frequent weather events will likely be reflected in rising risk premia for borrowing by small states, which could act as a long-term drag on needed investment to adapt to climate change. Because these costs stem from activity outside small states, the global community should continue to provide concessional insurance and other financing

subsidies to help small states manage climate vulnerabilities.

Providing specialized climate-related financing to small states is already a growing area of activity (Piemonte 2021). Numerous multilateral and bilateral climate financing facilities, such as the Green Climate Fund and the Global Environment Facility, are available to provide grant-based and concessional financing for disaster and climate resilience. With the support of the international community, several small states have been able to issue green (Fiji) and blue (Belize, the Seychelles) bonds to support environmental and climate resilience. However, commitments from these sources have been lower than needs and uneven across countries (Fouad et al. 2021).

With policy frameworks in place to help mobilize climate-related revenue streams and mitigate some lender risks through targeted guarantees, the private sector also has the potential to play a much larger role in providing climate- and disaster-related financing. For example, some small states may be able to develop effective carbon sequestration and offset programs, which can provide new revenue to fund up-front investments (Claes et al. 2022). The international community could also focus assistance on upstream technical capacity and early project preparation, to ensure a pipeline of bankable projects. Such measures could help ensure international financing supports domestic transitions to renewable energy, an area where small states are lagging relative to other EMDEs.

TABLE 4.1 **EMDE small states, by type**

	Tourism reliant (22)	Commodity importers (22)	Agriculture exporters (7)	Energy exporters (7)	FCS (6)	Islands (28)	Land-locked (2)	Fixed exchange rates (35)	Remittance reliant (9)
Antigua and Barbuda	X	X				X		X	
Bahamas, The	X	X				X		X	
Bahrain	X			X		X		X	
Barbados	X	X				X		X	
Belize	X		X					X	
Bhutan				X			X	X	
Brunei Darussalam				X				X	
Cabo Verde	X		X			X		X	X
Comoros			X		X	X		X	X
Djibouti		X						X	
Dominica	X	X				X		X	
Equatorial Guinea				X				X	
Eswatini		X					X	X	
Fiji	X		X			X		X	
Grenada	X	X				X		X	
Guyana				X				X	X
Kiribati		X				X		X	X
Maldives	X	X				X		X	
Marshall Islands	X	X			X	X		X	X
Mauritius	X	X				X			
Micronesia, Fed. Sts.	X	X			X	X		X	
Montenegro	X	X						X	X
Nauru		X				X		X	X
Palau	X	X				X		X	
Samoa	X	X				X		X	X
São Tomé and Príncipe			X			X		X	
Seychelles	X		X			X			
Solomon Islands			X		X	X		X	
St. Kitts and Nevis	X	X				X		X	
St. Lucia	X	X				X		X	
St. Vincent and the Grenadines	X	X				X		X	
Suriname								X	
Timor-Leste				X	X	X		X	
Tonga	X	X				X		X	X
Trinidad and Tobago				X		X		X	
Tuvalu		X			X	X		X	
Vanuatu	X	X				X		X	

Sources: UN World Tourism Organization; IMF Annual Report on Exchange Arrangements and Exchange Restrictions (AREAER) database; World Bank.

Note: FCS = fragile and conflict-affected situations. Tourism-reliant countries are those with inbound tourism expenditure as a share of GDP during 2015-19 above the 3rd percentile of the share in all EMDEs, based on UN World Tourism Organization data. Agriculture-exporting and energy-exporting economies are those where exports of agriculture or energy commodities accounted for 20 percent or more of total exports, on average, in 2017-19. Economies that meet these thresholds as a result of re-exports are excluded. The six countries classified as FCS as of the World Bank's fiscal year 2023 were also considered FCS for at least 10 years during fiscal years 2006-23. Fixed exchange rates include managed arrangements, pegs within horizontal bands, crawl-like arrangements, crawling pegs, stabilized arrangements, conventional pegs, currency boards, and the absence of a country-issued legal tender. Remittance-reliant countries are those with remittance inflows as a share of GDP during 2015-20 above the 75th percentile of all EMDEs (that is, above 8 percent of GDP), based on World Bank data.

TABLE 4.2 Real GDP for EMDE small states[1]

(Percent change from previous year)

Percentage point difference
from June 2022 projections

	2020	2021	2022e	2023f	2024f	2022e	2023f	2024f
EMDE small states (excluding Guyana)	-11.2	4.6	5.2	3.5	3.1	0.9	-0.2	-0.1
Bahamas, The	-23.8	13.7	8.0	4.1	3.0	2.0	0.0	0.0
Bahrain	-4.9	2.2	3.8	3.2	3.2	0.3	0.1	0.1
Barbados	-13.7	0.7	10.0	4.8	3.9	-1.2	-0.1	0.9
Belize	-13.7	16.3	3.5	2.0	2.0	-2.2	-1.4	0.0
Bhutan[2]	-2.3	-3.3	4.6	4.1	3.7	0.2	-0.6	-3.0
Cabo Verde	-14.8	7.0	4.0	4.8	5.7	-1.5	-1.3	-0.3
Comoros	-0.3	2.2	1.4	3.3	3.8	-1.4	0.2	0.1
Djibouti	1.2	4.3	3.6	5.3	6.2	0.3	0.1	0.0
Dominica	-16.6	6.5	5.8	4.6	4.6	-1.0	-0.4	0.0
Equatorial Guinea	-4.9	-1.6	3.2	-2.6	-3.4	1.4	0.0	-1.3
Eswatini	-1.6	7.9	1.1	2.6	2.7	-0.9	0.8	0.9
Fiji	-17.0	-5.1	15.1	5.4	3.4	8.8	-2.3	-2.2
Grenada	-13.8	4.7	5.8	3.2	3.0	2.0	-0.2	-0.1
Guyana	43.5	20.0	57.8	25.2	21.2	9.9	-9.1	17.4
Kiribati	-0.5	1.5	1.5	2.3	2.1	-0.3	-0.2	-0.2
Maldives	-33.5	41.7	12.4	8.2	8.1	4.8	-2.0	1.0
Marshall Islands[2]	-2.2	1.1	1.5	2.2	2.5	-1.5	-0.2	-0.1
Mauritius	-14.6	3.6	5.8	5.5	4.2	-0.1	-0.5	0.3
Micronesia, Fed. Sts.[2]	-1.8	-3.2	-0.5	3.0	2.5	-0.9	-0.2	0.6
Montenegro	-15.3	13.0	5.9	3.4	3.1	2.3	-1.3	-0.6
Nauru[2]	0.7	1.5	0.9	1.9	2.8	0.0	-0.7	0.4
Palau[2]	-9.7	-17.1	-2.5	18.2	4.5	-9.7	2.0	0.0
Samoa[2]	-3.1	-7.1	-6.0	4.0	3.5	-5.7	1.5	-0.3
São Tomé and Príncipe	3.1	1.8	1.1	2.1	2.4	-1.7	-0.9	-0.9
Seychelles	-7.7	7.9	11.0	5.2	4.8	6.4	-0.5	-0.2
Solomon Islands	-3.4	-0.2	-4.5	2.6	2.4	-1.6	-2.7	-1.4
St. Lucia	-24.4	11.9	8.9	4.4	3.2	2.5	-0.8	-0.1
St. Vincent and the Grenadines	-5.3	0.7	5.0	6.0	4.8	1.3	-0.4	1.6
Suriname	-16.0	-2.7	1.3	2.3	3.0	-0.5	0.2	0.3
Timor-Leste[3]	-8.6	2.9	3.0	3.0	3.0	0.6	0.2	0.0
Tonga[2]	0.5	-2.7	-1.6	3.3	3.2	0.0	0.1	0.0
Tuvalu	-4.9	0.3	3.0	3.5	4.0	-0.5	-0.3	0.0
Vanuatu	-5.4	0.5	2.2	3.4	3.5	0.2	-0.7	-0.2
EMDE small states memorandum items:[4]								
East Asia and Pacific	-10.1	-2.9	5.6	4.4	3.2	2.7	-1.2	-1.1
Latin America and the Caribbean (excluding Guyana)	-19.0	7.2	6.9	4.0	3.3	0.6	-0.2	0.2
Sub-Saharan Africa	-8.8	2.7	4.2	2.2	1.7	0.5	-0.2	-0.2
Tourism reliant	-12.9	5.7	6.1	4.3	3.8	1.1	-0.3	0.1
Commodity importers	-16.1	8.8	6.3	4.8	4.1	0.8	-0.3	0.3
Commodity exporters (excluding Guyana)	-7.1	1.4	4.3	2.4	2.2	1.0	-0.2	-0.6
Fragile and conflict-affected states	-4.1	1.2	-0.1	2.9	3.0	-0.9	-0.8	-0.3

Source: World Bank.

Note: e = estimate; f = forecast. World Bank forecasts are frequently updated based on new information. Consequently, projections presented here may differ from those contained in other World Bank documents, even if basic assessments of countries' prospects do not differ at any given date. Brunei Darussalam, Guyana, and Trinidad and Tobago are excluded from cross-country macroeconomic aggregates.

1. Headline aggregate growth rates are calculated using GDP weights at average 2010-19 prices and market exchange rates.

2. For the following countries, values correspond to the fiscal year: Bhutan (July 1-June 30); the Marshall Islands, the Federated States of Micronesia, and Palau (October 1-September 30); Nauru, Samoa, and Tonga (July 1-June 30).

3. Values for Timor-Leste reflect non-oil GDP.

4. East Asia and Pacific includes Fiji, Kiribati, the Marshall Islands, the Federated States of Micronesia, Nauru, Palau, Samoa, the Solomon Islands, Timor-Leste, Tonga, Tuvalu, and Vanuatu. Latin America and the Caribbean includes Antigua and Barbuda, the Bahamas, Barbados, Belize, Dominica, Grenada, St. Kitts and Nevis, St. Lucia, St. Vincent and the Grenadines, and Suriname. Sub-Saharan Africa includes Cabo Verde, Comoros, Equatorial Guinea, Eswatini, Mauritius, São Tomé and Príncipe, and Seychelles. Remaining groups include EMDEs as classified in table 4.1. Commodity exporters include agriculture, energy, and metal (Bhutan and Suriname) exporters.

References

Airaudo, M., E. F. Buffie, and L.-F. Zanna. 2016. "Inflation Targeting and Exchange Rate Management in Less Developed Countries." IMF Working Paper 16/55, International Monetary Fund, Washington, DC.

Al-Sadiq, A., P. Bejar, and I. Ötker. 2021. "Commodity Shocks and Exchange Rate Regimes: Implications for the Caribbean Commodity Exporters." IMF Working Paper 21/104, International Monetary Fund, Washington, DC.

Alwazir, J., F. Jamaludin, D. Lee, N. Sheridan, and P. Tumbarello. 2017. "Challenges in Correspondent Banking in the Small States of the Pacific." IMF Working Paper 17/90, International Monetary Fund, Washington, DC.

Arezki, R., R. Cherif, and J. Piotrowski. 2009. "Tourism Specialization and Economic Development: Evidence from the UNESCO World Heritage List." IMF Working Paper 21/104, International Monetary Fund, Washington, DC.

Armstrong, H., and R. Read. 2006. "Geographical 'Handicaps' and Small States: Some Implications for the Pacific from a Global Perspective." *Asia Pacific Viewpoint* 47 (1): 79-92.

ADB (Asian Development Bank). 2022. "2022 Annual Evaluation Review: Fragile and Conflict-Affected Situations and Small Island Developing States." Asian Development Bank, Manila.

Baffes, J., and P. Nagle, eds. 2022. *Commodity Markets: Evolution, Challenges, and Policies.* World Bank, Washington, DC.

Balasundharam, V., L. Hunter, I. Lavea, and P. Seeds. 2021. "Managing Fiscal Risks from National Airlines in Pacific Island Countries." IMF Working Paper 21/183, International Monetary Fund, Washington, DC.

Blanco, F., P. Saavedra, F. Koehler-Geib, and E. Skrok. 2020. *Fiscal Rules and Economic Size in Latin America and the Caribbean.* Latin American Development Forum Series. Washington, DC: World Bank.

Briguglio, L. 2022. "Economic Growth of Small Developing States—A Literature Review." Independent Evaluation Office Background Paper, International Monetary Fund, Washington, DC.

Brito, J. A. 2015. "Social Cohesion and Economic Growth: Small States vs Large States." MPRA Paper 66118, University Library of Munich, Germany.

Butkiewicz, J. L., and H. Yanikkaya. 2006. "Institutional Quality and Economic Growth: Maintenance of the Rule of Law or Democratic Institutions, or Both?" *Economic Modelling* 23 (4): 648-661.

Calvo, G. A., and C. M. Reinhart. 2000. "Fear of Floating." NBER Working Paper 7993, National Bureau of Economic Research, Cambridge MA.

Cantu-Bazaldua, F. 2021. "Remote but Well Connected? Neighboring but Isolated? Measuring Remoteness in the Context of SIDS." UNCTAD Research Paper 67, United Nations Conference on Trade and Development, Geneva.

Claes, J., D. Hopman, G. Jaeger. and M. Rogers. 2022. "The Potential of Coastal and Oceanic Climate Action." McKinsey and Company, Washington, DC.

Davidovic, S. E. Loukoianova, C. Sullivan, and H. Tourpe. 2019. "Strategy for Fintech Applications in the Pacific Islands." Departmental Paper 19/14, International Monetary Fund, Washington, DC.

Dieppe, A., ed. 2021. *Global Productivity: Trends, Drivers, and Policies.* Washington, DC: World Bank.

Drew, A. 2016. "The Role of Sovereign Funds in Pacific Island Nations." New Zealand Institute for Pacific Research, Auckland.

Easterly, W., and A. Kraay. 2000. "Small States, Small Problems? Income, Growth, and Volatility in Small States." *World Development* 28 (11): 2013-17.

Ehrlich, I., and G. S. Becker. 1972. "Market Insurance, Self-Insurance, and Self-Protection." *Journal of Political Economy* 80 (4): 623-648.

Espitia, A., N. Rocha, and M. Ruta. 2022. "How Export Restrictions Are Impacting Global Food Prices." *Private Sector Development* (blog), July 6, 2022. https://blogs.worldbank.org/psd/how-export-restrictions-are-impacting-global-food-prices.

FAO (Food and Agriculture Organization). 2020. "Small Island Developing States Response to COVID-19: Highlighting Food Security, Nutrition and Sustainable Food Systems." Food and Agriculture Commission of the United Nations, Rome.

FAO (Food and Agriculture Organization). 2022. "GIEWS Country Brief Cabo Verde." June 16. Food and Agriculture Commission of the United Nations, Rome.

Fouad, M., N. Novta, G. Preston, T. Schneider, and S. Weerathunga. 2021. "Unlocking Access to Climate Finance for Pacific Islands Countries." Departmental Paper 2021/020, Asia-Pacific and Fiscal Affairs Department, International Monetary Fund, Washington, DC.

Gibson, J., and D. McKenzie. 2011. "Eight Questions about Brain Drain." *Journal of Economic Perspectives* 25 (3): 107-128.

Government of Dominica. 2017. "Post-Disaster Needs Assessment: Hurricane Maria."

Government of Fiji. 2017. "5-Year and 20-Year National Development Plan: Transforming Fiji." Government of Fiji, Suva.

Guénette, J. D., M. A. Kose, and N. Sugawara. 2022. "Is a Global Recession Imminent?" EFI Policy Note 4, World Bank, Washington, DC.

Ha, W., J. Yi, and J, Zhang. 2016. "Brain Drain, Brain Gain, and Economic Growth." *China Economic Review* 38: 322-337.

Hale, T., N. Angrist, R. Goldszmidt, B. Kira, A. Petherick, T. Phillips, S. Webster, et al. 2021. "A Global Panel Database of Pandemic Policies (Oxford COVID-19 Government Response Tracker." *Nature Human Behaviour* 5: 529-38.

Hallegatte, S., J. Rentschler, and J. Rozenberg. 2019. *Lifelines: The Resilient Infrastructure Opportunity.* Washington, DC: World Bank.

Heller, P. S. 2022. "IMF Fiscal Policy Engagement in Small Developing States." International Monetary Fund, Independent Evaluation Office, Washington DC.

Hnatkovska, V., and F. Koehler-Geib. 2018. "Characterizing Business Cycles in Small States." Policy Research Working Paper 8527, World Bank, Washington, DC.

Horn, S., C. Reinhart, and C. Trebesch. 2019. "China's Overseas Lending." NBER Working Paper 26050, National Bureau of Economic Research, Cambridge, MA.

Imam, P. 2012. "Exchange Rate Choices of Microstates." *The Developing Economies* 50: 207-235.

IMF (International Monetary Fund). 2013. "Macroeconomic Issues in Small States and Implications for Fund Engagement." IMF Policy Paper, International Monetary Fund, Washington, DC.

IMF (International Monetary Fund). 2019. "Building Resilience in Developing Countries Vulnerable to Large Natural Disasters." IMF Policy Paper, International Monetary Fund, Washington, DC.

IMF (International Monetary Fund). 2021. *Fiscal Monitor: Strengthening the Credibility of Public Finances.* Washington, DC: International Monetary Fund.

IMF (International Monetary Fund). 2022. "Pacific Islands Monitor." Issue 16. International Monetary Fund, Washington, DC.

IPCC (Intergovernmental Panel on Climate Change). 2022. *Climate Change 2022: Impacts, Adaptation, and Vulnerability.* Cambridge, U.K., and New York, NY: Cambridge University Press.

IRENA (International Renewable Energy Agency). 2022. "Republic of Palau: Renewable Energy Roadmap: 2022-2050." IRENA, Abu Dhabi.

Izaguirre, C., I. Losada, P. Camus, J. Vigh, and V. Stenek. 2021. "Climate Change Risk to Port Operations." *Nature Climate Change* 11: 14-20.

Kose, A., P. Nagle, F. Ohnsorge, and N. Sugawara. 2021. *Global Waves of Debt: Causes and Consequences.* Washington, DC: World Bank.

Kumar, R., and P. Stauvermann. 2021. "Tourism and Economic Growth in the Pacific Region: Evidence from Five Small Island Economies." *Journal of the Asia Pacific Economy.*

Le Borgne, E., and P. Medas. 2007. "Sovereign Wealth Funds in the Pacific Island Countries: Macro-Fiscal Linkages." IMF Working Paper 07/297, International Monetary Fund, Washington, DC.

MacDonald, R. 2007. *Exchange Rate Economics: Theories and Evidence.* London: Routledge.

McIntyre, A., M. X. Li, and K. Wang. 2018. "Economic Benefits of Export Diversification in Small States." IMF Working Paper 18/86, International Monetary Fund, Washington, DC.

Mycoo, M., and M. Donovan. 2017. *A Blue Urban Agenda: Adapting to Climate Change in the Coastal Cities of Caribbean and Pacific Small Island Developing States.* Washington, DC: Inter-American Development Bank.

Nguyen, T. C., V. Castro, and J. A. Wood. 2022. "A New Comprehensive Database of Financial Crisis: Identification, Frequency and Duration." *Economic Modelling* 108 (March): 105770.

OECD (Organisation for Economic Co-operation and Development). 2021. "COVID-19 Pandemic: Towards a Blue Recovery in Small Island Developing States." OECD, Paris.

OECS (Organisation of Eastern Caribbean States). 2005. "Grenada: Macro-Socio-Economic Assessment of the Damages Caused by Hurricane Ivan." OECS, Castries, St. Lucia.

Ohnsorge, F., L. Quaglietti, and C. Rastogi. 2021. "High Trade Costs: Causes and Remedies." In *Global Economic Prospects*, June, 103-28. Washington, DC: World Bank.

Ohnsorge, F., and S. Yu, eds. 2021. *The Long Shadow of Informality: Challenges and Policies.* Washington, DC: World Bank.

Patil, P. G., J. Virdin, S. M. Diez, J. Roberts, and A. Singh. 2016. *Toward a Blue Economy: A Promise for Sustainable Growth in the Caribbean.* Washington, DC: World Bank.

Piemonte, C. 2021. "The Impact of the COVID-19 Crisis on External Debt in Small Island Developing States." Organisation for Economic Co-Operation and Development, Paris.

Pizzinelli, C., T. Khan, and K. Ishi. 2021. "Assessing Banking and Currency Crisis Risk in Small States: An Application to the Eastern Caribbean Currency Union." IMF Working Paper 21/276, International Monetary Fund, Washington, DC.

Pogliani, P., G. von Peter, and P. Wooldridge. 2022. "The Outsize Role of Cross-border Financial Centers." BIS Quarterly Review, June 2022, Bank for International Settlements, Basel.

Prasad, A., M. Pollock, and Y. Li. 2013. "Small States: Performance in Public Debt Management." Policy Research Working Paper 6536, World Bank, Washington, DC.

Ridderstaat, J., R. Croes, and P. Nijkamp. 2013. "Tourism and Long-run Economic Growth in Aruba." *International Journal of Tourism Research* 16 (5): 472-87.

Rivetti, D. 2021. *Debt Transparency in Developing Economies.* Washington, DC: World Bank.

Rustomjee, C., M. de Las Casas, A. Abrams, S. Balasubramanian, Y. Chen, and J. Li. 2022. "IMF Engagement with Small Developing States: Evaluation Report 2022." International Monetary Fund, Washington, DC.

Schiff, M., and Y. Wang. 2008. "Brain Drain and Productivity Growth: Are Small States Different?" IZA Working Paper 3378, Institute of Labor Economics, Bonn.

Schady, N., A. Holla, S. Sabarwal, J. Silva, and A. Y. Chang. Forthcoming. *Collapse and Recovery: How the COVID-19 Pandemic Eroded Human Capital and What to Do about It.* Washington, DC: World Bank.

Scott, D., M. Simpson, and R. Sim. 2012. "The Vulnerability of Caribbean Coastal Tourism to Scenarios of Climate Change Related Sea Level Rise." *Journal of Sustainable Tourism* 20 (6): 883-898.

Seetanah, R. 2011. "Assessing the Dynamic Economic Impact of Tourism for Island Economies." *Annals of Tourism Research.* 38 (1): 291-306.

Sy, M., A. Beaumont, E. Da, G. Eysselein, D. Kloeden, and K. R. Williams. "Funding the Future: Tax Revenue Mobilization in the Pacific Island Countries." IMF Departmental Paper 2022/015, International Monetary Fund, Washington, DC.

Taylor, L. 2022. "Covid-19: Lagging Vaccination Leaves the Caribbean Vulnerable, Says PAHO." *The BMJ* 376. https://www.bmj.com/content/376/bmj.o519.

Taylor, M., A. McGregor, and B Dawson. 2016. *Vulnerability of Pacific Island Agriculture and Forestry to Climate Change.* New Caledonia: Pacific Community.

UNCTAD (United Nations Conference on Trade and Development). 2022. *World Investment Report 2022.* UNCTAD, Geneva.

UNICEF (United Nations International Children's Emergency Fund. 2021. "COVID-19 Vaccine Hesitancy Survey Report 2021." United Nations International Children's Emergency Fund, New York.

UNWTO (United Nations World Tourism Organization). 2022. "Tourism Recovery Gains Momentum as Restrictions Ease and Confidence Returns." United Nations World Tourism Organization, Madrid. https://www.unwto.org/news/tourism-recovery-gains-momentum-as-restrictions-ease-and-con fidence-returns.

von Peter, G., S. von Dahlen, and S. Saxena. 2012. "New Evidence on the Macroeconomic Cost of Natural Catastrophes." BIS Working Paper 394, Bank for International Settlements, Basel, Switzerland.

Wenner, M. 2016. "Brain Drain: A Curse of Small States?" *Caribbean DEVTrends* (blog), September 26,

2016. https://blogs.iadb.org/caribbean-dev-trends/en/brain-drain-a-curse-of-small-states.

World Bank. Forthcoming. "Promoting Private Sector-led Growth to Foster Recovery and Resilience." Caribbean Regional Private Sector Diagnostic, World Bank, Washington, DC.

World Bank. 1985. "Terms of Lending to Small Island Economies Graduating from IDA." November (IDA/R85-134), World Bank, Washington, DC.

World Bank. 2016. "Climate and Disaster Resilience." *Pacific Possible* series, World Bank, Washington, DC.

World Bank. 2017. "Country Partnership Framework for Belize for the Period FY18-22." World Bank, Washington, DC.

World Bank. 2019a. "Addressing Debt Vulnerabilities in IDA Countries: Options for IDA19." World Bank, Washington, DC.

World Bank. 2019b. "Country Partnership Framework for the Republic of Cabo Verde for the Period FY20-25." World Bank, Washington, DC.

World Bank. 2021a. "Maldives Systematic Country Diagnostic Update." World Bank, Washington, DC.

World Bank. 2021b. "Recovery: COVID-19 Crisis Through a Migration Lens." Migration and Development Brief 35, World Bank, Washington, DC.

World Bank. 2021c. *Global Economic Prospects.* June. Washington, DC: World Bank.

World Bank. 2022a. "World Bank Group Support to Small States." World Bank, Washington, DC.

World Bank. 2022b. *Consolidating the Recovery: Semiannual Report for Latin America and The Caribbean.* Washington, DC: World Bank.

World Bank. 2022c. *Poverty and Shared Prosperity 2022: Correcting Course.* Washington, DC: World Bank.

World Bank. 2022d. *Commodity Markets Outlook: Pandemic, War, Recession: Drivers of Aluminum and Copper Prices.* Washington, DC: World Bank.

World Bank. 2022e. "Food Security Update." November 10. World Bank, Washington, DC.

World Bank. 2022f. "Wildlife Conservation Bond Boosts South Africa's Efforts to Protect Black Rhinos and Support Local Communities." Press release, March 23. https://www.worldbank.org/en/news/press-release/2022/03/23/wildlife-conservation-bond-boosts-south-africa-s-efforts-to-protect-black-rhinos-and-support-local-communities.

World Bank. 2022g. "Creating Markets in Fiji. Overview and Summary of Key Findings from Sector Deep Dives." Country Private Sector Diagnostic, World Bank, Washington, DC.

World Bank. 2022h. "Creating Markets in Eswatini. Strengthening the Private Sector to Grow Export Markets and Create Jobs." Country Private Sector Diagnostic, World Bank, Washington, DC.

World Bank. 2022i. "Climate and Development: An Agenda for Action-Emerging Insights from World Bank Group 2021-22 Country Climate and Development Reports." World Bank, Washington, DC.

World Bank. 2022j. "World Bank Support to Small States." World Bank, Washington, DC.

World Bank. 2022k. "Navigating Multiple Crises, Staying the Course on Long-Term Development: The World Bank Group's Response to the Crises Affecting Developing Countries." Global Crisis Response Framework Paper, World Bank, Washington, DC.

World Bank and IMF (International Monetary Fund). 2021. "Joint IMF-WBG Staff Note—DSSI Fiscal Monitoring Update: Supplementary Information." World Bank, Washington, DC.

World Bank and IMF (International Monetary Fund). 2022. "Making Debt Work for Development and Macroeconomic Stability." Development Committee Paper 2022-003, World Bank and IMF, Washington, DC.

World Bank and UNESCO (United Nations Educational, Scientific and Cultural Organization). 2022. "Education Finance Watch 2022." World Bank, Washington, DC.

World Food Program. 2021. "2021 Global Report on Food Crises: September 2021 Update." World Food Program, Rome.

STATISTICAL APPENDIX

Real GDP growth

	Annual estimates and forecasts [1] (Percent change)					Quarterly estimates [2] (Percent change, year-on-year)					
	2020	2021	2022e	2023f	2024f	21Q2	21Q3	21Q4	22Q1	22Q2	22Q3e
World	-3.2	5.9	2.9	1.7	2.7	12.1	4.8	4.9	4.4	3.0	..
Advanced economies	-4.3	5.3	2.5	0.5	1.6	12.7	4.4	5.0	4.2	2.9	2.3
United States	-2.8	5.9	1.9	0.5	1.6	12.5	5.0	5.7	3.7	1.8	1.9
Euro area	-6.1	5.3	3.3	0.0	1.6	14.2	4.0	4.8	5.5	4.3	2.3
Japan	-4.3	2.2	1.2	1.0	0.7	7.8	1.7	0.9	0.6	1.4	1.7
Emerging market and developing economies	-1.5	6.7	3.4	3.4	4.1	11.3	5.4	4.7	4.6	3.1	..
East Asia and Pacific	1.2	7.2	3.2	4.3	4.9	8.1	4.3	4.1	4.8	1.3	4.5
Cambodia	-3.1	3.0	4.8	5.2	6.3	..	..	..	..	..	..
China	2.2	8.1	2.7	4.3	5.0	7.9	4.9	4.0	4.8	0.4	3.9
Fiji	-17.0	-5.1	15.1	5.4	3.4	..	..	..	..	..	..
Indonesia	-2.1	3.7	5.2	4.8	4.9	7.1	3.5	5.0	5.0	5.4	5.7
Kiribati	-0.5	1.5	1.5	2.3	2.1	..	..	..	..	..	..
Lao PDR	0.5	2.5	2.5	3.8	4.2	..	..	..	..	..	..
Malaysia	-5.5	3.1	7.8	4.0	3.9	15.9	-4.5	3.6	5.0	8.9	14.2
Marshall Islands [3]	-2.2	1.1	1.5	2.2	2.5	..	..	..	..	..	..
Micronesia, Fed. Sts. [3]	-1.8	-3.2	-0.5	3.0	2.5	..	..	..	..	..	..
Mongolia	-4.4	1.6	4.0	5.3	6.4	-0.5	-1.2	-2.7	-3.8	6.9	6.9
Myanmar [3 6]	3.2	-18.0	3.0	3.0	..	..	..	..	..	..	..
Nauru [3]	0.7	1.5	0.9	1.9	2.8	..	..	..	..	..	..
Palau [3]	-9.7	-17.1	-2.5	18.2	4.5	..	..	..	..	..	..
Papua New Guinea	-3.2	0.1	4.0	3.5	3.3	..	..	..	..	..	..
Philippines	-9.5	5.7	7.2	5.4	5.9	12.1	7.0	7.8	8.2	7.5	7.6
Samoa [3]	-3.1	-7.1	-6.0	4.0	3.5	..	..	..	..	..	..
Solomon Islands	-3.4	-0.2	-4.5	2.6	2.4	..	..	..	..	..	..
Thailand	-6.2	1.5	3.4	3.6	3.7	7.7	-0.2	1.8	2.3	2.5	4.5
Timor-Leste	-8.6	2.9	3.0	3.0	3.0	..	..	..	..	..	..
Tonga [3]	0.5	-2.7	-1.6	3.3	3.2	..	..	..	..	..	..
Tuvalu	-4.9	0.3	3.0	3.5	4.0	..	..	..	..	..	..
Vanuatu	-5.4	0.5	2.2	3.4	3.5	..	..	..	..	..	..
Vietnam	2.9	2.6	7.2	6.3	6.5	6.6	-6.0	5.2	5.1	7.8	13.7
Europe and Central Asia	-1.7	6.7	0.2	0.1	2.8	13.7	5.6	6.6	5.1	0.7	..
Albania	-3.5	8.5	3.5	2.2	3.4	17.6	6.8	5.5	6.5	2.2	..
Armenia	-7.2	5.7	10.8	4.1	4.8	9.0	2.3	11.5	8.7	13.0	14.8
Azerbaijan	-4.3	5.6	4.2	2.8	2.6	..	..	..	..	..	..
Belarus	-0.9	2.6	-6.2	-2.3	2.5	6.0	1.7	1.3	-0.4	-7.8	..
Bosnia and Herzegovina [5]	-3.1	7.5	4.0	2.5	3.0	12.1	7.5	7.5	5.8	5.9	..
Bulgaria	-4.0	7.6	3.1	1.7	3.3	7.1	8.6	10.2	4.4	3.9	2.9
Croatia	-8.6	13.1	6.6	0.8	3.1	20.8	16.7	12.2	7.8	8.7	5.2
Georgia	-6.8	10.4	10.0	4.0	5.0	28.8	9.5	8.6	15.0	7.2	9.8
Hungary	-4.5	7.1	5.1	0.5	2.2	17.8	6.2	7.4	8.2	6.5	4.0
Kazakhstan	-2.5	4.1	3.0	3.5	4.0	6.3	6.1	5.4	4.6	2.7	..
Kosovo	-5.3	10.7	3.1	3.7	4.2	..	..	..	..	..	..
Kyrgyz Republic	-8.4	3.6	5.5	3.5	4.0	..	..	..	..	..	..
Moldova	-7.4	13.9	-1.5	1.6	4.2	16.8	11.7	18.3	1.1	..	..
Montenegro	-15.3	13.0	5.9	3.4	3.1	19.6	26.6	9.0	7.1	12.7	3.2
North Macedonia	-4.7	3.9	2.1	2.4	2.7	15.9	3.0	3.3	2.2	4.0	2.0
Poland	-2.0	6.8	4.4	0.7	2.2	12.2	6.5	8.5	8.6	5.8	3.6
Romania	-3.7	5.1	4.6	2.6	4.2	15.3	5.6	1.3	6.4	5.1	4.0
Russian Federation	-2.7	4.8	-3.5	-3.3	1.6	10.5	4.0	5.0	3.5	-4.1	-3.7
Serbia	-0.9	7.5	2.5	2.3	3.0	13.8	7.8	7.2	4.2	3.8	1.0
Tajikistan	4.4	9.2	7.0	5.0	4.0	..	..	..	..	..	..
Türkiye	1.9	11.4	4.7	2.7	4.0	22.2	7.9	9.6	7.5	7.7	3.9
Ukraine	-3.8	3.4	-35.0	3.3	4.1	6.0	2.8	6.1	-15.1	-37.2	-30.8
Uzbekistan	1.9	7.4	5.7	4.9	5.1	..	..	..	..	..	..

Real GDP growth *(continued)*

	Annual estimates and forecasts [1] (Percent change)					Quarterly estimates [2] (Percent change, year-on-year)					
	2020	2021	2022e	2023f	2024f	21Q2	21Q3	21Q4	22Q1	22Q2	22Q3e
Latin America and the Caribbean	**-6.2**	**6.8**	**3.6**	**1.3**	**2.4**	**17.2**	**7.3**	**4.2**	**3.8**	**4.5**	**..**
Argentina	-9.9	10.4	5.2	2.0	2.0	18.1	11.8	8.9	6.0	7.1	5.9
Bahamas, The	-23.8	13.7	8.0	4.1	3.0	..	..	..	..	..	..
Barbados	-13.7	0.7	10.0	4.8	3.9	..	..	..	..	..	..
Belize	-13.7	16.3	3.5	2.0	2.0	30.0	18.2	19.3	7.8	13.5	..
Bolivia	-8.7	6.1	3.3	3.1	2.7	23.1	5.5	0.2	4.0	4.3	..
Brazil	-3.3	5.0	3.0	0.8	2.0	12.4	4.4	2.1	2.4	3.7	3.6
Chile	-6.0	11.7	2.1	-0.9	2.3	18.9	17.2	12.0	7.4	5.6	0.3
Colombia	-7.0	10.7	8.0	1.3	2.8	18.3	13.8	10.8	8.7	12.8	7.0
Costa Rica	-4.1	7.8	4.1	2.9	3.1	10.2	12.6	10.4	8.3	6.1	2.4
Dominica	-16.6	6.5	5.8	4.6	4.6	..	..	..	..	..	..
Dominican Republic	-6.7	12.3	5.3	4.8	5.0	25.4	11.5	11.2	6.1	5.2	..
Ecuador	-7.8	4.2	2.7	3.1	2.8	11.6	5.5	4.9	3.8	1.7	..
El Salvador	-8.1	10.2	2.4	2.0	2.0	26.5	11.6	3.7	3.1	2.6	..
Grenada	-13.8	4.7	5.8	3.2	3.0	..	..	..	..	..	..
Guatemala	-1.8	8.0	3.4	3.1	3.5	15.4	8.1	4.7	4.5	4.1	..
Guyana	43.5	20.0	57.8	25.2	21.2	..	..	..	..	..	..
Haiti [3]	-3.3	-1.8	-1.5	-1.1	2.0	..	..	..	..	..	..
Honduras	-9.0	12.5	3.5	3.1	3.7	26.2	12.9	11.5	6.1	3.8	..
Jamaica [2]	-10.0	4.6	3.2	2.0	1.2	14.2	5.9	6.7	6.5	4.8	..
Mexico	-8.0	4.7	2.6	0.9	2.3	19.6	4.3	1.0	1.8	2.4	4.3
Nicaragua	-1.8	10.3	4.1	2.0	2.5	18.2	10.1	10.1	5.7	4.3	..
Panama	-18.0	15.3	7.2	4.5	4.5	40.0	25.5	16.3	13.6	9.8	9.5
Paraguay	-0.8	4.1	-0.3	5.2	4.2	14.1	2.6	0.2	-1.1	-3.4	..
Peru	-11.0	13.3	2.7	2.6	2.6	41.2	11.9	3.2	3.8	3.3	1.7
St. Lucia	-24.4	11.9	8.9	4.4	3.2	..	..	..	..	..	..
St. Vincent and the Grenadines	-5.3	0.7	5.0	6.0	4.8	..	..	..	..	..	..
Suriname	-16.0	-2.7	1.3	2.3	3.0	..	..	..	..	..	..
Uruguay	-6.1	4.4	5.0	2.7	2.5	10.2	6.2	5.9	8.5	7.9	3.7
Middle East and North Africa	**-3.6**	**3.7**	**5.7**	**3.5**	**2.7**	**5.2**	**6.8**	**6.4**	**6.6**	**7.9**	**..**
Algeria	-5.1	3.5	3.7	2.3	1.8	6.1	3.0	3.1	1.6	..	..
Bahrain	-4.9	2.2	3.8	3.2	3.2	5.5	2.1	4.3	5.4	6.9	..
Djibouti	1.2	4.3	3.6	5.3	6.2	..	..	..	..	..	..
Egypt, Arab Rep. [3]	3.6	3.3	6.6	4.5	4.8	7.7	9.8	8.3	5.4	3.3	..
Iran, Islamic Rep. [3]	1.9	4.7	2.9	2.2	1.9	..	..	..	..	..	..
Iraq	-11.3	2.8	8.7	4.0	2.9	..	..	..	..	..	..
Jordan	-1.6	2.2	2.5	2.4	2.4	3.2	2.7	2.6	2.5	2.9	..
Kuwait	-8.9	1.3	8.5	2.5	2.5	..	..	..	..	..	..
Lebanon [6]	-21.4	-7.0	-5.4	..	..	..	..	..	..	..	..
Libya [6]	-31.3	99.3	1.1	..	..	..	..	..	..	..	..
Morocco	-7.2	7.9	1.2	3.5	3.7	14.2	8.7	7.6	0.3	2.0	1.8
Oman	-3.4	3.1	4.5	3.9	2.4	..	..	..	..	..	..
Qatar	-3.6	1.5	4.0	3.4	2.9	4.0	2.4	2.2	2.3	6.3	..
Saudi Arabia	-4.1	3.2	8.3	3.7	2.3	1.9	7.0	6.7	9.9	12.2	8.8
Syrian Arab Republic [6]	-3.9	-2.9	-3.5	-3.2	..	..	..	..	..	..	..
Tunisia	-8.8	4.4	2.5	3.3	3.6	16.3	1.6	2.7	2.4	2.8	3.1
United Arab Emirates	-5.0	3.9	5.9	4.1	2.3	5.5	6.7	8.7	8.4	..	..
West Bank and Gaza	-11.3	7.1	3.5	3.0	3.0	19.3	6.7	11.2	5.7	3.3	..
Yemen, Rep. [6]	-8.5	-1.0	1.0	1.0	..	..	..	..	..	..	..

Real GDP growth *(continued)*

	Annual estimates and forecasts [1] (Percent change)					Quarterly estimates [2] (Percent change, year-on-year)					
	2020	2021	2022e	2023f	2024f	21Q2	21Q3	21Q4	22Q1	22Q2	22Q3e
South Asia	**-4.5**	**7.9**	**6.1**	**5.5**	**5.8**	**20.0**	**8.0**	**5.4**	**3.9**	**12.9**	**..**
Afghanistan [6]	-2.4	-20.7	..	..	..	..	..	..	..	..	..
Bangladesh [3][4]	3.4	6.9	7.2	5.2	6.2	..	..	..	..	..	..
Bhutan [3][4]	-2.3	-3.3	4.6	4.1	3.7	..	..	..	..	..	..
India [3][4]	-6.6	8.7	6.9	6.6	6.1	20.1	8.4	5.4	4.1	13.5	6.3
Maldives	-33.5	41.7	12.4	8.2	8.1	77.6	83.3	55.9	22.4	31.2	..
Nepal [3][4]	-2.4	4.2	5.8	5.1	4.9	..	..	..	..	..	..
Pakistan [3][4]	-0.9	5.7	6.0	2.0	3.2	..	..	..	..	..	..
Sri Lanka	-3.5	3.3	-9.2	-4.2	1.0	16.3	-5.8	2.0	-1.6	-8.4	-11.8
Sub-Saharan Africa	**-2.0**	**4.3**	**3.4**	**3.6**	**3.9**	**11.4**	**4.3**	**4.1**	**3.7**	**2.8**	**..**
Angola	-5.8	0.8	3.1	2.8	2.9	..	..	..	..	..	..
Benin	3.8	7.2	5.7	6.2	6.0	..	..	..	..	..	..
Botswana	-8.7	11.4	4.1	4.0	4.0	37.1	8.4	5.6	7.1	5.6	..
Burkina Faso	1.9	6.9	4.3	5.0	5.3	..	..	..	..	..	..
Burundi	0.3	1.8	2.1	3.0	4.0	..	..	..	..	..	..
Cabo Verde	-14.8	7.0	4.0	4.8	5.7	..	..	..	..	..	..
Cameroon	0.3	3.6	3.8	4.3	4.6	..	..	..	..	..	..
Central African Republic	1.0	1.0	1.5	3.0	3.8	..	..	..	..	..	..
Chad	-1.6	-1.2	3.1	3.3	3.3	..	..	..	..	..	..
Comoros	-0.3	2.2	1.4	3.3	3.8	..	..	..	..	..	..
Congo, Dem. Rep.	1.7	6.2	6.1	6.4	6.6	..	..	..	..	..	..
Congo, Rep.	-6.2	-2.2	1.9	3.7	4.5	..	..	..	..	..	..
Côte d'Ivoire	2.0	7.0	5.7	6.8	6.6	..	..	..	..	..	..
Equatorial Guinea	-4.9	-1.6	3.2	-2.6	-3.4	..	..	..	..	..	..
Eritrea	-0.5	2.9	2.5	2.7	2.9	..	..	..	..	..	..
Eswatini	-1.6	7.9	1.1	2.6	2.7	..	..	..	..	..	..
Ethiopia [3]	6.1	6.3	3.5	5.3	6.1	..	..	..	..	..	..
Gabon	-1.8	1.5	2.7	3.0	2.9	..	..	..	..	..	..
Gambia, The	0.6	4.3	3.5	4.0	5.5	..	..	..	..	..	..
Ghana	0.5	5.4	3.5	2.7	3.5	4.2	6.5	7.0	3.4	4.8	..
Guinea	4.9	3.9	4.6	5.3	5.6	..	..	..	..	..	..
Guinea-Bissau	1.5	5.0	3.5	4.5	4.5	..	..	..	..	..	..
Kenya	-0.3	7.5	5.5	5.0	5.3	11.0	9.3	7.4	6.8	5.2	..
Lesotho	-8.4	1.3	2.6	2.3	2.9	17.5	-1.2	1.5	1.5	0.1	..
Liberia	-3.0	5.0	3.7	4.7	5.7	..	..	..	..	..	..
Madagascar	-7.1	4.4	2.6	4.2	4.6	..	..	..	..	..	..
Malawi	0.8	2.8	1.5	3.0	3.4	..	..	..	..	..	..
Mali	-1.2	3.1	1.8	4.0	4.0	..	..	..	..	..	..
Mauritania	-0.9	2.4	4.0	5.1	7.9	..	..	..	..	..	..
Mauritius	-14.6	3.6	5.8	5.5	4.2	..	..	..	..	..	..
Mozambique	-1.2	2.3	3.7	5.0	8.0	2.1	3.5	3.6	4.1	4.6	3.6
Namibia	-8.0	2.7	2.8	2.0	1.9	5.6	5.6	4.3	6.6	6.0	4.3
Niger	3.6	1.4	5.0	7.1	10.1	..	..	..	..	..	..
Nigeria	-1.8	3.6	3.1	2.9	2.9	5.4	4.1	4.6	3.6	3.4	2.4
Rwanda	-3.4	10.9	6.0	6.7	7.0	20.6	10.1	10.3	7.9	7.5	10.0
São Tomé and Príncipe	3.1	1.8	1.1	2.1	2.4	..	..	..	..	..	..
Senegal	1.3	6.1	4.8	8.0	10.5	..	..	..	..	..	..
Seychelles	-7.7	7.9	11.0	5.2	4.8	18.6	7.9	-0.5	14.3	4.7	..
Sierra Leone	-2.0	4.1	3.7	3.7	4.4	..	..	..	..	..	..

Real GDP growth *(continued)*

	Annual estimates and forecasts[1] (Percent change)					Quarterly estimates[2] (Percent change, year-on-year)					
	2020	2021	2022e	2023f	2024f	21Q2	21Q3	21Q4	22Q1	22Q2	22Q3e
Sub-Saharan Africa (continued)											
South Africa	-6.3	4.9	1.9	1.4	1.8	19.5	3.0	1.7	2.7	0.2	4.1
South Sudan[3]	9.5	-5.1	-2.8	-0.8	2.1	..	..	..	..	..	..
Sudan	-3.6	-1.9	0.3	2.0	2.5	..	..	..	..	..	..
Tanzania	2.0	4.3	4.6	5.3	6.1	..	..	..	..	..	..
Togo	1.8	5.3	4.8	5.6	6.4	..	..	..	..	..	..
Uganda[3]	3.0	3.5	4.7	5.5	6.1	13.0	2.9	5.8	5.1	4.9	..
Zambia	-3.0	3.6	3.0	3.9	4.1	8.4	3.3	5.0	2.2	3.5	..
Zimbabwe	-5.3	5.8	3.4	3.6	3.6	..	..	..	..	..	..

Sources: World Bank; Haver Analytics.

Note: e = estimate; f = forecast. Since Croatia became a member of the euro area on January 1, 2023, it has been added to the euro area aggregate and removed from the EMDE and ECA aggregate in all tables to avoid double counting.

1. Aggregate growth rates calculated using GDP weights at average 2010-19 prices and market exchange rates.

2. Quarterly estimates are based on non-seasonally-adjusted real GDP, except for advanced economies, as well as Algeria, Ecuador, Morocco, and Tunisia. In some instances, quarterly growth paths may not align to annual growth estimates, owing to the timing of GDP releases. Quarterly data for Jamaica are gross value added. Quarterly data for Montenegro are preliminary. Data for Timor-Leste represent non-oil GDP.

Regional averages are calculated based on data from the following economies.

East Asia and Pacific: China, Indonesia, Malaysia, Mongolia, the Philippines, Thailand, and Vietnam.

Europe and Central Asia: Albania, Armenia, Belarus, Bosnia and Herzegovina, Bulgaria, Georgia, Hungary, Kazakhstan, Moldova, North Macedonia, Poland, Romania, the Russian Federation, Serbia, Türkiye, and Ukraine.

Latin America and the Caribbean: Argentina, Belize, Bolivia, Brazil, Chile, Colombia, Costa Rica, the Dominican Republic, Ecuador, El Salvador, Guatemala, Honduras, Jamaica, Mexico, Nicaragua, Panama, Paraguay, Peru, and Uruguay.

Middle East and North Africa: Bahrain, the Arab Republic of Egypt, Jordan, Morocco, Qatar, Saudi Arabia, Tunisia, and West Bank and Gaza.

South Asia: India, Maldives, and Sri Lanka.

Sub-Saharan Africa: Botswana, Ghana, Kenya, Lesotho, Mozambique, Namibia, Nigeria, Rwanda, South Africa, Uganda, and Zambia.

3. Annual GDP is on fiscal year basis, as per reporting practice in the country.

4. GDP data for Pakistan are based on factor cost. For Bangladesh, Bhutan, Nepal, and Pakistan, the column labeled 2022 refers to FY2021/22. For India and the Islamic Republic of Iran, the column labeled 2022 refers to FY2022/23.

5. Data for Bosnia and Herzegovina are from the production approach.

6. Forecasts for Afghanistan (beyond 2021), Lebanon (beyond 2022), Libya (beyond 2022), Myanmar (beyond 2023), the Syrian Arab Republic (beyond 2023), and the Republic of Yemen (beyond 2023) are excluded because of a high degree of uncertainty.

To download the data in this table, please visit www.worldbank.org/gep.

Data and Forecast Conventions

The macroeconomic forecasts presented in this report are prepared by staff of the Prospects Group of the Equitable Growth, Finance and Institutions Vice-Presidency, in coordination with staff from the Macroeconomics, Trade, and Investment Global Practice and from regional and country offices, and with input from regional Chief Economist offices. They are the result of an iterative process that incorporates data, macroeconometric models, and judgment.

Data. Data used to prepare country forecasts come from a variety of sources. National Income Accounts (NIA), Balance of Payments (BOP), and fiscal data are from Haver Analytics; the World Development Indicators by the World Bank; the World Economic Outlook, Balance of Payments Statistics, and International Financial Statistics by the International Monetary Fund. Population data and forecasts are from the United Nations World Population Prospects. Country- and lending-group classifications are from the World Bank. The Prospects Group's internal databases include high-frequency indicators such as industrial production, consumer price indexes, emerging markets bond index (EMBI), exchange rates, exports, imports, policy rates, and stock market indexes, based on data from Bloomberg, Haver Analytics, IMF Balance of Payments Statistics, IMF International Financial Statistics, and J. P. Morgan.

Aggregations. Aggregate growth for the world and all subgroups of countries (such as regions and income groups) is calculated using GDP weights at average 2010-19 prices and market exchange rates of country-specific growth rates. Income groups are defined as in the World Bank's classification of country groups.

Forecast process. The process starts with initial assumptions about advanced-economy growth and commodity price forecasts. These are used as conditioning assumptions for the first set of growth forecasts for EMDEs, which are produced using macroeconometric models, accounting frameworks to ensure national account identities and global consistency, estimates of spillovers from major economies, and high-frequency indicators. These forecasts are then evaluated to ensure consistency of treatment across similar EMDEs. This is followed by extensive discussions with World Bank country teams, who conduct continuous macroeconomic monitoring and dialogue with country authorities and finalize growth forecasts for EMDEs. The Prospects Group prepares advanced-economy and commodity price forecasts. Throughout the forecasting process, staff use macroeconometric models that allow the combination of judgement and consistency with model-based insights.

Global Economic Prospects: Selected Topics, 2015-23

Global Economic Prospects: Selected Topics, 2015-23

Growth and business cycles

Cross-border spillovers

Who catches a cold when emerging markets sneeze?	January 2016, chapter 3
Sources of the growth slowdown in BRICS	January 2016, box 3.1
Understanding cross-border growth spillovers	January 2016, box 3.2
Within-region spillovers	January 2016, box 3.3
East Asia and Pacific	January 2016, box 2.1.1
Europe and Central Asia	January 2016, box 2.2.1
Latin America and the Caribbean	January 2016, box 2.3.1
Middle East and North Africa	January 2016, box 2.4.1
South Asia	January 2016, box 2.5.1
Sub-Saharan Africa	January 2016, box 2.6.1

Productivity

How do disasters affect productivity?	June 2020, box 3.2
Fading promise: How to rekindle productivity growth	January 2020, chapter 3
EMDE regional productivity trends and bottlenecks	January 2020, box 3.1
Sectoral sources of productivity growth	January 2020, box 3.2
Patterns of total factor productivity: A firm perspective	January 2020, box 3.3
Debt, financial crises, and productivity	January 2020, box 3.4
Labor productivity in East Asia and Pacific: Trends and drivers	January 2020, box 2.1.1
Labor productivity in Europe and Central Asia: Trends and drivers	January 2020, box 2.2.1
Labor productivity in Latin America and the Caribbean: Trends and drivers	January 2020, box 2.3.1
Labor productivity in Middle East and North Africa: Trends and drivers	January 2020, box 2.4.1
Labor productivity in South Asia: Trends and drivers	January 2020, box 2.5.1
Labor productivity in Sub-Saharan Africa: Trends and drivers	January 2020, box 2.6.1

Investment

Investment growth after the pandemic	January 2023, chapter 3
Investment: Subdued prospects, strong needs	June 2019, Special Focus 11
Weak investment in uncertain times: Causes, implications, and policy responses	January 2017, chapter 3
Investment-less credit booms	January 2017, box 3.1
Implications of rising uncertainty for investment in EMDEs	January 2017, box 3.2
Investment slowdown in China	January 2017, box 3.3
Interactions between public and private investment	January 2017, box 3.4
East Asia and Pacific	January 2017, box 2.1.1
Europe and Central Asia	January 2017, box 2.2.1
Latin America and the Caribbean	January 2017, box 2.3.1
Middle East and North Africa	January 2017, box 2.4.1
South Asia	January 2016, box 2.5.1
Sub-Saharan Africa	January 2016, box 2.6.1

Forecast uncertainty

Scenarios of possible global growth outcomes	June 2020, box 1.3
Quantifying uncertainties in global growth forecasts	June 2016, Special Focus 2

Fiscal space

Having space and using it: Fiscal policy challenges and developing economies	January 2015, chapter 3
Fiscal policy in low-income countries	January 2015, box 3.1
What affects the size of fiscal multipliers?	January 2015, box 3.2
Chile's fiscal rule—an example of success	January 2015, box 3.3
Narrow fiscal space and the risk of a debt crisis	January 2015, box 3.4
Revenue mobilization in South Asia: Policy challenges and recommendations	January 2015, box 2.3

Other topics

Impact of COVID-19 on global income inequality	January 2022, chapter 4
Education demographics and global inequality	January 2018, Special Focus 2
Recent developments in emerging and developing country labor markets	June 2015, box 1.3
Linkages between China and Sub-Saharan Africa	June 2015, box 2.1
What does weak growth mean for poverty in the future?	January 2015, box 1.1
What does a slowdown in China mean for Latin America and the Caribbean?	January 2015, box 2.2

Global Economic Prospects: Selected Topics, 2015-23

Prospects Group:
Selected Other Publications on the Global Economy, 2015-23

Commodity Markets Outlook

Causes and consequences of metal price shocks	April 2021
Persistence of commodity shocks	October 2020
Food price shocks: Channels and implications	April 2019
The implications of tariffs for commodity markets	October 2018, box
The changing of the guard: Shifts in industrial commodity demand	October 2018
Oil exporters: Policies and challenges	April 2018
Investment weakness in commodity exporters	January 2017
OPEC in historical context: Commodity agreements and market fundamentals	October 2016
From energy prices to food prices: Moving in tandem?	July 2016
Resource development in an era of cheap commodities	April 2016
Weak growth in emerging market economies: What does it imply for commodity markets?	January 2016
Understanding El Niño: What does it mean for commodity markets?	October 2015
How important are China and India in global commodity consumption?	July 2015
Anatomy of the last four oil price crashes	April 2015
Putting the recent plunge in oil prices in perspective	January 2015

Inflation in Emerging and Developing Economies: Evolution, Drivers, and Policies

Inflation: Concepts, evolution, and correlates	Chapter 1
Understanding global inflation synchronization	Chapter 2
Sources of inflation: Global and domestic drivers	Chapter 3
Inflation expectations: Review and evidence	Chapter 4
Inflation and exchange rate pass-through	Chapter 5
Inflation in low-income countries	Chapter 6
Poverty impact of food price shocks and policies	Chapter 7

A Decade After the Global Recession: Lessons and Challenges for Emerging and Developing Economies

A decade after the global recession: Lessons and challenges	Chapter 1
What happens during global recessions?	Chapter 2
Macroeconomic developments	Chapter 3
Financial market developments	Chapter 4
Macroeconomic and financial sector policies	Chapter 5
Prospects, risks, and vulnerabilities	Chapter 6
Policy challenges	Chapter 7
The role of the World Bank Group	Chapter 8

Global Waves of Debt: Causes and Consequences

Debt: Evolution, causes, and consequences	Chapter 1
Benefits and costs of debt: The dose makes the poison	Chapter 2
Global waves of debt: What goes up must come down?	Chapter 3
The fourth wave: Ripple or tsunami?	Chapter 4
Debt and financial crises: From euphoria to distress	Chapter 5
Policies: Turning mistakes into experience	Chapter 6

Prospects Group:
Selected Other Publications on the Global Economy, 2015-23

Global Productivity: Trends, Drivers, and Policies	
Global productivity trends	Chapter 1
What explains productivity growth	Chapter 2
What happens to productivity during major adverse events?	Chapter 3
Productivity convergence: Is anyone catching up?	Chapter 4
Regional dimensions of productivity: Trends, explanations, and policies	Chapter 5
Productivity: Technology, demand, and employment trade-offs	Chapter 6
Sectoral sources of productivity growth	Chapter 7

The Long Shadow of Informality: Challenges and Policies	
Overview	Chapter 1
Understanding the informal economy: Concepts and trends	Chapter 2
Growing apart or moving together? Synchronization of informal- and formal-economy business cycles	Chapter 3
Lagging behind: informality and development	Chapter 4
Informality in emerging market and developing economies: Regional dimensions	Chapter 5
Tackling informality: Policy options	Chapter 6

Commodity Markets : Evolution, Challenges and Policies	
The evolution of commodity markets over the past century	Chapter 1
Commodity demand: Drivers, outlook, and implications	Chapter 2
The nature and drivers of commodity price cycles	Chapter 3
Causes and consequences of industrial commodity price shocks	Chapter 4

High-frequency monitoring
Global Monthly newsletter

ECO-AUDIT
Environmental Benefits Statement

The World Bank Group is committed to reducing its environmental footprint. In support of this commitment, we leverage electronic publishing options and print-on-demand technology, which is located in regional hubs worldwide. Together, these initiatives enable print runs to be lowered and shipping distances decreased, resulting in reduced paper consumption, chemical use, greenhouse gas emissions, and waste.

We follow the recommended standards for paper use set by the Green Press Initiative. The majority of our books are printed on Forest Stewardship Council (FSC)-certified paper, with nearly all containing 50-100 percent recycled content. The recycled fiber in our book paper is either unbleached or bleached using totally chlorine-free (TCF), processed chlorine-free (PCF), or enhanced elemental chlorine-free (EECF) processes.

More information about the Bank's environmental philosophy can be found at http://www.worldbank.org/corporateresponsibility.